COLLEAGUES
IN ORGANIZATION

D0826620

COLLEAGUES IN ORGANIZATION

The Social Construction
of Professional Work

Edited by Ralph L. Blankenship
University of Wisconsin-Platteville

John Wiley and Sons
New York/Santa Barbara
London/Sydney/Toronto

BOWLING GREEN UNIV. LIBRARY

Copyright © 1977, by John Wiley & Sons, Inc.

All rights reserved. Published simultaneously in Canada.

No part of this book may be reproduced by any means, nor transmitted, nor translated into a machine language without the written permission of the publisher.

Library of Congress Cataloguing in Publication Data
Main entry under title:

Colleagues in organization.

   Includes bibliographical references and indexes.
   CONTENTS: Perspective: Silverman, D. The action frame of reference. Lofland, J. Analyzing social settings. Bittner, E. The concept of organization. Bucher, R. and Stelling, J. Characteristics of professional organizations. [etc.]
   1. Organization—Addresses, essays, lectures.
2. Professions—Addresses, essays, lectures. 3. Professional socialization—
Addresses, essays, lectures.
I. Blankenship, Ralph L., 1937-
HM131.C7425   301.18′32   76-24899
ISBN 0-471-07952-9

Printed in the United States of America

10 9 8 7 6 5 4 3 2 1

ABOUT THE AUTHORS

CHARLES E. BIDWELL earned his doctorate degree in sociology at the University of Chicago where he is presently a professor in the Department of Education. His interests are in the sociology of education, organizational theory, and, especially, the social organization of schools. Professor Bidwell is co-author of *Administrative Relationships*.

EGON BITTNER is interested in social theory, sociology of knowledge, and social control. Among his publications is a major study of American police, *The Functions of the Police in Modern Society*. He teaches sociology at Brandeis University. Professor Bittner conducted his graduate studies at the University of California at Los Angeles.

RALPH L. BLANKENSHIP is professor and head of the Department of Sociology at the University of Wisconsin-Platteville. His graduate studies in sociology and social psychology were done at the University of Illinois at Urbana-Champaign. Professor Blankenship has published in the areas of deviance labeling, societal reaction, and organizational development.

M. RUE BUCHER received her doctorate degree in sociology from the University of Chicago. Her present appointment is in both the Department of Psychiatry (Medical Center) and the Department of Sociology (Chicago Circle) of the University of Illinois. Professor Bucher's interests are in professional socialization, professional organization, and processes of change in the professions and science. She is co-author of *Psychiatric Ideologies and Institutions* and currently, she is editor of *Sociology of Work and Occupations: An International Journal*.

THEODORE CAPLOW is author of *Sociology of Work* and *Principles of Organization*. He completed his doctoral studies at the University of Minnesota and is currently chairman of the Department of Sociology at the University of Virginia. His major interests are organizational studies, occupational mobility, and applied sociology.

MICHAEL CROZIER is Directeur du Centre de Sociologie des Organisations, in the National Center for Scientific Research, Paris, France. He is past president of the French Association of Sociology and is author of many works on organizations and bureaucracies, including *The World of the Office Worker.* His latest book is *The Stalled Society.*

JOHN LOFLAND is author of *Deviance and Identity* and is editor of the journal *Urban Life and Culture.* He is professor of sociology at the University of California at Davis. His graduate studies were conducted at the University of California at Berkeley and his primary interests are social organization, deviance, social control, and field research methods.

PETER K. MANNING received his doctoral degree from Duke University. He is presently completing a study of comparative policing for a forthcoming book, *Police Work,* and is interested in medical sociology, occupations and professions, and deviance and social control. He has edited two books, *Youth and Sociology* (with Marcello Truzzi) and *Youth: Divergent Perspectives,* and has published in many professional journals. He is an Associate Professor of Sociology and Psychiatry at Michigan State University.

WILLIAM J. McEWEN is a consulting anthropologist at the California State Health Department, in the Research Division, where he pursues his interests in epidemiological studies, community organization and processes, medical care delivery systems, and Latin American Studies. Dr. McEwen was trained in social anthropology at Cornell University.

REECE McGEE is a graduate of the University of Minnesota and is presently Master Teacher in the Department of Sociology at Purdue University. He is the author of *Social Disorganization in America, Academic Janus,* and *Points of Departure.* Dr. McGee is interested in large-scale social organization and in the sociology of higher education.

VIRGINIA OLESEN is currently professor of sociology and chairwoman of the Department of Social and Behavioral Sciences at the

University of California in San Francisco. She is now doing research on alienation in urban work styles.

THOMAS C. SCHELLING has published many books on the subjects of international conflict and arms control. He is a professor of economics at Harvard University where he earned his doctorate degree.

DAVID SILVERMAN is professor of sociology in the Department of Sociology of Goldsmith's College, the University of London. He has published widely in the area of organizations and is author of *The Theory of Organisations*.

JOAN STELLING is a graduate of the University of Chicago. She is currently located in the Department of Sociology of the University of Western Ontario. She has published in many professional journals and is interested in medical sociology, professional socialization and professional organizations.

JAMES THOMPSON graduated from the University of North Carolina. He became professor of sociology at Vanderbilt University where he worked in the areas of complex organizations and human ecology. His publications included *Comparative Studies in Administration*.

REBECCA VREELAND STAFFORD earned her doctorate at Harvard University. She is currently an associate professor of Sociology at the University of Nevada, Reno. Her primary interests focus on the social organization of higher education. She has written several articles on residential housing and on academic departments, and is author of *Effects of Academic Departments and Residential Houses on Student Attitudes*.

ELVI WHITTAKER holds her doctorate in anthropology from the University of California, Berkeley, and is currently located at the University of British Columbia. She is interested in phenomenological anthropology, theories of socialization, and cultural ecology, and her next book will be *The Malihini*.

KARL E. WEICK is professor of Psychology and Organizational Behavior at Cornell University. His graduate training was done at Ohio State University. Professor Weick is a social psychologist interested in developing new methodologies to study organizational behavior. His major publications include "Systematic Observational Methods" in the *Handbook of Social Psychology* and "Laboratory Experimentation with Organizations" in the *Handbook of Organizations.*

PREFACE

This book is about a kind of work organization within which professionals construct their careers. In a sense, we examine *colleges,* because the members of such organizations ordinarily relate to each other as colleagues. In these organizations, each member is enabled to work under conditions of relative autonomy and without some of the burdensome formal controls that typify bureaucracies, industries, and military organizations. Everyday life in collegial settings is vastly different from the experience of the worker in those other kinds of organizations, so it is fitting that there should be study materials available that focus on the conditions and the problems of collegial experience. This book does just that.

There are many more collegial settings today than in the past. The trend toward collegiality may be related to what one writer has termed "the professionalization of everybody." Professionalization movements have occurred in many occupations. In the postindustrial society, which some have asserted is already here, professionalized organizations will become more and more common. In this context it is prudent to add colleges to the existing set of organizational patterns studied by social scientists.

Few empirical situations may be found in which all of the members of an organization interrelate as equals. In most cases a compound structural scheme is found in which only certain members relate as peers. At the same time they function as superiors to other members whose roles are defined as ancillary, supporting, or paraprofessional. There often is a separate structural division for administration, to deal with matters that are not part of the professional's domain. Law firms, hospitals, universities, social service agencies, and even police departments and agencies of government share this common pattern. Some social scientists have described these settings as pseudo-bureaucracies, thus conceding that they are not truly bureaucratic. However, it is much more direct to classify them separately and in terms of their most dominant characteristics.

In recent years a sizable body of literature about collegial organizations and the processes and interactional forms prominent in collegial settings has been accumulating. The purpose of this book is to make a collection of these materials easily available to students of organizations and to the larger body of students who will spend their professional careers as members of collegial organizations.

The diversity of materials requires that an integrative theme or perspective be used to maintain a continuous focus on the topics under consideration. For this reason, the editor has included a series of introductory essays that describe a naturalistic perspective, drawing from the sociological and philosophical traditions of symbolic interactionism, ethnomethodology, pragmatism, and existentialism. The essays constitute less of an attempt to develop theory about organizations than an attempt to present the selected materials in a manner that follows naturally from the students' interests.

This book devotes considerable attention to the socialization of members, before and after recruitment, how members are selected, and how members use organizational resources to construct personal careers. Interpersonal conflict, negotiation, politics, and conceptions of competence and incompetence are some of the features of collegial settings that are considered. The issue of power in the everyday affairs of professionals also receives attention. In a previously unpublished study, the editor demonstrates the usefulness of these concepts in structuring and understanding a complex course of organizational events.

Above all this book is intended to offer the undergraduate student in the social sciences and the preprofessional student in many fields a useful perspective on a kind of organizational setting that is interesting in its own right and one that has special interest for those persons who become the next generation of colleagues.

Some personal acknowledgments are due. Norman K. Denzin taught me that organizations are places where people work. Peter K. Manning helped me to understand that organizations are the actions of members. During the preparation of this book, Tom Gay and Richard Baker at John Wiley and Sons offered encouragement and support. Finally, all of my family must be thanked for their understanding and cooperation.

Ralph L. Blankenship

Platteville, Wisconsin

July 1976

301. 1832
C698

CONTENTS

BOWLING GREEN UNIV. LIBRARY

COLLEAGUES
IN ORGANIZATION

INTRODUCTION:
PROFESSIONS, COLLEAGUES, AND ORGANIZATIONS

Today's reader of Marx might conclude that he was preoccupied with an apocalyptic vision—Western society under the threat of a system that reduced men and their labor to the status of mere commodities. Marx feared *the capitalization of everybody!* And when we read Max Weber today it might seem that he too was preoccupied with an apocalyptic vision —the common man falling under the tyranny of ordinary rules and regulations. Was Weber afraid of *the bureaucratization of everybody?*

More recently some social scientists have written about trends that did not concern the old masters. Some have suggested that modern man has steadily relinquished control over more and more aspects of his life and has turned these over to the control of an organization . . . organized religion, organized politics, even organized protest movements. Along with the recent trend to upgrade occupations and vocations and to emulate the image projected by doctors and lawyers, two more apocalyptic models are suggested. Imagine *the organization of everybody,* and then, *the professionalization of everybody!*

These latter two trends are the reason for this book. In recent years more and more persons have joined organizations of professionals where they work as part of a college of equals. For even more persons, their hope for the future is that some vexing occupational problems will be resolved by the professionalization of their fellow workers and their organizational situations. Almost never do we hear the cry that professionalization might be undesirable for everybody or that certain aspects of professional organizations are more vexing to members than would be expected. The main questions this book treats are: (1) What are the dynamics of organizations within which professionals do their work? (2) What is it like to be a member in these organizations?

Before proceeding to the selected readings it will be helpful for most students to know more about the study of professions and organizations. Actually there is quite a lot of theory and empirical research bearing on these subjects —far too much to be read by any but the most devoted. The intent of this introductory essay is to review the literature and touch upon some of the main points of agreement and disagreement among social scientists who investigate and explain organizations and the professions. In doing so we will develop an interactionist frame of reference.

The essay will be organized around a series of questions. First, we ask, what is a profession? Is there a professional trend in modern society? And, if so, does the professionalization trend converge with the trend toward organization? At that, it must be asked, what is an organization? Finally, we will ask what happens when professionals work in complex organizational settings.

WHAT IS A PROFESSION ?

The current definition of the term professional is confused because in recent decades the term has been used for diverse purposes. It has been *vulgarized;* its meaning is no longer precise and stable. It is often necessary to view the context in which the term is used to understand its meaning. The range of everyday meaning is too extensive for scientific discourse.

Some persons and some groups have used professional imagery to bolster bargaining positions in their competition for a share of the public resources of money and manpower. We commonly hear about professional wrestling, professional crime, and doing a professional job. Mothers urge their children to enter the professions to better their life chances. I recently read a human interest story in a local newspaper about a shoe store operator who claimed to feel satisfaction in his work because he offered a professional service—properly fitting shoes. So in addition to its instrumental value as a way of raising the value of one's good and services, the term has been used to make everyday or mundane work seem more important.

Professions, and those who train and certify professionals, may be accused of having *mystified* professionalism. Take for example the following, which is excerpted from a book on professional education:

> *Professions arose . . . when a group of men was recognized as having unusual abilities to assuage the hurts and calm the fears of others by mediating among them and between them and the powers of the universe. Those powers were everpresent; they had to be propitiated or disaster would befall . . . No lay person could command these powers; they were beyond ordinary control . . . Beginning, therefore, with the medicine man, the professional*

man has been a person of unusual gifts. His primary characteristic is special competence, his ability to act in certain useful ways which he has achieved by extraordinary dispensation or effort. . . . Because he has special competence, society allows the professional man to have a monopoly in his service. Only he and those with his skills and knowledge are permitted to practice. . . . Without this protection he can hardly function, for he would be placed in competition with others whose skills are less and whose training easier. (McGlothlin, 1964:2–3).

Perhaps the twentieth century emphasis on competence and altruism grew out of reaction to an even earlier distinction based on the gentlemanly tradition. As Elliott (1972) explained it:

professionalism at the end of the nineteenth century was a composite product of two trends. On the one hand there was a professional tradition claiming a right to social position rather than responsibility to perform any particular function. This claim was supported by a cultured and gentlemanly ideology and style of life. On the other hand changes in knowledge, economic and social organization created opportunities for occupations to meet specialized demands. Such professions seem to have been anxious to assert this knowledge and competence as a support for their claim to economic security and professional standing. (Elliott, 1972:56).

This attempt to legitimate the special status of the professions appears to have accelerated in the twentieth century. Take, for example, the six criteria given in 1915 by which professions were distinguishable from other and lesser occupations (Flexner, 1915). Dr. Flexner, a pioneer in medical education, declared that a profession is *intellectual,* it is *learned,* it is *practical,* it is based on *techniques,* it is *organized,* and it is guided by *altruism.* By these criteria, he argued, such occupations as social work were clearly inferior to the older and more prestigious professions of law and medicine.

Today, both the older and the newer professions draw on the tradition of gentlemanly status and the claim for specialized competence to support their claim for privileged treatment and economic security.

The mystification and vulgarization of professionalism has almost rendered the concept useless as a tool for classifying occupations and clarify-

BOWLING GREEN UNIV. LIBRARY

ing their similarities and differences. Some of the myths and false imagery have even become lodged in the thinking of many social scientists.

Talcott Parsons, for instance, first posited that professional and commercial attitudes were opposed. Initially, he argued that support for the professions was a means whereby larger social interests could be promoted. But in 1939 he switched his position and posited that both business and the professions were motivated by personal goals, especially security and success. Altruism and acquisitiveness were to be regarded as false motivational assumptions on the part of social scientists (Parsons, 1939).

It is important to know how this happened if we are to avoid making the same errors as we try to determine the social characteristics of professions and what differences exist between them and the other occupations.

It is always good practice to clarify terms, especially when a topic has become embedded in ideology and myth. The terms *profession, professionalism,* and *professionalization* have been treated by many social scientists, but there is little agreement about the precise meanings involved. Before attempting to offer a suitable answer to our question, what is a profession, we had better spend a moment listening to the messages being sent by these many others.

For example, professions are often identified on the exclusive basis of certain structural characteristics that make them different from other occupations (see Figure 1). The structural approach focuses on five factors: a profession must be a fulltime occupation, not a sideline, based on specialized knowledge, with its own training schools that are controlled by members of the profession, and with an association that defines membership and offers self-regulatory mechanisms. It is also important to have licensing or certification by a public agency and recognition from the community, and finally, a code of ethics that implies rights of autonomy and self-governance.

Other social scientists have argued that attitudes of a profession are most important. The attitudinal qualities of a professional are said to be a sense of commitment and identification with the professional association, a desire to dedicate oneself to service of the public rather than selfish pursuits, a sometimes fierce rejection of efforts of nonmembers to regulate the profession, a feeling that members are *called* to the profession by personal motives so that they would do their work even if they were not paid for it, a commitment to the principle that the complex and thorough training program and the exceptional quality standards set in recruitment make supervision and review of professional decisions unnecessary, and, finally, a belief that high rewards, material and subjective, are justified.

The demands placed on both recruits and members of the professions

FIGURE 1   CHARACTERISTICS OF PROFESSIONS[a]

	Carr-Saunders & Wilson (1933)	Foote (1953)	Greenwood (1957)	Goode (1957, 1960)	Bucher & Strauss (1961)	Wilensky (1964)	Barber (1968)	Hall (1968)	Gross (1969)
Attitudinal Qualities									
Colleagues as major reference group	X	X	X	X	X	X		X	X
Public service value	X					X	X	X	X
Self-regulation principle	X			X		X	X	X	
Sense of calling				X	X	X		X	
Autonomy principle						X		X	
Rewards justification	X						X		
Structural Qualities									
Full-time occupation, specialized knowledge	X	X	X	X	X	X	X	X	X
Own training schools	X	X	X	X		X		X	
Professional association	X	X	X	X	X	X	X	X	X
Licensing/certification, community recognition	X	X	X	X	X	X	X	X	X
Code of ethics	X	X	X	X	X	X	X	X	X

[a] Adapted from Morrow (1973), by permission of the author.

5

are very great. But the security and status of a profession is highly attractive when compared to most occupations. It is not surprising that many occupational groupings, from insurance agents to policemen, have become swept up in *professionalization movements* within which standards of *professionalism* have been extolled as a means to achieve social prestige and higher pay.

The recent rush of many occupations into professionalization movements has produced new, complex, and sometimes unexpected outcomes and problems. This is illustrated in Wilson's (1968) study of American police. Wilson found that changing social conditions in the twentieth century, especially in the larger cities, created strained relations between police officers and persons in their communities. This signaled a course of changes in the social organization of police work and police departments.

Since full enforcement of the laws is not feasible and since the statutes do not specify procedures for enforcement, discretion has always been an essential component of police work. Police officers must respond to undefined situations. Usually they cannot call on specific rules or supervisory opinion to guide their decisions. Yet their judgments become *law-in-practice* and are of great importance. So a parallel with the professions was drawn:

> *Occupations whose members exercise, as do the police, wide discretion alone and with respect to matters of the greatest importance are typically "professions"—the medical profession, for example. The right to handle emergency situations, to be privy to "guilty information", and to make decisions involving questions of life and death or honor and dishonor is usually, as with a doctor or priest, conferred by an organized profession. The profession certifies that the member has acquired by education certain information and by apprenticeship certain arts and skills that render him competent to perform these functions and that he is willing to subject himself to the code of ethics and sense of duty of his colleagues. . . . Failure to perform his duties properly will, if detected, be dealt with by professional sanctions—primarily, loss of respect. Members of professions tend to govern themselves through collegial bodies, to restrict the authority of their nominal superiors, to take seriously their reputation among fellow professionls, and to encourage some of their kind to devote themselves to adding systematically to the knowledge of the profession through writing and research. (Wilson, 1968:29–30).*

But on many key points—lack of emphasis on academic training, lack of a professional association, subordination to the authority of senior officers, and failure to produce a systematic body of police knowledge—the police are clearly not a profession. Nor is it likely that full professionalization of the police could be achieved because of a countertrend toward increased accountability which had arisen as a means of eliminating the corruption permitted under older patterns of discretion. On the one hand, policemen were insisting on greater discretionary powers under the banner of professionalization; on the other hand, administrators and public agents were seeking to reduce the amount of discretion an officer could sell.

Bureaucratization (which is a process of increasing reliance on rules and regulations to accomplish the efficient coordination of an organization's parts to achieve a formally sanctioned goal) and professionalization became alternate modes of development which vied for dominance in different police departments. We will consider bureaucracy at a later point. However, Wilson observed that police work could not be bureaucratized any more fully than it could be professionalized, because it is a *craft*—lacking both generalized knowledge and routinized procedures:

> *An attempt to change a craft into a bureaucracy will be perceived by the members as a failure of confidence and a withdrawal of support and thus strongly resisted; efforts to change it into a profession will be seen as irrelevant and thus largely ignored.*
>
> *Faced with these difficulties, it is tempting to devise ways whereby the police can be bureaucratized for some purposes, professionalized for others, and left alone for still others. (Wilson, 1968:283).*

So the avenue of professionalization may lead to an elusive paradise, not at all like the reformer's vision. Indeed, one result of professionalization may be the development of new and mixed configurations of older patterns of organization, caused by the forced imposition of structural and attitudinal conditions onto activities and purposes that are highly resistive.

Not all of the outcomes of professionalization are pleasant and desirable from the member's point of view, as shown in Figure 2, which summarizes some studies of professionalization movements.

The studies of professionalization show that divisive issues within the occupation, power struggles, and status problems are salient concerns for participants. Since these factors do not dissipate during the course of a

FIGURE 2   CHARACTERISTICS OF PROFESSIONALIZATION MOVEMENTS[a]

	Tae-usch (1926)	Hughes (1952, 1958)	Blau-ner (1960)	Goode	Wilensky (1961, 1964)	Bucher & Strauss (1961)	Strauss (1963)	Ber-ger (1964)	Per-row (1967)	Beck-er (1968)
Power struggles			X							
Status strivings				X	X	X	X	X		
Segments within profession						X				
Desires for autonomy	X								X	X
Technology					X	X			X	
Competition		X					X			
Personal gain	X							X		
Service	X									

[a] Adapted from Morrow (1973), by permission of the author.

professionalization movement, they can become a permanent fixture of the occupational situation. Similarly, it is reported that professionalizing occupations show greater concern about perceived incursions against their autonomy. They may place undue emphasis on technological advances. Competition may develop among members who favor one "best way" of working. A moral dilemma, personal interests versus the value of service, may engage the attention of some.

We originally set out to clarify three terms. Professions were defined in terms of sets of structural and attitudinal characteristics. Together these characteristics describe a mode of doing work that was highly attractive to a wide range of occupations. In response, many occupational groupings launched themselves on courses of development that we refer to as professionalization movements. The outcomes of these movements were not always as predicted nor have they always been satisfying in terms of anticipated rewards and greater security.

The third term is professionalism. In treating this term, we must be very cautious. There is a great risk of circular reasoning—of moving from the premise of one's definition of a profession through the salient concerns of professionalization movements to a definition of professionalism that mirrors or reflects the premise. If we do this, there is no way we can use these theoretical constructs in a general explanatory scheme. For example, if we accept that a code of ethics and a professional association to enforce it are essential structural characteristics of a *profession,* that desires for autonomy are salient components of *professionalization* movements, and that acceptance of the statement "a person who violates professional standards should be judged by his professional peers" (Hall, 1968) is a measure of *professionalism,* we may have made the equivalent of a definition that declares that happiness is a feeling of being happy. This message above all, we must hear: the social science literature draws us perilously close to a tautological position.

There may be a distinct advantage in reconceptualizing the subject matter slightly. In doing so I would insist that the theoretical constructs be reflective of certain social–psychological differences in the object of reference. In other words, we should create our explanation by observing the objects themselves and noting their unique characteristics. Now this seems both simple and obvious. Yet the structural and attitudinal explanations of professions, professionalization, and professionalism were based largely on metaphors—on the assumption that these objects were like *something else.*

To begin with, it seems clear that a profession lacks material substance and therefore cannot be treated as if it were a bridge or a gearbox consisting of structural components linked together in some physical or metaphysical system. Further, it stands to reason that a materialistic conception cannot merely be replaced by a metaphysical conceptualization based on attitudinal ethos. A profession can be neither defined as a structure nor a state of mind, if one's purpose is serious and directed toward explanation. These conceptualizations are metaphors that distort the nature of the object under consideration; they are equivalent to saying that an organization is like a good woman, or like a bad debt. (Personally, I find my mind jumping ahead to find the punch line.)

Although there is no opportunity to go into extensive detail in this essay, I would like to suggest that a profession can be understood as a social object (Strauss, 1956: 117–119, 180–181; McCall and Simmons, 1966:50–52); that is, its reality is constructed through the act of creating it symbolically and subsequently treating the symbolic organization as a determinant of further activities. If that sounds like jargon, let me put it differently. When we speak of a profession such as medicine or law, we do not refer merely to the existence of offices, hospitals, framed degrees on waiting-room walls, and the like. Nor do we refer to an attitude of moral repulsion against "socialized medicine," any more than to the old-fashioned practice of making rounds of homebound patients. It is not the rules governing medical training, for example, but the activity of going through medical training as a legitimate, voluntary, self-imposed precondition of setting up a medical practice that gives the profession its social reality. When a number of persons agree to the existence and legitimacy of a profession and then act accordingly, using the symbolic profession to account for their activities and give meaning to their activities, the consequence is the construction of the profession as a social object.

If they subsequently perceive the profession as real and as capable of both action and independent existence, they may treat it as if it were also capable of causing them to act. In that case, their own action may indeed be determined, but only by their belief that such reality exists and can determine members' activities directly.

Since there is no literal professional body, all contacts with the profession are in the form of interactions with other professional members. Perceiving himself as a member and the others as either members or nonmembers, a professional can refer to the significant symbols of his profession as his basis for appropriate role action. In so doing, the professional confirms the symbolizations and makes them socially real (Mead, 1932:180–191). A major social component of a profession is the development and support of the social roles of colleague and noncolleague. A professional's competence may be judged by his colleagues primarily in terms of his finesse in role playing (cf. Heiny, 1969). We will return to these matters in each of the following parts of the book. Let us continue with the clarification of terms.

If we agree to the reconceptualization of professions sketched so briefly here, professionalization becomes more readily dealt with. Instead of looking at professionalization in terms of its outcome, the development of new professions, I would like to suggest that it is a process. The model created in the study of social movements can most readily be applied— professionalization movements can be studied independently of their products. Indeed, Bucher and Strauss (1961) suggest that all professions and many occupations present ongoing processes of internal change that resemble those of social movements. Professionalization may be conceptualized as an ongoing process of development and change in response to internal and external conditions.

This view frees the conceptualization from its interdependence with the substantive and attitudinal components of professionalism. It becomes possible to treat professionalism then as a set of sanctioned attitudes, an ideological tool for use in professionalization movements, and as a social outcome of negotiations among members.

Members need some kind of a cognitive map in order to evaluate their personal and collective progress as a profession. Am I a professional? Am I as professional as I should be? Are "we" a profession? How can "we" become more professional? The answer to these questions can be made by reference to an emerging world-view or perspective that provides both a model and a prescriptions for its achievement. Professionalism and the shortcomings it reveals can be useful as a source of direction for further change—it can motivate members to mobilize in further professionalization movements.

Up to this point we have asked only what a profession *is.* The section should close on another question—what does a profession *mean?* The meaning of a profession may be found in its *mandate.* Freidson (1970) stresses that of all professions, medicine has established the greatest monopoly and the most extensive mandate over their domain of work. A mandate provides the power to define and to set the terms of the problems and services involved, to control admission to their ranks, to fix limits of their responsibility, to define legitimate and desirable problems and clients, to determine the distribution of services, and set the level and mode of payment (Thorne, 1973a: 36). In short, a profession means power to control one's work, including the roles of others who may rely on the profession for valued services. But Bucher and Strauss (1961) caution us to bear in mind that mandates shift, vary, divide, and generate conflict.

Thus, far from being the model of stability and order, professions more often resemble "loose amalgamations of segments more or less delicately held together under a common name, at a particular period in history" (Bucher and Strauss, 1961:326).

The above perspective on professions will be further elaborated in the articles that follow in this book. Let us proceed to the second question.

IS THERE A PROFESSIONAL TREND ?

Historical eras have been characterized by dominant patterns of work organization. The ancient world was one in which crafts and craft-guild organization were dominant (Whitehead, 1948). In the modern world, some would argue, industrial organization is dominant. Others insist that we have entered a postindustrial era; the new era is characterized by the professions and their organizations (Bell, 1973; Lynn, 1963). Accordingly, many social scientists have explored the apparent trend toward professionalization (Lynn, 1963; Wilensky, 1964; Akers and Quinney, 1968; Hodge, et al., 1968; Moore, 1970; Goode, 1969; Engel and Hall, 1971). Let us consider first the argument in favor of professional centrality and dominance in modern society and then the manpower trends that support the argument. Finally, we will examine the historical process of professionalization and the arguments for acceptance of the postindustrial hypothesis.

The Centrality of the Professions

Talcott Parsons (1939) posited that "the professions occupy a position of importance in our society which is . . . unique in history" (Parsons, 1954:-34). Indeed, he argued, the professions must be allowed to function smoothly if modern society would avoid great structural change. The position of the professions is too often eclipsed, in social science, by concern about the business economy. However, such diversion of attention, based on an assumption that professionals and businessmen are differently motivated, is in opposition to the empirical evidence—namely that both forms of work organizations have developed in the same society. Parsons argued in favor of a viewpoint that sees both professionals and businessmen acting in response to the same motivation—acquisitiveness and altruism being mainly the product of institutional arrangements in the larger social structure. Both the professional and the businessmen seek high financial reward, but the professional, unlike the businessman, must assume a commitment to serve others as a condition of his professional status (Parsons, 1954:34–39).

What Parsons provides is a way of explaining a professionalization trend without entering into a debate over whether professions or the business economy is dominant; professions are seen as part of the business economy. But that argument does not rule out the possibility that, since 1939, the professions might be outstripping the rest of the business economy in rate of growth, so that an eventual displacement could occur. A "professional economy" is a distinct possibility. Some data on manpower trends may be helpful at this point.

Expansion of the Professions

Victor Fuchs (1968) offered the hypothesis that the service sector of our economy has increased over the past century, resulting in a "service economy." Since that sector includes the professions, his point is relevant.

FIGURE 3   MANPOWER TREND BY ECONOMIC SECTOR, 1870–1965[a]

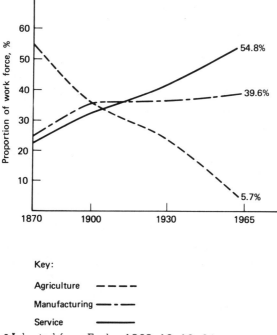

Key:

Agriculture   — — — —

Manufacturing — · — · —

Service   ————————

[a]Adapted from Fuchs, 1968: 18, 19, 24.

Fuchs' data offers graphic evidence that the service sector is outstripping all other sectors (See Figure 3). Agriculture may soon reach its low point, for some labor will continue to be required to produce food. And the industrial sector is expanding too slowly to offer much in the way of new opportunities for displaced workers.

Along with the rise of service occupations, the same period also presented increasing urbanization of the work force and a tendency toward entry into the labor market at a later age. Harris (1972:411–423) claimed that over one-half of the present cohort of high school students will go to college. Once there, they will demand expert training and preparation for subsequent work roles. Clark Kerr (Hughes, et al., 1973: xii) posited that "the increase in the numbers of professionals as a proportion of the labor force has exceeded that of all other categories except that of clerical workers. And more and more students expect professional education to prepare them for their life work." Using the Census Bureau's narrow definition of professional, that category comprised 14% of the nation's employed labor force in 1969 (Hughes, et al., 1973:2).

Neal Rosenthal (1973) offers a projection of the trend over the twenty-five-year period, 1960 to 1985. He divided the labor force into white-collar workers, blue-collar workers, service workers, and farm workers (service workers, in his case, meant household workers, waiters, etc., and is not the same as Fuchs', cited above). His projections were: Farm workers will decline from 8% (1960) to 2% (1985); service workers will remain constant at 13%; blue-collar workers will decline from 36% (1960) to 33% (1985); white-collar workers will rise from 43% (1960) to 53% (1985). Within the latter category, professional and technical workers will rise from 11% (1960) to 17% (1985) (Rosenthal, 1973:9). In sum, the manpower trend data suggests that society is experiencing a professionalization trend. But if so, what is happening besides the proportionate shifts in the labor force? Particularly, are the "true professions" expanding or is it the case that "new professions" are coming into being?

Rising Occupations

Wilensky (1964) made the observation that by analyzing the developmental patterns of those professions to which most people would grant "true" professional status, a natural history of professionalization could be revealed. The natural history would then be useful as a model by which emerging professions could be gauged. The following steps were revealed:

1.   The work becomes a full-time activity.

2.   University training schools are established.

3. Local and then national professional associations are formed.

4. The task is divided into preferred work and dirty work—the latter being delegated to others.

5. Those members who seek to upgrade the professions win power over the older members.

6. Neighboring occupations are brought under professional dominance.

7. Legal protection is sought through political influence.

8. A code of ethics is generated.

Not all professions fit the model perfectly, but as a whole, the established professions are included. Further, some of the steps may occur simultaneously. Figure 4 summarizes the argument.

Figure 4 shows that new professions are emerging over time, and that their progress closely resembles the development of the older ones. This raises a question: if new professions emerge and claim the rewards and statuses accorded to the older professions, must the older ones give up a share, or can the society generate enough new rewards and statuses to absorb the professions? In short, is professionalism a zero-sum game or can society become relatively more professionalized? This point was raised by Goode (1969), who settled in favor of an expanding market for professional services:

> *Thus, over a longer time perspective in which a profession becomes recognized, its greater eminence is not likely to have been taken away from that of another profession, but has rather been earned independently, through transactions in which in fact it has begun to contribute more to the society. (Goode, 1969:-270–71).*

If this expanding market position were true, it would follow that a professionalizing society could have an increasing set of professions, yet the favored status of older professions could remain unaffected. Indeed,

FIGURE 4   THE PROCESS OF PROFESSIONALIZATION[a]

	Became Full-Time Occupation	First University School	First National Professional Association	First State Licence Law	Formal Code of Ethics
Established:					
Accounting (CPA)	19th cent.	1881	1887	1896	1917
Architecture	18th cent.	1868	1857	1897	1909
Civil engineering	18th cent.	1847	1852	1908	ca.1910
Dentistry	18th cent.	1867	1840	1868	1866
Law	17th cent.	1817	1878	1732	1908
Medicine	ca.1700	1779	1847	Before 1780	1912
Others in progress, some marginal:					
Librarianship	1732	1897	1876	Before 1917	1938
Nursing	17th cent.	1909	1896	1903	1950
Optometry	—	1910	1897	1901	ca.1935
Pharmacy	1646	1868	1852	1874	ca.1850
School teaching	17th cent.	1879	1857	1781	1929
Social work	1898(?)	1904	1874	1940	1948
Veterinary medicine	1803	1879	1863	1886	1866
New:					
City management	1912	1948	1914	None	1924
City planning	19th cent.	1909	1917	1963	1948
Hospital administration	19th cent.	1926	1933	1957	1939
Doubtful:					
Advertising	1841	1909	1917	None	1924
Funeral direction	19th cent.	1914	1882	1894	1884

[a] Adapted from Wilensky, 1964:143.

this contention is upheld by the findings of a study (Hodge, et al., 1968) of occupational prestige in the United States between 1925 and 1963. The researchers noted a very high correlation of prestige rankings across time. The professions as a whole showed very slight upward movement, but the greatest upward movement was among blue-collar workers.

> *Occupational morphology, at least insofar as prestige is concerned, remained remarkably stable. To be sure, systematic patterns of change could be detected, but one would miss the import of this paper if one failed to recognize that these changes were minor relative to the overall stability. (Hodge, et al., 1968: 302).*

In answer to our question, then, there is a professionalization trend in society, the evidence is positive. The trend, furthermore, is diffused across the breadth of the work force and has produced a more professionalized social order.

The meaning of the trend can be regarded as twofold. For the individual, the most important consequence is not the end-product. More or fewer professions is not as important as the process of upgrading one's occupation, the pursuit of greater rewards, and heightened social status. In a professionalizing society it is the process of professionalization itself that has the greatest meaning for the individual and for his occupational fellows.

On the other hand, taking a broad societal view, the meaning of the trend is very much a function of the product. Taking much of the data presented above as evidence, one can argue that our society has become a postindustrial society (Bell, 1973; Touraine, 1971). In a postindustrial society, it is knowledge, rather than capital, that enables men to exercise power and to project new enterprise. Knowledge is, by definition, monopolized by professionals.

According to Bell (1973) five dimensions characterize a postindustrial society and distinguish it from earlier forms of social organization:

1. The emergence of a service economy.

2. The preeminence of a professional and technical class.

3. The primacy of theoretical knowledge.

4.   A planned technology.

5.   The development of an intellectual technology.

We have already documented the first two dimensions. The third dimension, primacy of theoretical knowledge, is supported by the extent to which new inventions, new industries, and new social programs are no longer based on isolated and serendipitous advances, but are the products of systematic research and development. Electronics, nuclear technology, and even warfare are now matters of theory, controlled and developed by professional and technological experts. This advance makes the fourth dimension, planned technology, feasible. It is currently feasible to include considerations of social and ecological impact in the planning and development of new enterprise. No longer need we wait until harm is done before being aware of risks in technological progress. The fifth dimension also follows; problems can be solved by the application of problem-solving rules in the place of older models based on intuition and hunch (see Hall, 1975, for a more detailed discussion; also Bell, 1973, and Touraine, 1971, for the original exposition).

Whether we are yet fully into a postindustrial social order or not, the sound of Bell's argumentation has an already familiar ring. The professions are rising in prominence and power. The future development of our society must be considered in light of the heightened importance of knowledge, the professions, and their organizations. We must now direct our attention to the next question.

IS THERE A CONVERGENCE OF PROFESSIONS AND ORGANIZATIONS?

Another way of asking this question is, whatever happened to the good old free professional in solo practice? Barrie Thorne, discussing the medical profession, observes:

> *Doctors and lawyers have traditionally regarded solo practice as an ideal, in which services are delivered on a one-to-one basis, in a private transaction between professional and client, with the client paying a fee for the services received. This ideal reflects not only the values of individualism and autonomy, but also the entrepreneurial side of the professional's role. . . . (Thorne, 1973a:38).*

However, traditions sometimes must give way before changing conditions. Thorne describes a new professional context:

> *Individualism remains a deep-seated value in the professions, even though there have been extensive changes in the context of medical practice since the nineteenth century, a result of changes in technology, processes of institutionalization, and shifts in financing. There has been a steady decline in the number of physicians both in solo and in general practice, and more physicians work in organized settings. The medical division of labor has become increasingly complex; rather than an individual practitioner, there is frequently now a team of workers (or more accurately, a hierarchy of health workers under the control of the doctor). The private office is giving way to clinics and hospitals, and medical centers and teaching complexes have assumed strong institutional power, especially in urban areas. (Thorne, 1973A:38–39).*

We have, in Thorne, a wide-ranging set of social changes culminating in the abandonment of solo practice in favor of a variety of forms of organizational membership within which nearly all contemporary professionals do their work (see also Parsons, 1951:436; Hughes, 1963; Zald, 1971; Freidson, 1970; etc.). We will consider some of the bases of professional organizing; in part, it is a matter of finding the limits of solo practice in a complex social order.

Thorne's commentary on the medical profession will not hold universally for all professions. Some—law, for example— have relatively more solo practitioners while others, such as social work, have always been identified with organizational structures and institutions. But a comparison of these two professions, which are commonly regarded as being very different, will show that although differences exist, there is an increasing similarity among professions.

First, the case of lawyers: In 1967, it was reported, a low 44% of the graduating class from the Harvard Law School entered *private* practice, a level far below the norm. That year, 14% entered business and government, 12% took judicial clerkships, 7% remained in academia, and 3% entered public service roles (Harvard Law Record, 1971). After a brief lull at or near the 1967 level, the proportion entering into private practice rose to former levels (near 60%); in 1972, when the public service sector "tightened" more graduates were "forced" into private practice (nearly 75%), which set a new high point (*New York Times*, 1972).

In contrast, Golton reports that of approximately 42,000 social workers practicing in 1967, only 8 to 10% were in private practice (1971:952). Most of that number were believed to be either part-time professionals with no other professional post, or moonlighters, who engaged in private practice as an adjunct to a full-time organizational post.

The comparison, based on private practice, may be somewhat misleading, however. There is a difference between private practice and solo practice; the latter may be regarded as the stronger indicator of individualistic orientation. Private practice actually refers to the mode of payment for professional services—direct payment by the client with no intermediaries or third parties. It does not always follow that private practice is solo practice and in recent times both are becoming more rare, if rigorous criteria are applied. For example. many of the lawyers described above are *employees* of rather large law firms, thus raising serious problems of validity for the claim of great differences between professions.

A law firm may become large as a result of having many partners who share the work and the rewards equally, according to shares. Or a few partners may generate a large firm by hiring lawyers and paraprofessionals to work for salary or wages. For example, "the lawyer appointed to chair the American Bar Association Special Committee on Lay Assistants works in a three-attorney office employing over 20 subprofessionals" (Yegge, et al., 1971). Smigel (1969) described a Wall Street law firm that employed over 100 lawyers and had a staff of 240 paraprofessionals. Clearly, private practice is moving in the direction of organizational practice, resulting in less difference between professions.

To blur the distinction even further, many of the larger law firms now conduct part of their law practice on a *pro bono* basis. This includes such public service projects as maintaining "slum branch offices" where poor clients can recive legal services and pay according to a sliding scale based on income and ability to pay. Add to this the expansion of publicly supported legal aid and public defender's agencies; the latter doubled in number between 1964 and 1967 (Bellow, 1968), and then doubled again by 1969 (Harvard Law Record, 1971). In medicine, much the same effect was created by the advent of medical insurance programs associated with industry, and especially the publicly financed Medicare program which introduced third-party arrangements between the health service vendor and his patient.

The result is a definite blurring of the conventional view which sets private practice and organizational membership at opposing ends and equates the former with solo practice. A new model, the salaried professional, must be considered. We would define the new model broadly, to include professionals who collect part or all of their fees from third parties, as well as those who depend on a salary.

William Kornhauser (1962) reported that the rate of growth of a profession during the period 1900 to 1960 was directly proportional to the number of salaried members. *The greater the increase in the size of a profession, the higher the proportion of its members will be salaried.* For example, the medical and legal professions have grown less than 100% over the time span, and are also less than 40% salaried. Professors, scientists, accountants, and engineers, on the other hand, have increased more than 1000%, and are more than 80% salaried (see also Zald, 1971:32). Growth implies organizing.

We have seen that even the legal profession has moved away from the older traditions of private and solo practice and has become more like the social work profession. The typical professional today is likely to work in a large organization and to depend on a third party, either the organization itself or an external government bureaucracy, for his financial security. At this point we will probe deeper to examine the underlying bases of the trend. Perhaps this can be accomplished by searching for the working limits of solo practice in a complex social setting.

The Limits of Solo Practice

Even today there are some professionals who continue, either by choice or by necessity, to maintain the solo/private-practice model. We would expect to find this pattern whenever the social context was insufficient to support a higher level of organization as, for example, in rural areas of low population density. Such communities might be lucky to have even one member of the basic professions. Indeed, it is claimed that more than 5000 American communities have no doctor at all (Michaelson, 1971). Within most large metropolitan areas, similar problems exist for the poor, low-status groups who cannot either attract or support professionals. They, too, are likely to have no professional services, or to be served by professionals in solo practice (the urban poor, however, have also been the traditional training population for many professions, including law and medicine).

If there were a rational system of deploying professionals throughout society to provide optimal accessibility for all citizens, solo practice would probably be much more common. But such a system does not exist. Professionals exercise choice in both the location of their practice and the form of organization. Most often they choose to work among substantial populations of financially secure clients, and to affiliate with other professionals in some form of group practice. We will see that this choice is not entirely free, however, but is determined by conditions of increased social complexity; we will consider complexity in relation to work, the social context, technology, political organizations, social change, and social organizations.

SOCIAL CONTEXT, WORK, AND TECHNOLOGY

Paralleling their growth in size, western societies have also grown in the total amount and variety of knowledge. Increases in knowledge have made it possible to sustain growth in population; by increasing the level of knowledge about agriculture, for example, it has been possible to simultaneously increase productivity and reduce the commitment of manpower to that sector of the economy, freeing some for industrial production and others for service roles. The result has been a rising standard of living for a growing population.

This achievement has not been without its cost. Growing food, an activity that once was understood by most members of society, is now a specialized activity, requiring knowledge and techniques possessed by very few—not to mention the increased burden of capitalization presently needed to compete in the agricultural sector. The ability to produce food is only part of the specialized knowledge—one must also know how to raise capital and manage the overall enterprise. Those who lack the requisite knowledge have been pressed to find other lines of work. Let us set this situation in theoretical terms in order to understand more fully what has occurred.

Neil Smelser (1968) might see this as a problem in explaining social change. Drawing on the earlier work of Spencer and Durkheim, he offers what he calls the differentiation/integration tradition in social theory. Briefly, it is maintained that some forces in social life divide a society and others unify it. In the face of increasing differentiation, society must respond with suitable increases in integration, or the result would be hazardous to the continued survival of the social order.

Both rising population and rising knowledge base are likely to have a differentiative effect on society, through the generation of specialization and a complex division of labor. The principle holds true for smaller social units as well, including organizations and professions. For example, a small company may be able to function smoothly when the owner manages the overall enterprise. But if the company grows and the operation becomes more complex, it may become necessary to sell stock in order to raise capital to purchase equipment and to hire engineers, marketing experts, and varied staff personnel. The functions once met by one person would then be divided between specialists. The stockholder contributes only capital; the engineer contributes only technical skill, the personnel manager only his expertise, and so on.

The question then arises, how can all of these specialized members be unified into an effective collective entity? The answer, in our example, might lay in the development of a system of formal controls that would achieve the rational coordination necessary to offset the differentiative effects of complexity. The form, in our example, would probably be some variation of a centralized authority system utilizing formal offices, and legalistic rules and regulations that set forth the limits of individualistic action and prescribe appropriate penalties for violations.

Has something comparable happened in the professions? Everett C. Hughes has argued that this is so (1963). According to Hughes, professional training in earlier times was characterized by intense competition between students, who were encouraged toward individualistic orientations. Not so any longer, though, he claims. Today's professional training is directed toward the development of "organization men"; from the first day of graduate school the student is treated as a "member of the family" of fellow professionals. This has occurred naturally in response to changes in the work, the social context, and the advances in technology. Hughes notes that even the "free" professions must work in organizational settings, including courtrooms, hospitals, and so on. Further, the modern professional must direct and oversee the work of many paraprofessional co-workers, whose efforts constitute part of a "system" of professional service.

The number of paraprofessional workers has increased in relation to the size of the profession. In 1900, for example, there was a ratio of one paraprofessional to one physician. By 1975, the ratio has changed to 20 paraprofessional workers for each physician (Schreckenberger, 1970). There are now over 100 separately designated occupations in the health field, with more than 200 further subdivisions (Thorne, 1973b: 75–76). In 1968, the American Bar Association moved to actively encourage the development and training of legal paraprofessionals (Yegge, et al., 1971).

Hughes (1963) continues his argument that professionals are trained to be organization men, noting that specialization within professions makes them more interdependent. Older patterns of referring a client to a specialist for special problems have given way to group practice, a system in which a client can walk in the front door and be directed to the member with the required specialized expertise (cf. Freidson, 1963:304). This is a great advance, from the client's viewpoint, for it would otherwise be very difficult to find the "right" professional. Further, some specializations are practicable only in organizational settings. Otherwise, the supply of cases might be insufficient to sustain the professional.

Changes in the work, the social context, and technology have altered the older problem of whether professional work can be done in an organizational setting. The problem facing the professional now is, more aptly, finding a place in an organizational system in order to be free to do professional work. A professional in an organization may be freer than his solo/private practice counterpart who depends on local reputation, local customs, and the goodwill of his fellow members. He may choose his work, his clients, and his problems. "As the professions become more organized, business organizations become more professionalized. The result is the development of new patterns of organization" (Hughes, 1963:11).

POLITICAL AND SOCIAL CHANGE

Following the increasing complexity of society and the emergence of specialization, the organizations in which professional work is done, courtrooms, hospitals, universities, etc., constitute a valuable and necessary resource which must be available in order to do professional work. Scarce resources offer an arena in which men can develop and exercise political power. Without a hospital, a physician cannot work; without the support of his colleagues, a physician cannot use a hospital. Thus physicians must become political:

> *Members of the medical profession always had to obtain hospital privileges to have a successful practice. . . . The medical center provides the practicing physicians not only the technical support he requires, but also the access to other specialists he needs to supplement his own knowledge and skills. . . . Practicing physicians are involved in circles of colleagues who control the appointments to hospitals in their community . . . and determine patient referrals between themselves. . . . Simply, dependence on colleagues in one way or another is the rule. . . . (Zola and Miller, 1971:159–160; see also Coleman et al., 1966; and Freidson, 1963).*

Political influences are also present in the relationship of a profession to the larger environment—especially to the government, which serves as a regulator and a source of outside funding for research and training. The *Medical World News* (1966) notes that medical research has been thwarted by governmental reactions to public opinion demanding greater direct service programs. Political influence has generated programs to establish service systems for populations that could not compete in the older solo/private practice model. In this way, many of the "free" professions have come to resemble the professions, like social work, that service clients who cannot afford to pay. Included in this set are professions whose client is the public (public health), or the poor (social welfare), or the profession itself (science). Also included might be the clergy, whose client is a divine force.

The involvement of politics in professional work is intimately interwoven with the growth of the salaried professional and the rise of professional roles in government. It should be noted before passing on, that a problem of role conflict is present in many cases. Salaried professionals, social welfare workers for example, may be uncertain whether they owe their primary loyalty to the client, who cannot pay, or the government agency, who does pay. Is it his responsibility to pursue his clients' interests, if those interests come into conflict with those of the agency? Often a physician, for example, orders the medical procedures for which Medicare will pay, rather than those that he might otherwise prefer, based on his appraisal of his patient's needs. The resolution of such conflicts may require even greater attention to political influences from within and without the profession. As society continues to change, these conflicts may become more and more severe and may lead to further changes in the definition of professional roles.

THE SOCIAL ORGANIZATION OF PROFESSIONS

Within each profession, patterns of differentiation are present that do not follow lines of specialization, but can determine the forms of organization and make solo/private practice more or less possible. From the beginning, one benefit of professional status has been the power to determine one's associates and one's clients. This remains a strong incentive and is reflected in "a stable system of social stratification." Take, for example, the legal profession:

> In a study of the New York City bar, Jerome Carlin (1966) found that lawyers differed in social standing, income, types of clientele and work settings. The differences clustered into a stable system of social stratification. The elite (21 percent of the bar) were lawyers in large firms, with business clients (largely corporations in heavy industry and major finance) and individual clients who were typically affluent Protestants; their contacts with courts and agencies centered on the federal level. Over three-fourths of them had incomes of $35,000 or more. The middle stratum of lawyers (15 percent) practiced in medium-sized firms, while the lowest

stratum (64 percent of all lawyers) were in small firms or individual practice, represented the least affluent and lowest status clients (including blacks and Puerto Ricans), dealt with the lower courts and government agencies, and had lower incomes (only 13 percent of the individual practitioners earned $35,000 or more). Lawyers entered these different types of practice through a complex process of recruitment and self-selection. (Thorne, 1973b:111).

We can see that not all lawyers are equal in their opportunity to join those organizations in which the greatest rewards can be earned. So it is also in other professions. The choice of organizational form can be a determinant of the professional's chances to interact with those colleagues and clients who can enhance or detract from his chances of gaining success, prestige, and recognition for professional achievement. This is even the case in professions which, like professional science and academia, have a high proportion of salaried members (see Crane, 1965, for a study of productivity and recognition of scientists at major and minor universities).

One last aspect of the social organization of professional work is the need for appropriate audiences. Unlike those occupations that produce tangible goods, the professions rely on audiences, who view performances of the professional role, as the primary source of feedback by which competence can be established and identity can be affirmed. Without audiences of colleagues and clients, professional work, and thus the professional himself, is largely invisible. Organized practice eliminates much of the uncertainty in this respect, providing a valuable and reliable supply of colleagues and clients and enabling the professional to enact his role and create his self-identity in a social arena (Blankenship, 1973; Manning, 1970).

We have examined the limits on solo practice in a complex society; now we must consider, at least briefly, the other side of the question. What are the limits on organizing professional work? We will consider three: the setting in which professional work is done, the complexity of the work itself, and the relationship between professional and client.

LIMITS ON ORGANIZING PROFESSIONALS

If professional work is done in the central setting of an organizational structure, then the potential for organizational development is relatively great. If the work is done elsewhere, on the client's premises for example, it may be impossible to organize the profession to any great degree. As Thorne has put it:

Hospitals became a setting for the integration of healing activity into a central institutional complex. In law, several institutions—the courts, law firms and legal aid offices—may serve as organizing institutions, though no legal institution has a position as central as the hospital (and hence the legal work system may never be as tightly controlled as that in medicine (Thorne, 1973a:116).

Thorne's point dovetails with the problem of work that is so complex that unique solutions are necessary. Often this calls for working on the client's premises. Interior decorators, for example, may successfully operate from a very small organizational base, since their work calls for unique and personalized services suited to the conditions set forth by the client's home or office and personal taste.

The professional service that calls for a special and unique relationship between professional and client, psychoanalysis for example, is also highly resistive to large-scale organizing. Once the special relationship is set, it may function as a strong barrier against organizing.

Our initial intent, in this section of the essay, was to treat the question, is there a convergence of professions and organizations? We have endeavored to show that the old solo/private practice model of professional work has given way to newer forms of organizations, including the emergence of the salaried professional. Increasing social and technological complexity was cited as a limit on solo practice, as was a course of political and social changes. Further, the social organization of the professions themselves tend to direct members into organized patterns. Although some limits on organizing were noted, the preponderance of opinion and data confirm the convergence of professions and organizations in our complex, modern society. The result is a new professional model shown in Figure 5.

At this juncture our focus shifts to the problem of defining organization —before undertaking a description of the characteristics of collegial organizations.

WHAT IS AN ORGANIZATION?

The social sciences have generated a multitude of terms to delineate social categories into meaningful order. The result is another of those problems of definition similar to what we faced with the term professional. Max Weber is generally conceded to be the person who opened up organizations as an area of study, and he referred to them as social organizations. This seems very sensible. A social organization was defined as a set of social relationships that is closed to or limited to certain members with

FIGURE 5   EVOLVING PROFESSIONAL CHARACTERISTICS [a]

Traditional Characteristics	Modified Characteristics
1. Isolated individual provides service	Teams provide service
2. Knowledge from a single discipline typically utilized	Knowledge from diverse fields typically utilized
3. Remuneration predominantly fee for service	Remuneration predominantly by salary
4. Altruism: selfless service limited by entrepreneurialism	Increased opportunity for selfless service
5. Restricted colleague evaluation of product	Increased opportunity for colleague evaluation of product
6. Privacy in client–professional relationship	Decreased privacy in client–professional relationship

[a] Adapted from Engel and Hall, 1971:85.

specific rules enforced by particular others. The definition shows that Weber did not choose to characterize organizations as something unique and apart from other groups. Organizations were seen as corporate groups—as one of the variety of forms groups can take. But this catholicity did not prevail and others have chosen to stress different language and different characteristics.

In current usage "social organization" refers generally to the ordering of behavior among individuals into regular and predictable patterns. The study of social organization would include societies, culture, roles, relationships, community, institutions, groupings, and groups. So the qualifying term social is now not appropriate for the focus on organizations. We frequently see the qualifying terms *formal* and *complex* in use to specify social organizations of a smaller order that did not emerge spontaneously but were deliberately established for a particular purpose (cf. Blau and Scott, 1962:2–8). Formal and complex are used to point out that these are not natural or *crescive* organizations but were *enacted,* to borrow on Sumner's language (Sumner, 1907). They do not function, as it might appear, as a marker of a critical difference of degree. A formal organization is not necessarily highly formalized, and a complex organization may be fairly simple. Formalization, a matter of how extensively an organization's activities are rationalized for efficient goal-attainment, can vary and it is a very worthy phenomena for serious study. Complexity, the extent to which an organization is internally differentiated into specialized roles, also varies and is also open for empirical study. By responding to qualifiers as more than mere names, some students of organization became preoccupied with the task of reconciling formal organizational structure with informal structure (see Dalton, 1959). The latter is an implied residual category that often looms larger and more important than formal structure. Paradoxically, we still lack standard measures of either formalization or complexity for research purposes and *an understanding of the theoretical significance* of these organizational features.

One reason for the retarded level of theory of organizations is that social scientists depend on the managerial class for access to research settings. This has resulted in some oversensitivity to the world-view of management. Consequently studies of formal/informal structure (why don't the workers follow our approved scheme?) or effects of specialization on productivity (how can the worker be made to produce more value at less cost?) have primarily served the interests of managers who seek to expand their base of power over subordinates and increase the efficiency with which formally approved goals are pursued. Even the most rigorous pursuit of *commonsense concepts* has failed to produce good theory.

Another common approach, based on functional analysis, builds organizational theory from inferences about *why* men create organizations. For example, Parsons' position might be that an organization comprises a collective effort to ensure that certain functional dilemmas will be resolved satisfactorily and predictably through "structuring" and institutionalizing actions. In this view, functional dilemmas—such as minimizing potentially disruptive behavior and the motivation to disrupt, the problem of order including the problem of opportunity, the problem of prestige allocation and the problem of power—motivate the development of roles, norms, etc., in any social system. Most simply, then, organizing is done to solve problems affecting the social system (Parsons, 1951:29–33; 1956).

Selznick was too impressed with the importance of ongoing actions of members to accept the purely sociological view taken by Parsons. Instead, Selznick combined two views to produce a perspective in which men organize because they need a way to integrate their capacity for individual action with the supports and sanctions available in the external social and economic environment. In short, men create organizations as a means of achieving union with the social system and thereby gaining personal ends (Selznick, 1948).

An implicit theme of rationality is present in these positions. Each of them characterize man as being knowledgeable to outcomes and alternatives and as electing a course of action based on criteria of self-interest. Rationality was even more clearly drawn in the work of Weber, who seems to explain the existence of bureaucratic organization as an artifact of man's capacity for ends–means reasoning. Bureaucracy as a form of social organization could focus more power and more resources on a given goal with greater efficiency than any previous sytem. And the key was the rationalization of personal action in accord with collective purpose through legalistic authority, rules, and regulations (Weber, 1947). More recently, a psychologist offered the following definition of an organization, which is typical of many that follow in the Weberian line:

> *An organization is the rational coordination of the activities of a number of people for the achievement of some common, explicit purpose or goal, through the division of labor and function, and through a hierarchy of authority and responsibility. (Schein, 1965:8).*

Similarly, Etzioni (1964:5–19; 1975) indicates that men develop organizations to promote goal-attainment. Actually, this position is so widespread that it may be classified as a modern platitude. Few make the effort to question its truth or its significance (see Wilson, 1970).

Even Erving Goffman, whose work is not commonly grouped with those discussed above, offers a variant of the rational goal-attainment theme. If we were to expand upon his social psychology of everyday encounters, and especially with reference to his discussion of joint performances (Goffman, 1959:77–105), we could sketch a conception of organizations as congeries of overlapping moral orders created and re-created in the course of social interactions that are constructed in order to facilitate the work of making a self; although a single actor could only be engaged in a small number of interactional relationships and thus privy to only part of the fabric of moral meanings, his limited participation could contribute to team performances of massive dimension that could produce ample rewards for all of the members to share.

We could examine other theorists' views of organizations in search for an answer to the question of motivation, but even these few reveal some common elements. In each of these perspectives there is a similar functional conclusion (or perhaps it is an assumption)—the rewards and benefits men recognize and perceive are those that motivate them to action. If a worker reports that he feels happy when he picks up his paycheck we are likely to conclude that men are motivated to work by monetary incentives. If a worker tells us that he likes to work at XYZ Industries because they take an interest in their workers we might produce the pretentious proposition that worker morale is a function of personnel policy.

All of social science is subject to this particular problem of theorybuilding because we depend so heavily on finding the meaning of our observations from the subjects of our study. It becomes difficult to sort out those explanations that our subjects use to make order of and give meaning to their everyday lives from those explanations that are sufficient for the purpose of building science. In other words, our subjects offer us commonsense concepts and it is our job to transform them into theoretical concepts. We operate in the midst of a thick soup of taken-for-grantedness; our task is to isolate a kernel of general knowledge that can be tested against observable phenomena.

The success of our enterprise will depend on the commitment we make to treat both the commonsense and the theoretical aspects of reality without inadvertently mixing them and mistaking one for the other. In this, our guidelines may come from Weber, who called for a sociology that takes note of the interplay between the subjective and the objective, the material and the ideal, the purpose and the function.

It is not our purpose in this essay to attack the work of Parsons, Selznick, or any of the others mentioned above, but merely to highlight their functionalist bias and show the resulting insufficiency of their theory. Functional analysis is an excellent tool but it makes a poor theory. In order to understand the world of the professional we should seek definitions of order and meaning from members; if a physician tells us that he joined with others to form a clinic to reduce his clerical and accounting expense, let us listen and note the place of such concerns in his world. But let us avoid making the theoretical generalization that economy is the motive for organizing or the root of complex organizations. Instead, these more theoretical concerns should be approached from an objective analysis of the acitivity in sociological and psychological terms.

A number of social scientists take the position that *general systems theory* offers the best approach to the problem (cf. Parsons, 1956). Objectivity is one claim made in favor of this perspective. Systems theories are developed by elevating functional relationships to the status of maxims or laws; in form they emulate the model of Newtonian physics. Generally an observable empirical relationship, measured by statistical tests, is stated as a proposition which attributes causal power to one or more conditions over an outcome. For example, a series of industrial studies produced the following complex causal chain: *an increase in work group cohesiveness (indicated by greater homogeneity of task and attitude) is positively related to the rate of joint payoff transactions (indicated by degree to which managerial changes have roughly the same positive or negative effect on all of the workers) which is positively related to union mobilization to oppose managerial decisions* (cf. Whyte, 1969:479–513).

Functional theory makes certain assumptions about the objects it would explain. First among these assumptions is that *the phenomena of a system are interrelated in such a way that a change in one part produces or causes changes in other parts.* Every "structure" is functionally important as a potential causal agent for effects observed in other structures. The social scientist need only determine the constant interrelationships within a discrete set of "organizational indicators" to establish control over the organization in the same fashion as a physical engineer controls a powerful steam-generating plant. The second assumption follows—that *persistence of the system requires balance or equilibrium between the various parts.* Naturally, this assumption favors a conservative stance that is highly compatible with managment attitudes and lends an air of legitimacy to reactionary, paternalistic, and manipulative policies. Change is difficult to accommodate in systems theories, although open-systems theory (Katz and Kahn, 1966) improves performance in that area by allowing for ongoing interchanges between the system and its environment. As a theory of organization, though, systems theory is not sufficient for the simple reason that although organizations develop systems and are in some ways *systematic,* they are not merely systems.

A general explanation of organizational settings cannot be based on either commonsense concepts or on metaphors. It is fair to say that *we do not now really have a general theory of organizational settings.* What we do have are a number of partial theoretical statements of widely divergent scope and focus, a number of nontheoretical accounts of organizational phenomena, and a whole lot of unsorted empirical findings and generalizations.

Within this melange of materials it is possible to identify several lines of thematic development.[1] Which of these lines offers the greatest potential for general understanding is a question that can raise a furor of controversy among social scientists. For the purposes of this book, however, the author chooses to select a line that emphasizes the fluxiveness rather than the orderliness of organizational settings because that characteristic seems most typical of collegial organizations. The line begins in the work of Max Weber, who described the ideal bureaucracy and also stressed the need to consider the knowledge, the attitudes, and the feelings of members as part of the organization. Phillip Selznick extended the line further by describing organizations as an interface of rational action and networks of interpersonal relationships. A third extension of the line is found in the work of Anselm Strauss and his co-researchers, who defined the organization as a negotiated order plus an interactional arena within which members enact everyday work.

Max Weber

It is fitting that the first theorist should be Weber, for he broke the ground and his statement on bureaucracy remains unsurpassed in its significance and its effect on others' thinking. Weber comes nearest to offering a complete theory of organizations and the tools for their empirical analysis (cf. Weber, 1947).

An organization represents a legitimated order within which stable patterns of interactions, expressed as relationships, occur between members. Power is a feature of the relationships; power is merely the ability to get another person to do your bidding. Power that is perceived as legitimate is termed authority. Power can be legitimated through tradition, charisma, or rules. However, traditional and charismatic authority are unstable and tend to evolve toward legalistic authority over time. This process, the routinization of authority, has contributed to the increasing development of bureaucracy in Western society. Like Marx had done before him with capitalism, Weber drew an ideal type, *bureaucracy,* to be used as a benchmark against which the critical features of real bureaucracies would stand out more clearly. The administrative significance of bureaucracy is in its capacity to focus a great deal of manpower in a controlled and highly rationalized program of goal-attainment.

The ideal characteristics of organizations based on rational–legal order include:

1. The organization is guided by a set of explicit and specific

purposes from which a system of rules and regulations is derived that governs the behavior of officials.
2.   There is a distribution of activity among offices so that each incumbent has a specified sphere of competence.
3.   The offices are arranged in a hierarchical pattern so that each official exercises authority over those subordinate to him and is subject to the authority of his superiors, but only in his capacity as an office-holder and within the limits established by organizational rules.
4.   Officials are personally free, bound to their offices only by a contractual relationship that involves services in return for compensation.
5.   Candidates for positions are selected on the basis of technical competence, and they are promoted on the basis of seniority, performance, or both.
6.   Officials must carry out their functions in a disciplined and impersonal manner.
7.   The organization maintains detailed written records, the contents of which are often treated as "official secrets."
8.   The individual's commitment to his office is his primary work commitment. (CRM Books, 1973:153).

Weber saw the ideal-type function as a means of objectifying organizational analysis and facilitating comparative analysis, but he also urged that the perspective of members be sought and incorporated into the total explanation. Organizational reality was to be located in the interplay between the subjective worlds of the members and the objective characteristics of the corporate group.

Weber serves as a watershed. Principal among the criticisms of his theory is his failure to recognize the dysfunctional aspects of bureaucratic structure. The same features that are proposed as means of achieving greater efficiency have proven to contribute inefficiency and irrationality to the organization. As Merton pointed out (1940), bureaucracies have negative effects on the psychological patterns of members, resulting in decreased capacity for goal-attainment. Some "bureaucrats" appear to have displaced formal organizational goals in favor of compulsive performance of ritualized means.

Other critics claim that Weber overemphasized the importance of formally approved goals. Some studies have shown that most workers are unaware of the formal goals, which are often stated in terms of unanalyzable abstractions that could not provide direction, even if known. Health care and prevention of disease, for example, must be broken down into concrete tasks such as cleaning hospital equipment and administering particular medical tests to particular persons; it is these lower-order programs and activities that are used to order organizations. Some organizations, because of unanticipated success, find that new goals must be identified if the organization is to persist. This suggests that unattainable goals may be the best and most durable formal goals of all and that rationalization per se is more important than goal attainment.

Others claim that Weber ignored the importance of informal structure. Ignored may be too strong a word. Although it is clear that the ideal type was based on elements of formal structure to the exclusion of informal structure, Weber's insistence on including members' subjective viewpoints in the explanation of organizations certainly permits the consideration of informal structure. This potential was shown in the work of Phillip Selznick.

Phillip Selznick

Selznick (1948) presents his conception of organization in a study of the TVA project, an early effort at socialistic delivery of services to American citizens. The TVA faced two main problems—the lack of prior models and the lack of grassroots ideological support. Thus many of the taken-for-granted processes of organizational development were problematic and were more readily observed by Selznick. Blocked goals, for example, resulted in abandonment, modification, or simply ignoring of the goals.

Selznick proposes that trade unions, government agencies, and businesses are all rationally ordered structures; a single organizational theory would be superior to separate theories. The general and common characteristics of organizations would provide the basis of a general theory; an organization could be described as *an arrangement of persons for the purpose of accomplishing some agreed-upon program or goal through the allocation of functions and responsibilities.* An organization is the structural expression of rational action, but a dialectic tendency renders the structure vulnerable to nonrationality. No amount of rational scheming can ensure that the way things are supposed to be done and the way they are truly done will coincide. At best, what is achieved is a more-or-less coordinated interface between a rational scheme of order and an informal and nonrational interpersonal network of members and activities. Cooperation between members who interact within the organizational setting makes possible the maintenance of a system of functionally interrelated roles. On a larger scale, the informal structure functions in an adaptive sense to articulate the formal structure and the environment.

This more fluxive view of organizations was a high-water mark in organizational theory which was not surpassed for many years. The combined work of Weber and Selznick afford a very rich beginning point for further development by others.

Strauss, Schatzman, Ehrlich, Bucher, and Sabshin

An interdisciplinary group of research scholars collaborated on a study of mental hospitals (Strauss et al., 1964). A model for the study of hospitals and other organizations was generated; it has become known as the interactive arena model. The arena model bears on:

> ... how a measure of order is maintained in the face of inevitable changes (derivable from sources both external and internal to the organization). Students of formal organization tend to underplay the processes of internal change as well as to overestimate the more stable features of organizations—including its rules and its hierarchical statuses. Contracts, understandings, agreements, rules—all have appended to them a temporal clause. . . . In short, the bases of concerted action (social order) must be reconstituted continually; or as remarked above, "worked at".
>
> Such considerations have led us to emphasize the importance of negotiation—the processes of give and take, of diplomacy, of bargaining—which characterizes organizational life. (Strauss, et al., 1963:148).

A hospital was characterized as a geographical site on which professionals and others, including lay workers and patients, meet in the ongoing activity of health care, which as a goal is strikingly nondirective and incapable of being directly rationalized. Order is the product of negotiations between members—negotiations conditioned by ideology, power, and situational considerations, but only slightly limited by rules or formal guidelines. While some agreements were of long standing, others were called into question or ignored after only a short time; although some negotiation was deliberate and produced explicit contracts, other understandings emerged from apparently insignificant interactions between virtual strangers and remained essentially tacit.

When an organization is viewed as an interactive arena its substance consists of an emerging set of interactional products:

With an eye on practicality, one might maintain that no one knows what a hospital "is" on any given day unless he has a comprehensive grasp of what combination of rules and policies, along with agreements, understandings, pacts, contracts and other working arrangements, currently obtains. In any pragmatic sense, this is the hospital at the moment; this is its social order. (Strauss et al., 1963:165).

As a rapidly evolving phenomenon the social order is subject to persistent change in response to shifts in its external or internal conditions. The primary mechanism in the construction of the social order and the primary mechanism of its presentation and its change is the same negotiation process.

In criticism of the arena model it must be noted that exclusive emphasis given to the symbolic character of the social order works to the detriment of understanding negotiation as a process and as an activity. Organizational action must be considered in both its ideal sense and its material sense. Symbols may be both the cause and the effect of interactions, but, even so, interactions themselves are necessary.

In this essay a perspective was proposed beginning with the suggestion that professions be considered social objects and professionalization considered an ongoing process that resembles social movements. Professionalism was relegated to the role of ideology—a set of concerns that define membership, competence, and the like. As social objects, professions lack existence independent of members' interactions with themselves and with significant audiences. The interactions are necessary as means of confirming the profession and reaffirming such critical matters as membership. The functional dilemma thus raised may account in part for the development of organizations by professionals. It was argued that conventional explanations of organizations cannot serve theoretical needs because of their reliance on commonsense concepts and mischievous metaphors. Weber and Selznick are suggested beginning points for a more adequate organizational theory. The interactive arena model, with some minor revision, offers a useful way of looking at organizations in which some or all of the members operate in a professional mode. In closing, consider a fuller definition of organizational situations, one which stresses the interdependence of members, interactions, and symbols:

The enacted organizational situation is the interactions of members with members and with others in the social environment, the tangible products of the interactions, the meanings, the careers, the sytems and the selves thus created and defined, and the projections of interactions yet to come.

This definition is excerpted from the closing paper of this volume where it is developed more fully in the context of a study of power in a collegial organization. Our attention can now shift to the last question:

WHAT ARE COLLEGIAL ORGANIZATIONS LIKE?

This is truly the central question that led to the development of this book. A full answer is not feasible within the limits of this introductory essay; if it were, the remainder of the book would be unnecessary. The questions that have preceded this closing section of the Introduction are necessary background for what follows. Accordingly, the closing section offers only a brief sketch of the scheme around which the remaining material is organized.

Collegial organizations are different from bureaucracies and other organizational setting. Many past social scientists have discussed the work settings of professionals in terms of a difficult and conflict-prone interface between individualistic professional interests and bureaucratic organizational interests.[2] Implicit in such a conceptualization is a commitment to the outdated models of solo/private practice and industrial bureaucracy. We agree, however, with Harries-Jenkins (1970) in his assertion that the contemporary professional who works in an organizational setting is quite likely to feel at home and at ease there because profession and organization are fused into a new social form.

The essential characteristic of the new form is the centrality of the individual member and his interaction with others, most importantly with his colleagues. Papers for the first part of this book were selected on the basis of their contribution in making the reader more sensitive to the ever-changing interactional phenomena which, together with more durable patterns and tangible products, make up the organization.

The second part is built around this direct concern with members. Professional membership and organizational membership are seen as parallel social processes—continuous, overlapping, sometimes complementary, and sometimes in conflict. A professional works within two institutions, the profession and the firm. His socialization into the complex role he will enact must begin long before he joins the firm—in professional school. The profession is significant throughout his career in the organization, including control over his recruitment and placement, his acceptability as a colleague, his eventual acceptance within the community of fellow professionals, and even the degree to which he can become productive and gain recognition for his achievement. In all of these ways, the professional community influences the organizational setting and directs the professional worker into lines of activity that must be supported by organizational resources. A special relationship is likely to develop between a professional and the organization based on the utility of the setting as a base for the construction of the professional career. When the organization provides the necessary resources, the professional member is enabled to establish lines of professional activity through which both he and the organization can benefit.

A third aspect of collegial dynamics refers to the ways in which organizational problems are typically handled. Professionals are highly resistive to rules, regulations, and commands. This is not to say, however, that professionals are resistive to socially organized activities. Participation is the key word—participation in planning, decision making, development, and so on. Bargaining processes and reciprocal systems of give and take in the everyday course of events are regarded as very important—important enough to stir vigorous defensive action in the face of perceived threatening conditions. The result is a virtual paucity of issues and concerns within collegial settings that can be regarded as closed, resolved for good and all. The typical organizational affair is reminiscent of the old-fashioned soup-kettle which was kept on the back of the stove; although the soup changes with the bounty of each passing day, it is somehow much the same after all.

The final portion of the book treats the question of power and control. How, in the face of flux and change, can individualistic members be checked and guided toward acceptable lines of activity. The relationships of peer to peer and professional to manager draw our attention. The former, however, and not the latter will be given the greater attention. To be accepted as a colleague means to be controlled; the power to check and balance is held by the collegial peer group.

Footnotes

[1] Each author of a book on organizations typically constructs a typology of organizational theories and offers a summary of each one which he regards as important. We will not attempt to replicate what is already available in profusion. The student who wishes to read further is urged to consider the following: Silverman, 1970:26–125. Haas and Drabek, 1973:23–94; Champion, 1975:24–76; Mouzelis, 1968:7–165.

[2] There is an extensive body of literature on the topic of professionals in bureaucracy. The interested reader might wish to consider the following: Scott, 1966; Kornhauser, 1962; Etzioni (ed.), 1969; Glaser, 1964.

REFERENCES

AKERS, RONALD L., AND RICHARD QUINNEY
1968   "Differential Organization of Health Professions: A Comparative Analysis," *American Sociological Review* 33:104–21.

BARBER, BERNARD
1968   "Some Problems in the Sociology of the Professions," pp. 15–34 in Kenneth S. Lynn (ed.), *The Professions in America*. Boston: Houghton Mifflin Company.

BECKER, HOWARD L., AND ANSELM L. STRAUSS
1968   "Careers, Personality and Adult Socialization," pp. 21–34 in Barney G. Glaser (ed.), *Organizational Careers: A Sourcebook for Theory*. Chicago: Aldine Publishing Company.

BELL, DANIEL
1973   The Coming of Post-Industrial Society. New York: Basic Books.

BELLOW, GARY
1968   "The Extension of Legal Services to the Poor: New Approaches To the Bar's Responsibility," in A. Sutherland (ed.), *The Path of the Law from 1967*. Cambridge, Mass.: Harvard University Press.

BERGER, PETER L.
1964   "Some General Observations on the Problem of Work," pp. 230–247 in Peter L. Berger (ed.), *The Human Shape of Work*. New York: The Macmillan Company.

BLANKENSHIP, RALPH L.
1973   "Organizational careers: An interactionist perspective," *The Sociological Quarterly* 14 (Winter): 88–98.

BLAU, PETER M., AND W. RICHARD SCOTT
1962   *Formal Organizations.* San Francisco: Chandler.

BLAUNER, ROBERT
1960   "Work Satisfaction and Industrial Trends in Modern Society," pp. 339–360 in Walter Falenson and Seymour M.
Lipset (eds.), *Labor and Trade Unionism: An Interdisciplinary Reader.* New York: John Wiley and Sons, Inc.

BUCHER, RUE, AND ANSELM STRAUSS
1961   "Professions in Process," *American Journal of Sociology*
66:325–334.

CARLIN, JEROME
1966   *Lawyers' Ethics: A Survey of the New York City Bar.* New
York: Russell Sage Foundation.

CARR-SAUNDERS, ALEXANDER, AND P. A. WILSON
1933   *The Professions.* Oxford: Clarendon Press.

CHAMPION, DEAN
1975   *The Sociology of Organizations.* New York: McGraw-Hill.

COLEMAN, J. S., E. KATZ, AND H. MENFEL
1966   *Medical Innovation: A Diffusion Study.* Indianapolis:
Bobbs-Merrill.

CRANE, DIANA
1965   "Scientists at Major and Minor Universities: A Study of Productivity and Recognition," *American Sociological Review*
30:699–714.

CRM BOOKS
1973   *Society Today.* Los Angeles: CRM Books.

DALTON, MELVILLE
1959   *Men Who Manage.* New York: John Wiley and Sons, Inc.

ELLIOTT, PHILLIP
1972   *The Sociology of the Professions.* New York: Herder and
Herder.

ENGEL, GLORIA V., AND RICHARD H. HALL
1971   "The growing industrialization of the professions," in Eliot Friedson (ed.), *The Professions and Their Prospects*. Beverly Hills, California: Sage Publications: 75-88.

ETZIONI, AMITAI (ED.)
1969   *Readings on Modern Organizations*. Englewood Cliffs, N. J.: Prentice-Hall.

ETZIONI, AMITAI
1975   *A Comparative Analysis of Complex Organization*. New York: Free Press.

ETZIONI, AMITAI
1964   *Modern Organizations*. Englewood Cliffs, N. J.: Prentice-Hall.

FLEXNER, ABRAHAM
1915   "Is Social Work a Profession?" *Proceedings of the National Conference of Charities and Corrections*. Chicago.

FOOTE, NELSON M.
1953   "The Professionalization of Labor in Detroit," *American Journal of Sociology* 58:371-380.

FREIDSON, ELIOT (ED.)
1963   *The Hospital in Modern Society*. New York: The Free Press of Glencoe.

FREIDSON, ELIOT
1970   *Professional Dominance: The Social Structure of Medical Care*. New York: Aldine-Atherton.

FUCHS, VICTOR
1968   *The Service Economy*. New York: National Bureau of Economics Research.

GLASER, BARNEY G.
1964   *Organizational Scientists: Their Professional Career*. Indianapolis: Bobbs-Merril.

GOFFMAN, ERVING
1959   *The Presentation of Self in Everyday Life.* Garden City: Doubleday Anchor.

GOLTON, MARGARET
1971   "Private Practice in Social Work," *Encyclopedia of Social Work,* Vol. 2, pp. 949–955.

GOODE, WILLIAM J.
1969   "The Theoretical Limits of Professionalization," pp. 266–313 in Amitai Etzioni (ed.), *The Semi-Professions and Their Organizations.* New York: The Free Press.
1960   "Encroachment, Charlatanism, and the Emerging Professions: Psychology, Sociology, and Medicine," *American Sociological Review* 25:902–914.
1957   "Community Within a Community: The Professions," *American Sociological Review 22:194–200.*

GREENWOOD, ERNEST
1957   "Attributes of a Profession," *Social Work* 2:44–55.

GROSS, EDWARD
1969   "Changes in Technological and Scientific Development and Its Impact upon Occupational Structure," pp. 17–45 in Robert Perrucci, et al. (eds.), *The Engineers and the Social System.* New York: John Wiley and Sons, Inc.

HAAS, J. EUGENE, AND THOMAS E. DRABEK
1973   *Complex Organizations: A Sociological Perspective.* New York: The Macmillan Company.

HALL, RICHARD
1975   *Occupations and the Social Structure.* 2nd Edition. Englewood Cliffs, N. J.: Prentice-Hall.
1968   "Professionalization and Bureaucratization." *American Sociological Review* 33:92–104.

HARRIES-JENKINS, G.
1970   "Professionals in Organizations," pp. 51–108 in J. A. Jackson (ed.), *Professions and Professionalization.* Cambridge: Cambridge University Press.

HARRIS, SEYMOUR E.
1972   *A Statistical Portrait of Higher Education.* New York: McGraw-Hill.

HARVARD LAW RECORD
1971   Vol. 53, No. 5, October 29, 1971.

HEINY, ROBERT
1969   *Student Role Performances: A Case Study in the Professionalization of Special Educators.* Ph.D. dissertation, University of Illinois at Urbana-Champaign.

HODGE, ROBERT W., PAUL M. SIEGEL, AND PETER H. ROSSI
1968   "Occupational Prestige in the United States, 1925–63," *American Journal of Sociology* 70:286–302.

HUGHES, EVERETT C.
1973   "Introduction," pp. 1–16 in Hughes et al., *Education for the Professions of Medicine, Law, Theology and Social Welfare.* New York: McGraw-Hill.
1963   "Professions," pp. 1–14 in Kenneth S. Lynn (ed.), *The Professions in America.* Boston: Houghton-Mifflin.
1958   *Men and Their Work.* Glencoe, Ill.: The Free Press.
1952   "The Sociological Study of Work: An Editorial Foreword." *American Journal of Sociology* 57:423–426.

HUGHES, EVERETT C., BARRIE THORNE, AGOSTINE M. DEBAGGIR, ARNOLD GURIN, AND DAVID WILLIAMS
1973   *Education for the Professions of Medicine, Law, Theology, and Social Welfare.* New York: McGraw-Hill.

KATZ, DANIEL, AND ROBERT L. KAHN
1966   *The Social Psychology of Organizations.* New York: John Wiley and Sons, Inc.

KERR, CLARK
1973   "Foreword," p. xiii in Hughes, et al., *Education for the Professions of Medicine, Law, Theology and Social Welfare.* New York: McGraw-Hill.
1963   Godkin Lectures, Harvard University (Spring).

KORNHAUSER, WILLIAM
1962   *Scientists in Industry.* Berkeley: University of California Press.

LYNN, KENNETH S.
1963   "Introduction," pp. ix–xiv in Kenneth S. Lynn (ed.), *The Professions in America.* Boston: Houghton-Mifflin.

MCCALL, GEORGE J., AND J. L. SIMMONS
1966   *Identities and Interactions.* New York: Free Press.

MCGLOTHLIN, WILLIAM J.
1964   *The Professional Schools.* New York: Center for Applied Research in Education.

MANNING, PETER K.
1970   "Talking and Becoming: A View of Organizational Socialization," in Jack D. Douglas (ed.), *Understanding Everyday Life.* Chicago: Aldine.

MEAD, GEORGE HERBERT
1932   *The Philosophy of the Present.* Chicago: Open Court.

MEDICAL WORLD NEWS
1966   "Is Basic Research Threatened?" 7 (December 2): 108–119.

MERTON, ROBERT K.
1940   "Bureaucratic Structure and Personality," *Social Forces* 18:560–568.

MICHAELSON, MICHAEL G.
1971   "The Coming Medical War," *New York Review of Books,* pp. 32–38, July 1.

MOORE, WILBERT E.
1970   *The Professions: Roles and Rules.* New York: Russell Sage Foundation.

MORROW, GLORIA
1973   *The Professionalization of Insurance Agents.* Unpublished

M.S. thesis. Virginia Commonwealth University.

MOUZELIS, NICOS
1968   *Organisation and Bureaucracy.* Chicago: Aldine.

PARSONS, TALCOTT
1964   *Structure and Processs in Modern Societies.* Glencoe: Free Press.
1956   "Suggestions for a Sociological Approach to the Theory of Organizations, I, II," *Administrative Science Quarterly* 1:63–85, 225–239.
1954   *Essays in Sociological Theory.* New York: The Free Press of Glencoe.
1951   *The Social System.* Glencoe: Free Press.
1939   "The Professions and Social Structure," *Social Forces* 17:457–467.

PERROW, CHARLES
1967   "A Framework for the Comparative Analysis of Organizations," *American Sociological Review* 32 (April): 194–208.

ROSENTHAL, NEAL H.
1973   "The United States Economy in 1985: Projected Changes in Occupations," *Monthly Labor Review* 96 (December): 18–26.

SCHEIN, E. H.
1965   *Organizational Psychology.* Englewood Cliffs, N.J.: Prentice-Hall.

SCHRECKENBERGER, PAUL C.
1970   "Playing for the Health Team," *Journal of the American Medical Association* 213 (July 13): 279–81.

SCOTT, W. RICHARD
1966   "Professionals in Bureaucracy—Areas of Conflict," pp. 265–274 in Howard M. Vollmer and Donald L. Mills (eds.), *Professionalization.* Englewood Cliffs, N.J.: Prentice-Hall.

SELZNICK, PHILLIP
1948   "Foundations of the Theory of Organizations," *American*

Sociological Review 13:25–35.

SILVERMAN, DAVID
1970   *The Theory of Organisations.* New York: Basic Books.

SMELSER, NEIL
1968   "Toward a General Theory of Social Change," pp. 192–280 in *Essays in Sociological Explanation.* Englewood Cliffs, N.J.: Prentice-Hall.

SMIGEL, ERWIN O.
1969   *The Wall Street Lawyer.* Bloomington, Ind.: Indiana University Press.

STRAUSS, ANSELM (ED.)
1956   *The Social Psychology of George Herbert Mead.* Chicago: The University of Chicago Press.

STRAUSS, ANSELM, LEONARD SCHATZMAN, DANUTA EHRLICH, RUE BUCHER AND MELVIN SABSHIN
1964   *Psychiatric Ideologies and Institutions.* New York: The Free Press.
1963   "The Hospital and Its Negotiated Order," in Eliot Friedson (ed.), *The Hospital in Modern Society.* New York: Free Press.

STRAUSS, GEORGE
1963   "Professionalism and Occupational Associations," *Industrial Relations* 2:1–15.

SUMNER, WILLIAM GRAHAM
1907   *Folkways.* Boston: Ginn and Company.

TAEUSCH, CARL F.
1926   *Professional and Business Ethics.* New York: Henry Holt and Company.

THE NEW YORK TIMES
1972   March 14.

THORNE, BARRIE
  1973a   "Professional Education in Medicine," pp. 17–100 in Hughes et al., *Education for the Professions of Medicine, Law, Theology and Social Welfare.* New York: McGraw-Hill.
  1973b   "Professional Education in Law," pp 101–68, ibid.

TOURAINE, ALAIN
  1971   *The Post-Industrial Society: Tomorrow's Social History: Classes, Conflicts and Culture in the Programmed Society.* New York: Random House.

WEBER, MAX
  1947   *The Theory of Social and Economic Organizations.* Glencoe: Free Press.

WHITEHEAD, ALFRED NORTH
  1948   *Adventures of Ideas.* Great Britain: Pelican Books.

WHYTE, WILLIAM F.
  1969   *Organizational Behavior: Theory and Applications.* Homewood, Ill.: Richard D. Irwin, Inc.

WILENSKY, HAROLD L.
  1964   "The Professionalization of Everyone?" *American Journal of Sociology* 70:137–155.
  1961   "Orderly Careers and Social Participation: The Impact of Work History in Social Integration in the Middle Mass," *American Sociological Review* 26:521–539.

WILSON, BRYAN (ED.)
  1970   *Rationality.* New York: Harper and Row.

WILSON, JAMES Q.
  1968   *Varieties of Police Behavior.* Cambridge: Harvard University Press.

YEGGE, ROBERT B., WILBERT E. MOORE, AND HOWARD HOLME
  1971   "New Careers in Law," 1969, in *Report of the A.A.L.S. Curriculum Committee.*

ZALD, MAYER N.
1971   *Occupations and Organizations in American Society.* Chicago: Markham Publishing Co.

ZOLA, IRVING KENNETH, AND STEPHEN J. MILLER
1971   "Time Erosion of Medicine from Within," in Eliot Freidson (ed.), *The Professions and Their Prospects.* Beverly Hills: Sage Publications.

CHAPTER ONE:
PERSPECTIVE

OVERVIEW

It is usual for a first chapter to introduce the reader to the general outlines and conceptions that will follow throughout a book. So it will be here. Four papers have been selected for this section; they move from the most general question of what should be the nature of social science to the more specific question of what are the typical characteristics of collegial organizational settings.

SOCIAL ACTION AND MEANING

Whenever we set out to create an explanation of something, whether that something is a chemical change, an attitude, or a revolution, our task calls for an answer to the question—why? But the form of the question, why, is not always the same. The key to understanding the transformation of why is in the nature of the object being explained. The more complex the object, the less precise and less stable the explanation. The scientific study of physical objects has produced a set of universal laws to explain the "behavior" of inanimate and unconscious phenomena of nature. Biologists, on the other hand, have had to develop less precise explanations of organic systems and processes of change, including adaptation to environmental conditions. The shift holds true also in the cases of psychology and sociology, the latter producing the least precise and the most unstable explanations of all the sciences. This fact among others has led to much borrowing of explanatory models and research methods from the more respectable sciences. This in turn has forestalled the day when sociologists must face up to the most difficult of questions—what kind of social science is possible?

David Silverman argues that basic differences in the objects of study preclude the usefulness of the physical sciences as a model for the social sciences. Behaviorism is considered and rejected as being too limiting, or as merely insufficient to handle the fullness of social reality. Silverman calls for a social science that is capable of explaining how subjective meanings become involved in the actions of self-conscious persons and what part meaning plays in the whole of social reality. Social science should explain how meanings arise and how they change. Mere causal relatedness in the model of positivism is insufficient.

The model one can generate when organizational order is treated as problematic and when professional membership is treated as honorific and temporally limited is much more dynamic and fluxive than older, more conventional approaches have suggested. A research methodology is needed that can accommodate the quality of fluxiveness.

John Lofland is an advocate of field research in the participant–observation tradition. As a methodology, that tradition calls for flexibility and responsiveness to changing situations. The field researcher must observe when the opportunity is present, but he must also be prepared to shift to focused interviewing or documentary analysis if indicated by the flow of events in their social setting. The result is often a massive body of unsorted and uncomparable materials which he must use as data. In the selection, Lofland uses a variety of published research materials to illustrate the various levels of research analysis. Acts and activities can be studied, and each of these offers both static and phase varieties. A common activity, such as having lunch, involves many acts—ordering, preparing, tasting, eating, etc. One might choose to concentrate on the static aspect of lunching, by treating the activity as a class of events and looking for different conditions associated with its variations. Or the phase analysis approach might sensitize the researcher to patterned order within the activity—the sequence of acts or the existence of stages within the activity. In addition Lofland suggests considering meanings, relationships, participation patterns, and settings in their totality, as well as seeking out interesting or theoretically meaningful relationships between acts and meaning, activities and relationships, or other combinations.

ORGANIZATIONS

In a paper that focuses on the concept of organization, Egon Bittner points up the pitfalls which lay before those guilty of intellectual shortcutting. The false debate about informal and formal organization structure, he maintains, is attributable to Weber's indolence, his willingness to call upon commonsense concepts such as rationality and efficiency to do the work of theoretical concepts.

Rue Bucher and Joan Stelling offer a merger of the process perspective on professions and the arena model on organizations. They set forth a model built around the clustering of five characteristics common in professional organizations: roles are interactive rather than rigid or deterministic, diverse groups arise around common interests, such groups enter into competition for the organization's resources, members are integrated into the organization through political interdependence, and power shifts from group to group as conflicts arise over issues.

ONE
THE ACTION
FRAME OF
REFERENCE
David Silverman

Many writers have made use of an Action approach and the works that are discussed here include Weber (1964), Schutz (1964), Berger (1966), Berger and Luckmann(1967), Berger and Pullberg (1966), Rose (1962), Goffman (1959), Cicourel (1964) and Cohen (1968). Instead of providing a summary, at this point, of these various views, I shall try to present an ideal-typical action theory. This will fail to do justice to the separate arguments of each author, but it will have the advantage of presenting clearly the essential features of the perspective.

Seven propositions are presented below and the rest of the chapter will be devoted to a discussion of them.

1. The social sciences and the natural sciences deal with entirely different orders of subject-matter. While the canons of rigour and scepticism apply to both, one should not expect their perspective to be the same.

2. Sociology is concerned with understanding action rather than with observing behaviour. Action arises out of meanings which define social reality.

3. Meanings are given to men by their society. Shared orientations

Source: Chapter 6 of *The Theory of Organisations,* by David Silverman. © 1970 by David Silverman, Basic Books, Inc., Publishers, New York.

become institutionalized and are experienced by later generations as social facts.

4.   While society defines man, man in turn defines society. Particular
constellations of meaning are only sustained by continual reaffir-
mation in everyday actions.

5.   Through their interaction men also modify, change and transform
social meanings.

6.   It follows that explanations of human actions must take account of
the meanings which those concerned assign to their acts; the
manner in which the everyday world is socially constructed yet
perceived as real and routine becomes a crucial concern of sociological analysis.

7.   Positivistic explanations, which assert that action is determined by
external and constraining social or non-social forces, are inad-
missible.

The Distinction Between
the Social and Natural Sciences

The view that the natural sciences provide the most appropriate model for
the study of social life has a long and distinguished history in sociology.
It suffers, however, from the fatal defect that it fails to take into account
whether social and natural phenomena are the same in kind. The behaviour of matter may be regarded as a necessary reaction to a stimulus. Matter
itself does not understand its own behaviour. It is literally meaningless until
the scientist imposes his frame of reference upon it. There is no possibility
of apprehending its subjective intentions and the logic of its behavior may
be understood solely by observation of the behaviour itself. The action of
men, on the other hand, is meaningful to them. While the observer perceives water boiling when it has reached a certain temperature, men
themselves define their situation and act in certain ways in order to attain
certain ends. In doing so, they construct a social world,. Social life, therefore, has an internal logic which must be understood by the sociologist;
the natural scientist imposes an external logic on his data. As Weber
(1964) and Schutz (1964) have observed, this situation is both a source
of problems *and* a distinct help to the social scientist.

   If social action derives from the meanings which those concerned attribute to their social world, the observer is limited by his inability to experience the experience of another. Schutz points out that the scientist's individual biography and view of society may make him perceive what is going on in a way which distorts its meanings to those involved.[1] His best defence is to develop a "scientific" frame of reference, for the distinction between the natural and social sciences does not affect the common rules of procedure which they share (rigour, scepticism and so on). But this is very little use if the observer fails to come to grips with the problem of the subjective meanings that the actors themselves attach to their acts. Fortunately, the social scientist has one distinct advantage. He is not limited merely to the observation of uniformities of behaviour: "In the case of social collectivities," Weber suggests, "we can accomplish something which is never attainable in the natural sciences, namely the subjective understanding of the action of the component individuals" (1964, p. 103).

The generalizations which the social sciences develop are also fundamentally different from the laws of the natural sciences. The former are based on the probability that actors will act in terms of certain typical motives or intentions, the latter on the necessary reaction of matter to a stimulus (providing other stimuli are controlled for). Both the data and the form of explanation of the two types of science are thus fundamentally different: they share only a commitment to a systematic and rigorous analysis of their material.[2]

Action Not Behaviour

According to one view, observable patterns of behaviour provide the social scientist with his most reliable source of data. While what goes on in the minds of people is difficult to assess, their behaviour is concrete, quantifiable and easily susceptible to scientific analysis. Such a position has been taken by behaviourists generally, and is also favoured by those who take the Interactionist view of organizations which, while taking account of attitudes, concentrate mainly on interpersonal contacts ("interaction") and work tasks ("activities") (Whyte, 1959).

However, the mere observation of behaviour has its own set of difficulties. In order to make sense of an act, the observer must place it within a category which he can comprehend. He might distinguish, for instance, between an act associated with work and, say, an act of friendship. At the same time, however, the act will have a certain meaning to the person who carries it out and to the people to whom it is directed. What the observer takes to be merely the repetition of the same physical action may imply totally different meanings to those concerned according to the way in which they define each situation. By concentrating on the behaviour itself, it is possible to miss totally its significance to the people involved and, therefore, to be unable to predict with any accuracy the way in which those at whom it is directed will react to it. This difficulty has made itself felt most strongly among anthropologists who have to come to terms with a culture very different from their own, in which the subjective significance of actions is difficult to grasp. Even in his own society, however, the observer is still frequently an untutored outsider unable, without further knowledge of the commonsense assumptions being used, to comprehend the implications of the behavior he is observing.

As has already been suggested, problems of this nature are specific to the social sciences. Matter, on the other hand, does not act, it "behaves." Moreover, the logic of its behavior may be understood through an observation of the behaviour itself. The action of men, however, stems from a network of meanings which they themselves construct and of which they are conscious.[3] Weber put the relationship between social science and action clearly when he argued that sociology is concerned with: "The interpretation of action in terms of its subjective meaning" (1964, p. 94), where action is "all human behaviour when and in so far as the acting individual attaches a subjective meaning to it" (p. 88).

Action Arises From Meanings

Behaviourists argue that behaviour can be broadly explained as a response to a stimulus whose objective characteristics are perceived by the scientist. The reaction of subjects to this stimulus (e.g. "expressive" supervision) may thus be observed and laws formulated which relate the observed response to the stimulus (e.g. expressive supervision tends to be associated with a high level of morale among those who are exposed to it).

This fails to take account, however, of the "internal" logic of the situation. People assign meanings to situations and to the actions of others and react in terms of the interpretation suggested by these meanings.[4] Thus they may respond differently to the same objectively defined stimulus: the same supervisory behaviour may be interpreted as a friendly act by one group of workers (who, because they also desire supervision of this nature, react in a favourable way), or as an illegitimate attempt to win their sympathy in order to accomplish objectives opposed to their own. The same individual even may, at different times or in different situations, assign varying meanings to what appears to an observer to be the same act.

Action occurs, therefore, not as a response to an observable stimulus but as a product of what Parsons (1951) has called a "system of expectations" arising out of the actor's past experiences and defining his perception of the probable reaction of others to his act. At the level of cognition,[5] the actor defines his situation in this way and becomes aware of alternative courses of possible action. Since action is goal-oriented, that is concerned with the attainment of certain subjectively perceived ends, the actor chooses, from among the means of which he is aware, the action that seems most likely to produce what he would regard as a satisfactory outcome. At this analytical level, to use Parsons's term, he is concerned with "evaluation." Any instance of action (a unit act) thus stems from the ends that the actor is concerned to attain, his definition of the situation, including the range of alternative actions that he perceives to be available to him, and his choice of a means which is likely to be effective, bearing in mind the likely reaction of others to his act.

Meanings as Social Facts

Since action stems from meanings, it is legitimate to pose the question— "from where do these meanings arise?" One valid answer would be that meanings are given to men by their society and the past societies that preceded it. Such a reply would draw heavily on the perspective of Durkheim, who argued that men are constrained by social facts which determine their actions and consciousness. The suicide rate, to take Durkheim's favorite example, is separate from the intentions of individual men. It is a social fact which stems from the organization of society and is thus both external and constraining to individual actors.

If we follow Durkheim, it seems clear enough that meanings reside in social institutions. Society is composed of an interrelated series of institutional orders each of which is composed of a hierarchy of status positions of which are attached rights and obligations. This hierarchy usually persists even though the occupants of offices change. Meanings are, therefore, associated with an institution itself, both in terms of the general areas within which its members are supposed to act (e.g. the economy, the law) and of the specialized expectations attached to each office. Individuals are thus located on a particular social map. They live in a particular society and play roles in some at least of its component institutional orders. By participating in society they are given expectations about the appropriate acts of themselves and of others when in various status positions. They are able to apprehend the meanings associated with the actions of other people and to form a view of self based on the responses of others.

The question that now arises is why people should meet the expectations of others; one comprehensive answer to this has been offered by Parsons. According to Parsons (1951), society motivates its members, while respecting their personalities and biological needs; by this means it is able to prevent too much deviance from expected ways of behaving. People *learn* the expectations contained in different social roles through the process of socialization. They *conform* to them because these expectations become part of their definitions of themselves (or are "internalized," as Parsons put it) and because they want to retain the good opinion of those around them. Conformity thus expresses a set of shared values which is central to the existence of any society. While Parsons acknowledges that people can engage in interaction for their own private purposes, he holds that, unless one is prepared to be led "straight to the Hobbesian thesis [of a war of all against all]," common values must predominate if the system is to survive.[6] Action thus necessarily derives not only from shared expectations or norms, but also from shared values. "Considering that we are talking about the conditions of relatively stable interaction in social systems," he writes, "it follows from this that the value-standards which define institutionalized role-expectations assume to a greater or less degree a *moral* significance" (Parsons, 1951, p. 41, my italics).

The meaning of the social world is given to us by the past history and present structure of our society. Social reality is "pre-defined" in the very language in which we are socialized. Language provides us with categories which define as well as distinguish our experiences. Language allows us to define the typical features of the social world and the typical acts of typical actors—it gives us a set of what Schutz (1964) calls "typifications." Typifications deal with symbols, highly abstracted from everyday experience (e.g. art, religion, science); with categories of people and the implied pattern of behaviour in which each may legitimately indulge (e.g. policeman, friend, neighbour); and with particular people with whom one has had the opportunity to interact face-to-face (e.g. a helpful policeman, a reliable friend, an unpleasant neighbour). These typifications may be viewed as composing a set of concentric circles of knowledge which vary in diameter according to our degree of familiarity with the person or object involved. Typifications provide the individual with a frame of reference which he can use to shape his own actions and to make sense of the acts of others.

Meanings are Socially Sustained

It is true that society constrains us; it is also true that society provides us with the belief that, rather than bowing to constraints, we are acting in a manner which expresses what common sense suggests. Even in our routine compliance with role-expectations, we believe we are acting "naturally" in the only way which it is possible to act. Society, as Berger (1966) has pictured it, is both a prison and a puppet-theatre, in which we are manipulated while maintaining that we are doing "what any reasonable man would expect."

In viewing society as a social fact, sociologists reflect the common-sense view of members. Man experiences the social world as an external and unquestioned reality. People have always acted in a certain way, they will go on acting in that way because it is "natural" that they should do so, and an individual's wants and intentions are as nothing before "what has to be." Society is perceived to be something out there and we believe we have no choice but to meet its requirements. The social world is a taken-for-granted world governed by what we understand as "the laws of nature." "We experience the objects of our experience," Laing puts it, "as *there* in the outside world. The source of our experience seems to be outside ourselves" (1967, p. 33).

We can best apprehend the limitations of the commonsense view of the nature of society by asking how it is that members come to perceive the social world as an external, routine, nonproblematic facticity.

To answer this question we need to take account of two phenomena: men "know" the social world through a shared stock of knowledge and the "correctness" of this knowledge is continually made apparent in the actions of other men. The social stock of knowledge is a series of assumptions about appropriate behaviour in different contexts. I know how I ought to behave as a teacher and I know how my students ought to behave towards me. I know what purposes may underlie their actions and I know how my purposes may appear to them. Moreover, my view is usually confirmed by the everyday actions of others which appear to stem from the same set of assumptions. I do not doubt that I am a teacher and that this man is a student because he continues to act as I imagine a student should and, by responding to my actions in the way that I expect, he confirms my impression of myself. As such reciprocal typifications develop out of interaction, expectations become institutionalized and social roles are objectified or made part of the "natural order of things." In this way, it becomes thought necessary, proper and natural that the roles of student and teacher should be defined in a particular manner; it is no longer noticed when subsequent generations of actors continue to meet these assumptions—after all, what other way could they behave?

This glimpse at an aspect of the everyday world, while it stresses the routine nature of interaction, paradoxically makes social order seem more problematic. To be believable, the reality of the world-taken-for-granted must be continually reaffirmed in the actions of men. Meanings are not only given, they are socially sustained. "The realization of the drama," as

Berger and Luckmann point out, "depends upon the reiterated performance of its prescribed roles by living actors. The actors embody the roles
and actualize the drama by presenting it on the given stage. Neither drama
nor institution exist empirically apart from this recurrent realization" (1967,
p. 75).

Social order depends upon the cooperative acts of men in sustaining
a particular version of the truth. In conversation, for instance, we find it
convenient to accept the prevailing definition of reality within a group and
not to question the major aspects of the views of self which are being
presented. When actors act in unexpected ways, however, or when, as
Goffman (1959) shows, events occur which cast doubt upon an agreed
definition of a situation, that part of the social order is, for the time being,
no more.[7] The fact that the stock of knowledge upon which action is based
tends to change rather slowly reflects the vested interest that we all have
in avoiding anomie by maintaining a system of meanings which daily
confirms the non-problematic nature of our definitions of ourselves.

Man makes the social world. The existence of society depends upon
it being continuously confirmed in the actions of its members. Social structure, therefore, "has no reality except a human one. It is not characteriza-
ble as being a thing able to stand on its own . . . [and] exists only in so far
and as long as human beings realize it as part of their world" (Berger and
Pullberg, 1966, p. 63). We reify society if we regard it as having an
existence which is separate from and above the actions of men: social roles
and institutions exist only as an expression of the meanings which men
attach to their world—they have no "ontological status," as Berger and
Pullberg put it (p. 67).

The phenomenological position adopted by Berger, Luckmann and
Pullberg has clear parallels with the view of social relationships presented
by the Symbolic Interactionists. If, as Rose (1962) notes, man lives in a
"symbolic environment" and acts in terms of the social meanings that he
ascribes to the world around him, then roles are merely "clusters of related
meanings" perceived to be appropriate to certain social settings (Rose, p.
10); structure, once more, refers only to meanings, in this case the meanings that define the social setting itself and the appropriate relationships
between the role-players that are expected to be part of it. Both roles and
structure merely provide a framework for action; they do not determine it.
Both "are the product of the activity of acting units and not of 'forces' which
leave such acting units out of account" (Blumer, 1962, p. 189). Industrialization, to take one example, does not determine the family form. This will,
as Blumer points out, depend on the interpretations which the actors
concerned place on the industrialization process.

If society is socially constructed, then the logic behind some sociological investigations becomes highly questionable. For to relate one structural variable to another, for instance organizational form and economic environment, may fail to take account of the orientations of the people involved and the meanings which they attach to 'efficiency', 'the economy' and so on. It is out of factors like these that action is generated: to pay insufficient attention to them can involve the sociologist in an empty determinism in which things happen and processes occur apparently without the direct intervention of human purposes. Indeed, what has already been said should indicate a need to extend what have been regarded as the canons of satisfactory explanation of social phenomena; a need, as Berger and Luckmann argue, for "more than the casual obeisance that might be paid to the 'human factor' behind the uncovered structural data." Instead, we must be concerned with a "systematic accounting of the dialectical relation between the structural realities and the human enterprise of constructing reality—in history" (1967, p. 170).

Meanings are Socially Changed

If the reality of the social world is socially sustained, then it follows that reality is also socially changed—by the interaction of men. Indeed, the only alternative to explaining social change by an historical examination of past interaction is to assume an evolutionary scheme through which the needs of social systems are "necessarily" met.

The most obvious instance of changed meanings resulting from interaction is when disruptive events occur which bring into question a certain aspect of reality. Goffman gives the example of an inquisitive guest who wanders into a room where he is not expected and discovers pulp magazines which he reveals to the others present, much to the consternation of his host who had successfully defined himself as a great intellectual. The implication that roles are not just given but socially sustained and changed casts some doubt on Parsons' emphasis on the socialization-internalization process as a non-problematic source of social order. Roles are normally only defined to a limited extent, and there are varying motives which underlie compliance to role-expectations.

Our behaviour is not completely determined by role-expectations. Even when we accept the conventions associated with social roles as constraining, there remains, as Dahrendorf (1968) has pointed out, an element of choice in role-playing. Role demands may refer to role behaviour or role attributes (dress, manner and so on). Since the latter are usually defined in a far more imprecise manner than the former, the actor's individual biography becomes important in shaping his particular pattern of behaviour. Role demands are also usually defined by exclusions rather than prescriptions and this permits the "arts of impression-management" to be used by an individual as he presents an image of himself to others (Goffman, 1959). The components of a role in fact include varying levels of perceived compulsion, each of which is supported by different kinds of sanction and reward. It is necessary to distinguish, therefore, between the actor's perception of "must," "should" and "can" expectations (Dahrendorf). Failing to meet a "must" expectation usually involves breaking the law; social exclusion usually results from breaking a "should" expectation; one merely loses popularity by failing to comply with a "can" expectation. This allows an element of choice in role-playing and implies the possibility of change through interaction. Dahrendorf does not directly dispute, however, Parsons's assumption that men are socialized into a common value-universe. Only when we question the notion that learning a norm necessarily implies a valued attachment to it, can we fully explain social change. This argument is taken up in an important paper by Wrong.

Wrong (1967) points out that Parsons and others may have exaggerated the extent to which conformity derives from the shared values which men learn. Even if social norms are internalized, one ought not necessarily to expect them to be expressed in behaviour. Men can act in a certain way and feel guilty about offending their conscience only retrospectively. At the same time, there may be internal conflicts in the values that men learn in society. While men may generally seek approval, they may also be more concerned with the approval of certain types of men than of others and be prepared to offend the latter in the hope of satisfying the former. In doing so they continually re-define social reality as experienced by themselves and others. Parsons may, therefore, be criticized for having adopted an "over-socialized conception of man" which overlooks the fact that role-expectations are not just given by society but arise from and depend upon on-going human interaction. Social order is, therefore, problematic. A more complete analysis would need to take account of the range of motives underlying conformity to the expectations of others, and to pay attention to the possible role of coercion in *imposing* a normative definition of the situation on others.

Weber had already noted, many years previously, that in social relationships the parties may (and to some extent always do) attach different meanings to their interaction. It is certainly true that interaction may involve shared values (Weber gives the example of a father-child relationship) but very frequently the meanings involved may not be shared and the relationship will then be, as he puts it, "asymmetrical."[8] What is to the shop steward, for instance, a means of "delivering the goods" to the workers he represents, may be regarded by the manager as a necessary relationship in order to settle disputes with the minimum interruption to production. The shop steward and the manager come together not because they have the same values (indeed, each may hope one day to overturn the authority of the other) but because, for a while at least, their differing ends may be served by the same means.

Social relationships, then, need only involve the ability of the actors to predict the likely actions of others by means of the common stock of knowledge which they share. At the same time, there always exist which Schutz call "finite provinces of meaning," sets of orientations which govern the nature of the involvement in any particular social relationship and derive from the various experiences of different actors (their "individual biographies," to use Schutz's term). Moreover, if conformity to the expectations of other partners in this relationship is not generated by shared values then analysis of its origins may reveal that it derives from the attempts of certain actors to attain their own personal ends and is merely tolerated by others. To take an extreme example, the relationship between the slave and master in a plantation society, while occurring on the basis of common expectations of the likely behaviour of the other, may originate in the ability of the master to impose his definition of the situation upon the slave. It need not, therefore, involve shared values, while the degree of attachment to it (and hence the measure of commitment to its continuation) may vary considerably between the participants. It becomes necessary to examine, in a similar manner, the processes through which any body of knowledge comes to be socially established as reality (i.e. institutionalized) and to take account, as Berger and Luckmann (1966) put it, of the fact that: "He who has the bigger stick has the better chance of imposing his definitions" (p. 101).[9]

The existence of different definitions of situations indicates the advantages of an action perspective and reveals certain limitations of analysis from the point of view of the system. As Berger (1966) has noted, in an extremely useful little introduction to sociology, the System approach tends to be concerned with analysis from the viewpoint of the authorities and is primarily concerned with the problems involved in the management of social systems. However, what is a problem to one actor is often a more or less efficient means to an end from the point of view of another.[10] A situation may, therefore, be usefully examined from the vantage points of "competing systems of interpretation," and this will provide important clues as to how it arose, why it continues in its present form, and what circumstances may make it change.

It is important to recognize that the social order is threatened not only by particular circumstances, such as revolutionary change, culture contact or marginal groups (Berger and Pullberg), but by its very nature. "*All* social reality is precarious," as Berger and Luckmann put it, "*All* societies are constructions in the face of chaos" (1966, p. 96). While people take everyday life as non-problematic, as reality, they continually step into situations that create problems which have not yet become routinized. Our normal reaction is to seek to integrate the problematic sector of reality into what is already unproblematic: we look around for an already learned definition of the situation to apply to the "new" reality. However, this is not always possible ; "certain problems 'transcend' the boundaries of everyday life and point to an altogether different reality" (p. 24).

Explanations in Terms of Meanings

The form of explanation which the foregoing analysis suggests is concerned with *Verstehen,* that is, it begins with "the observation and theoretical interpretation of the subjective 'states of mind' of actors'.[11] This may take the form of 'the actually intended meaning for concrete individual action . . . [or] the average of, or an approximation to, the actually intended meaning" (Weber, 1964, p. 96). More usually, however, explanations are in terms of ideal-typical actors whom we take to be pursuing certain ends by choosing appropriate means on the basis of a subjective definition of the situation. "It is not even necessary," Schutz argues "to reduce human acts to a more or less well known individual actor. To understand them it is sufficient to find typical motives of typical actors which explain the act as a typical one arising out of a typical situation" (1964, vol. 2, p. 13). He goes on to suggest how the acts of priests, soldiers and so on, may be explained in this way.

Ideal-typical explanations, according to Weber, must be adequate on the level of meaning and also causally adequate. They must make use of what is known about the actor's definition of the situation and his ends. They must show that the action to be explained is in practice related to these meanings: that is, where the act is present, so must be the meaning. Ideal-typical explanations usually involve the assumption of rational action or the continuous weighing by the actors of means, ends and the secondary consequences of their actions (Weber calls this type of action '*zweckrational*'). It then becomes possible to examine the non-rational elements in actual behaviour—the extent to which those concerned diverge in practice from such a weighing process. As Schutz notes, it is easiest to come to grips with the subjective meanings of actors where their behaviour is most rational and, therefore, most standardized and anonymous.

Action explanations make a great deal of what Schutz calls "in order to" motives. An action is explained when the meaning which the typical actor attributes to it has been demonstrated. At the same time, action is motivated on the basis of the actor's background and environment: this is its "because" motive. I act in a certain way, therefore, not only in order to attain certain desired ends but also because I see myself as the sort of person who engages in acts of this nature. However, it is illegitimate to say that my action is *caused* by certain characteristics of mine which only the observer perceives. "One reifies action," as Berger and Pullberg put it, "by claiming that it is performed *because* [. . .] the actor is an X-type person" (1966, p. 66). This is to detach an act from its performer, who is viewed merely as a collection of roles. In the same way, "roles are reified by detaching them from human intentionality and expressivity, and transforming them into an inevitable destiny for their bearers" (p. 67).

The Rejection of Positivism

In equating the methods of studying social and natural reality, positivism may take any one of three approaches. It may try to explain human behaviour in terms of universal psychological forces (e.g. aggression), non-social factors (climate or technology), or reified social constructs (social facts). Since most contemporary sociologists reject the first two, the discussion here will be concerned with the third.

Berger (1966) has accused much Sociology of viewing society as a "prison" or as a "puppet-theatre." According to the former position, society is external to men and constrains them through the operation of impersonal social facts; according to the latter, society enters into the minds of men through the process of socialization which gives them their social roles and determines how they will in future respond. "That this sort of intellectual edifice is inviting to many orderly minds," he remarks, "is demonstrated by the appeal that positivism in all its forms has had since its inception" (p. 190). None the less, there is an alternative view. Society may be seen as populated by living actors and its institutions regarded as dramatic conventions depending on the cooperation of the actors in maintaining a definition of the situation. As he puts it, the way in which this position "opens up a passage out of the rigid determinism into which sociological thought originally led us" (p. 160), is best illustrated by the methodology of Weber.

Weber stands firmly against the reification of concepts by the observer. The State, for instance, does not itself act; it is merely a representation of certain meanings held by actors and is reducible to those meanings. When these meanings change, the State changes: "for sociological purposes there is no such thing as a collective personality which "Acts.""

When reference is made in a sociological context to a 'state' [. . .] a 'corporation' [or] a 'family' [. . .] what is meant is [. . .] *only* a certain kind of development of actual or possible social actions of individual persons" (Weber, 1964, p. 102). Such sets of meanings constrain only in the sense that they are objectified by actors who orient their actions to them: "The social relationship thus *consists* entirely and exclusively in the existence of a *probability* that there will be, in some meaningfully understandable sense, a course of social action" (p. 118, his italics). He goes on: "It is vital to be continually clear about this in order to avoid the reification of these concepts."

In attributing a causative role to the constructs of the observer (system needs, system dynamics) and losing sight of the meanings which actors attach to their actions, many contemporary sociologists have cheated themselves of a rich source of data. Parsons, in his introduction to Weber's most substantial work, accuses him of failing to use the insights of a functionalist system perspective; but it is clear that Weber very sharply saw the difficulties involved in explanations in terms of the nature of the whole and, in particular, its need for survival.[12]

The Action Frame of Reference and the Systems Approach

The Systems approach tends to regard behaviour as a reflection of the characteristics of a social system containing a series of impersonal processes which are external to actors and constrain them. In emphasizing that action derives from the meanings that men attach to their own and each other's acts, the Action frame of reference argues that man is constrained by the way in which he socially constructs his reality. On the one hand, it seems, Society makes man; on the other, Man makes society. It is hardly surprising, therefore, that each approach should appear to stress merely one side or another of the same coin. When the relative merits of the two approaches are discussed, it is usually suggested that they are complementary to each other. This appears to be the argument in a recent work by Percy Cohen (1968).

Cohen distinguishes a "holistic" from an "atomistic" approach: the former seeks to explain the action of parts of a system in terms of the nature of the whole, while the latter views the system as an *outcome* of the action of the parts. The tension between the two is provided by the fact that knowledge of the social system does not tell one everything about the action of its parts, just as information about its human parts does not in itself provide a complete description of the nature of the system. Cohen argues that this is because the members of society have biological and other characteristics which are separate from the nature of the whole system. Secondly, individuals have choice over which aspect of the whole to respond to, especially where it makes demands which are mutually inconsistent (Cohen, 1968, p. 14).[13] Thus both approaches have difficulty in explaining facts which the other is able to take for granted: the Action approach tends to assume an existing system in which action occurs but cannot successfully explain the nature of this system, while the Systems approach is unable to explain satisfactorily why particular actors act as they do.

The way in which each approach is affected by these sort of limitations has been taken up in a paper by Wagner (1964). Wagner distinguishes two sorts of atomistic model: "Reductionist" theories explain the behaviour of the parts in terms of their individual biological or psychological make-up and, because they apply the same general laws to the parts and the whole, have no difficulty in also explaining the characteristics of society. Social action theories, on the other hand, are concerned with explanations in terms of interpersonal human action and are, therefore, best fitted to explain "micro" problems involving particular patterns of action. When they seek to comprehend "macro" processes, action theorists at once come up against "the apparent machine-like character of large social systems which seem to follow their own mechanical laws." It is almost impossible, in this situation, "to submit adequate interpretations of large-scale societal structures and processes, without resorting to non-voluntaristic (i.e. positivist) explanation" (Wagner, 1964, p. 583). Attempts to do so, from an action position, inevitably raise the problem of what he calls "a displacement of scope."

As Touraine puts it, however, the view that: "The action approach says little about the characteristics of the social system" (1964, p. 7) and, therefore, "does not attempt to substitute for an analysis of social systems but to complement it" (p. 11), is severely challenged by several of the writers who have been discussed in this chapter. The work of Berger, Luckmann and Pullberg, for instance, supports the argument that, by its examination of the sense in which society *does* make man, the Action approach can offer a means of explanation of the nature of social systems and need not depend on Systems analysis for, as it were, the other half of the picture. "The paradox," as Berger and Luckmann note, "is that man is capable of producing a world that he then experiences as something other than a human product" (1966, p. 57).

The possibility that Action and Systems explanations offer conflicting rather than complementary frames of reference is strengthened by the view that they are concerned with different types of problem. Cohen argues that holism and atomism are alternative means of coming to grips with the same basic issue: the problem of moral order. However, as Dawe (1969) suggests, contemporary sociology is also concerned with a second problem—"the exertion of human control over hitherto- inviolable institutions" (Dawe, 1969, p. 116). This latter issue was a major concern, as he points out, of the Enlightenment and it underlies Berger and Pullberg's discussion of "objectivation" and reification.[14] A commitment to the insights of phenomenology may in practice prove difficult to reconcile with an acceptance of the positivist position. Even if both approaches are ultimately concerned with social order, their views of its nature and consequences are very different.

Footnotes

[1] The problems to which this gives rise have been vividly expressed by Laing: "If, however, experience is evidence, how can one ever study the experience *of the other*? For the experience of the other is not evident to me, as it is not and never can be an experience of mine. . . . Since your and their experience is invisible to me as mine is to you and them, I seek to make evident to the others, through their experience of my behaviour, what I infer of your experience, through my experience of your behaviour. This is the crux of social phenomenology" (1967, pp 16-17).

[2] Laing has also pointed out the error of attempting to follow blindly the approach of the natural sciences in the study of the social world: "The error fundamentally," he suggests, "is the failure to realize that there is an ontological discontinuity between human beings and it-beings. . . . Persons are distinguished from things in that persons experience the world, whereas things behave in the world" (1967, p. 53).

[3] Schutz (1964) notes that: "The distinguishing characteristic of action is precisely that it is determined by a project which precedes it in time. Action then is behaviour in accordance with a plan of projected behaviour: and the project is neither more nor less than the action itself conceived and decided upon in the future perfect sense" (vol. 2, p. 11).

[4] Rose (1962) points out that: "All social objects of study . . . are 'interpreted' by the individual and have social meaning. That is, they are never seen as physical 'stimuli' but as 'definitions of the situation' " (p. x). Similarly, Cicourel (1964) argues that "the actor's awareness and experience of an object are determined not only by the physical object as it is . . . given, but also by the imputations he assigns to it " (p. 220).

[5] This discussion is not concerned with "cathection"—or reaction in terms of

innate personality drives—which Parsons takes as another level of human response.

[6] Parsons acknowledges that an actor's sentiments may not be involved in his action: "But, in a general sense in social situations, the circumstances of socialization preclude that this should be the predominant situation in permanent social systems which involve the major motivational interests of the participant actors" (1951, p. 40).

[7] Goffman considers the definition of the situation which the actors project in face-to-face interaction. He goes on: "we can assume that events may occur within the interaction which contradict, discredit, or otherwise throw doubt upon this projection. When these disruptive events occur, the interaction itself may come to a confused and embarrassed halt. Some of the assumptions upon which the responses of the participants had been predicated become untenable, and the participants find themselves lodged in an interaction for which the situation has been wrongly defined and is now *no longer defined*" (Goffman, 1959, p. 12, my italics).

[8] "The subjective meaning," he notes, "need not necessarily be the same for all the parties who are mutually oriented in a given social relationship. . . . 'Friendship,' 'love,' 'loyalty,' 'fidelity to contracts,' 'patriotism,' on one side, may well be faced with an entirely different attitude on the other. In such cases the parties associate different meanings with their actions and the social relationship is in so far objectively 'asymmetrical' from the points of view of the two parties. . . . A social relationship in which the attitudes are completely and fully corresponding is in reality a limiting case" (Weber, 1964, p. 119). The appeal of the "non-routine," in the form of a charismatic leader, was also a central concern of Weber's sociology.

[9] What the "stick" actually consists of will vary according to the meanings attached to various sanctions by the actors' stock of knowledge. Excommunication, for instance, is at certain times a far more significant threat than more material "sticks."

[10] "Organizations," as Touraine puts it, "can be thought of as social systems, but also as means limiting or providing the opportunity for the actor to attain his ends" (1964, p. 7).

[11] Parsons, introduction to Weber (1964, p. 87, footnote 2).

[12] Weber notes that sociologists have used an organic analogy in discussing society and goes on: "this functional frame of reference is convenient for purposes of practical illustration and for provisional orientation . . . at the same time, if its cognitive value is overestimated and its concepts illegitimately 'reified,' it can be *highly dangerous*" (1964, p. 103, my emphasis). Similarly, Berger and Luckmann term functionalism "a theoretical legerdemain" and suggest that: "A

purely structural sociology is endemically in danger of reifying social phenomena" (1966, p. 170).

[13] The same point is made by Rose (1962), who argues that actors possess choice especially where a culture is internally inconsistent. Of course, if reality is socially constructed, then the maintenance of any definition of a situation is the outcome of choice by the actors—however much they may experience the situation as constraining.

[14] While the problem of order "gave rise to a social system approach," Dawe remarks, " . . . the problem of control gave rise to a social action approach, with its emphasis on the actor's definition of and attempts to control his situation, and upon a distinctively 'social science' view of the nature of social inquiry" (1969, pp. 116–17).

REFERENCES

BERGER, P. L., (1966), *Invitation to Sociology*, Penguin.

BERGER, P. L., AND LUCKMANN, T. (1967), *The Social Construction of Reality: A Treatise in the Sociology of Knowledge*, Allen Lane, the Penguin Press.

BERGER, P. L. AND PULLBERG, S. (1966), "Reification and the socological critique of consciousness", *New Left Rev.*, vol. 35, no. 1, pp. 56-71.

BLUMER, H. (1962), a paper in A. M. Rose (ed.), *Human Behaviour and Social Processes: An Interactionist Approach*, Houghton Mifflin.

CICOUREL, A. V. (1964), *Method and Measurement in Sociology*, Free Press.

COHEN, P. S. (1968), *Modern Social Theory*, Heinemann.

DAHRENDORF, R. (1968), *Essays in the Theory of Society*, Stanford University Press.

DAWE, A. (1969), book review, *Sociology*, 3, no. 1, pp. 115-17.

GOFFMAN, E. (1959), *The Presentation of Self in Everyday Life*, Doubleday.

LAING, R. D. (1967), *The Politics of Experience*, Penguin.

PARSONS, T. (1951), *The Social System*, Free Press.

ROSE, A. M. (ed.) (1962), *Human Behaviour and Social Processes: An Interactionist Approach*, Houghton Mifflin.

SCHUTZ, A. (1964), *Collected Papers* (in three volumes, edited by M. Natanson), Nijhoff.

TOURAINE, A. (1964), "Pour une sociologie actionnaliste", *Europ. J. Sociol.*, vol. 5, no. 1, pp. 1-24.

WAGNER, H. R. (1964), "Displacement of scope: a problem of the relationship between small-scale and large-scale sociological theories", *Amer. J. Sociol.*, vol. 69, no. 6, pp. 571-84.

WEBER, M. (1964), *The Theory of Social and Economic Organization,* Free Press.

WHYTE, W. F. (1959), "An interaction approach to the theory of organizations", in M. Haire (ed.), *Modern Organization Theory,* Wiley.

WRONG, D. W. (1967), "The over-socialized conception of man", in N. J. Demerath and R. A. Peterson (eds.), *System, Change and Conflict,* Free Press.

TWO
ANALYZING SOCIAL SETTINGS
John Lofland

Inquiry or analysis is usefully thought of as the attempt to answer one or more of only three questions:

1. What are the *characteristics* of a social phenomenon, the forms it assumes, the variations it displays?

2. What are the *causes* of a social phenomenon, the forms it assumes, the variations it displays?

3. What are the *consequences* of a social phenomenon, the forms it assumes, the variations it displays?

As simple as it may seem, social inquiry and social theory reduce basically to the attempt to provide *answers* to these three *questions.*

This chapter is devoted to some suggestions on how one might go about providing answers to the first question, the question of characteristics.

I have tried in what follows to present a large number of examples of accomplished qualitative analyses. In order to emphasize analytic structure, the examples are stripped down to the basic categories that constitute their analytic thrust. It is hoped that through contemplating what others have done with qualitative materials, the novice observer-analyst can better figure out how to use his own.

Source: Abridged from *Analyzing Social Settings* by John Lofland. © 1971 by Wadsworth Publishing Company, Inc., Belmont, California 94002. Reprinted by permission of the author and the publisher.

Six Units

In thinking about presenting the examples in an orderly fashion, it seemed best to arrange them along a continuum from the most *microscopic* social phenomenon to the most *macroscopic*. While the materials in fact shade one into another, in order to be more crisp, I have chopped the continuum into six categories. Ranging from microscopic to macroscopic, these are as follows:

1. *Acts.* Action in a situation that is temporally brief, consuming only a few seconds, minutes, or hours.

2. *Activities.* Action in a setting of more major duration—days, weeks, months—constituting significant elements of persons' involvements.

3. *Meanings.* The verbal productions of participants that define and direct action.

4. *Participation.* Persons' holistic involvement in, or adaptation to, a situation or setting under study.

5. *Relationships.* Interrelationships among several persons considered simultaneously.

6. *Settings.* The entire setting under study conceived as the unit of analysis.

The vague term "social phenomenon" used above can now be seen to translate into at least six more specific categories. Instead of asking "What are the characteristics of a social phenomenon, the forms it assumes, the variations it displays?", we can now ask:

> What are the characteristics of acts, activities, meanings, participation, relationships, and settings, the forms they assume, the variations they display?

Let me emphasize, however, that there is nothing magic or immutable in this set of six terms. It is merely a device, useful, I hope, in making an orderly and therefore more understandable presentation of many years of accomplished qualitative analysis in sociology.

Within each of these six units a distinction may be made between whether an analysis provides a static depiction of a social phenomenon or reports phases or sequences through which a phenomenon passes over the course of time. This is rather like the difference between a photograph and a motion picture. A photograph captures the standing arrangement of an object under view, while a motion picture can capture the moving arrangement of an object under view. Static versus phase analysis will be the major internal principle of organizing the explication.

Throughout I shall employ the term *"social setting"* as a single designation for what are otherwise quite dissimilar forms of human association. The single term social setting encompasses the following associations: formal organizations, or locales therein such as an industrial workshop, a typing pool, or a civic improvement club; loose "worlds that transcend space" such as a homosexual milieu in a large city, the rock hound world, or the stamp collector world; and similar circumstances of life wherein the relevant persons do not have direct contact with one another, such as visibly handicapped persons, persons new to the city, or persons who have a schizophrenic family member. These settings vary in many ways, but they are alike in that they provide for those involved a *similarity of circumstance of action.* This similarity of circumstance of action is accessible to direct engagement by means of intensive interviewing and/or participant-observation.

ACTS   The term "act" refers to human emissions of short temporal duration encompassing a relatively narrow sector of an actor's total activity. As developed in qualitative studies, this analytic focus is of a "one-sided" character. The analyst adopts the point of view of the actor looking out onto the world. The imagery is that of actor as strategist, maneuvering among other strategists. These other strategists tend to be taken as simply given and treated only as posing the problems to which the actor as a strategist must respond. (This is also the point of view of the units here labeled activity, meaning, and participation. Only when we come to "relationships" will we pass from the central emphasis of looking over the shoulder of one set of actors.)

The simplest analysis of acts isolates only a *single* type, specifying neither more detailed forms or variations nor phases or sequences through which it might move. Thus, Erving Goffman's observations of merry-go-rounds and hospital surgery revolve around the type of act he calls "role distance." Defining role distance as any act which suggests "that the actor has some measure of disaffection from, and resistance against, the role," Goffman offers a variety of concrete occurrences as illustration (Goffman, 1961b:108).

More typically, analysts have not contented themselves with a single status type, but go on to suggest *multiple* static acts. The most phenomenological strategy is that of explicitly adopting as the concepts of analysis the linguistic terms used by the participants themselves in designating their own acts. The aim is then to decipher more concretely the acts to which the participants' terms do and do not apply.

Depending somewhat more heavily on the analyst's patterning powers, there is a large middle range of acts that are more or less recognized by the participants but remain without explicit naming. These are likely to be instantly recognizable to the participants but simply "something I never thought much about." In a study of cab drivers Fred Davis noted that these urban types could be seen to engage in certain acts calculated to ensure themselves what they considered to be a proper tip. Watching for incidents of such acts, he reports that their tactical gambits include:

1. Fumbling in the making of change.

2. Giving the passenger a hard-luck story.

3. Making fictitious charges for service.

4. Providing a concerted show of fast, fancy driving.

5. Displaying extraordinary courtesy (Davis, 1959;163).

Observing that enlisted men of the United States Army Reserve seemed strongly oriented to avoiding task assignments during their spate of weekend warriorship, Mark Krain focused on acts employed in order to decline an assignment in the unlucky event of actually being asked to do something. He observed that the *compleat* decliner of assignments went about his weekend rather self-consciously equipped with one or more of these means of deflecting orders:

1. *Prior Assignment.* The enlisted man already has a task, making it impossible to start a new one.

2. *Urgent Situation.* A long-standing foul-up, with which the Army abounds, is related to the superior as an urgent situation that must be attended to now.

3. *Incapacity.* The assignment cannot be accepted for reasons of sickness (relatively rare in use), permanent medical restrictions, lack of technical knowledge, or lack of legal right (as in driving a vehicle or operating a projector).

4. *Shunning.* The assignment is laughed off as "not serious" and the decliner withdraws. (Krain, 1967:72-80).

The distinction between static types and sequences or phases in the analysis of acts refers not to the way the world really is "out there" but to the form of presented analysis. Thus, any of the examples of types given above could conceivably have been developed in terms of sequence, as, for example, in "phases of role distance."

We may distinguish two forms of phase analysis of acts. These are:

1. Phases leading up to a single class of performed act.

2. Phases of (or within) a single performed act.

Relative to the first, an effort is made to discern any typical stages through which action and actor-definition pass in the process culminating (or not culminating) in a particular kind of act. A paradigmatic instance of this type of effort is provided by Donald Cressey's work on embezzlement. Performing intensive interviews with imprisoned embezzlers, Cressey attempted to formulate the general sequence of the actor's definition of his situation that seems to eventuate in the act of violating a position of financial trust. Through a process of successive revision (see Cressey, 1950), he provides what appears to be a generally applicable series of three stages:

Trusted persons become trust violators when they:

1. Conceive of themselves as having a financial problem which is nonsharable.

2. Are aware that this problem can be secretly resolved by violation of the position of financial trust.

3. Are able to apply to their own conduct in that situation verbalizations which enable them to adjust their conceptions of themselves as trusted persons with their conceptions of themselves as users of the entrusted funds or property (Cressey, 1953:30).

While Cressey was concerned with the causal efficacy of a sequence, it is also possible simply to focus on "mini natural histories" without strong reference to causality. Among acts, this may simply involve phases of an act, although it must be recognized that the present concept of the act is sufficiently ambiguous to have it rightfully charged that each phase might itself be conceived as an independent act. One such mini natural history is provided us in Lyn Lofland's observational analysis of phases of the act of entering a public establishment.

There is first a stage of "checking for readiness," involving numerous variations on ways in which the individual "checks out and, if necessary, rearranges his body presentation to make certain nothing in his appearance will jar the image he wishes to convey."

Second there is the phase of "taking a reading," or quickly familiarizing himself with the setting. Four major ways of taking a reading were observed:

1. Tunneling, or taking a quick look around and proceeding in as though wearing blinders.

2. Blasé pausing at the entrance and taking in the scene.

3. Partial reading, or concentration on some small part of the setting.

4. Avoiding a reading, for example by walking into the setting backward.

Third and last is the phase of securing a stopping place in the setting. The forms of this final stage are determined by the tactics used in the previous stages, producing multiple sequences within the third stage.

Two major forms of this stage (linked to the previous variations) are:

1. The beeline tactic, a further prosecution of the tunneling stance of the second stage.

2. The object concentration tactic, a further prosecution of the partial reading behavior of the second stage. (Summarized and quoted from L. Lofland, 1973:140–146)

Relative to acts; then, the observer analyst might ask himself these kinds of questions:

1. What static acts seem to recur and to have some importance among all or various types of participants in this setting?

2. What are phases of recurring acts among various participants in this setting?

ACTIVITIES Although the distinction is not as clear as it might be, I want to distinguish "acts," just discussed, from activities. Activities refer to collective conduct that (1) takes days, weeks, or months to play through, (2) encompasses a relatively large segment of actors' time, and (3) is likely to be engaged in collectively and conjointly in a social setting, instead of more individualistically and privately.

Although often conceived and phrased in organizational terms and as the actions of formal organizations, many studies of organizations are perhaps better viewed as patterns of activities. Among classic efforts, Philip Selznick's explication of what he terms "cooptation" stands as one of the more bold and useful static depictions. He defines cooptation as "the process of absorbing new elements into the leadership or policy-defining structure of an organization as a means of averting threats to its stability or existence." This idea evolved out of Selznick's immersing himself in the structure of the Tennessee Valley Authority, finding, further, that it was useful to conceive

> this general mechanism . . . [as assuming] two basic forms: Formal cooptation, when there is a need to establish the legitimacy of authority or the administrative necessity of the relevant public; and

informal cooptation, when there is a need for adjustment to the pressure of specific centers of power within the community (Selznick, 1953:259).

Thus conceived and distinguished, an infinite variety of acts could then be viewed as instances of these two basic types of activities, becoming thereby the major organizing principle in analyzing the TVA.

The documentations of activities of a more "narrow" character border on being "acts," in the previous sense, but are still distinguishable in terms of their more drawn out time for playing through. In a study of relations between staff and line personnel in manufacturing establishments, Melville Dalton documents how

Actual or probable line rejection of their ideas provokes staff groups to

1. Strengthen their ties with top line.

2. Adhere to the staff role, but "lean over backward" to avoid trouble down the line that could reverberate to the top.

3. Compromise with the line below top levels (Dalton, 1959:101ff).

On occasion, patterns of activity (or other units) seem to possess some more systematic interrelations. Such systematic interrelation is often found by specifying a small number of variations whose *conjoint* variation accurately encompasses various patterns already discerned and points up yet others not yet fully contemplated. For example, in analyzing a proselytizing religious group, I found that the members' strategies for attempting to contact prospective converts seemed to revolve around:

1. Whether or not to impart information and make new contact in a face-to-face manner or to employ mediated means such as radio and newspapers.

2. Whether or not to make clear initially that the group believed in a new Christ and the imminent end of the world or to withhold revelation of these beliefs.

3. Whether or not to attempt contact in religious places (e.g., chur-
    ches) or secular places (e.g., street corners) (J. Lofland, 1966:
    Chapters 5–6).

The cross-classification of these three dichotomous distinctions produces
eight basic patterns or possibilities as shown in Figure 1. A certain degree
of systematic coherence is thus provided in the analysis. Such a device can
also serve importantly to call attention to existing but still unnoticed patterns or to the virtual absence of a logically possible pattern, raising the
question of why it is absent. (See further, Barton and Lazarsfeld, 1955;
McKinney, 1966.)

FIGURE 1   Example of a Typology: Types of Proselytizing Strategies

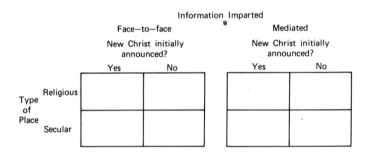

It must be cautioned that this procedure of constructing "typologies"
can easily become a sterile exercise revealing little if it is not performed
within the context of a full and extensive knowledge of, and sensitivity to,
the empirical materials themselves.

While any pattern of activity is likely amenable to phase explication,
attempts to discern phases have been notably lacking. Among existing
efforts we may point, however, to the excellent study by Burton Clark on
phases of what he terms "the reorienting process" whereby junior college
aspirants for four-year college degrees are gradually guided to quitting
school at the end of two years. Clark explicates five steps in this "cooling
out process."

1. Intensive pre-entrance testing and assignment to remedial work,
    the facts of which are recorded in a counselling folder.

2. A counselling interview at the beginning of each semester in which the student's record of failure is brought to his attention with increasing force.

3. Entrance into an "Orientation to College" course designed to surface occupational ambitions and appraise them in light of performance.

4. If B.A. ambitions remain unsurrendered, "need for improvement" and "request for conference" notices are issued by counsellors who "delicately . . . but persistently" confront the overambitious student.

5. Finally, the student may be put on a drawn-out probation, in a "slow killing-off of the lingering hopes of the most stubborn . . . [failing] students" (Clark, 1960).

Regarding activities, then, the observer-analyst can be attuned to questions of these kinds:

1. What are the most broad kinds of activities carried on by the participants in this setting?

2. What are more specialized and delimited kinds of activities carried on by all or various types of participants in this setting?

3. What are phases or stages of activities carried on by all or various types of participants in this setting?

MEANINGS The term "meaning" is intended to single out participants' verbal productions as a significant unit of comprehension in itself. In discussing acts and activities a distinction was drawn between actor and observer categories in the construction of analyses, based on the different meanings acts and activities have for actors and observers. We may now take one further step. Previously we focused upon actor (or observer) designated acts and activities as topics of the observer's analysis. Now we want to focus upon actors' verbal productions as patterns which transcend behavior (acts, activities, etc.), forming the distinctly hu-

BOWLING GREEN UNIV. LIBRARY

man phenomenon of definitions of "objects, events, and human nature"
(Shibutani, 1955: 564).

Observer Articulation.

Even in the study of meanings *per se* we again encounter the possibility
of a certain discrepancy between the members' and observer's constructions. This discrepancy or discontinuity is primarily dependent on the
degree to which a meaning is *explicitly articulated* by members. Members
can be seen to employ a given meaning, but they are simply not all that
clear themselves as to their own usages. This is well illustrated in David
Sudnow's analysis of what he calls the "normal crime" as a complex
meaning in the world of the Public Defender (P. D.).

> I shall call *normal crimes* those occurrences whose typical features,
> e.g., the ways they usually occur and the characteristics of persons
> who commit them (as well as the typical victims and typical scenes),
> are known and attended by the P. D. For any of a series of offense
> types the P. D. can provide some form of proverbial characteriza-
> tion. For example, *burglary* is seen as involving regular violators,
> no weapons, low-priced items, little property damage, lower class
> establishments, largely Negro defendants, independent operators,
> and a non-professional orientation to the crime (Sudnow,
> 1965:260).

While the precise term "normal crime" is not likely locatable in the
lexicon of public defenders, more narrow working terms do seem present.
P.D.'s refer easily to "such cases," "crimes such as this," "it's the same kind
of case as the others," as well as to "burglars," "petty thieves," "narcos,"
etc. Sudnow invents the term "normal crime" as a more encompassing
designation of this class of member meanings.

Life-Encompassing Meanings.

The analysis of meanings can encompass the most general themes of
definition that pervade all the members' situations or it can focus on meanings attached to more delimited aspects of members' lives.

In attempting to capture very broad meanings, Walter B. Miller
(1958) strove to delineate what he called the "focal concerns" of low-
income adolescent males growing up in an urban slum.

Possessed of a similar concern, Bennett Berger tells us that (in 1966–
1967):

For a few months I've been going around the San Francisco Bay Area asking hippies what the New Morality is all about . . . I've been doing more than my share of café-sitting, digging the moral feeling of the young as it comes across through their talk (Berger, 1967:19).

Taking on an earlier formulation by Malcolm Cowley, Berger argues that the hippie system of meanings is composed of "eight basic ideas":

1. Salvation by the child.

2. Self-expression.

3. Paganism.

4. Living for the moment.

5. Liberty.

6. Female equality.

7. Mind expansion and transcending the realities that hang one up.

8. Romantic love of the exotic (Berger, 1967:19–20).

What are here called meanings are often labeled "ideology," or "world view" in studies of societies, social movements, groups and the like. In book-length studies, these frequently appear in a separate and early chapter. Because a social movement especially is likely to have a written creed, platform, set of demands, or the like, such treatment in a separate chapter appears quite logical, for members themselves have a designated body of written material which *they* refer to as their "position," "point of view," etc. The analyst is therefore coding such a body of written material just as do the members. Indeed, in order that any subsequent rendition of acts, activities, participation, and the like can make sense it is entirely reasonable that there be early-on such a summary and recounting of the elements of belief, ideology, etc.—that is, the meanings.

Middle-Range meanings.
But meanings can also be more discrete, in that they can be attached to

more delimited aspects of the members' round of life, although still rather general in their application.

Analyses of meanings often center on the question of how members define for themselves a given problematic topic. That which is seen as problematic may be so defined by the observer, the members, or both. Thus in observing a religious group that strongly believed they were destined to make thousands of new converts and who worked hard to achieve that goal I found them failing time after time. They themselves perceived this failure as well. How, then, did they define this chronic gap between aim and actuality? Members of the group seemed to possess three basic definitions or explanations of the disparity.

> *First,* the American group was an offshoot of the Korean founding body, which had gone for years without success before beginning to make large numbers of converts. They would remind themselves that they were perhaps only following "the Korean pattern."
>
> *Second,* they would apply their general "principle of restitution" which held that God and Satan alternated in their influence. Current failure was due to Satan's dominant influence, which would later be counterbalanced by God's good influence on prospects in the making of converts.
>
> *Third,* members believed that God would deliberately withhold his help from them in order to see how well they could do on their own. Current failure was testing their strength (J. Lofland, 1966:244-245).

Situated Meanings.

On the more narrow side, meanings can be attached or applied to only a small part of members' full round of activities. A pioneering work here is that of Gresham Sykes and David Matza in their attempt to formulate definitions that youth appear to apply to their (occasional) delinquent acts. Calling these "techniques of neutralization," Sykes and Matza formulate what appear to be five "definitions favorable to the violation of law."

1. The denial of one's personal responsibility for the act.

2. The denial of anyone's being injured by the act.

3. The denial of the victim's right to protection, because he is a disreputable person.

4. The denial of the condemners' rights to condemn the perpetrator, because they are hypocrites and the like.

5. The claim that loyalties to one's friends or other groups supersede loyalty to legal rules (Sykes and Matza, 1957).

Viewed in the broadest manner, all social and personal change entails phases or changes of meaning. Even when viewed more narrowly— within the context of specified social situations—phases or changes of meaning can occur at the level of acts, activities, participation, relationships; and settings.

At this juncture, a single—almost pure—example of phases of meaning analysis may be described. Sensitive to the processual aspects of social life and experience, Howard S. Becker sought to provide an explanation of "becoming a marihuana user" that transcended static depictions of "kinds of people" predisposed to the behavior. He took as his problem the task "of describing the set of changes in the person's conception of the activity and of the experience it provides for him." He attempted "to describe the sequence of changes in attitude and experience which lead to the use of marihuana for pleasure" (Becker, 1953:235, italics omitted). The finished statement asserts three things that must be *learned,* a term we can here take to indicate necessary changes in meaning.

No one becomes a user without:

1. Learning to smoke the drug in a way which will produce real effects.

2. Learning to recognize the effects and connect them with drug use (learning, in other works, to get high).

3. Learning to enjoy the sensations he perceives (Becker, 1953:242).

Becker's further comments on phases of meaning in marihuana use provide a useful guide to more general study.

> If a stable form of a new behavior toward . . . [an] object is to emerge, a transformation of meanings must occur, in which the person develops a new conception of the nature of the object. This happens in a series of communicative acts in which others point out new aspects of experience to him, present him with new interpretations of events, and help him achieve a new conceptual organization of his world, without which the new behavior is not possible (Becker, 1953:242).

Concerning meanings, then, the observer-analyst can be attuned to the following questions:

1. What life-encompassing meanings occur among the participants in this setting?

2. What relatively circumscribed meanings occur among the participants of this setting?

3. What situationally-specific meanings are employed by the participants in this setting?

4. What phases of meaning seem to occur among participants in this setting?

PARTICIPATION The foregoing units of comprehension deemphasize persons *per se* by focusing upon highly selected sets of their acts and activities or their transpersonal meanings. In turning to participation, we focus directly upon the person as a unit upon holistic patterns of involvement they have in a social setting. Stated differently, participants in settings tend to vary in the manner in which they forge careers and the ways in which they adapt to settings. Here, more than elsewhere, elements of actors' "personal styles" can enter the sociological picture.

We need again to draw a distinction between the observer's attempts to discern participation patterns already identified and employed by the natives of the setting, and those that he constructs out of the existing but unarticulated patterns of participation found in the setting.

Member-Identified Types.

Member-identified or folk types vary along dimensions of the degree of centrality and the degree of longevity in a social setting. Although perhaps important to members, some participation patterns are short-term, situational, and *relatively* peripheral to a given organized system. In observing the clinical activities of medical students, Becker, Geer, Hughes, and Strauss found these students using the term "crook" to "refer to patients who disappoint them by failing to have pathological findings" (Becker et al., 1961:328). This student-identified pattern of patient participation then provided clues as to what constituted, in the students' minds, more "proper" patterns of patient participation.

Within the social setting provided by formal organizations, there typically develops a lush undergrowth of what are sometimes called "argot roles." Such roles have been studied most extensively in encompassing organizations where people live out their days literally walled in; namely, in prisons. Typically recurring and member-identified patterns of participation in male prisons include the right guy, wolf, tough, gorilla, hipster, and ball buster (Giallombardo, 1966:285).

Moving into broader social contexts, participants in more "free" social worlds regularly distinguish informal patterns of participation among themselves. At one point in the history of San Francisco's Haight-Ashbury district, hippies drew among themselves a distinction between "heads" and "freaks."

> While a whole penumbra of allusive imaginery surrounds these terms, a "head" essentially is thought to be someone who uses drugs—and here, it is mainly the hallucinogens that the speaker has in mind—for purposes of mind expansion, insight, and the enhancement of personality attributes, i.e., he uses drugs to discover where "his head is at."
> By contrast, the term "freak" refers usually to someone in search of drug kicks as such, especially if his craving carries him to the point of drug abuse where his health, sanity, and relations with intimates are jeopardized (Davis and Munoz, 1968:160).

Among any socially identified category, there are likely to arise a wide range of internally identified "types" that are indicative, to use Samuel Strong's terms, of the participants' "axes of life." "Axes of life are crucial lines of interest in the life of the group . . . and constitute frames of reference according to which the group categorizes some of its members" (Strong, 1943:565). The collection and classification of such natively identified patterns of participation is one "means of learning the run of attention of a community, its main problems, and the definitions made of issues, crises, and special situations." "Social types stand for what the members who live in . . . various social worlds believe to be critical and important and refer to what they approve or reject" (Strong, 1946:23; 1943:564).

Observer-Articulated or Constructed Types.

Patterns of participation vary in the degree to which participants have themselves articulated and designated variance in participation. At one remove from instances such as those just recounted are participant-designated patterns for which the analyst assumes the task of articulation of uncrystallized participation identifications. At the farthest remove from participant-articulated designations, the analyst assumes the task of *constructing* patterns that appear to exist but remain unconceived in the phenomenology of the participants. It is this latter task of observer construction that is the most hazardous and most subject to the legitimate charge of imposing a world of meaning on the participants that better reflects the observer's world than the world under study. When the observer constructs participation patterns he is more likely to impute participation than to discern it. Nonetheless, it still seems worthwhile to attempt construction. As previously mentioned, the best and most stringent test of observer constructions is their recognizability to the participants themselves. When participants themselves say "Yes, that is there, I had simply never noticed it before," the observer can be reasonably confident that he has tapped into extant patterns of participation.

Attempts to articulate or construct may themselves be distinguished in terms of the duration and scope of the pattern of participation. At the temporally brief and situationally specific end of these variables, Lyn Lofland, in observing waiting behavior in public places, noted that "waiters" tended to vary in the degree to which their behavior was restricted or self-protective. (L. Lofland, 1973:146–151)

In a more expanded context, patterns of participation relate to the diversity of ways in which persons can adapt to the pressures of their jobs. Writing of the peculiar difficulties faced by Navy disbursing officers, Ralph Turner reports four modes of handling the conflicting forces of disbursing work.

1. The *Regulation* type approximates the true bureaucrat in that he remains impervious to rank, informal structures, and the orders of his superiors . . .

2. Opposite is the type who doubts the potency of the General

Accounting Office and . . . will do anything for a friend or superior without debate . . .

3. On a different axis . . . is the *Sincere* type . . . [who] fails to recognize conflicts between regulations and orders from superiors and is unaware of the importance of informal systems . . .

4. The commonest type is the *Realist.* Regulations are seen as illogical concatenations of procedures . . . [which] often, when strictly applied, defeat . . . the purpose for which they were constructed . . . They [can] assume the regulation facade . . . but know how any payment may be made "legally" if the request comes from an important enough source (Turner, 1947:347).

Patterns can be further expanded to delineate long-term stances toward, or types of, careers themselves. Studying medical careers, Oswald Hall found three main styles of being a doctor.

The prominent features of a [*friendly* career] are loyalty to patients and solicitude toward the careers of a few colleagues who [are] defined as friends. [The *individualistic* career] . . . is characterized by open competition with other doctors for clientele and by an implicit acceptance of the medical career as a commercial venture. [The *colleague*] . . . career differs from both in its close identification with the medical institutions of the community . . . It involves meticulous etiquette as far as a group of similarly placed colleagues is concerned (Hall, 1949:246).

Lastly, one may point to works which attempt to document relatively diffuse and broad patterns of participation that transcend formally organized contexts. Among these is Alvin Gouldner's analysis of the difference between cosmopolitans and locals in college teaching.

1. *Cosmopolitans:* those low on loyalty to the employing organization, high on commitment to specialized skills, and likely to use an outer reference group orientation. [Further divided into:]

   a. The Outsiders.
   b. The Empire Builders.

2. *Locals:* those high on loyalty to the employing organization, low on commitment to specialized skills, and likely to use an inner reference group orientation. [Further divided into:]

    a. The Dedicated.
    b. The True Bureaucrat.
    c. The Homeguard.
    d. The Elders (Gouldner, 1957:290; 1958:446–450).

All the foregoing examples of participation analysis are static in character. No attempt is made to search out time-oriented stages, phases, or sequences of participation in a social setting. Analyses that do have a stage or phase focus are not untypically oriented to stages or phases of socialization to or in a social setting. Observing first year medical students, Becker, Geer, Hughes, and Strauss found these "boys in white" to *begin* their school careers with an idealistic view of medicine as "The best of All Professions," in "An Effort to Learn It All." But the overwhelming amount of information presented them leads to a *second* stage of realizing that "You Can't Do It All." By the end of the freshman year, this has crystallized into a *third* and final stage oriented around "What They Want Us to Know" (Becker, Geer, Hughes, and Strauss, 1961: Part Two).

Likewise attuned to socialization, Fred Davis has focused on stages of student nurses undergoing what he calls "doctrinal conversion . . . the social psychological process whereby students come to exchange their own lay views and imagery of the profession for those the profession ascribes to itself." His focus was on "those feelings, states, inner turning points, and experimental markings which, from the perspective of the subject, impart a characteristic tone, meaning, and quality to his status passage" (Davis, 1968:237). The phenomenological experience and empirical materials of exchanging one self for another are organized into six stages.

1. Initial innocence.

2. Labeled recognition of incongruity.

3. "Psyching out."

4. Role simulation.

5. Provisional internalization.

6. Stable internalization (Davis, 1968:241–251).

Expanding the temporal reference from a few months or years to include many years or perhaps entire lives, concern can be given to the typical stages of the *careers* of persons found in a social setting. Thus, in interviewing medical doctors, Oswald Hall suggests the existence of four central "stages of the medical career," each with its associated causes, consequences, and contingencies. In bare essentials these are:

1. Generating an ambition.

2. Incorporation into the institution of medicine.

3. Acquiring a clientele.

4. Entering the inner fraternity (Hall, 1948).

Regarding participation, then, an observer-analyst can be sensitive to these types of questions:

1. What member-developed and designated static patterns of participation are found in this social setting?

2. What static patterns of participation may I, as observer, reasonably articulate or construct on the basis of member activities I observe?

3. What phases or stages of participation are either already designated by participants here or might I as observer articulate or construct?

4. What cycles of participation might exist among the participants of this setting?

RELATIONSHIPS   Almost all of the strategies and notions explicated above are phrased in terms of the emissions of individuals. We move now to a unit that by its nature transcends individuals. We turn to relationships.

A sense of static depictions of relationships may be provided by reference to analyses of hierarchy, alliance, and conjoint awareness.

1. Hierarchy.

Participants in social settings tend formally or informally to rank one another and to process different degrees of influence over one another. Collectively considered, these personal differences in power, influence, and centrality tend to form a social hierarchy. Even if there is struggle over placement in the social hierarchy, struggle over the hierarchy itself, or a struggle between two or more social hierarchies in the same setting, there nonetheless tends to exist, even if fluid and changing, a ranking system. Such a system among a street corner group that William Whyte calls "The Nortons" (1955) . . . illustrates the most fundamental and primitive structural meaning of the concept of relationship.

2. Alliance.

But concepts of relationship are possible on a variety of other bases. In observing several commercial and industrial firms, Melville Dalton noticed that webs of informal ties among executives tended to assume a variety of forms. Calling them by their traditional name—cliques—Dalton classified these forms in terms of their relations to the formal structure of the organization harboring them.

1. *Vertical Cliques* usually occur in a single department . . . between a top officer and some of his subordinates. They are vertical in the sense that they are up-and-down alliance between formal unequals.

    a. *Vertical Symbiotic Cliques.* The top officer is concerned to aid and protect his subordinates . . . The subordinates fully advise him of real or rumored threats to his position . . . There is a satisfying exchange of services.

    b. *Vertical Parasitic Cliques.* The exchange of services between the lower and higher clique members is unequal. The lower ranked person or persons receive more than they give and may greatly damage the higher officer.

2. *Horizontal Cliques* . . . cut across more than one department and

embrace formal equals for the most part.

    a.   *Horizontal Defensive Cliques.* It is usually brought on by what its members regard as crises . . . [and] is strong for only the limited time necessary to defeat or adjust to a threat.

    b.   Horizontal Aggressive Cliques. Their action is a cross-departmental drive to effect changes rather than to resist them, to redefine responsibility, or even directly to shift it.

3.   *Random Clique.* As compared with the more functional cliques this one is random in the sense that its members may come from any part of the personnel, managers and managed, and that they do not anticipate important consequences of their association (Dalton, 1959:57–65).

3. Conjoint Awareness.

Finally, an elegantly analytic example of a concept of relationship may be mentioned. Concerned with situations of dying, Barney Glaser and Anselm Strauss noticed considerable variation in who knew what about a person's impending death. Contemplating this variation, they formulated the idea of awareness context, by which they mean "the total combination of what each interactant in a situation knows about the identity of the other and his own identity in the eyes of the other" (Glaser and Strauss, 1964:-670). This central idea is then elaborated into four types of awareness contexts.

1.   An *open* awareness context obtains when each interactant is aware of the other's true identity. [E.g., both the doctor and the patient know and say they know that the patient is dying.]

2.   A *closed* awareness context obtains when one interactant does not know either the other's identity or the other's view of his identity. [E.g., the doctor but not the patient knows that the patient is dying.]

3.   A *suspicion* awareness context is a modification of the closed one; one interactant suspects the true identity of the other or the other's view of his own identity, or both. [E.g., the doctor believes the patient is dying but will not admit this to the patient, who, in his

turn, suspects that the doctor believes that he is dying.]

4. A *pretense* awareness context is a modification of the open one:
    both interactants are fully aware but pretend not to be. [E.g., both
    the doctor and the patient believe the patient to be dying, but
    neither will openly admit this to the other.] (Glaser and Strauss,
    1964:670; and 1965:Chapters 3–6.)

Note the way in which each of these example analyses employs concepts which by their nature require simultaneous and conjoint specifica-
tion of a plurality of persons. Thus, one cannot speak of awareness contexts
without equal and simultaneous attention to at least two persons.

A second form of conceiving relationships focuses upon sequential
stages (or phases of interchange) between two or more parties. What are
phases through which relationships can move? Thus, in interviewing a set
of visibly handicapped people, Fred Davis sought "to delineate in transac-
tional terms the stages through which a sociable relationship" between a
normal and visibly handicapped person may typically pass. Three such
stages are explicated.

1. *Fictional Acceptance.* Unlike earlier societies . . . in which a
    visible handicap automatically relegates the person to a caste-like,
    inferior status . . . in our society the visible handicapped are
    customarily accorded . . . the surface acceptance that democratic
    manners guarantee to nearly all.

2. *"Breaking through"—Facilitating Normalized Role-Taking.* In
    moving beyond fictional acceptance, what takes place essentially
    is a redefinitional process in which the handicapped person pro-
    jects images, attitudes, and concepts of self which encourage the
    normal to . . . take his role . . . in terms other than those associated
    with imputations of deviance.

3. *Institutionalization of the Normalized Relationship.* Having disa-
    vowed deviance and induced the other to respond to him as he
    would to a normal, the problem then becomes one of sustaining
    the normalized definition in the face of the many small amend-
    ments and qualifications that must frequently be made to it. (Davis,
    1961:125–131).

One of the more complex and insightful phase analyses of relationships has been performed by Edwin Lemert on interactional processes
leading up to a person's being labeled and hospitalized as a "paranoid."
Lemert's account of relationships that promote the growth of a paranoid
"delusion" is of the following character.

1. The person who is conducively oriented to participate in subse-
    quent stages already displays one or another kind of interper-
    sonal difficulty with his work associates, in particular a tendency
    to disregard primary group loyalties, to violate confidences, and
    to presume on privileges not accorded him.

2. His associates tend for a time to perceive the person as a variant
    normal, but one or more events precipitate a reorganization of the
    associates' views, seeing him now as "unreliable," "untrust-
    worthy," "dangerous," or someone with whom others "do not
    wish to be involved."

3. Associates begin to engage in patronizing, evasive, and spurious
    interaction with the person, to avoid him, and to exclude him from
    interaction.

4. The person perceives the associates' tendencies to patronize,
    avoid, and exclude him from interaction, strengthening his initial
    tendencies to disregard confidences, etc. (1 above) and promot-
    ing his demands to know what is happening.

5. The associates deal with the increasing difficulties posed by the
    person by strengthening their own patronizing, avoidance, and
    exclusion (2 above). They begin, moreover, to *conspire* among
    themselves in developing means to deal with the person.

6. The person senses this conspiracy, but it, and all other difficulties,
    tend to be denied by the associates. The person's situation
    becomes increasingly one of declining flow of information to him,
    a widening discrepancy between expressed ideas and affect
    among his associates, and increasing ambiguity for the person as
    to the nature of situations and his associates.

7. These three phases (4, 5, and 6 above) *concatenate*. The person
    and the associates mutually respond to the difficulties posed by

the other, in a process that spirals and feeds upon itself, a process that is *mutually* constructed.

8. Finally, if all the associates' efforts to discharge or transfer the person fail, sick leave, psychiatric treatment, or, in the extreme case, mental hospital commitment may be accomplished (summarized and quoted from Lemert, 1962).

Regarding relationships, then, the observer can be attuned to these kinds of questions:

1. What types of standing or static relationships exist among participants in this setting?

2. What phases do various kinds of relationships go through among participants in this setting?

3. What kinds of cycles do the relationships in this setting display?

SETTINGS   Finally, one may point to the temporally longest and spatially largest of observational-analytic units. Considering collectively and globally the emissions of the participants, one can ask: What pattern or patterns does this setting *itself* display? Put somewhat differently: Of what more general category or conceptual construction may this setting be legitimately viewed as an instance?

Let me point, first, to the well-known notion of the "total institution." Observing a mental hospital, Erving Goffman began to contemplate ways in which that establishment resembled organizations not typically classified as similar to mental hospitals. Cogitating also on TB sanitaria, monasteries, boarding schools, and the like, he began to conceive the mental hospital of his acquaintance as an instance of a more general *type* of setting.

When we review the different institutions in our Western society, we find some that are encompassing to a degree discontinuously greater than the ones next in line. Their encompassing or total character is symbolized by the barrier to social intercourse with the outside and to departure that is often built right into the physical plant, such as locked doors, high walls, barbed wire, cliffs, water,

forest, or moors. These establishments I am calling *total institutions*
. . .

A basic social arrangement in modern society is that the individual tends to sleep, play, and work in different places, with different copariticipants under different authorities, and without an overall rational plan. The central feature of total institutions can be described as a breakdown of the barriers ordinarily separating these three spheres of life (Goffman, 1961a:4–6).

Having formulated and explored the general characteristics of this abstract type, Goffman could go on to trace out and explicate what seemed to follow from the more general features. The minutiae of social life in the hospital he observed could then take on a more general meaning and relevance as typifying all total institutions.

Attuned to Max Weber's ideal type of what constitutes a "bureaucracy," Jerry Jacobs came away from a year's employment as a "social case worker" in a public welfare department with the distinct sense that he had been exposed to something quite different from the bureaucracy portrayed by Weber and his followers, despite the fact that governmental organizations are always depicted as prototypes of bureaucracies. Studying the contrast between the Weberian idea of a bureaucracy and what he had actually observed, Jacobs concluded that the disparity was so great that a new type needed to be formulated adequately to capture what in fact goes on in some organizations ostensibly labeled bureaucracies.

It is possible for an organization to conform little or not at all to the conditions of bureaucracy, while maintaining an image of complete adherence to bureaucratic ideals. The existence of such a situation will hereafter be referred to as "symbolic bureaucracy" (Jacobs, 1969:414).

Armed with this more abstract concept, Jacobs could then review the materials of his organization in terms of the degree to which it might be said to be a "symbolic bureaucracy," as distinct from the classic one of Weber's formulation.

Reflecting on the logic of his anlysis of the communist party, Philip Selznick has commented on the origin and status of the idea of the *combat party* as a more abstract type employed to order and interpret his concrete historical materials.

The major concern is to identify the system, to state what the "nature of the beast" is. The task is to construct a conceptual model of a functioning institutional system. But this is also an exercise in typology. We view the structure we are studying as an instance of a class of objects whose general features are to be explored. The class may have only one member, but it is the *kind* of thing we are dealing with that interests us. We ask: What kind of a social system is the Communist party? We answer by developing a model of the "combat party," including its strategies (Selznick, 1960:xiv).

This logic is, of course, easily extended to the conceiving of numerous types. Where more than one concrete setting is under observation, the variance that exists in the world is likely even to make multiple typing necessary.

The phase analysis of one or more settings begins to link up with the more conventional notion of history. Indeed, there is little lack of historical accounts of this or that reasonably discrete setting, such as social movements, organizations, milieux, and the like. However, such accounts almost without exception fail to qualify as *sociological* analysis. They fail primarily because they do not attempt *articulately* to classify the materials of a historical record into one or another kind of *stages, phases,* or *periods.* This is not to say that writers of histories do not in fact possess such schemes. It *is* to say that they most often leave their schemes implicit or, in the tradition of literati, even try to deemphasize their existence or to hide the fact of their covert employment. The quest of sociology is altogether different. The attempt is to discern patterns and clearly to communicate what one has discerned.

In addition to calendar-based and member-recognized setting cycles there are revolving regularities of a more unplanned, unrecognized, and less scheduled nature. Thus, in observing some three years in the history of a small end-of-the-world religion, it seemed to me that the group went through four cycles of collective hope and despair over their problem of making converts. The cult was committed to the prediction and the activity of making many thousands of converts. In stark contrast to this prediction and operating goal was the fact that very few people could even be interested, and fewer still could be converted. The four cycles in the three years studied had the character of:

1.   Some event occurring or plan devised that provided for them a collective sense of hope that many converts would soon be made;

2. Action would be organized around the event or plan which;

3. Eventually failed by their own estimation, leading to;

4. A collective sense of despair of ever attaining their goal.

5. The group then came full circle back to a new event or plan (J. Lofland, 1966: Chapter 12)

Such analyses can be further combined with an effort to specify, at a middle level of generalization, activities, meanings and the like upon which cycles are predicated. Thus, in this cult example, four kinds of activities and definitions provided the materials necessary to initiate the first state of a new cycle.

> New hope was generated when the entire believership decamped and migrated *en masse,* a rather common strategy in religious history.
> New hope was generated by announcing to the believers the imminent but unspecified arrival on the scene on their messiah.
> New hope was generated by defining present time as preparatory, planning, and organizing time for a later time, when, aided by things done now, goals will really be achieved.
> New hope was generated by geographical dispersion of believers on missionary quests. A sense of expansion and potency was derived from new places and people, if not from larger membership (adapted from J. Lofland, 1966: Chapter 12).

Concerning settings, then, the observer-analyst can be attuned to these kinds of questions:

1. Of what more general conception might this setting be an example? What type of setting is this?

2. If more than setting is under observation, or the setting contains subsettings, what varying patterns do these settings display?

3. Through what stages, phases, or periods has this setting passed?

4. Through what cycles might this setting itself be passing?

These units in no way constitute the general outline of a given study. There might be some temptation simply to adopt these six categories as the section outline of a paper or the chapter outline of a longer work. To do so would be to misconstrue the intention and import of the preceding description and discussion. What have been outlined above are, rather, *elements* with which to sort and classify observations and to build some *other kind* of analytic scheme for one's observational materials. These are building blocks that can be utilized in designing one's own building and-/or in portraying the building that has been constructed in or by some social setting. The creative and organizing capacities of the observer-analyst remain a fundamental necessity. Nonetheless, his creative task is presumably facilitated by a familiarity with the kinds of construction materials at his disposal.

REFERENCES

BARTON, ALLEN, AND PAUL F. LAZARFELD, "Some Functions of Qualitative Analysis in Social Research," *Frankfurter Beitrage Zur Soziologie*, Band 1, 1955, pp. 321–361. (Also available as a Bobbs-Merrill Reprint in Sociology, Number 336.)

BECKER, HOWARD S., "Becoming a Marihuana User," *American Journal of Sociology*, 59:235–242 (November, 1953).

BECKER, HOWARD S., BLANCHE GEER, EVERETT HUGHES, AND ANSELM STRAUSS, *Boys in White: Student Culture in Medical School*, Chicago: University of Chicago Press, 1961.

BERGER, BENNETT, "Hippie Morality—More Old Than New," *Transaction*, 5, 2:19–23 (December, 1967)

CLARK, BURTON R., "The 'Cooling-out' Function in Higher Education," *American Journal of Sociology*, 65:569–576 (May, 1960).

CRESSEY, DONALD R., "The Criminal Violation of Financial Trust," *American Sociological Review*, 15:738–743 (December, 1950).

CRESSEY, DONALD R., *Other People's Money: A Study in the Social Psychology of Embezzlement*, New York: The Free Press, 1953.

DALTON, MELVILLE, *Men Who Manage: Fusions of Feeling and Theory in Administration*, New York: John Wiley, 1959.

DAVIS, FRED, "The Cabdriver and His Fare: Facets of a Fleeting Relationship," *American Journal of Sociology*, 65:158–165 (September, 1959).

DAVIS, FRED, "Deviance Disavowal: The Management of Strained Interaction by the Visibly Handicapped," *Social Problems*, 9:120–132 (Fall, 1961).

DAVIS, FRED, "Professional Socialization as Subjective Experience: The Process of Doctrinal Conversion among Student Nurses," in Howard Becker, Blanche Geer, David Riesman, and Robert Weiss, eds., *Institutions and Persons: Papers Presented to Everett C. Hughes,* Chicago: Aldine Publishing Co., 1968, pp. 235–251.

DAVIS, FRED, WITH LAURA MUNOZ, "Heads and Freaks: Patterns and Meanings of Drug Use among Hippies," *Journal of Health and Social Behavior,* 9:156–164 (June, 1968).

EVAN, WILLIAM, "On the Margin—The Engineering Technician," in Peter L. Berger, ed., *The Human Shape of Work: Studies in the Sociology of Occupations,* New York: Macmillan Co., 1964, pp. 83–112.

GIALLOMBARDO, ROSE, "Social Roles in a Prison for Women," *Social Problems,* 13:268–288 (Winter, 1966).

GLASER, BARNEY G., AND ANSELM L. STRAUSS, "Awareness Contexts and Social Interaction," *American Sociological Review,* 29:669–679 (October, 1964).

GLASER, BARNEY G., AND ANSELM L. STRAUSS, *Awareness of Dying,* Chicago: Aldine Publishing Co., 1965.

GOFFMAN, ERVING, *Asylums: Essays on the Social Situation of Mental Patients and Other Inmates,* Garden City, N.Y.: Doubleday & Co., 1961a.

GOFFMAN, ERVING, *Encounters: Two Studies in the Sociology of Interaction,* Indianapolis: Bobbs-Merrill Co., 1961b.

GOULDNER, ALVIN, "Cosmopolitans and Locals: Toward an Analysis of Latent Social Roles—I," *Administrative Science Quarterly,* 2:281–306 (December, 1957).

GOULDNER, ALVIN, "Cosmopolitans and Locals: Toward an Analysis of Latent Social Roles—II," *Administrative Science Quarterly,* 2:444–480 (March, 1958).

HALL, OSWALD, "The Stages of a Medical Career," *American Journal of Sociology,* 53:327–336 (March, 1948).

HALL, OSWALD, "Types of Medical Careers," *American Journal of Sociology,* 53:243–253 (November, 1949).

JACOBS, JERRY, " 'Symbolic Bureaucracy': A Case Study of a Social Welfare Agency," *Social Forces, 47:413–422 (June, 1969).*

KRAIN, MARK, "On Staying Loose: Task Avoidance in the U.S. Army Reserve," Manuscript, University of Michigan, 1967.

LEMERT, EDWIN M., "Paranoia and the Dynamics of Exclusion," *Sociometry, 25:2–20 (March, 1962).*

LOFLAND, JOHN, *Doomsday Cult: A Study of Convension, Proselytization, and Maintenance of Faith,* Englewood Cliffs, N.J.: Prentice-Hall, 1966.

LOFLAND, LYN H., *A World of Strangers,* New York: Basic Books, 1973.

MC KINNEY, JOHN C., *Constructive Typology and Social Theory,* New York: Appleton-Century-Crafts, 1966.

MILLER, WALTER B., "Lower-Class Culture as a Generating Milieu of Gang Delinquency," *Journal of Social Issues, 14:5–19 (1958).*

SELZNICK, PHILIP, *The Organizational Weapon: A Study of Bolshevik Strategy and Tactics,* New York: Free Press, 1960, with a new Preface by the author (original copyright, 1952).

SELZNICK, PHILIP, *TVA and the Grassroots: A Study in the Sociology of Formal Organization,* Berkeley and Los Angeles: University of California Press, 1953.

SHIBUTANI, TAMOTSU, "Reference Groups as Perspectives," *American Journal of Sociology,* 60:562–569 (May, 1955).

STRONG, SAMUEL, "Negro–White Relations as Reflected in Social Types," *American Journal of Sociology,* 52:23–30 (July, 1946).

STRONG, SAMUEL, "Social Types in a Minority Group: Formulation of a Method," *American Journal of Sociology,* 48:563–573 (March, 1943).

SUDNOW, DAVID, "Normal Crimes: Sociological Features of the Penal Code in a Public Defender Office," *Social Problems, 12:255–276 (Winter, 1965).*

SYKES, GRESHAM M., AND DAVID MATZA, "Techniques of Neutralization: A Theory of Delinquency," *American Sociological Review,* 22:664–670 (December, 1957).

TURNER, RALPH H., "The Navy Disbursing Officer as a Bureaucrat," *American Sociological Review,* 12:342–348 (June, 1947).

WHYTE, WILLIAM F., *Street Corner Society: The Social Structure of an Italian Slum,* enlarged edition, Chicago: University of Chicago Press, 1955 (original copyright, 1943).

THREE
THE CONCEPT
OF ORGANIZATION
Egon Bittner

In recent years a good deal of the very best sociological work has been devoted to the study of organization. Although the term, organization, belongs to the category of expressions about which there is maintained an air of informed vagueness, certain special conventions exist that focus its use, with qualifications, on a delimited set of phenomena. In accordance with these conventions, the term applies correctly to stable associations of persons engaged in concerted activities directed to the attainment of specific objectives. It is thought to be a decisive characteristic of such organizations that they are deliberately instituted relative to these objectives. Because organizations, in this sense, are implementing and implemented programs of action that involve a substantial dose of comprehensive and rational planning, they are identified as instances of formal or rational organization in order to differentiate them from other forms.[1]

It has been one of the most abiding points of interest of modern organizational research to study how well the programmatically intended formal structures of organizations describe what is going on within them, and what unintended, unprogrammed, and thus informal structures tend to accompany them.

How do sociologists go about distinguishing the facts of formal organization from the facts of informal organization? There seem to be two things that matter in the ways this distinction is drawn. There is, in the first place, a certain scholarly tradition in which the distinction is rooted. It dates back to Pareto's definition of rationality, Tönnies' typology, Cooley's concept of

Source: "The Concept of Organization" by E. Bittner. *Social Research*, 32, 3 (Autumn 1965): 239–255.

primary-group, and—tracing through the seminal achievement of the Hawthorn studies—the tradition is very much alive today. Being steeped in this line of scholarship allows a sociologist to claim his colleagues' consent to the decisions he makes. In this way the distinction is a fact of life in sociological inquiry, and perceiving it correctly is a trademark of professional competence. Although this is undoubtedly a potent factor in many decisions, it does not furnish a clear-cut rule for the distinction.[2]

The rule, which is the second consideration, can be stated as follows: In certain presumptively identified fields of action, the observed stable patterns of conduct and relations can be accounted for by invoking some *programmatic constructions* that define them prospectively. Insofar as the observed stable patterns match the dispositions contained in the program they are instances of formal organizational structure. Whereas, if it can be shown that the program did not provide for the occurrence of some other observed patterns which seem to have grown spontaneously, these latter belong to the domain of the informal structures.

Despite its apparent cogency, the rule is insufficient. The programmatic construction is itself a part of the presumptively identified field of action, and thus the sociologist finds himself in the position of having borrowed a concept from those he seeks to study in order to describe what he observes about them.

In general, there is nothing wrong with borrowing a commonsense concept for the purposes of sociological inquiry. Up to a certain point it is, indeed, unavoidable. The warrant for this procedure is the sociologist's interest in exploring the commonsense perspective. The point at which the use of common-sense concepts becomes a transgression is where such concepts are expected to do the analytical work of theoretical concepts. When the actor is treated as a permanent auxiliary to the enterprise of sociological inquiry at the same time that he is the object of its inquiry, there arise ambiguities that defy clarification. Now, if the idea of formal structure is basically a common-sense notion, what role can it have in sociological inquiry?

The Theoretical Sense of
Formal Structures of Organization

In an influential essay published fifteen years ago, Philip Selznick explicitly addressed the problem of the theoretical significance of formal constructions by relating them, as facts of life, to functional imperatives of organizations conceived as cooperative-adaptive systems.[3] Arguing along the lines of structural-functional analysis, he showed convincingly why "formal administrative design can never adequately or fully reflect the concrete organization to which it refers," but is nevertheless a relevant element in the sociological study of organizations. In his view, the design represents that particular conception of organization which management technicians seek to explicate. Even though there may attach to these explications some descriptive or analytic intent, they are primarily active elements of the concrete phenomenon of organization rather than disinterested statements about it. As such, the presence of rational organizational design in social systems of action is a source of tension and dilemma. These consequences arise out of the "recalcitrance of the tools of action," relative to the "freedom of technical or ideal choice" reflected in plans and programs.

It is important to note that in this new and rich context the old conception of formal organization, which is traceable to Max Weber, remained intact. Together with Weber, Selznick assumes that the formal structures represent an ideally possible, but practically unattainable state of affairs. While Weber outlined the contents of the normative idealization in general terms, Selznick pointed out that the normative idealization, to be an effective source of restraint, must be constantly adapted to the impact of functional imperatives of social systems. Thus he furnished the necessary theoretical argument for an entire field of sociological investigations by directing attention to a sphere of adaptive and cooperative manipulations, and to the tensions typically found in it.

Despite the gain, the argument retains a certain theoretical short circuit. While Selznick quite clearly assigns the formal schemes to the domain of sociological data, he does not explore the full range of consequences arising out of this decision. By retaining Weber's conception of them as normative idealizations, Selznick avoids having to consider what the constructions of rational conduct mean to, and how they are used by, persons who have to live with them from day to day. It could be, however, that the rational schemes appear as unrealistic normative idealizations only when one considers them literally, i.e., without considering some tacit background assumptions that bureaucrats take for granted.

In the following we shall endeavor to show that the literal interpretation of formal schemes is not only inappropriate but, strictly speaking, impossible. We shall further show that the tacit assumptions are not simply unspecified, but instead come to the fore only on occasions of actual reference to the formal scheme. Finally, we shall argue that the meaning and import of the formal schemes must remain undetermined unless the circumstances and procedures of its actual use by actors is fully investigated.

Critique of Weber's Theory of Bureaucracy

We shall introduce our argument by considering Weber's work critically because the short circuit in theorizing occurred first in his work and because most of contemporary research in formal organization claims to stand in some sort of relationship to the definitions formulated by him. We shall be discussing the theory of bureaucracy as the most general case of many possible, more specific, rational schemes. But what we say about the general form is applicable to such specific instances as manuals of operations, tables of organization or programs of procedure.

Weber used the concept of organization to refer to a network of authority distribution.[4] As is well known, he asserted that such a network may be said to exist when and insofar as there prevails a high degree of correspondence between the substance of commands and conditions favoring compliance with them. Confining our interest to bureaucracy, we note that the condition favoring compliance with its authority structure lies in its acceptance as being efficient.[5] From this premise, pure bureaucracy obtains when the principle of technical efficiency is given overriding priority above all other considerations. The ideal type of bureaucracy is, consequently, the product of ostensibly free conceptual play with this principle.

To say, however, that the resulting scheme is a meaningful conceptualization indicates that the ideal of efficiency is exercised over a domain of objects and events that are known to exist and that are known to possess independent qualities of their own. The efficiency principle merely selects, identifies, and orders those existing elements of a scene of action that are perceived as related to it. The relevance of the known qualities of things becomes very apparent when one considers that it must be at least possible for them to be related in ways that the idealization stipulates. What sorts of things are taken for granted may vary, but it is not possible to have any rational construction of reality that does not rest on some such tacit assumptions.[6]

It could be said that this is not an unusual state of affairs. In scientific inquiry it is always the case that in order to assert anything one must leave some things unsaid. Such unsaid things stand under the protection of the *ceteris paribus* clause. The use of this clause is, however, restricted and its contents are always open to scrutiny.[7]

When one lifts the mantle of protection from the unstated presupposition surrounding the terms of Weber's theory of Bureaucracy one is confronted with facts of a particular sort. These facts are not sociological data, or even theoretically defensible hypotheses. Instead, one is confronted with a rich and ambiguous body of background information that normally competent members of society take for granted as commonly known. In its normal functioning this information furnishes the tacit foundation for all that is explicitly known, and provides the matrix for all deliberate considerations without being itself deliberately considered. While its content can be raised to the level of analysis, this typically does not occur. Rather, the information enters into that commonplace and practical orientation to reality which members of society regard as "natural" when attending to their daily affairs. Since the explicit terms of the theory are embedded in this common-sense orientation, they cannot be understood without tacit reference to it. If, however, the theorist must be persuaded about the meaning of the terms in some prior and unexplicated way, there then exists collusion between him and those about whom he theorizes. We call this unexplicated understanding collusive because it is a hidden resource, the use of which cannot be controlled adequately.

Some examples will help to clarify this point. Consider the term "employee." There is little doubt that Weber presupposed, rather than neglected, a whole realm of background information in using it. Certainly employees must be human beings of either the male or female sex, normally competent adults rather than children, and in many ways familiar types of persons whose responsiveness, interests, inclinations, capacities and foibles are in a basic sense known as a matter of course. All this information is obvious, of course, but does not by any means coincide with the scientifically demonstrable or even scientifically tenable. Rather, the full meaning of the term "employee," as it is used in the theory of bureaucracy, refers to that understanding of it which fully franchised persons in society expect from one another when they converse on matters of practical import. That is, insofar as the term refers meaningfully to some determinate object, it does so only in the context of actors making common sense of it in consequential situations.

Let us consider the ideal of efficiency itself. While Weber is quite clear in stating that the sole justification of bureaucracy is its efficiency, he provides us with no clear-cut guide on how this standard of judgment is to be used. Indeed, the inventory of features of bureaucracy contains not one single item that is not arguable relative to its efficiency function. Long-range goals cannot be used definitively for calculating it because the impact of contingent factors multiplies with time and makes it increasingly difficult to assign a determinate value to the efficiency of a stably controlled segment of action. On the other hand, the use of short-term goals in judging efficiency may be in conflict with the ideal of economy itself. Not only do short-term goals change with time and compete with one another in indeterminate ways, but short-term results are of notoriously deceptive value because they can be easily manipulated to show whatever one wishes them to show. [8] Clearly, what Weber had in mind when speaking about efficiency was not a formally independent criterion of judgment but an ideal that is fully attuned to practical interests as these emerge and are pursued in the context of every-day life. The standard itself and the correct way to use it are, therefore, a part of the selfsame order of action that they purport to control. The power and right to judge some procedure as more or less efficient require the same kind of sensitivity, responsiveness and competence that using the procedure presupposes in the first place. Only those who have serious business in doing what must be done are also franchised to judge it.

Weber, of course, intended to achieve an idealized reconstruction of organization from the perspective of the actor. He fell short of attaining this objective precisely to the extent that he failed to explore the underlying common-sense presuppositions of his theory. He failed to grasp that the meaning and warrant of the inventory of the properties of bureaucracy are inextricably embedded in what Alfred Schutz called the attitudes of every-day life and in socially sanctioned common-sense typifications. [9]

Thus, if the theory of bureaucracy is a theory at all, it is a refined and purified version of the actors' theorizing. To the extent that it is a refinement and purification of it, it is, by the same token, a corrupt and incomplete version of it; for it is certainly not warranted to reduce the terms of common-sense discourse to a lexicon of culturally coded significances to satisfy the requirements of theoretical postulation. This is the theoretical shortcut we mentioned at the beginning of our remarks.

The Study of the Concept of Organization as a Common-Sense Construct

Plucked from its native ground, i.e., the world of common sense, the concept of rational organization, and the schematic determinations that are subsumed under it, are devoid of information on how its terms relate to facts. Without knowing the structure of this relationship of reference, the meaning of the concept and its terms cannot be determined.

In this situation an investigator may use one of three research procedures. He can, for one thing, proceed to investigate formal organization while assuming that the unexplicated common-sense meanings of the terms are adequate definitions for the purposes of his investigation. In this case, he must use that which he proposes to study as a resource for studying it.

He can, in the second instance, attach to the terms a more or less arbitrary meaning by defining them operationally. In this case, the relationship of reference between the term and the facts to which it refers will be defined by the operations of inquiry. Interest in the actor's perspective is either deliberately abandoned, or some fictitious version of it is adopted.

The investigator can, in the last instance, decide that the meaning of the concept, and of all the terms and determinations that are subsumed under it, must be discovered by studying their use in real scenes of action by persons whose competence to use them is socially sanctioned.

It is only the last case which yields entirely to the rule specifying the relevance of the perspective of the actor in sociological inquiry. This is so because in order to understand the meaning of the actor's thought and action, which Weber sought, one must study *how* the terms of his discourse are assigned to real objects and events by normally competent persons in ordinary situations.

Insofar as the procedures and considerations actors invoke in relating terms of rational common-sense construction to things in the world exhibit some stable properties, they may be called a method. It is, of course, not proper to assume that this method is identical with, or even similar to, the method of scientific inquiry. Garfinkel proposed that in order to differentiate the study of this method from the study of the methods of scientific inquiry it be called ethnomethodology. [10]

In the following we shall propose in brief outline a program of inquiry which takes as its object of interest the study of the methodical use of the rational constructions subsumed under the concept of organization. We shall also present examples of this program. The concept itself and its methodical use are, of course, defined as belonging entirely to the domain of facts.

We must emphasize that our interest is in outlining a program of inquiry, not in producing a theory of organization. It has to be this way because the inquiry cannot get under way without first employing the very sensibilities that it seeks to study, i.e., the common-sense outlook. At the outset the phenomenon or organization comes to our attention in just the way it comes to the attention of any normal member of our linguistic community. Even as we turn to the investigation of the common-sense presuppositions in which it is embedded, and from which it derives its socially sanctioned sense, other common-sense presuppositions will continue to insinuate themselves into our thinking and observation. The important point in the proposed study is that we must be prepared to treat every substantive determination we shall formulate as a case for exploring the background information on which it in turn rests.

By way of defining our task we propose that *the study of the methodical use of the concept of organization seeks to describe the mechanisms of sustained and sanctioned relevance of the rational constructions to a variety of objects, events and occasions relative to which they are invoked.*

In order to free ourselves progressively from the encumbrance of presumptive understanding we shall take two preliminary measures. First, the author of the rational scheme, typically the managerial technician who deals with organization in the "technical sense," will not be treated as having some sort of privileged position for understanding its meaning. By denying him the status of the authoritative interpreter we do not propose to tamper with the results of his work in the least. From our point of view he is merely the toolsmith. It seems reasonable that if one were to investigate the meaning and typical use of some tool, one would not want to be confined to what the toolmaker has in mind.

Second, we will not look to the obvious or conspicuous meaning of the expressions used in the scheme to direct us to objects and events which they identify. Rather, we will look for the way the scheme is brought to bear on whatever happens within the scope of its jurisdiction. The consequence of this step is that the question of what the scheme selects and neglects is approached by asking how certain objects and events meet, or are made to meet, the specifications contained in the scheme.

After denying the technician and his scheme the authority to organize the field of observation for the sociologist, the question of how they, nevertheless, organize it in some other sense is open for investigation.

If one suspends the presumptive notion that a rational organizational scheme is a normative idealization with a simple import, i.e., demanding literally what it says it demands; and if one views a rational organizational scheme without information about what it is ostensibly meant to be, then it emerges as a *generalized formula to which all sorts of problems can be brought for solution.* In this sense there is no telling what determinations a formal organizational scheme contains prior to the time that questions are actually and seriously addressed to it.

More important than the open capacity and applicability of the formula is, however, the fact that *problems referred to the scheme for solution acquire through this reference a distinctive meaning that they would not otherwise have.* Thus the formal organizational designs are schemes of interpretation that competent and entitled users can invoke in yet unknown ways whenever it suits their purposes. The varieties of ways in which the scheme can be invoked for information, direction, justification, and so on, without incurring the risk of sanction, constitute the scheme's methodical use. In the following we propose to discuss some examples of possible variations in the methodical use of organizational rationalities.

Examples of Variation in the Methodical Use of the Concept of Organization

THE GAMBIT OF COMPLIANCE[11]   As we have noted earlier, the concept of rational organization is often regarded by sociologists and management technicians as a normative idealization. Even though one finds only *"is"* and *"is not"* in the substantive determination, there attaches the sense of *"ought"* to the entire scheme.

Conceived as a rule of conduct, the concept of organization is defined as having some determining power over action that takes place under the scope of its jurisdiction. This power to produce an intended result is uncertain and depends for its effectiveness on complex structural conditions. Hence, research informed by the conception of organization as a rule of conduct will seek to procure estimates of its effectiveness, and will relate the findings to factors that favor or mitigate against compliance. All such research is necessarily based on the assumption that the relationship of correspondence between the rule and the behaviors that are related to it is clear. A cursory consideration of the significance of rules as social facts reveals, however, that their meaning is not exhausted by their prospective sense. Aside from determining the *occurrence* of certain reponses under suitable conditions rules are also invoked to clarify the *meaning* of actions retrospectively. For example, one knows what a driver of an automobile signaling intent to make a left turn is doing in the middle of an intersection because one knows the rule governing such procedures. Indeed, it is a readily demonstrable fact that a good deal of the sense we make of the things happening in our presence depends on our ability to *assign them* to the phenomenal sphere of influence of some rule. Not only do we do this but we count on this happening. That this is so is richly documented in the work of Goffman who has shown how persons conduct themselves in such a way as to enable observers to relate performances to some normative expectation.

When we consider the set of highly schematic rules subsumed under the concept of rational organization, we can readily see an open realm of free play for relating an infinte variety of performances to rules as responses to these rules. In this field of games of representation and interpretation, the rule may have the significance of informing the competent person about the proper occasion and form for doing things that could probably never be divined from considering the rule in its verbal form. Extending to the rule the respect of compliance, while finding in the rule

the means for doing whatever need be done, is the gambit that characterizes organizational acumen.

We propose that we must proceed from the theoretical clarification of
the essential limitation of formal rules achieved by Selznick to the investigation of the limits of maneuverability within them, to the study of the skill and
craftsmanship involved in their use and to a reconsideration of the meaning of strict obedience in the context of varied and ambiguous representa-
tions of it. This recommendation is, however, not in the interest of
accumulating more materials documenting the discrepancy between the
lexical meaning of the rule and events occurring under its jurisdiction, but
in order to attain a grasp of the meaning of the rules as common-sense
constructs from the perspective of those persons who promulgate and live
with them.

THE CONCEPT OF FORMAL
ORGANIZATION AS A MODEL
OF STYLISTIC UNITY   It is often noted that the formal organi-

zation meets exigencies arising out of the complexity and large scope of
an enterprise. The rationally conceived form orders affiliations between
persons and performances that are too remote for contingent arrangement, by linking them into coherent maps or schedules. The integration
transcends what might result from negotiated agreements between con-
tiguous elements, and lends to elements that are not within the sphere of
one another's manipulative influence the character of a concerted action.
As a consequence of this, however, each link derives its meaning not so
much from the specific rule that determines it, but from the entire order of
which the rule itself is a part. Each link is intrinsically a member of a chain
or fabric of links which conducts a reproducible theme. In this context,
many specific instances or elements can be compared with each other as
variations of a single pattern. For example, a simple polarization of authority pervades the whole order of an organization and can be found as
a redundant thematic focus in many segments of it. A rational principle of
justice may prevail in the entire structure while governing differentially
correct associations between particular performances and rewards. The
varieties of demeanors that are appropriate to a particular status within the
system may be perceived as variations of a more general pattern.

We are suggesting the possibility of a principle of discipline that
derives from the formal style of the rational scheme and which works
against centrifugal tendencies and heterogeneity. The resulting coherence will be in evidence as outwardly proper conduct and appearance.
One would then ask how the sensibility of esthetic appreciation is sum-

moned for direction, information and control in various concrete situations. The dominant consideration underlying this constructon would not be found in the field of means-ends relations but in an all-pervading sense of piety (i.e., in accordance with Burke's definition of the term, a sure-footed conviction of "what properly goes with what").[12]

The question whether the syntactic composition of the formal scheme is the leading metaphor for the interpretation of the composition of actual performances and relations is obviously difficult to investigate. A tentative approach may be in the investigation of ties and performances that appeal to bureaucrats as incongruous or in bad taste, and the study of those observed proprieties and tolerated licenses that are restricted to "on the job" circumstances. In further development the problem could lead to experimental studies. For example, the features of the stylistically normal could be studied by having subjects perform tasks that are not related or even contrary to their routine activities. The subjects would be induced to perform these tasks under the gaze of their work associates, and would be penalized for attracting attention and rewarded for remaining unnoticed.

THE CONCEPT OF ORGANIZATION AS CORROBORATIVE REFERENCE

There is another problem which is related to the problem of stylistic unity. A large-scale and complex organization is often composed of fragmented tasks and relations that are not capable of acquiring a phenomenal identity of their own or, at least, it is thought to be extremely difficult to value them for their intrinsic merits. Whether it is enough to relate these tasks to work obligations, and whether work requires any corroboration of worth beyond pointing to its market price is an open question. If it does, however, the formal scheme could be invoked to attest to it.

When from the perspective of a fragmentary involvement the actual contingent outcome of one's work cannot be appraised, or appears senseless, then it can be understood and judged in terms of its over-all functional significance by invoking the formal scheme. For example, mismanagement and waste could be defined as merely accidental or perhaps even justified, relative to the total economy of the enterprise. This consideration of the formal scheme not only persuades the participants of some correct or corrected value of their duties, but can also be used as a potent resource for enforcing prohibitions when interest dictates that such prohibitions should be justified.

In this construction, the formal scheme is used as a resource for bringing anything that happens within an organization under the criterion of success or failure when real results are not visible, or must be discredited. This is not a simple matter, of course, because the scheme does not promote a single ideal of economy but specifies a field of economy in which various aspects of an operation may compete for priority. For example, in an industrial enterprise certain ways of doing things may have one value relative to interest in production and an altogether different value relative to interest in maintenance. The problem that requires investigation is how various evaluations can be used as credits, and what sorts of credits have the consequence of assimilating some partial performance closer to the larger enterprise. The investigation of this problem would reveal the negotiable relationship between policy and politics.

Conclusion

We have cited the gambit of compliance, stylisic unity, and corroborative reference merely as examples of the possible methodical use of the concept of organization by competent users. The examples are based on reflections about ethnographic materials depicting life in large-scale and formally programmed organizations.[13] We have indicated earlier that such formulations must be regarded as preliminary at best. Whether what we have tentatively called the reference through the sensibility of esthetic appreciation exists effectively or not, is a matter to be decided by empirical research. Without doubt, these suggestions will have to be revised and amplified, but they must suffice to illustrate the ethnomethodological study of rational organization.

In conclusion, we should like to mention that there remains for this inquiry one more problem that we have mentioned in passing but have not discussed adequately. We have noted that the methical use of the concept of organization must be studied by observing *competent* users. We mean, of course, socially recognized competence. Consequently it is not within the prerogative of the researcher to define competence. Instead, while he looks for the right way to use the rationalities subsumed under the concept or organization, he must also be looking for the rules governing the right to use the concept.

Footnotes

[1] These characteristics are generally noted when the task is to identify real instances of "formal organization." *Cf.* Talcott Parsons, *Structure and Process in Modern Societies* (New York: Free Press, 1960), pp. 16–96; Amitai Etzioni, *Complex Organizations* (New York: Free Press, 1961); P. M. Blau and W. R. Scott, *Formal Organizations* (San Francisco: Chandler Publications, Inc., 1962).

Various authors have studied such organizations in ways that seem to disregard the identifying characteristics, or to subordinate them to other interests. To study a phenomenon while suspending the relevance of that feature by which it is recognized is not an unusual procedure, though it produces peculiar problems. G. E. Moore and Edmund Husserl have explored these problems from substantially different perspectives.

[2] It should not be thought that such grounds are wholly particular to the procedures of sociological inquiry. The distinguished physical chemist G. N. Lewis pointed out that a traditional conception of causality has led to an arbitrary interpretation of Maxwell's equations with the consequent development of a special electromagnetic theory of light. On purely theoretical grounds an entirely different development was equally justified and did occur later, making possible the development of quantum electromechanics. See G. J. Whitrow, *The Natural Philosophy of Time* (New York: Harper Torchbooks. 1963). pp. 25–35.

[3] Philip Selznick, "Foundations of the Theory of Organization," *American Sociological Review,* 13 (1948). pp. 25–35.

[4] Unfortunately there exists some confusion on this point. Weber himself uses the term organization as we have stated, *cf.* "Herrschaft durch 'Organisation,'" *Wirtschaft und Gesellschaft* (4th edition by J. Winckelmann, Tubingen: J. C. B. Mohr, 1954), Kapitel IX, Abschnitt I, #3. The German term "Organisation" is translated by Shils and Rheinstein as "organization" in M. Rheinstein, ed., *Max Weber on Law in Economy and Society* (Cambridge, Mass.: Harvard University Press, 1954), Ch. XII, sect. 3. On the other hand, Henderson and Parsons translate Weber's German term "Betrieb" as "organization." The reason for this choice is that Weber's definition of "Betrieb" coincides with Alfred Marshall's definition of "organization" in economic theory. More important than the question of "authenticity" is, however, the fact that Weber's statement on "Betrieb" is almost never cited in modern organizational studies while his work on authority is widely used.

[5] H. H. Gerth and C. W. Mills, eds. and trans., *From Max Weber: Essays in Sociology* (London: Routledge and Kegan Paul Ltd., 1948), pp. 214–216

[6] It has been proposed that this restriction extends to all types of rational constructions. For a critique of Russell's mathematical logic along these lines see M. J. Charlsworth, *Philosophy and Linguistic Analysis* (Pittsburgh: Duquesne University Press, 1959). Ch. 2.

[7] Concerning the role of the *ceteris paribus* clause in economic analysis see Felix Kaufman, *Methodology of the Social Sciences* (New York: Humanities Press, 1958). Ch. XVI.

[8] *Cf.* Mason Haire, "What Is Organized in an Organization?" Mason Haire, ed., *Organization Theory in Industrial Practice* (New York: John Wiley & Sons, 1962), especially pp. 8–10.

[9] Alfred Schutz, "Common Sense and Scientific Interpretation of Action," *Philosophy and Phenomenological Research*, 14 (1953), pp. 1–38.

[10] The term "ethnomethodology" does not appear in Garfinkel's writings; he invented it, however, and uses it sometimes to refer to a program of inquiry that he has formulated; cf. his "Common Sense Knowledge of Social Structures," J. M. Scher, ed., *Theories of the Mind* (New York: Free Press, 1962), pp. 689–712; and "Studies in the Routine Grounds of Everyday Activities," *Social Problems*, 11 (1964), pp. 225–250.

[11] We should like to point out that this example corresponds to what Selznick suggests when he urges the study of the "manipulation of the formal processes and structures in terms of informal goals." *Op. cit.*, p. 32.

[12] Kenneth Burke, *Permanence and Change* (2nd revised edit., Los Altos, Calif.: Hermes Publications, 1954), pp. 74. ff.

[13] Some prominent examples of works containing excellent ethnographic descriptions of conduct in formal organizations are, Chester R. Barnard, *The Functions of the Executive* (Cambridge, Mass.: Harvard University Press, 1938); F. J. Roethlisberger and W. J. Dickson, *Management and the Worker* (Cambridge, Mass.: Harvard University Press, 1939); Philip Selznick, *TVA and the Grass Roots* (Berkeley: University of California Press, 1949); Melville Dalton, *Men Who Manage* (New York: John Wiley & Sons Inc., 1959).

FOUR CHARACTERISTICS OF PROFESSIONAL ORGANIZATIONS *
Rue Bucher and Joan Stelling

For some years, we have been bothered by discrepancies between our observations in the organizations in which we were doing research and material found in the literature of formal organizations. Approaches to formal organizations dominated by Weberian concepts of bureaucracy simply did not fit organizations dominated by professionals. Our original focus of research was on the professions, but most of the professionals included were carrying out their work within formal organizations. Gradually, our research interest shifted toward concern with what kind of an organization results when professionals are doing the work of the organization. It was evident that a totally new kind of organizational model was required. This paper represents an attempt to outline the major features and requisites of such a model. (The reader can discern the initial outlines of this model in Strauss, et al., 1964, and Strauss, et al., 1963).

As the above remarks imply, we had been thinking of an organization dominated by professionals as a distinctive type of formal organization.

*This work was supported in part by a Public Health Service Career Development Award, K3MH-25,203, from the National Institute of Mental Health and by a research grant from the National Insitute of Mental Health, MH 10391. Support for part of this investigation was provided by a Public Health Service General Research Support Grant. Support for previous research cited in this paper is acknowledged in the indicated publications.
Source: "Characteristics of Professional Organizations" by Rue Bucher and Joan Stelling, *Journal of Health and Social Behavior,* 10 (March 1969): 3–15.

However, a number of recent studies have emphasized fluidity and emerging forms in organizations, and it appears that not even industrial firms are as bureaucratized as was formery believed. (Bennis, 1966; Dalton, 1959; Goldner, 1967; Goldner and Ritti, 1967.) Therefore, it is likely that the characteristics described here as typical of professional organizatious occur in other organizations as well. These characteristics are probably particularly developed and clustered within organizations in which professionals work. The term 'cluster' is used deliberately, in that we suspect that these characteristics are highly interrelated and that given some of them, the others will tend to follow. All the organizations studied have the full cluster, which is presented below. This makes it impossible to tender any hypotheses about which items in the cluster pull in others. Also, the reader should keep in mind that, as an initial strategy in building our model, the emphasis has been on ferreting out *similarities* among the different organizations known to us, and the differences have not been taken into consideration. Thus, the presentation does not reflect a complete comparative analysis. It does, however, highlight features which distinguish these organizations from conventional bureaucracies.

Our observations extend over a period of ten years. The data consist of both intensive depth interviews with professionals and other organizational participants, and participant observation field notes. The professionals studied include various medical specialists, scientists of diverse disciplines, nurses, social workers, occupational therapists, and clinical psychologists. The organizations include a general hospital, a university hospital, one state mental hospital, two psychiatric sections of general hospitals, and a medical school. (Publications from this research most relevant to the topic of this of this include: Bucher and Strauss, 1961; Bucher, 1962; Strauss, et al., 1964; Schatzman and Bucher, 1964. The medical school study is ongoing, and no data have yet been published.)

Professional or Not

Observing professionals and aspiring professionals in various organizational contexts reinforces the viewpoint that being "professional" is an honorific status, which arises out of interaction among *specific* audiences.[1] Occupational label is no necessary indicator of professional status; the status of people of particular occupational titles can vary markedly in different formal organizations. Presumably, in our society, the physician should be able to command prestige and respect wherever he goes. But in each of the institutions observed, there have been situations in which physicians were in decidedly subordinate positions with respect to other professionals. In all of these cases, the status of the physician was relative to specific arena of action within the organization. Being accorded professional status thus involves the following contingencies:

1. The professional makes *claims* to competence in particular areas. He claims that he, uniquely, possesses the knowledge and skills to define problems, set the means for solving them, and judge the success of particular courses of action within his area of competence. To the extent that others accept these claims, the professional is accorded the license and mandate which Hughes has written of as central to being professional (Hughes, 1958:78-87).

2. Having his claims accepted in one area does not necessarily mean that the professional will have his claims accepted in other areas. By areas we mean both subject matter areas and different sectors or arenas of action within an organization. The competence or *expertise* claimed by the professional is *specific;* it is not necessarily generalized to other areas.

3. Having one's claims accepted is not a one-shot affair. The professional does not earn his status once and for all. Rather, it is a continuous process in which his claims to competence are being tested every day in interaction with others and he can lose the respect of others.

4. Even if one is accorded professional status, impinging on other people's areas of work can lead to challenges of claims.

The concept of professional status as generalizable and a matter of commonly held values is plausible insofar as the focus is upon a "professional" group's relation to a lay public. It begins to obscure important processes when the focus is upon the group's relations with other professional groups, and the organization in which they all work. In this kind of situation, the professional is dealing with others who are in a better position to judge his credentials than the lay public. What one sees in many organizations is the struggle of different groups for varying levels of professional recognition, with differential success in different locales. (For instances of variable success, see Schatzman and Bucher, 1964.) The reward for success is autonomy and influence: the group is accorded the competence to define problems, determine solutions, and monitor the functioning of the system.

The reader should keep the above four points in mind in reading the description of characteristics of professional organizations. They are the rules of the game, as it is played among the professionals studied. These rules may well apply in other organizations as well, where people are not labelled as professional. in any case, we think that when the above processes are at work in an organization, the following chacteristics emerge.

The Professional in the Organization

The two primary attributes of a professional organization are *role-creation* and *negotiation*. They are two sides of the same coin; when one is present so is the other. When a person who has been acknowledged as professional enters an organization, he does not step into a clearly defined and pre-existing role. Rather he builds his own place in the organization and creates the role that he plays there. In the medical school, for example, we have never seen a case in which a new faculty member took over the role of his predecessor. Even within the same discipline, faculty members differ in their conceptions of their responsibilities, their interests, and their ways of organizing their time. For example, the particular research interest of a faculty member is a determining factor in the type and amount of space he needs, and for how he organizes his time. One of our respondents requires a room in which temperature can be held constant. Another needs animal quarters where light can be held constant or varied by design. A third, engaged in dream research, needs a suite of rooms, *and* control of temperature. In all three of these cases, also, the researcher must have control of his time once the research begins—else the experiment is lost. Hence the new faculty member negotiates for work space and resources, and proceeds to set up his work as he conceives it.

Hospitals provide many instances of role-creation. During our observation of hospitals, many new chiefs of service have been appointed, but we have yet to find a case in which the new chief carries on the same activities as the former chief; indeed, the appointment of a new chief frequently results in a complete change in the way the service is run. In teaching hospitals, role-creating occurs on a scheduled basis along with the rotation system. As new interns, residents, and attending men rotate through a service, each works out his role on the service in interaction with the others.[2] In psychiatric units the appointment of a new member of the "team," in any position, results in a period of sounding each other out, new rounds of negotiation, and the eventual forgoing of new roles. (Schatzman and Bucher, 1964; for another discussion of role-creating, see Rushing, 1964).

Role creation is a direct consequence of the according of professional status. The professional is the person who has the right to say what should be done and what is necessary to get it done. Professionals thus enjoy considerable success in controlling their working conditions; and, characteristically, they attempt to insure the working conditions which they consider necessary to implement their own set of professional values. The effort to control working conditions is not unique to the professional or to the professional organization; it has been observed among many different types of workers. However, there are some crucial differences in the behavior of the professional which distinguish him from other workers.

First, the professional has a greater stake in the outcome of his efforts. Whether or not he is able to do the work which he has set himself and achieve his career goals depends upon whether he can command the proper working conditions. To do research, one must have the necessary time, facilities, equipment and personnel. To train students one must be able to insure that they have particular kinds of experiences. With other types of workers the stakes usually have to do with convenience and ease on the job, rather than success. Whereas with the professional, his self-respect, reputation, and career are at stake. To put it even more sharply, the career of the professional, both within and without the organization, depends on his ability to control his working conditions, whereas in other organizations one's career may depend on how well one can accept and work within the conditions set by the organization.

Second, in the process of trying to control his working conditions, the professional engages in *open* negotiation and bargaining. This is in contrast to the industrial worker, for example, whose efforts in this direction are frequently covert. In addition, the negotiation takes place from a position of professional worth and values and involves a whole rhetoric of professional claims. It may be primarily focused on the professional's own 'work space'—the actual physical facilities and equipment, as well as the human resources, with which he must deal daily in order to get his work done. As indicated above, the kind of laboratory facilities and equipment needed by those engaged in research are determined not so much by the discipline as by the specific type of research. In negotiations of this type, the arena involved is usually the professional's own department or sector of the institution. But he may also be drawn into negotiations concerning characteristics of larger segments of the organization. This is very likely to happen when these negotiations have consequences for his work space or when they relate to or threaten his professional values and claims. In the medical school, for example, proposals to establish a new research center and to set up a new graduate program drew a number of faculty members into negotiation with others from throughout the university. This type of negotiation is not confined to academic institutions; it has occurred many times in the hospitals we have studied.

There are some structural conditions which appear, at first, to set limits to role-creation on the part of the professional. These situations deserve special attention, in that they may shed some light upon how much role-creation can occur within an organization.

One kind of situation is well known both in academic institutions and in hospitals. This occurs when a particular set of skills or kind of person is sought for a position, usually in order to cover some area defined as necessary for the program of the organization. For example, a physiology department may be seeking a neurophysiologist or a cell physiologist. However, even in the case of supposedly necessary functions, both the individual professional and the organization have more options than appear on the surface. The department of medicine in the medical school study has been attempting to recruit a cardiologist and an endocrinologist in order to supervise clinical services and teaching in these areas. It is well understood among the staff that if the recruiting is successful, each of these men will have set his conditons and will be given *carte blanche* to build his area as he sees fit. If the recruiting is not successful, the department may decide to ride with a weak service, utilizing trainees and outside consultants. They may decide, too, that they should emphasize and specialize in other areas in which they are strong. Indeed, this department of medicine appears to be moving toward this kind of compromise. In short, the program can be shifted to accommodate the movement of different kinds of professionals through the organization.

Second, there are situations in which one group of professionals within an organization has specific views as to the place and functions of other groups, and the groups concerned are not able to make their own claims and definitions prevail. The task of such a group is to work to alter the first group's definition of their place. This is a task which many scientists moving into medical school settings have had to tackle. This kind of not-so-quiet struggle is frequent, also, among groups such as social workers, who do not enjoy uniform success in having their claims to professional status accepted.

"Teams" provide particularly dramatic instances of the consequences of these kinds of divergent views in inter-professional relations. Interaction in teams not only sets conditions affecting role-creation, but also can affect professional identity. The phenomenon of "the team" is replete with struggles over professional claims. There is a considerable hortatory literature on "teams," and many elegant defintions of what they should be. We will only say that a team is brought together to pursue a supposedly shared goal, to which each of the members is presumed to have a potential contribution. This does not mean that they have common understandings of what their tasks should be, or how the goals should be pursued. Upon further probing, they are also likely to discover that they do not even really share the same goals. It has been a frequent observation in hospitals that when these kinds of difficulties have reached an unbearable stage, someone can be counted upon to remind the group that it is the welfare of the patient which is all important. Temporarily, then, they move away from conflicts over what their goals may be. (For material on teams, see: Schatzman and Bucher, 1964; Jungman and Bucher, 1967).

Participation in a team can be highly fateful for professional persons. It is an arena of action in which the work spaces of the different team members usually crisscross. What one person does is likely to affect the work of another, and to do what one wants to do requires that one's professional claims be accepted. The trick is to achieve a situation in which each person's professional identity is acknowledged throughout the team, and mutually acceptable and complemenary activities are arranged. In our observations the only teams that appear at all successful have been together for extended periods of time. Persons who are unsuccessful in achieving recognition generally move away from the areena; they either resign or go off on their own, essentially abdicating team work.

On the other hand, it would seem that the classic team of hospital wards—attending man, resident, intern, head nurse, etc.—is an example of a team in which prearranged and generally understood roles are taken. From the point of view of the attending man, or the rotating resident, this is so; they have to take for granted that the team will carry out its conventional tasks. This may be characteristic of teams of fleeting existence, but momentous tasks. However, the attending man is not on the scene enough to perceive how the team is really working. As indicated before, the resident and interns are working out their relationships to one another, and the head nurse is keeping a close watch upon them, prepared to move in or not, as events prove.

In any case, teams can be the making or breaking of a professional. He may be able to utilize them to forward his professional values, or he may be forced to retreat. But there is another highly important resolution of team conflict: professional values may be altered, and new identities taken on. Whether former identities are strengthened, or new ones adopted, teams can be a major agency for further professional socialization through organizational participation.

The Collectivity of Professionals

The discussion above shows that one major condition of working in organizations is that professionals have to take others into account in ways which are not covered by theories of professions which tend to focus upon professionals *vis à vis* clients or a lay public. Role-creation and negotiation proceed as an interactive process, with outcomes for any one role-creator dependent upon the particular collectivity. Some degree of size of organization and some diversity among professionals may be necessary before the full cluster of characteristics develops. As the observations do not include any small or 'single profession' organizations, we do not know what degree of diversity or how many professionals are necessary, but to the extent that there is some number of different kinds of people calling themselves professionals and who are recognized as such by their colleagues, there are a series of consequences for the form which the organization will take.

First, there is a more or less continually unfolding internal differentiation or *segmentalization* within the organization, which arises out of differences in professional interest and professional identity. A segment usually begins as a small group of professionals allied together because of a mutuality of interests or to achieve some particular purpose. There have been many instances of this in the medical school. There was, for example, a group of three endocrinologists who were closely allied by virtue of their research interests. In the biochemistry department there is one segment consisting of the people involved in two sets of laboratories. They not only meet together on a regularly scheduled basis, but there is more or less continual unscheduled consultation and association between them. Segments are frequently interdisciplinary, as is the case with one in the department of psychiatry which includes two child psychiatrists, two social workers, and a psychologist. This internal differentiation is an ongoing process, and there is considerable fluidity in the segments in that new ones arise and existing ones shift and even disappear, as professionals move into or out of the organization, as research interests shift, or as the particular purpose on which a segment was based is accomplished or abandoned. The resignation of one of its members was a key factor in the dissolution of one of the earlier segments in the medical school.

It is implicit in these remarks, but we want to emphasize the emergent quality of segmentalization. In most cases it is *not* something which is initiated by the administration, but rather the impetus comes from the professionals involved in it. Indeed, the higher administration is frequently unaware of developing segments, at least in the earlier stages. But as a segment develops and gains strength, it may agitate for administrative recognition. The department of psychiatry has two relatively new divisions, one in child psychiatry and one in sociology. These divisions came into being after the department brought in a sociologist and a child psychiatrist, each of whom managed to recruit some associates and achieve administrative recognition. Similarly, an interdisciplinary group may labor to create a center or a newly emerging discipline may request departmental status—biophysics is one of the newer disciplines which appears to be approaching this threshold, as did biochemistry several years ago. There are some cases in which the administration does initiate a new segment. This happened at one of the psychiatric hospitals when the administration decided to establish a research unit and recruited a psychiatrist specifically for that purpose. But our observations indicate that this is an exception—that the establishment of a new administrative unit usually means the bestowal of administrative recognition on an already existing segment. The data cited are primarily from the medical school, and indeed, segmentalization is most obvious in universities, with their proliferation of schools, colleges, divisions, departments, centers and institutes. But it is also present in other professional organizations. It happened in one of the psychiatric hospitals, for example, when a group of professionals were successful in setting up an adolescent unit. It can be easily observed in hospitals and research organizations, where groups of people cluster around particular laboratories or sections.

   With segmentalization along lines of professional interests, there inevitably comes the potentiality of competition and conflict between sectors and subgroupings. Organizational budget and space are obvious areas of competition. In professional schools a place in the curriculum is a vital area of competitition. The journals of medical specialties are replete with essays and personal anecdotes referring to the speciality's earlier battles for recognition in the curriculum and exhorting the membership either to hold its position against all assaults or to widen its place in the curriculum. (Bucher, 1955.) We were fortunate to observe a classic instance of this kind of competition in the medical school under study. A proposal for changing the curriculum of the clinical years was put before the faculty for discussion at a special meeting. The heart of the proposal gave the students more free time at the expense of cutting into the time allotted for almost all the specialties. One by one, the professors of medicine, surgery, neurology, dermatology, and orthopedics came to the podium and delivered an impassioned plea for their own speciality. Each stressed the importance of his speciality in patient care and the unique contribution that exposure to the particular speciality makes in the education of a physician.

Conflict within professional organizations has its roots in the divergence of professional values and interests. There are at least two general types of context in which conflict is most likely to become open and acute. One context is when the "work spaces" of different groups overlap. The other major context is the influencing of organizational policy. The pitfalls of overlapping work space are illustrated most sharply in the problems which "teams" encounter. This happens most frequently in psychiatric hospitals, particularly in those which are also teaching institutions. In such places trainees and staff in nursing, social work, psychology, occupational and activity therapy, and psychiatry all vie for some part of the patient, and they usually have differing notions as to what should be done, with consequent frazzled tempers. Considerable ruffling of poise also occurs in situations where scientists share the same equipment or animal quarters.

Undoubtedly the conflicts of greatest import to the organization, as well as its professionals, occur over the formulation of policy. With a sizeable collectivity of different kinds of professionals, each of these groupings has its own notions as to what directions the organization should be taking, and where it needs changing. They frequently take differing positions on policy matters. There are two organizational contingencies of great importance to how policy conflicts arise and unfold. These contingencies are not peculiar to professional organizations, but complicate the working out of conflict within the special conditions of professional organizations. The first contingency is that what are problems for one group may not be problems for other groups. Second, and related, policy decisions are likely to have differential consequences for different sectors of the organization. (Smith, 1958.)

There are examples of both these contingencies in the medical school data. Indeed, of the nine policy issues which brought about general faculty arousal over a five-year period, only one was seen as a problem throughout the faculty. However, the consequences of policy decisions on that one issue were perceived by the participants as different for different departments. In all nine cases, the consequences of policy differed depending upon the sector of the school.

The reform of medical education was a policy issue which was recognized as a problem by some sectors of the faculty and not others, and it also was—and is—a distinctively diffferent issue for different sectors. The reform of medical education is a general movement sweeping through many of the schools of medicine in the nation. Among the clinical faculty of this medical school, it was generally agreed that something needed to be done about the system by which they were educating future physicians. It was too rigid, too lockstep, contained too many meaningless exercises, and did not provide the conditions under which students could develop special interests in depth. It is high time, many of these faculty members thought, for a new Flexner report. Thus, the clinical faculty perceived an important problem and proceeded to take steps to change the situation. The major focus of their thrust toward change was upon medical education.

At the same time, these concerns of the clinical faculty were largely irrelevant to the basic science faculty (the faculty of the first two years). They also wanted change, but their focus was upon "excellence," "scholarship"—an atmosphere emphasizing research values. They took their obligation to teach medical students seriously, but they assumed that efforts to improve their teaching program were their prerogative. However, it came about that the first efforts to reform the curriculum were aimed at the first two years. We cannot go into the series of events and their consequences here. Suffice it to say that the major consequences were that the basic science faculty increasingly began to perceive themselves as being victimized, "pushed around," with their own values and contributions misunderstood; whereas the clinical faculty saw the basic science faculty as "obstructionistic" and "conservative." The bitterness aroused over this particular issue has colored many of the other issues which have arisen.

Considerable bitterness can also arise when policy issues have differential consequences for different groups in the ongoing organization. Our data suggest that conflict becomes bitter when what is deemed good for one group or number of groups actually is detrimental to other groups— or is *defined* by them as detrimental. In one example of this, the parties concerned *perceived* the consequences of a projected large increase in student enrollment quite differently. Some of the departments took the position that the only way in which they could obtain a significant increase in their resources was through an expansion of enrollment, and the structure of these departments was such that the faculty could envisage the means for handling the increase in number of students without altering their accustomed patterns of doing things. Other departments, however, were pessimistic over whether an increase in resources would really occur; but even so, they could not imagine how the increased enrollment could be handled within their present system. Some of these faculty thought that such an eventuality would be the destruction of their teaching and research programs.

In another case, the consequences are still being worked out, but the perspectives of the antagonists are clear. The issue was whether this school should annex a neighboring hospital. Polar sentiments developed between four of the major departments in the school. Medicine and surgery were in favor of taking over this hospital because they badly needed the beds for their teaching programs. Pathology and psychiatry, on the other hand, wanted no part of it. For both these departments, there was nothing that they stood to gain, and it would involve a tremendous increase in their service burdens, thereby taxing their other programs.

We have said that the differential perception of problems and the differential consequences of policy for the various sectors of the organization take on a special significance in professional organizations. Presumably, in a bureaucratic organization policy decisions are made within top management, and the various sectors re-tooled to accomplish the objectives decreed from above. This is true only to a very limited extent in professional organizations, e.g., in the Manhattan project or this nation's space program. In general, professional organizations consist of a number of professional groupings, each working in ther own directions, implementing their own professional vaues. How, then, is any measure of integration achieved in professional organizations? Such integration as exists tends to be of a loose and fluid kind. Problems of integration generally arise only in the context of the competition and conflict of sectors noted above. Then, under these conditions of diverse values and competing interest, integration occurs *through a continual political process.*

An informant in the medical school once remarked that, "the College is just like Congress." Academic institutions have developed the most elaborate machinery for the playing out of this political process. University statutes define the rights and privileges of the faculty and administration, and provide forums, through a committee structure, senates, and faculty meetings, for a resolution of the contention of viewpoints and interests. This particular school of medicine is part of a university, and thus subject to its statutes. (Typically, however, the statutes are invoked when some parties to a dispute see an advantage to invoking them.) The political arenas provided in this institution include intra- and inter-departmental committees. The recommendations of the inter-departmental committees go to an executive committee, composed of each of the department heads plus a number of members elected from the faculty, whose deliberations are subject to faculty approval.

Our data suggest that there is a tendency for non-academic professional organizations to develop some of these legislative forms. For example, in hospitals there are meetings of the medical staff (and staffs of services) which follow parliamentary procedures. Then the establishment of committees seems to be a virtually ubiquitous phenomenon in professional organizations of any size. In some clinical settings there are powerful figures reminiscent of the traditional "Chief." But even these figures utilize and are subject to the forums of a collegium. The two strongest "chiefs" whom we have followed each had an international reputation. One of them described to us at length how he utilized the younger men for ideas, and had just appointed a committee to work out some basic innovations in operating room technology and procedures. The other has within the past two years suffered at least two stunning defeats delivered through the legislative forum of his medical staff.

Whether there is a visible legislative apparatus or not, the political process in professional organizations involves a *party* phenomenon. Persons sound out colleagues in a search for allies. This is both an intra and inter-departmental (or whatever the sectors are named) phenomenon. One of our major informants in the medical school who was a department head has told us, on a series of occasions, how he has been approached by the head of medicine, the head of surgery, the head of preventive medicine, etc. In each instance, they were sounding him out as to his views on issues, and whether they might make common cause. This informant frequently alluded to the norm of *pro quid quo* in describing these encounters—if he could help out the head of medicine in something of importance to that department, he would expect similar assistance when he needed it. These types of encounters occur at every level of seniority in the professional organizations we have studied, not just at the higher levels. As faculty members, we have engaged in numerous "deals" with trusted colleagues from other sectors of the university in faculty elections, and it is clear that others are doing this also. In every troubled "team" situation in our sample, cliques of team members have banded together to try to work out some position with respect to their dealings with others on the team.

This seeking of allies leads to the growth of parties, or factions. Factions may be the better term, in that these alliances have a relatively fluid existence, as compared to the parties of national politics. Such factions represent groups of people who, perhaps only temporarily, share perspectives, who see common problems and common consequences of events. Alliances following lines of pervasive and deep professional differences appear to be the most stable factions. Thus, the cleavage between the basic science faculty and the clinical faculty of the medical school runs deep and influences faculty response to most issues. Similarly, a distinction exists between M.D.'s and non-M.D.'s in three of the psychiatric hospitals in which we have observed. When issues arose which touched upon this sensitive spot, all Ph.D.'s locked forces. On the other hand, we have seen members of one of these basic factions join forces with the other side in response to specific issues; and we have seen the dissolution of alliances.

For example, a department head who had strongly pushed certain educational reforms gradually shifted his position, and began siding with the opposition forces. Hence new alliances may be formed, and factions may shift, in response to different issues and changing conditions. (Descriptions of this kind of 'politiking' may be found in Dalton, 1959; Strauss et al.,1964; Schatzman and Bucher, 1964. But perhaps the best description can be found in literature, in Snow, 1959.)

Factions can engage in all of the political tactics of national parties, but the rhetoric is more gentle. One does not, outside of small groups of close allies, cast aspersions upon the motives or competence of the opposition. While our model places competition and conflict at the core of the functioning of a professional collectivity, we do not mean to imply that it is cutthroat. It generally proceeds in a gentlemanly fashion, with a genuine reluctance to do damage to other factions. (Goldner, 1967, describes something similar in an industrial organization—that sectors do not try to eradicate other sectors unless threatened by them.) Within the legislative apparatus of the medical school, an attempt is made to avoid bringing to the vote an issue over which there is great and bitter opposition. On the few occasions when such an issue has come to a vote, considerable fence-mending has ensued. Thus, the tactics most favored in the professional organization involve face-to-face negotiations among key political figures, some caucusing, and working out of more or less acceptable compromises. Heavy handed tactics, such as packing meetings and log-rolling, are avoided as much as possible, and tend to occur only when there is an issue of great consequence. After the smoke of battle has cleared, and the bitterness has abated, fence-mending and compromising come into play again.

The goal of this political activity is to bring to bear sufficient power to influence policy. Through concerted political activity, the various allies and factions seek to influence events so as to protect their vital interests and implement their professional values.

The question of which persons and groups influence the setting of goals and practices in professional organizations points to a complex and probably fluid phenomenon. Power to determine policy is not clearly located in specific positions. It is more diffuse, and the locus and balance of power often shifts in response to different issues and as different persons and groups move through the organization.

We have not explicitly discussed the nature of power and authority in professional organizations. Authority, at least in the sense in which this concept has been used in most organizational theory, is relatively rare in such organizations. Briefly, authority is generally defined as a relationship in which the subordinate voluntarily surrenders his own judgment and ability to make decisions and bases his actions on the commands of his superior. (For a discussion of some concepts of authority see Blau and Scott, 1962, pp. 27–40; Simon, 1961, pp. 123–153; Barnard, 1953, pp. 161–199.) This type of relationship is something rarely seen among professionals in professional organizations. Moreover, the idea of a hierarchical structure in which authority is vested in the position or office, and in which the positions on each level have authority over those on lower levels and are subordinate to those on higher levels is clearly irrelevant here. Power, on the other hand, is extremely important, since the extent to which individuals and groups can control their working conditions is a function of the power which they can bring to bear. Power is broadly defined here, to include different types of influence, as it is not yet completely clear what constitutes power or its varieties in professional organizations.

Power is not identical with professional label, although some types of professionals seem to have more of it than others and contending for power is a prominent activity in situations involving multiple professions. Academicians firmly believe that their value in the market place is the basis of their power, but the instances when this conception has boomeranged on people are part of the common lore also. (Caplow and McGee, 1958). Reputation among colleagues probably is an extremely important component of power, but more research is needed to discover how it operates and what it can do. Key positions within a professional organization, while they do not automatically bestow authority or power, do offer greater opportunity to amass power. Certainly, control over resources is one source of power, and this is built into some positions. (Bierstedt, 1950) Department heads, for example, usually have control over some funds; in some organizations, it is also the department head who makes or withholds recommendations for promotions. The size of a group of professionals undoubtedly also has an effect on its degree of power, in that the larger groups have greater potential power than the smallest, but we are not sure how important this is. The two largest departments in the medical school have, on occasion, 'packed' faculty meetings when crucial issues were coming to a vote, but this is a tactic used only *in extremis*. In any case, the origin and operation of power in professional organizations remain central questions for further research.

Summary and Discussion

The major characteristics which appear to cluster in organizations dominated by professionals may be summarized as follows:

1. *Role-creation and negotiation:* The professional typically builds his own role in the organization rather than fitting into preset roles, and role-creation proceeds through negotiation with relevant figures in the organization.

2. *Spontaneous internal differentiation:* There is a tendency for internal differentiation to occur in relation to the particular professionals who are moving through the organization. Typically, such differentiation is not legislated from the top, but occurs as the consequence of the building of work interests among congeries of professional workers.

3. *Competition and conflict for resources:* The different types of professionals in an organization each have their own requirements for carrying out their mission. They also are likely to have differing ideas about where the organization is going and what are its problems. This sort of differentiation sets up the conditions for more or less open competition and conflict among distinctive groups within the organization.

4. *Integration through a political process:* The various professionals engage in a number of activities which are more appropriately described using the language of politics than the language of social structure. A major aim of the participants in this political process is to influence the setting of goals and policies of the organization.

5. *The locus of power shifts:* Power is not identical with office in the organization. Rather, power seems to be a fluid phenomenon, shifting as various professionals move through the organization, and in response to different issues.

There are some marked contrasts between the preceding picture of professionals in organizations and most of the growing body of literature on this problem. The major differences arise because we do not begin with the assumption that the organizations in which professionals work are bureaucratic in nature. The theoretical equipment which many researchers bring to this area predisposes them to the idea that there is something contradictory in the idea of a professional working in a formal organization. (Goss, 1963; Marcson, 1960; Kornhauser, 1962; Blau and Scott, 1962; also see the *Administrative Science Quarterly* 10, 1965, for a special issue on professionals in organizations.) By formal organization, they understand an organization modeled along bureaucratic lines. Such an organization would be characterized by a hierarchical chain of command, clearly defined duties and obligations associated with each office, with goals and procedures determined at the top and conveyed down the chain of command—a type of system which would discourage autonomy and innovation among the ranks. (Thompson, 1965.) A professional, on the other hand, is presumably a person who derives his aims and methods from a professional body, works independently, and who commands the privilege to autonomously determine what should be done and how it should be done. Thus, should a professional find himself operating within the confines of a formal organization, inevitable tensions and conflicts can be expected between the requirements of the bureaucratic system, and the values of the professional.

This type of thinking juxtaposes two entirely separate bodies of theory, and finds them incompatible. The organizational theory is dominated by a Weberian notion of bureaucracy, in which the professional is seen as a bureaucratic functionary. The theory of professions utilized emphasizes the independent professional, guided in his relationship to a client by a professional subculture and normative system. The *organization* of professional work and the institutional framework of professional work are overlooked. Neither the bureaucratic nor the professional theories provide adequate guides to the analysis of the types of organizations in which we have observed professionals at work.

The posing of questions in terms which pit the professional against the organization obscures many important features of the institutions in which professionals work. It is both more realistic and more heuristic to view the professional as one who has a very great stake in the organization, in terms of its influence on his career and his professional identity and values. Our conception of professional organizations reflects this view of the professional in that it views them as establishments on which people *identified* as professional exert a considerable measure of control and influence. Such an organization may be identified by (1) the extent to which professionals control the policies and operations of their own sector of an institution; and (2) the extent to which professionals influence goal setting and policy making for the whole institution. Such a definition includes three critical elements: (1) identifying specific groups as professional, and paralleling this, (2) the extent of professional control, and finally, (3) the notion of professional sectors of larger organizations. (For other definitions of professional organizations see Scott, 1965; Litwak, 1961; and Etzioni, 1961; 51–52.)

We have discussed in some detail our conception of professional status as an honorific one arising out of interaction between specific audiences, but our analysis does not allow us to specify the conditions under which a group succeeds or fails in the achievement of professional status. This is primarily because the focus has been on those who have already achieved some measure of professional status, and has not systematically taken into account the participation of those who are still engaged in a struggle for professional status. A comparative analysis focusing more on those latter groups, pulling out the differences between those who succeed in this struggle and those who fail, would lead to a delineation of the conditions under which professional status is accorded and would result in a fuller and more complex picture of professional organizations.

As indicated above, different occupational groupings achieve more or less professional status, and with their measure of success, they achieve more or less control and influence in an organization. We have seen more than one situation in which social workers control the operations of their own sector, but have practically no influence over other professional sectors or policy making in the organization as a whole. We have also observed a hospital in which the research sections were almost totally separate from clinical functions and thoroughly autonomous in their operations. Usually, the scientists did not participate in policy making for the institution as a whole, but they exerted considerable influence when issues arose which vitally affected them.

These observations indicated that the extent and degree of professional control in a larger organization can be highly variable. (Hall's data also support the idea that professional control is highly variable; 1968.) They also suggest that it is extremely difficult to draw sharp boundaries around the notion of a "professional organization" and that to do so may obscure important and distinctive processes occurring in organizations manned by professionals. The basic argument of this paper, however, is that to the extent that professionals exert control in an organization, the organization will show the characteristics which we have described.

Finally, it may be that the separation of professional sectors from other sectors of an organization is characteristic of professional organizations. We do not think that there is any *necessary* conflict or great distinction in value orientations and goals between professional and non-professional sectors. (See also Tagiuri, 1965.) Nor are other sectors necessarily bureaucratic, in a strict definition of the term. We may take this position because the organizations observed are what might be considered traditional and prototypical bailiwicks for professionals—organizations which Scott would term "autonomous." (1965) Professionals frequently were the initiators of such organizations, rather than being brought in at a later stage.

The emphasis in this paper has been on the extent to which the professional molds the organization and the ways the organization is re-shaped and modified in response to the varying groups of professionals moving through it. But it is clear that the influence operates in both directions. That is, the organization, in the form of a collectivity of colleagues, molds the professional, too. It has already been pointed out that professional identities and values may be altered as a result of participation in a team. The extent of the organization's influence on the professional is probably contingent upon several factors, including the stages of the professional's career that are spent in the institution, the types and groupings of other professionals included in the institution, the locus and distribution of power, and the flow of opportunities, as resources change and other professionals move through the organization.

Although this analysis is based on a limited range of organizations, the approach may prove fruitful in other types of organizations and help overcome some of the difficulties encountered in organizational analyses. Thinking in terms of political process is of great value in understanding the many areas of professional behavior which do not fit into the rational bureaucratic model. (Also, see Zald, 1965.) It may also prove a useful tool in studying business and industrial organizations, particularly as the management of these organizations becomes increasingly professionalized. Another area in which some of the concepts used above may prove useful is that of "informal organization." One of the factors involved in the original distinction between "formal" and "informal" organization was the failure of the rational bureaucratic model to fit the organizations being studied. Today this seems to us to be an analytical distinction which more often impedes than facilitates our understanding of organizations. Much of the material which has been subsumed under the rubric "informal organization" may well yield to the concepts used in this analysis. Indeed, it seems likely that if one substituted the word 'expert' for 'professional', most of the analysis would be relevant to other kinds of organizations.

Footnotes

[1] We consider it fruitless to enage in debates over absolute criteria for according professional status. In our conception of the symbolic character of this status, we agree with Becker (1962). We depart from him, however, on the point that once a group achieves this honorific status in any particular situation, the attributes associated with being professional become its due. The status is highly fateful, both for individual and group. The state mental hospitals we have studied provide a plethora of data on the inadequacy of professional label as a predictor

of professional status and influence. In large state hospitals, physicians tend to be immigrants, held in bondage by their inability to pass American certifying examinations, while those who really influence policy are likely to be psychologists and social workers.

2 Anselm Strauss (1955), in an unpublished manuscript, describes a similar period of 'sizing each other up' on the part of interns, residents, attending staff, and nurses, with subsequent working out of a division of labor. Our own recent observations of medical services so far confirm Strauss' findings.

REFERENCES

BARNARD, CHESTER I.
1953   The Functions of the Executive. Cambridge; Harvard University Press.

BECKER, HOWARD
1962   "The nature of a profession." Pp. 27–46 in Education for the Professions. Chicago: Sixty-first Yearbook of the National Society for the study of Education.

BENNIS, WARREN G.
1966   Changing Organizations. New York: Mc-Graw-Hill.

BIERSTEDT, ROBERT
1950   "An analysis of social power." American Sociological Review 15:730–738.

BLAU, PETER M., AND W. RICHARD SCOTT.
1962   Formal Organizations. San Francisco: Chandler.

BUCHER, RUE
1955   Unpublished and untitled series of "Notes" on the medical Specialties.
1962   "Pathology: a study of social movements within a profession." Social Problems 10:40–51.

——AND ANSELM STRAUSS
1961   "Profession in process." American Journal of Sociology 66:325–334.

CAPLOW, THEODORE, AND REECE J. MCGEE
1958   The Academic Marketplace. New York: Basic Books.

DALTON, MELVILLE
1959   Men Who Manage. New York: Wiley.

ETZIONI, AMITAI
1961   A Comparative Analysis of Complex Organizations. New York: The Free Press of Glencoe.

GLASER, BARNEY
1964   Organizational Scientists: Their Professional Careers. Indianapolis: Bobbs-Merrill.

GOLDNER, FRED H.
1967   "Role emergence and the ethics of ambiguity." Pp. 245–266 in Gideon Sjoberg (ed.), Ethics, Politics, and Social Research. Cambridge: Schenkman.

——— AND R. R. RITTI
1967   "Managers and professionals in complex organizations." Paper Presented at the 62nd Annual Meeting of the American Sociological Association in San Francisco, 1967.

GOSS, MARY E. W.
1963   "Patterns of bureaucracy among hospital staff and physicians." Pp. 170–194 in Eliot Freidson (ed.), The Hospital in Modern Society. New York: The Free Press of Glencoe.

HALL, RICHARD H.
1968   "Professionalization and bureaucratization." American Sociological Review 33:92–104.

HUGHES, EVERETT C.
1958   Men and Their Work. Glencoe: The Free Press. Pp. 78–87.

JUNGMAN, LYNNE, AND RUE BUCHER
1967   "Ward structure, therapeutic ideology, and patterns of patient interaction." Archives of General Psychiatry 17:407–415.

KORNHAUSER, WILLIAM
1962   Scientists in Industry. Berkeley: University of California.

LITWAK, EUGENE
1961   "Models of bureaucracy which permit conflict." American Journal of Sociology 67:177–184.

MARCSON, SIMON
1960   The Scientist in American Industry. New York: Harper.

RUSHING, WILLIAM A.
1964   The Psychiatric Professions. Chapel Hill: University of North Carolina.

SCHATZMAN, LEONARD, AND RUE BUCHER
1964   "Negotiating a division of labor among professionals in the state mental hospital." Psychiatry 27:266-277.

SCOTT, W. RICHARD
1964   "Reactions to supervision in a heteronomous professional organization." Administrative Science Quarterly 10:65–81.

SIMON, HERBERT A.
1961   Administrative Behavior, Second Ed., New York: The Macmillan Company.

SMITH, HARVEY
1958   "Contingencies of professional differentiation." American Journal of Sociology 63:410–414.

SNOW, C. P.
1959   The Masters. Garden City: Doubleday Anchor Books, Doubleday.

STRAUSS, ANSELM
circa
1955   "The House Staff's World of Responsibility, Rules, and Decisions", unpublished manuscript.

—— ET AL.
1963   "The hospital and its negotiated order." Pp. 147–169, in Eliot Freidson (ed.), The Hospital in Modern Society. New York: The Free Press of Glencoe.
1964   Psychiatric Ideologies and Institutions. New York: The Free Press of Glencoe.

TAGIURI, RENATO
1965   "Value orientations and the relationship of managers and

scientists." Administrative Science Quarterly 10:39–51.

THOMPSON, VICTOR A.
1965   "Bureaucracy and innovation." Administrative Science Quarterly 10:1–20.

ZALD, MAYER N.
1965   "Who shall rule? A political analysis of succession in a large welfare organization." Pacific Sociological Review 8:52–60.

CHAPTER TWO:
MEMBERS

INTRODUCTION:
MEMBERSHIP AND CAREERS

My personal interest in the subject matter of this book is partially the result of work and research experience in several "new" organizations. Two of these were in higher education and the other was in the health services field. Along with shifting influences from the larger political and economic systems, the personal characteristics of the new members appeared to shape the course of those newly emerging and developing organizations. Success or failure in goal-attainment, the priorities that were set, the very goals that were recognized were the result of decisions which members made. Although there were some rather definite political and economic influences from outside of the organizations, members' decisions were made from anong a set of alternatives.

A proper understanding of an organizational setting must begin with a careful scrutiny of the characteristics of its members. Members are neither universal nor interchangeable. They are not passive, indifferent, or mute. Aside from the few common human and cultural similarities, members bring with them a diverse set of unique and personal differences. These differences lead to the deviations that always seem to appear no matter how comprehensive or how rational the initial organizing scheme might be. Members have their own purposes, motives, and preferences, and their own personal histories, which motivate action intended to bring a situation around to favor their interests.

Let us put the matter a bit differently. If we wished to create an organization, why not being by finding and hiring some good members? Hypothetically, as soon as the members began to interact, the process of organizing would be underway, leading to the definition and construction of the orderly acts, activities, meanings, relationships, and patterns of participation that comprise ordinary organizational settings. If the members were to already share a common professional orientation the process would be greatly aided and the result would follow more predictably.

The position we take is by no means new, although many social scientists have opted to focus mainly on how the organization affects members. Organizational effects are a very real and important phenomenon; it may be argued, however, that since the organization is dependent on members' ability to act, it is more valid to conceptualize the matter in such a way that members receive their due attention. Rather than to think in terms of organizational effects and member effects, we prefer thinking in terms of interactions between members. The organization, consisting of goals, programs, roles, offices, and the like, comprises a symbolic setting for these interactions. The resulting activity is partly conditioned by the unique and personal interests of the interacting members, and partly conditioned by their perceptions of symbolic order. We can gain a glimpse of the members' part by considering the literature bearing on work motivation, and job satisfaction. The other side of the question, how institutions and organizations limit the member, will also be considered.

Victor Vroom (1964) has examined the question of why men work. He posits that men are motivated to work by five factors:

1. Men work to gain wages and other extrinsic benefits including insurance and pensions.

2. Men work as a means of expending energy, both physical and mental.

3. Men work to achieve intrinsic satisfaction from altering and manipulating the environment.

4. Men work to achieve intrinsic satisfactions from social interaction, including the development and exercise of power.

5. Men work to achieve higher social status.

The reader may note that Vroom's first two factors refer to man's physiological and biological nature; without food, shelter, health care, and physical activity man's survival is problematic. But the remaining factors are expressions of culture. We *learn* to derive satisfaction from such things as changing our environment, controlling others, and being "looked up to." These factors, then, are not universal, but depend on a person's individual course of social learning.

Abraham Maslow (1954) also offers a set of five motivational factors. There is a certain similarity between the two sets, but Maslow's set is based on a hierarchical principle: Maslow posits that man's lower order needs for food, shelter, safety, and security operate as motivators, but only when they are unfulfilled. Once these needs are met they no longer act as motivators to work. At that point higher order needs come to bear, in the following order:

1. Men need love, companionship, and affection.

2. Men need self-esteem and the respect of others.

3. Men need to express and develop their self to its fullest potential.

Maslow's position has been criticized from two angles. Some have argued that the order of his hierarchy is not universal—that some men need self-esteem, for example, whether or not their need for love is fulfilled. Others have charged that his higher-order needs are descriptive of academicians, and professionals generally, but not of all workers. The latter charge, however, does not diminish the value of Maslow's position if one's concern is with professionals.

Frederick Herzberg offers a third approach to work motivation—a dual-factor theory of job satisfaction and job dissatisfaction (Herzberg, 1966; Herzberg et al., 1959). According to Herzberg, men derive satisfaction from factors associated with the work itself. The work-related or intrinsic factors include achievement, recognition, responsibility, advancement, and the pleasure of doing the work itself. Dissatisfaction, on the other hand, stems from the worker's relationship to the work setting. Policies and procedures that produce inefficiency or reduce effectiveness, or poor management and supervisory practices can produce dissatisfaction. When dissatisfactions are absent, it does not automatically follow that workers will be satisfied. The two factors can operate independently. Let us attempt, now, to apply these perspectives to our earlier position—that organizations are the product of motivated members' activities.

Most researchers who have conducted comparative studies of job satisfaction report a high level of satisfaction among professionals (Inkeles, 1960). Being relatively free from problems of economic and physical security, professional workers are more concerned about conditions of the work itself. Professionals lay claim to rights of autonomy which decreases the sources of dissatisfaction. They find their work interesting and they have a high degree of social interaction with clients and other colleagues. Establishing a professional reputation and developing political relationships with colleagues may be prime sources of motivation for professionals. These concerns contribute naturally to the professional's interest in his organizational situation, resulting in a higher commitment to the organization's goals and programs and reducing the conflict of interests that might otherwise generate dysfunctional antagonisms (Etzioni, 1964). The organization is a necessary means by which motivated professional workers may promote their own interests. Each professional tries, accordingly, to join the particular organization that will enhance his personal career to the greatest degree, just as the organizational body tries to recruit new members who will add to the collective worth of the organization as a setting for work and a base for further personal advancement.

Matching members and organizations is a complex problem. However, orderly institutional arrangements aid greatly in reducing the part played by chance. The case of university-based scientists is reported in a study by Diana Crane; she asks, "Are scientific productivity and recognition entirely the result of achievement, or does the scientists' environment significantly influence his performance and the extent to which he receives credit for it?" (Crane, 1965:699). Crane reports that the older, established universities have the greatest share of outstanding scientists on their faculties. Consequently, they attract the best students and recruit the best graduates of other outstanding universities. Membership in these universities enables a scientist to receive greater stimulation to productivity, provides better research support, enables greater continuity of research and places a "halo" over the scientist's work which enhances its acceptability and increases his chances of professional recognition.

Crane concludes (712–713) that productivity is most strongly associated with the school where the scientist was trained, but recognition is most strongly associated with the school where he works. Given the pattern of recruiting major university faculty from other major university graduates, the two outcomes are closely related.

We can interpret these findings as supportive of the hypothesis that the character of an organization is given in the characteristics of its members, but organizational factors can either impede or enhance a member's chances to construct an outstanding professional career.

How members carry out campaigns to make personal liveable worlds within organizational settings is considered in the following chapters, which deal with negotiation and power. The present chapter focuses mainly on how nonmembers *become* members, and how membership is manifested in longer-term forms, including organizational careers. Membership and careers are concerns that occupy much of the attention of professionals in organizations, and they are used here as the central core of our analytic scheme. What is membership all about? The person who aspires to membership must know where to go for his training and preparation for memberships in both the profession and the organization of his choice. Becoming a member is a complex process involving many kinds of learning and also involving the intricate coordination of many different organizations—the profession, the university, the various levels of government—and many individuals in addition to the aspirant-member. Once professional and organizational membership is achieved in the formal sense, the process of membership is only just begun. Unlike a college degree, which is only conferred once and is good for life, membership must be worked at continually. In the process of its construction, careers are formed, altered, modified, and ended.

The primary focus on membership and careers reveals the essential political character of professional organizations and the extent to which personal interests function as the source of incentive toward action. Given the conflict base upon which organizations of professionals are built, two other aspects of organizations become especially problematic; how can any member get other members to contribute toward the advancement of his personal career, given that his personal interests are in competition and conflict with theirs? And secondly, what arrangements can be made to ensure that each member will have the optimum chance to advance his own career while at the same time the minimum chance of being adversely affected by his colleagues' ambitions or failures? Thus, while Chapter Two of this book will examine membership and careers, later parts will treat the questions of how order is negotiated and maintained among equals in a state of conflict, and how power is related to the control of equals.

REFERENCES

CRANE, DIANA
    1965   "Scientists at major and minor universities: A study of pro-
            ductivity and recognition," *American Sociological Review*
            30:699–714.

ETZIONI, AMITAI
    1964   *Modern Organizations,* Englewood Cliffs, New Jersey:
            Prentice-Hall.

HERZBERG, FREDERICK
    1966   *Work and the Nature of Man.* Cleveland, Ohio: World Pub-
            lishing Company.

HERZBERG, FREDERICK, B. MANSEN, AND B. SNYDERMAN
    1959   *The Motivation to Work.* 2nd Edition. New York: John Wiley
            & Sons.

INKELES, ALEX
    1960   "Industrial man: The relation of status to experience, per-
            ception and value," *American Journal of Sociology* 66
            (July): 1–31.

MASLOW, ABRAHAM H.
    1954   *Motivation and Personality.* New York: Harper and Row.

VROOM, VICTOR
    1964   *Work and Motivation.* New York: John Wiley & Sons.

OVERVIEW

Membership and the conditions that affect it begin far from the organizational scene and long before the collegial aspirant arrives to take up his role. Just how far and how much prior is not always clear. But for the usual case it is helpful to begin by studying the university-based professional schools. It is there that the first stage of *socialization* begins.

Chapter Two will consider the process of *professional socialization,* which begins on campus and extends into the rituals of recruitement and subsequently through "learning the ropes" on the job. Finally, a long-term view of *organizational careers* will conclude the chapter.

In the first paper Olesen and Whittaker comment on the authoritarian role-structure of university-based schools of nursing. How, they ask, does authoritarianism fit with the formal goal of preparing students to make independent professional decisions? In their view, the conflict underlying the student–faculty relationship enables students to establish a strong measure of independence from their mentors, early on. But at the same time, a special kind of dependence is generated—dependence on the judgment of one's peers.

Olesen and Whittaker argue that professional socialization is best understood as a give-and-take between faculty and students. In summary, the faculty, patients, peers, family, and even old friends contribute to a cumulative change process in which the student learns the information, the skills, the self-concept, and the generalized attitudes of the professional. The student himself is of great importance in the process, for he remains conscious of every performance and its reception by others, and he continually tries to improve his effectiveness in his own eyes as well as the eyes of his significant audiences.

The Caplow and McGee essay treats the elaborate rituals involved when professionals seek out new colleagues. Their case-in-point is academia.[1] Recruiting calls for the expenditure of large blocks of time by faculty members in the pursuit of the "right man." The time is given because of the importance of selecting a member who will fit in and who will contribute to the collective prestige of each member. What the faculty wants to know is actually impossible to know. One cannot guarantee, by any amount of discussion and consideration, that a person will be a congenial and productive colleague. Yet the discussion and consideration is functionally desirable, for it permits the negotiation of consensus . . . the generalized agreement that the "right man" has been found.

During all of this, the candidate does not remain passive. As a professional student nears graduation, he typically begins to plan carefully and talk with his peers and mentors in anticipation of the recruitment experience. His first exposure to his potential future colleagues is usually during a visit to their campus for two or three days of formal and informal interviews. He knows that every encounter is a significant encounter in which he "gives off" information that might be used against him in following faculty meetings. The trick, he is told, is to "psych out" the department and to know as much as possible about the faculty before the visit, so exactly the right face can be worn. An offhand comment in an unguarded moment is sure to be reported in later meetings; on such errors, recruitment decisions can rest, or fall.

Job interviews are subject to careful staging and skillful role playing on both sides. But the length and complexity of academic recruiting makes the experience substantially different from lesser interview situations. Many consider this experience to be the most important part of one's professional socialization . . . the dramatic status passage from student to professional. The student learns to view himself as a peer among professionals and he is treated in that role by his potential colleagues. He is *there,* and the feeling is good.

Having been accepted, the young professional becomes a member of his new organizational group. He may be surprised to find that the new status he enjoys was not guaranteed to last by his mere appointment.

Socialization is continuous and does not end at graduation. Organizational socialization replaces professional socialization as the main focus after graduation and recruitement. The next paper in this chapter views organizational socialization from the unusual approach of sociolinguistics. If you think about the problem of becoming a member of any organization, you may imagine yourself in dialog with other members, in the ongoing activity of some everyday organizational event. Years ago a popular magazine carried a regular feature article in which two workmen were doing something. In the caption, they spoke in vocational jargon and the reader was challenged to guess what work they did. The results were often humorous, but the unspoken lesson was clear. If you can't call things by their "right" name, you don't belong to the work group—you are an outsider.

Manning begins his paper with a review of the Weberian tradition in which rationality is *given* as an attribute of organizational *structure* and actors are cast in appropriate roles, which *determine* their conduct. This view he rejects as both unrealistic and intellectually misguided. Rationality is problematic; rules, for example offer a resource for action, which may be used or ignored. Rules are often invoked after the fact to *explain* conduct, but conduct is itself decided upon grounds that are principally situational. Within the context of a particular situation, an actor puts together a course of action that appears promising in terms of his purposes and the available opportunities.

The contextual basis for action is mainly the existent sets of names for significant objects. By using the names properly, an actor creates the potential for joint action with others. Manning offers: "Becoming a socially sanctioned member of an organization, by implication, involves displaying, adhering to, and being sanctioned for use of an ordering scheme or subschemes." In any organization such a lexicon of terms, names, and role-terms exists as part of the knowledge taken for granted by its members. Newcomers are introduced to the lexicon through reflexive dialog with "regulars." When competence in the lexicon is achieved, the constraints of the novice role fall away and membership status is achieved.

The chapter moves to a close in the final essay on organizational careers. Careers in organizations are described as being highly problematic, just as much so as any other phase of becoming a professional. Having come this far, though, our typical young professional will probably discover that he is becoming increasingly committed to the very lines of activity that will bring the dual ends of professional competence and organizational tenure. The successful enactment of a professional career in the setting of an organization depends on the member's ability to get and keep the ongoing approval and support of his colleagues. This can only be done through the presentation of an acceptable professional self in the course of everyday work.

Footnotes

[1] In earlier times, when a few universities trained nearly all of the doctoral students, placement by personal referral was a sufficient system for all but those unfortunate students who were unable to establish themselves with a powerful sponsor. But the radical expansion of the number of degree-granting universities and the body of students and professors has left the marketplace in comparative disorder.

Some of the traditionalism and elitism of earlier days was lost as a result of the infusion of university faculties by professors who lack conventional academic orientations. These are a young and aggressive lot, given to an achievement ethic, that the worth of a person is determined by his productivity. Once the academician's "real work," research publication, no longer flows, senility is assumed.

According to Caplow and McGee, academic recruitement is becoming more open; that is, more competitive and less bound by personal and social ties. A recent inspection of several hundred vitae, professional resumes submitted by students nearing their doctoral degrees, revealed how far the achievement ethic has penetrated. Graduate students now read research papers at professional meetings and publish articles in professional journals. One's professional worth must be proven *before* professional membership can follow. In other fields, such as medicine and law, the pressure appears in the form of increased student demands for opportunities to ''practice'' their skills, as in neighborhood clinics and poverty law offices, law permitting.

The university's growing dependence on federal funding agencies has contributed an unexpected windfall of openness. The demand for *affirmative action* toward the deliberate and systematic recruitement of women and minority candidates is backed by the power to withhold research and program funds. Waspishness and maleness, especially during the early stages of screening and selecting candidates, are a distinct disadvantage. The full extent of affirmative action policies cannot be presently assessed, except in the degree of ambivalence it has added to the recruitement process.

In the main, however, the dynamics of academic recruitment have changed only slightly.

FIVE CHARACTERISTICS OF PROFESSIONAL SOCIALIZATION
Virginia L. Olesen and Elvi W. Whittaker

Students in professional socialization are subordinate to their teachers in the role arrangements of the professional school. The faculty roles, after all, are those in which the institution and profession invest the authority and responsibility to pace, order, and sanction the progress of the aspirants to the profession.

It is, however, possible to grant this aspect of the organizational arrangments and at the same time to recognize that the young people who take the student role, unlike the submissive zombies of our caricature, do in fact shape the role and take an active part in their own education. As recent studies of medical students indicate, students do assess faculty demands, elect certain strategies, and behave in ways that they believe will deliver what the faculty wants.[1] Such ways of getting through the professional school represent not only alternatives for individual choices, but well-organized strategies and perspectives, a part of the norms and perspectives sometimes hidden from faculty view: "There was always *something* the students could block off privately. If they were being taught Marx and 'Fats' Domino, perhaps they were pursuing Racine and Mozart on the sly. In any case, they had some underground culture the faculty would do best not to know about. . . ."[2]

We think the image of the student who participates in shaping his

Source: "Characteristics of Professional Socialization" by Virginia L. Olesen and Elvi W. Whittaker. From *The Silent Dialogue,* © 1968 by Jossey-Bass Inc., San Francisco, California 94111

education is more useful for research in professional socialization than the one earlier sketched in our caricature, partly because the idea of student as participant comes closer to students' own report.

Young students in any professional school participate in their own education by making choices to meet faculty demands, to handle non-institutional pressures, and to work out situations of their own creating. Students may choose foolishly or wisely, depending on the perspective they or the faculty take. They may later regret or be satisfied with their choices, but they are constantly choosing among the degrees and ranges of alternatives open to them and those which they open for themselves in the institutional setting.[3] The students do more than simply talk back: they are, in fact, actively involved in the shaping of existential situations in which acquisition of professional and adult role behaviors occur.

To describe student professionals thus is to speak only of one sector of the socialization process during the student years. The student encounters others who have many roles both within and outside of the formal institutional structure. Medical students, for example, may learn from their patients a great deal that the instructors do not wish them to assimilate; furthermore, such knowledge may be more easily learned from the faculty.[4] Thus there is in every profession a kind of bootlegging, in which the student, unwittingly or not, acquires from non-official vendors the ideas, values, and ways of behaving and thinking that are attributed, sometimes legitimately and sometimes not, to the profession.[5]

These multiple agents of socialization function in yet a different way for the student professional. They view, and act toward, the student as a professional in ways that need not necessarily concur with what the student thinks of himself, or what the faculty wants him to think of himself, as amusingly suggested in the following newspaper account of college undergraduates:

> The student goes home for Christmas vacation only to find that his previously perfectly okay parents have suddenly become stupid, overbearing, narrow-minded, selfish, childish and generally unwilling to acknowledge the student's individuality and independence and the need for a complete, immediate and radical revolution in the United States.[6]

Thus in several ways professional socialization is multidimensional: the student, in his role as student and as beginning professional, finds many sources of information about the profession other than faculty sources, with which they are sometimes congruent, sometimes discrepant. The occupants of these other roles—clients, family, and friends—view and act toward the student as a new professional in ways that may or may not harmonize with his view of himself. The growth of the student's ability to place in perspective the views of those in other roles, both in their functions as sources of information and as ratifiers of a professional self, is an important aspect of student separation from the world of laymen.

Needless to say, the influences of persons who occupy roles in the student's role set do not commence merely with the entry to formal schooling, nor do they cease with graduation. Indeed, a most interesting question in the study of professional socialization is the issue of learning that takes place at the hands of these multiple others before and after formal schooling. For example, studies on lawyers and school-teachers affirm that significant role learning does take place after graduation.[7] In this book, however, the institutional years are of primary concern.

Yet another facet of professional socialization merits note, that having to do with the students' roles which are undergoing socialization. Most usually in the United States professional education occurs when the student makes the transition from adolescence to adulthood, as well as from layman to professional.[8] These years of becoming a professional are both "developmental socialization"—acquiring an adult role and self—and "resocialization" from layman to professional.[9]

Both types of socialization occur simultaneously but not necessarily smoothly or harmoniously for the young student. The lateral life roles may blend quite uncomfortably with the roles in professional education, the trade-off between the two types of roles sometimes having a discernible effect. Although educators recognize this reciprocal influence, they do not always agree that lateral role socialization and learning the professional role are mutually beneficial.[10]

Traditionally, sociological studies of adult socialization neglect problems in occupational socialization, while analyses of professional socialization overlook events in lateral life roles. Historically, sociological investigators have failed to account for lateral facets of vocational socialization, perhaps because the professions—law, medicine, egineering, and theology—recruited males almost exclusively, in whose life roles the resolution of problems was supposedly not relevant.[11] Paradoxically, however, two male professions, the priesthood and the military, have historically recognized the reciprocal influence of lateral and professional roles, for their training schools, the seminary and the academy, have in the past and still do demand celibacy of their candidates during the student years. This very issue and the matter of continued celibacy were matters of controversy among Roman Catholic clergy and laity at the time this book was written.

Professional socialization is also multidimensional in that students simultaneously acquire new views of self along with role behaviors. (These distinctions are, of course, matters of conceptualization.) Most sociologists would grant that the student's inner world is shifting and changing, even as his outer world is observable, for example, in changing role performances. In the main, however, phenomenological aspects of professional socialization have been merely assumed and passed over, rather than being systematically explored and related to objective events in socialization or external variables. Interestingly, these questions have had attention from educators in certain fields where increasing self-awareness is regarded as critical to learning and carrying out the professional role.[12] Some recent writing on expressive gestures and subjective aspects in professional socialization has also begun to redress this inadequacy, but for the most part the dialogue within the student's inner world remains, at this writing, an unknown but fertile field of inquiry.[13]

Any description of professional socialization would be incomplete without acknowledgment of the differences among the persons who become students, and of the differences among their instructors. By no means can students be thought to be homogeneous upon entry into (or graduation from) professional school. On the American scene, the workings of a more or less open class system with the attendant educational opportunities bring a variety of students even into those educational institutions where access is highly restricted—for example, the military academy.[14] In sum, not every student starts from the same baseline, either with respect to his qualifications or, indeed, the awareness he has of the profession and the self as a professional.[15]

If the student's role can be conceptualized as having varied attributes, a similar observation can be made of faculty. Differences in age, life style, social class, marital status characterize faculty, even as they do students. Differences in outlook may also characterize faculties who have experienced changes in their schools. Rapid change may generate divisiveness among faculty on how the student should be educated, what curriculum emphasis should be, and what should be expected of the student.

From this description of the multiple roles involved in the process and the variegated quality of the occupants' roles, we may infer that the student's progress in becoming a professional may be continually problematic, beset with halts and starts and even backsliding from time to time. These different rates of progress apply to the collectivity of students in professional schools—within any given class of students at any point in the formal span of the curriculum, including the very day of graduation, there will be different types of role assimilation, various degrees of self-awareness, and differences in professional behavior and knowledge. Even in such a total institution as the military academy, student attitudes vary on central professional problems.[16] Students in general do more or less assimilate a central core of values emphasized by the faculty and the profession, but within a collectivity of graduate students there can be found wide divergences.

Thus, different students may display different rates and levels of progress; any individual student may accelerate at one time, only to falter at another. In part, the variegated aspects of professional socialization may be understood in light of the ever increasing role demands on the student. The student seeks to meet these levels of role knowlege and self-awareness, only to find that once these levels are attained, another equally or more difficult level lies ahead.

In sum, with respect to the configuration of roles involved, we assume that professional socialization is multidimensional. In terms of the attributes of the occupants of the roles we regard these characteristics as variegated. From the standpoint of the candidates' progress and outcome, the movement forward is constantly and continually problematic. These descriptive statements constitute a set of assumptions or a model about professional socialization, regardless of whether it occurs in students in a military academy or an art school. These assumptions in turn generate other questions about professional socialization. To some of these questions, the ones that are at issue in this study, we now turn.

Questions at Issue

A genealogy of mixed ancestry must be written for the questions of interest in this study and at issue in the book. In some respects they are the natural children of symbolic interaction, with the emphasis on the problems of self and other, emerging configurations of role and self.[17] To imply, however, that these questions stood crystal clear in our minds on the opening day of the study would be to falsify our own past. Yet, it is in general true that the broad contours of these questions were in the background as we began our three-year immersion in the world of student nurses in the fall of 1960. The buffeting which we, like the students, took during those years served to sharpen and sometimes to mute these questions. We acknowledge this in passing, reserving the minute details of how and what changed the questions for face-to-face collegial discourse.

The questions understandably derive partially from the assumptions we have just described. Like the progress of the students themselves, however, the questions, too, were emergent. For this reason, the book is a natural history, reconstructing the ongoing development and becoming of the student through institutional and personal time, rather than starting from a series of propositions and hypotheses derived from theory. Perhaps as influential as any other factor in the sharpening and emerging of the questions was our growing realization that the assumptions we had initially made about professional socialization failed to tell us important parts of the story about how the students became, and how to put together various pieces of the socialization puzzle—for example, the relationship of phenomenological and objective progress.

Although we thought that students had multiple encounters with persons in other roles during their institutional years and that persons in some non-faculty roles may be significant for students, we knew very little about the meaning and implications of these encounters, both sanctioned and otherwise, for the students. We could assume that they contributed in some ways to the development of a central and necessary facet of the professional role, namely self-awareness, but we did not know in what ways self-awareness emerged nor to what extent the various members of the student role set were implicated. A first line of questions, then, is: How did our students become aware of themselves in their various roles—as nurses, as students, as women, as adults? How did they learn to be aware of being aware?[18] How did they come to see themselves as nurses as well as laymen? The question of awareness was a critical one in this research.

A second line of questions has to do with the problematic and variegated quality of professional socialization. The institution and its faculty representatives, as well as others, made of the students demands which the students defined and acted on in various ways. Many of these demands were problematic, no easy or simple solution being available, such as how much of the reading list to do, whether to take a summer job in nursing, whether to ask for an easy or difficult patient, what clinical area to specialize in, how to manage an important or difficult faculty member. Noting these concerns, we were led to ask what strategies the students worked out for themselves personally and in company with their fellow students for managing the vicissitudes of the institution, and how these strategies related to becoming.

Recalling that our students were not only undergoing professional socialization, but were also becoming young adults, we note a third set of questions which have to do with the intermeshing of these roles. Although our earlier discussion, based on observation and evidence from professions other than nursing, suggested that there is a reciprocal influence between life roles and professional roles, we were not certain as to what the interplay of these roles was for the student. How does the student accomodate and integrate multiple facets of roles and selves? This became a focal question.

THE EXISTENTIAL
PERSPECTIVE AND METHOD   These issues of self-aware-

ness, situational management, and integration of multiple roles and selves demand a perspective that would allow us to work with concepts of self, awareness, role relationships, and the connections between these variables. If there is a single theoretical position in this book, it is that of symbolic interaction, a position that permits analysis of the students' existential encounters in which the students defined, chosen, and acted on their choices. This particular position allows us to note that once the student has defined, chose, and acted on her choices, her action not only has implications for behavior with respect to others and her own view of herself, but also has consequences that become a part of the experience and a basis for further choice.[19] In short, we are concerned with the "human condition" of the student, a variable neglected in some studies.[20]

Footnotes

[1] Howard S. Becker, Blanche Geer, Everett Hughes, and Anselm Strauss, *Boys in White: Student Culture in a Medical School.* Chicago: University of Chicago Press, 1961. Part Two, "Student Culture in the Freshman Year," and Part Three, "Student Culture in the Clinical Years," pp. 62-273.

[2] Stanley Edgar Hyman, "Ideals, Dangers and Limitations," *Daedalus,* 89 (Spring 1960), p. 384.

[3] This image of the student professional assumes an underlying philosophy of "soft determinism," "foresight," or "prehension." Among the many sources which analyze this position are David Matza, *Delinquency and Drift,* New York: Wiley, 1964, especially p. 11; Harry Stack Sullivan, "Tensions Interpersonal and International: A Psychiatrist's View, " in Helen S. Perry (ed.), *The Fusion of Psychiatry and Social Sciences,* New York: Norton, 1964, especially p. 303; Alfred North Whitehead, *Adventures of Ideas,* New York: Macmillan, 1933; Roger W. Sperry, "Mind, Brain and Humanist Values," in John R. Platt (ed.), *New Views of the Nature of Man,* Chicago: University of Chicago Press, 1964, pp. 71-92, especially p. 87.

[4] Everett Hughes, *Men and Their Work,* Glencoe, Ill.: Free Press, 1958, p. 121.

[5] On parents as sources of information and support, see Sanford M. Dornbusch,

"The Military Academy as an Assimilating Institution," *Social Forces,* 32 (March, 1955), p. 321.

[6] *San Francisco Examiner,* December 19, 1965, p. 8.

[7] See in particular Dan C. Lortie, "Laymen to Lawmen," *Harvard Educational Review,* 29 (Fall, 1959), pp. 352-69; Miriam Wagenschein, "Reality Shock: A Study of Beginning School Teachers" (unpublished master's thesis, Sociology Department, University of Chicago, 1951); Howard S. Becker, "The Career of the Public Schoolteacher," *American Journal of Sociology,* 57 (March, 1952), pp. 470-77.

[8] Medical education in France has certain effects for students precisely because French medical students are beyond the adolescent crisis. Jean-Daniel Reynaud and Alain Touraine, "Deux Notes à Propos d'une Enquête sur les Étudiants en Médecine," *Cahiers Internationaux de Sociologie,* XX, Novelle Série, Troisième Année, 1956, p. 124.

[9] Stanton Wheeler, "The Structure of Formally Organized Socialization Settings," in Orville Brim, Jr. and Stanton Wheeler, *Socialization After Childhood,* New York: Wiley, 1966, pp. 68-69.

[10] Thoughtful statements may be found in Charlotte Towle, *Education for the Professions, As Seen in Education for Social Work,* Chicago: The University of Chicago Press, 1954, p. 106; H. Richard Niebuhr, Daniel Day Williams, and James J. Gustafson, *The Advancement of Theological Education,* New York: Harper, 1957, p. 167; Editorial, "Domesticity in Our Seminaries," *Christian Century,* 75 (January-June, 1958), p. 485; N. E. Hulme, "The Seminary Student and His Family Life," *Pastoral Psychology,* 11 (September, 1960), p. 35; David Feldman, "Social Class and Achievement in Law School" (unpublished Ph.D. dissertation, Department of Sociology, Stanford University, 1960).

[11] Curiously, the effect of lateral roles is much discussed in folk culture with respect to the performance of men and women on similar jobs. This facet of professional life in post-school years has been sytematically explored by André Biancone, "Les Instituteurs," *Revue Française de Science Politique,* 9 (Decembre, 1959), pp. 935-50 and by Ida Berger, "Instituteurs et Institutrices, Hommes et Femmes dans une Même Profession," *Revue Française de Sociologie,* I (Avril–Juin, 1960), pp. 173-85.

[12] Some essays by educators in the professions on subjective socialization in students include J. P. Dowling, "Stages in Progress of First-Year Students in Veterans' Administration," *Social Casework,* 33 (January, 1952), pp. 13-18, G. Hamilton, "Self-Awareness in Professional Education," *Social Casework,* 35 (November, 1954); Thomas W. Klink, "The Career of Preparation for the Ministry," *Journal of Pastoral Care,* 18 (Winter, 1964), pp. 200-207; Penrose St. Amant, "The Private World of Theological Students" *Religion in Life,* 31 (Autumn, 1962), pp. 497-506; Sister Madeleine Clemence Vaillot, *Commitment to Nursing,* Philadelphia: J. B. Lippincott, 1963; Rodney Coe, "Self Conceptions

and Professional Training," *Nursing Research,* 14 (Winter, 1965), p. 49; Jean Tomich, "Home Care: A Technique for Generating Professional Identity," *Journal of Medical Education,* 41 (March, 1966), pp. 202-207.

[13] Work along these lines has been done by Virginia Olesen and Elvi Whittaker, "Adjudication of Student Awareness in Professional Socialization: The Language of Laughter and Silences," *The Sociological Quarterly,* VII (Summer, 1966), pp. 381-96; Fred Davis, "Professional Socialization as Subjective Experience: The Process of Doctrinal Conversion Among Student Nurses," in Robert S. Weiss, *et al.* (eds.), *Essays in Honor of Everett C. Hughes,* Chicago: Aldine, 1968; Ida Harper Simpson, "Patterns of Socialization into the Professions: The Case of Student Nurses," *Sociological Inquiry,* 37 (Winter, 1967), pp. 47-54.

[14] John P. Lovell, "The Professional Socialization of the West Point Cadet," in Morris Janowitz (ed.), *The New Military,* New York: Russell Sage Foundation, 1964, p. 120.

[15] On differential backgrounds in law students, American and French, see Seymour Warkov with Joseph Zelan, *Lawyers in the Making,* Chicago: Aldine, 1965, especially Chapter 1, "Recruitment," pp. 1-52; André Sauvegeot, "Les Origines de la Magistrature d'Aujourd'hui," *Le Pouvoir Judicatre* (Octobre, 1954), quoted in *Revue Française de Science Politique,* 9 (Decembre, 1959), pp. 951-54.

[16] Lovell, *op. cit.,* p. 129.

[17] Classic works on symbolic interaction are Charles Horton Cooley, *Human Nature and the Social Order,* Glencoe: The Free Press, 1956, and Anselm Strauss (ed.), *The Social Psychology of George Herbert Mead,* Chicago: University of Chicago Press, 1946.

[18] The significance of being aware about awareness is implied in a report indicating that stability in professional–client relationships depends in part on mutual empathy which, for the professional, derives from awareness of being aware. Charles Kadushin, "Social Distance Between Client and Professional," *American Journal of Sociology,* 67 (March, 1962), pp. 517-31.

[19] See George Herbert Mead, *The Philosophy of the Present,* Chicago: Open Court, 1932, especially Chapter Three, "The Social Nature of the Present," pp. 57-67, and Howard S. Becker, "Personal Change in Adult Life," *Sociometry,* 27 (March, 1964), pp. 40-53.

[20] This objection has been raised by Daniel Levinson, "Medical Educators and the Theory of Adult Socialization," paper presented to a special meeting of the section of medical sociology, American Sociological Association, August, 1965.

SIX PROCEDURES OF ACADEMIC RECRUITMENT
Theodore Caplow and Reece J. McGee

The process of faculty recruitment cannot be understood or adequately described without attention to the details of hiring procedures, which turn out to be extraordinarily complex and elaborate. . . . The analysis of hiring procedures may clarify our general view of the values held in the academic profession.

Open and Closed Hiring

A distinction must be made between the two kinds of recruitment in general use—"open," or competitive, hiring and "closed," or preferential, hiring. In theory, academic recruitment is mostly open. In practice, it is mostly closed.

In the theoretical recruiting situation, the department seeking a replacement attempts to procure the services of an ideal academic man. Regardless of the rank at which he is to be hired, he must be young. He must have shown considerable research productivity, or the promise of being able to produce research. He must be a capable teacher with a pleasing personality which will offend neither students, deans, nor colleagues. In order to secure the very best man available, the department simultaneously announces the opening in many quarters and obtains a long list of candidates named by their sponsors. When a sufficient number

Source: Chapter 6 of *The Academic Marketplace,* by Theodore Caplow and Reece J. McGee. © 1958 by Basic Books, Inc., Publishers, New York.

of high-caliber candidates have applied for the position, the department members sift and weigh the qualifications of each most carefully in order to identify the one who best meets their requirements. This is the model hiring situation. It is a stereotype of the profession, and it actually occurs in a small percentage of cases. Indeed, some elements of the model situation are present in almost every vacancy-and-replacement, but the outlines are blurred and distorted by a host of other factors.

The most common of these distorting factors is the preferential treatment of some candidates, based on an association between themselves and the hiring department. For want of a better term, it may be called nepotism, although the work is perhaps excessively strong. According to one of the dictionary definitions, it is the "bestowal of patronage by reason of relationship rather than merit." . . .

It is not difficult, despite the taboo, for a man with the appropriate disciplinary connections to go soliciting a position. The taboo, it would appear, is quite real (since there are statements that men who solict positions are rejected from candidacy in some departments), but it can certainly be evaded if things are done discreetly. The technique is to solicit while avoiding the appearance of solicitation.

The crucial factor here is possession of the appropriate acquaintances in the discipline to whom one's availability may be indicated. These are the connections by means of which one is freed of local institutional ties. . . .

Discrimination on racial or religious grounds is a luxury in the hiring process which seems to be practiced only when there is a surplus of candidates of quality. It is *always* institutional. We know of no instance of a disciplinary discrimination system. As suggested elsewhere, women tend to be discriminated against in the academic profession, not because they have low prestige but because they are outside the prestige system entirely and for this reason are of no use to a department in future recruitment.

With the exception of a few disciplines which enjoy the privilege of hiring in a truly international market (Spanish studies, for example), the importation of scholars from abroad is a sign of a very tight market in a specialty. The major universities may seek men from abroad before they will seek them from the minor league at home. Failing to discover a candidate to their taste in a foreign land, they may decide not to hire at all; or they may even hire a woman, who, being outside the prestige system, cannot hurt them. Not even as a last resort will they recruit from institutions with prestige levels much below their own.

The Process in Practice

If we turn from the model recruiting situation to examine what usually occurs, it may first be noted that there is a considerable evidence that both vacancies and appointments are disturbing to academic departments and often result in a cumulative turnover of personnel. This is to say that the occurrence of a vacancy, especially when coupled with a search for a replacement, increases the probability of future vacancies in the same department. . . .

The apparent explanation of this circumstance is that the personnel process frequently provides an evaluation of either the departed man or a candidate which is inconsistent with the self-evaluation of some other member of the department, thereby turning his thoughts to greener, or less stony, pastures.

Another event which occurs frequently in the personnel process is the intrusion of outside influence upon the department. For example, a nepotistic appointment may be blocked when an outsider, usually the dean, requests the reopening of the field for further candidates. Factions within a department will often do the same thing, seldom opposing the man whom their rivals have put up for candidacy but muddying his inside track or obstructing it completely by the insistence that other candidates, better qualified, may be found if the search is extended somewhat.

We may also note that many academic men seem to be, as one respondent put it, "passively on the market" all the time. This is to say that they are not soliciting positions actively but will listen to any proposal which comes their way. This is, of course, one way for the individual professor to resist institutional authority, and it is sometimes cited as one of the academic subsistutes for unionization. . . .

There is, as a matter of fact, a great deal of coyness in the recruiting process, but mostly on the side of the hiring parties, encouraged by higher administrators. It is very seldom seen in candidates. Ideally, both parties to the negotiation are supposed to be mutually friendly and ingratiating. The candidate usually is, and genuinely so. The university cannot be. It believes it has too much at stake, and the uncertainties of buying a less-than-perfectly-known quantity loom too large. This institutional anxiety can lead to coyness on a grand scale.

> "His name had been brought to the attention of the President there. They met at the home of a friend of his, by accident, seemingly. The President then made him an offer when he went there to make a talk."

Festina Lente

When we examine the specific procedures of hiring in the American university, they turn out to be almost unbelievably elaborate. The average salary of an assistant professor is approximately that of a bakery truck driver, and his occupancy of a job is likely to be less permanent. Yet it may require a large part of the time of twenty highly-skilled men for a full year to hire him. The reader is invited to consider the following report:

"We had discussed the problem many times in staff meeting. We did a great deal of thinking on this. Our first step was to bring together a committee. They met a number of times trying to decide the qualities to be looked for and then to dig up suitable people to fill the role. After a number of meetings, it was boiled down to five men. One man notified us he couln't be considered. The other four were brought here at intervals of a week or two. They met with each member of the staff and discussed their speciality. Lastly we invited each to give a paper. We brought in heads of other departments and members of the administration to hear them. They added their impressions to our own. We quickly centered on two men. It was difficult to decide, they had highly contrasting interests, abilities, and accomplishments. There were two or three staff meetings before the vote. The needs of the department were examined. We asked ourselves, 'Do we need glamour or promise?' "

"The four men who came each spent about half a week with us. The committee had got out an elegant and complete biography on each man prior to his visit. The vote was taken the week following the appearance of the last man. The Chairman saw the Dean the day afterward, and the Dean said, 'Go to it,' so the letter was sent that day. The level and approximate salary had been settled between the Chairman and the Dean previously, but it wasn't inflexible. The vote included the assistant professors, since it was made at that level."

Hiring procedures of approximately this complexity and duration are not the exception but the rule. Since they have no apparent ritual function in most cases, the best explanation we can offer is that these lengthy procedures reflect anxieties attendant upon the comparison of candidates by estimation of their disciplinary prestige. The appointment of an assistant professor or an instructor for two or three years does not seem to be of enough importance to the university to justify so complex a system on other grounds. . . .

Some Recruiting Agents

In many academic specialties within disciplines there are one or two men who are nationally recognized as leaders. These men sometimes become informal deans in their fields. Through their wide acquaintance, they can place almost anyone in the specialty, although they can seldom deny placement to anyone, since they do not control all the vacancies existing. . . .

The Slave Market, an inaccurate (although beloved) figure of speech in wide use among professors, refers in general to the academic labor market and is used in particular reference to professional meetings and conventions. It is a misnomer in most disciplines, for it suggests the sale of professor-flesh upon the block with particularly high value being placed upon muscles and endurance. It is specifically applicable only to a few fields, such as English, where there is a great deal of routine and unavoidable undergraduate instruction to be done.

Appearing only infrequently, but dramatically when it does, is an especially elaborate form of procedural elaboration which might be called the Puppet Show. It occurs when a department *really* wants a specific man and is uncertain about being permitted to hire him. In general, it seems to develop in colleges where deans exercise their authority capriciously, for in the cases reported there is no definite evidence that the dean would have opposed the appointment had it been broached directly to him. The department, however, took no chances.

> "In the meantime we'd brought another man in as a Visiting Professor. In June, I talked to him to see if he'd be interested in staying on. He said 'No.' But he spent the summer with us and had a wonderful time. Well, by that time we'd picked out four more men including two we couldn't get at less than associate with $2,000 more than the Dean said we could have. We looked them all over and weren't particularly interested. Then one day this visiting man intimated it wouln't be impossible to interest him in the permanent post. He asked what I thought the Dean might say. I wrote the Dean a letter, about the four men, only this time I headed the list with the weakest and worked up to the strongest of the four. Then I added a paragraph to this effect: 'If the administration should wish to do something outstanding for this department, to bring it once more to

the ranks of the best in the country, they might be able to bring in our Visitor as a permanent member.' I saw the Dean about two weeks later. He said, 'That was a very clever letter. I wouln't hire the first two people on your list and after finishing your letter I could come to only one conclusion. " . . .

The role of the department chairman in the hiring process is an uncertain one. He may be a servant or a tyrant. . . .

[Interviewer]: "Was this an open vote?"
"Certainly the discussion was open. I think I may have requested closed ballots. I believe that's what I did. That's what we're doing now on promotions; they want that secret so if there's any complaint they can't say, 'The chairman didn't do it right.' I believe I have their votes in their own handwriting on file, in case there's an error or ever any cause to defend it before the Dean."

This example of closed but not secret balloting illustrates rather neatly the role of the chairman who is a servant of the servants. One other aspect of the chairman's role in the hiring process needs comment. In a good department, to concentrate the hiring in the hands of the chairman is often to allow him to build a feudal empire. Many medical school departments offer excellent examples. They may be, and often are, professionally excellent but their members, whatever their private feelings toward the chairman, are never likely to forget they owe their positions and their prospects to him. To be the chairman of a bad department and to be solely responsible for hiring, on the other hand, is to be gray of hair and ulcerous of stomach from the constant and frustrating effort to secure suitable candidates or approval for unsuitable ones.

As far as the data of this study permit us to judge, the presence of a university committee in the hiring process is likely to impede the already complex procedures, sometimes to the point of breakdown. The situation is often recognized by the working professor. . . .

"The Dean has a committee that does these things [evaluation of candidates] all over again. It's a farce, in my opinion. It should work, but it doesn't. They've made some awful appointments. And they've made some mistakes and promoted the wrong people."

There seems to be no sure way for men who are members of one discipline to check their judgments of a man in another. Knowing neither the prestige nor the bases of judgment the men recommending the candidate, the members of the committee must resort to their own friends in the discipline or to marginal persons in it (who are more likely to talk freely to outsiders) to arrive at an appraisal themselves. These appraisals will almost certainly be distorted (from the department viewpoint) by the pressure of interdisciplinary rivalries. . . .

The function of placement bureaus in the recruiting process of major universities can be summarized by saying that prestige is attached to the nonuse of their services. This is less true of the university's own placement service than of commercial agencies (which exist somewhere in the darkness of an academic limbo beyond Siberia), but even these are mostly patronized by aspirants with degrees in education, a discipline which, in the view of many academic men, occupies a special Siberia of its own. The contamination of these users has passed to the bureau itself, for reasons which become evident upon analysis.

Recommendations are read primarily in the attempt to ascertain the disciplinary prestige of the candidate. The first consideration for any hiring department is to safeguard itself against a ridiculous choice, the public-knowledge of which could lower the departmental reputation at one blow. The unwritten, essential, and elemental rule of hiring, then, is that the candidate must be disciplinarily respectable before he will be considered at all. It is exactly this elemental respectability which no placement service can guarantee, unlike the private letter of recommendation which demonstrates the subject's respectability by the very fact of its existence. As a result, there is a tendency in most fields for only the weakest candidates to use the services of a placement agency. Only where the ''slave market'' prevails can the placement bureau safely be used by a major department. In such cases, the prestige of the departments depends upon the senior men and is relatively unaffected by the juniors.

Hiring Procedures in Perspective

When academic hiring procedures are viewed in perspective, their most striking feature is the time and effort which most departments devote to appointments, including the appointments of junior men, who tend to be transient and unimportant to the department. It has been noted that in most cases the procedure seems to have no ritual significance, although there are some instances of its being used to manipulate a dean. We should also note that if the procedure is too prolonged and agonized, it may pass the point of no return, and the department will find itself unable to make a replacement because any candidate suggested will be vetoed by a remark to the effect: "But is he as good as that young Smith whom we turned down three years ago?"

We have suggested that what the department attempts to do in hiring is to establish the candidate's prestige-potential—his value for future staff procurement. The elaboration of procedures is in part explained by the fact that there are no objective means by which future prestige can be measured. Prestige, it must be remembered, is subjective, consisting, in essence, of what other people think about a man. It may be more important to the department than the qualities of the man, observed in themselves. The academic labor market is an exchange where universities speculate in future prestige values, based on yet undone research. By attempting to hire men whose value will increase at more than the normal rate, they hope to purchase future institutional prestige below the market price. However, since most universities and most departments tend to get the candidates whom their actual prestige deserves, and since they are normally subject to the Aggrandizement Effect, they are very frequently dissatisfied with their purchases. . . .

The Merits of Candidates

As part of the hiring process often hidden within the overlapping layers of procedures is the actual evaluation of candidates on their merits. The following sensible nonsense is an excellent summary of the way the market for futures is viewed by many of its most active traders.

"We take a good look at their letters and then when they're down here we look at them and talk to them and then we take a good look into our crystal ball and pull out the best man. In other words, we're completely subjective about the whole thing.
"It's usually fairly simple. You can tell from a ten-minute conversation if a man will be a good teacher. The thing that is perturbing is trying to forecast what their scientific career is going to be like on the basis of the same conversation. What counts is drive and imagination. You can have pretty good luck, though, this way. We hired a man this way three years ago who has proved to be the outstanding man in the country of those who were available at that time.
"We can't afford to hire any other way. There is no other way of judging a man's research and scholarly capacities. It's extremely time-consuming, but it works."

Despite the occasional recognition that the process of evaluation is subjective, the overelaboration of procedures which characterizes the whole system of recruiting often represents a dogged attempt to achieve consensus at any price.

"We pass the recommendations and vita and stuff around to the whole staff—everyone on the full-time staff—and they look it over. If there are too many applicants, I may do a little weeding first and throw out the obviously unsuitable ones. Then we write and get opinions from the men we know we can trust with whom they've worked or in their home departments. Then we invite two or three of them down here in a rank order of preference, and everyone gets a chance to see them and talk to them, and we ask them to give a seminar paper for an hour at a staff seminar. Sometimes during the time they're here, a day or two, everyone gets a chance at them and really works them over, in particular with regard to what they have done and are doing in research, what their research attitudes are, that kind of thing. Of course, if they have publications, everyone reads those, or most of us do. And we have a party and pour a couple of drinks into them if they'll take them, and see how they are when they're loosened up a bit. Then we take them into the Deans of the College of Letters and the Graduate School and let them have a look at them. Then after they go home, we have a staff meeting and really chew them over and everyone gets a chance to have a say and contribute what he thinks of the man. Every man in the department has the blackball privilege, although of course he has to be able to state his reasons. We respect them, too; doesn't matter who they come from if they make sense. We can't afford to have brawls within the department."

The blackball device, mentioned above may help to insure department harmony, but it probably tends to favor men with neutral characteristics. This is not always an asset, even in a democratic department.

Throughout the information on candidate evaluation, the human element obtrudes in singular ways, sometimes comic, and often pathetic.

"We had one young woman come down here from one of the Big Ten. She had the M.A. and was working on her doctoral dissertation and we would have very much like to have gotten her, but when she saw the Dean, he turned her down. He didn't like the way she was turned out, thought she was too stylishly dressed. We had thought she looked very lovely." . . .

One of the most time-hornored of all of the evaluative devices in use is that of having all the staff members of the department above the rank at which the replacement is to be made meet to decide upon a man. This keeps the hierarchy hierarchical and reduces the probability of invidious comparison between the emoluments offered the new man and those of present members of the same rank.

Even under the best conditions, the evaluation of candidates is beset with uncertainty. If judgment is made on the basis of a visit, the judges get no view of that research ability which is chiefly sought. If the candidate is judged on the basis of his recommendations, the judge must not only determine what those recommendations really mean but must evaluate the disciplinary prestige of the recommending scholars.

The Decision-making Procedure

As for the actual credentials used in decision making, it is not an overgeneralization to say that departments do not, as a rule, consider teaching, academic records, or theses. Why theses are not read is a puzzling question, since the thesis is usually the only major work which a young man can show and probably represents the best current effort of which he is capable. But they are not read—in the same way that publications are not generally read in the course of his candidacy for a position. Of course, they may be taken out of the library and piled upon the chairman's desk so that anyone who wishes to do so may look at them.

The reason why publications, all protestations to the contrary, are not really *read* has been suggested before: because men are hired for their repute, and not for what that repute is purportedly based upon. Men are hired, to put it baldly, on the basis of how good they will look to others. It is assumed that the long, grueling training demanded for the Ph.D. guarantees a satisfactory quality of teaching and the quality, if not the quantity, of a man's research. There is very little point in trying to determine how good the man *really* is, or even how good the department opinion of him may be. What is important is what others in the discipline think of him, since that is, in large part, how good he is. Prestige, as we have remarked before, is not a direct measure of productivity but a composite of subjective opinion. . . .

It may also be said, in the light of the analysis above, that an academic man's career is pretty well determined by the time he has reached the age of forty. Opinions of him by then will have crystallized and will be so widely diffused that the possibilities of changing them will be slight. Disciplinary prestige is a feature of a social system, not a scientific measurement. It is correlated with professional achievement but not identical with it. A man may, for example, publish what would be, in other circumstances, a brilliant contribution to his field, but if he is too old, or too young, or located in the minor league, it will not be recognized as brilliant and will not bring him the professional advancement which he could claim if he were of the proper age and located at the proper university. Disciplinary prestige, then, has a social and institutional locus. There are men to whom this has happened in every discipline, and many readers will be able to supply specific examples.

A further illustration of the nature of the prestige order is that a man's prestige in his discipline is often measured by the number of citations he receives from other authors—yet the number of citations received is in part a consequence of high prestige. And lest the reader who is a physical scientist believe himself exempt, let it be pointed out that, although the scientist's prestige is presumed to depend upon the quality of his work, the quality is often a function of the equipment to which he has access—which is at least partly dependent on his prestige. High-energy accelerators are not available to unknown instructors.

The haunting uncertainties and anxieties of the selection process are reduced in a few specialities in which professional skill—and, hence, prestige—can be determined by audition. Music is such a field. In these areas we find none of the elaborate procedures which prevail elsewhere in the academic profession. . . .

A final point of interest is that many of the people most concerned with hiring do not seem to know precisely what the hiring procedures at their universities are. In the same department, procedures often vary from one appointment to the next. It is not unusual for the dean to initiate all personnel, actions for one department of his college and scarcely to be consulted in another. The formal procedures of appointments are often unfamiliar to people who make appointments.

Perhaps the precise method of selection makes so little difference to the university because all methods are used to measure, very imperfectly, the same variable, and none of them measures it well. . . .

The results . . . suggest that departments get the replacements to which their place in the prestige order entitles them.

Hazards of the Market

There is a ceremonial way of canvassing for a roster of candidates. It consists of seeking nominations from the big names, both human and institutional in the discipline. The ceremony is almost always carried out when time allows, but men are hired where they are found and contracts with them are made in such a variety of ways as to defy cataloguing.

We have spoken before of nepotism in the hiring process. Our data on the extent to which closed, or preferential, hiring occurs indicate that for the replacements made in the sample universitities 40 percent of instructors and assistant professors and 61 percent of associate and full professors had some contact with the department before their candidacy. There is a statistically significant positive association between two variables. This is to say that as the rank of the replacement increases, the probability that he had some contact with the department to which he goes also increases. In a sense, of course, this is to be expected because the greater the rank, the greater the likelihood that the individual will at least have met someone from the hiring department before. However, in most of these cases, the reported contact was much more than casual acquaintance.

We also note in the interviews a steady insistence that prior contact does not make any difference—*i.e.,* does not unduly influence the selection of candidates. . . .

For purposes of formal evaluation, prior association between the candidate and the hiring department probably does not make much difference, since it does not affect his prestige, but, as we have already suggested, certain reasons exist why familiar candidates are preferred to unknowns. In departments rated high by their chairmen, 59 percent of the candidates had prior contact before the replacement was hired, whereas in low-rated departments only 38 percent had such contact. . . .

This is to be expected if our analysis of the rating process is correct; better departments seek men with more prestige; men with more prestige are better known and have a wider acquaintance in the discipline.

Prestige is not rank—which is definite and discrete. One has a given rank or one has not; there can be no ambiguity about it. Prestige, being a kind of average of opinions about a man, is, like any average, subject to distortion by extreme values. Hiring departments, therefore, are most sensitive to sharply negative opinions. A mildly critical opinion may be balanced by laudatory reports, but a sharply negative opinion from someone of high prestige is usually sufficient to destroy a candidate's chances.

It is our impression, however, that negative opinions referring to personality factors are less likely to be fatal than those referring to professional ability.

The compilers of rosters are haunted by uncertainty about finding and evaluating men. We suggested earlier that disciplinary respectability is so urgent a requirement in a candidate that some canvassing techniques are not used for the sole reason that they cannot assure this. The result of the uncertainty, of course, is often nepotism, since departments are apt to prefer anyone who is at all familiar to someone who is totally unknown.

There is another uncertainty to be taken account of: the fear of the "Bogie-man Replacement." There appear to be two kinds of bogie-men whom departments fear. The first is the temperamental prima donna, who can wreck a department by his mere presence. He is especially dangerous in the tenure ranks since prima donnas—as visualized—will do anything to get what they want. The second, and more conspicuous, bogie-man is the "man who won't fit in." Among the most common qualities sought in candidates are "the right personality," "someone whom we can live with," and the like. The frequent reliance upon the blackball, or the senatorial courtesy principle, is illustrated by one or two of the interviews that we have quoted previously. This concern with getting replacements with whom the department can live, and the rule that a candidate must be *persona grata* to everyone in the department, reflect the fear of the man who won't fit in. On the part of the candidate, "fitting in" involves the acceptance of the values of the department as a peer group and a willingness to defend it under attack from without, especially from higher administrators, whom the department often regards as enemies.

This conception of the department as an embattled band is especially strong in expanding disciplines, in which the process of professional growth makes recurrent demands upon the administration for further funds for new positions, promotions, and research support. The department must, in this situation, be a conflict group, constantly striving to acquire a larger share of the finite institutional budget at the expense of competitiors. Such departments are especially wary of "traitors" who will betray departmental secrets to the administration or to its disciplinary enemies. Equally dangerous is the nonconformist, who cannot be assimilated into the defensive structure of the department and who threatens its prestige by operating as a detachable Achilles' Heel.

These threats are given the weight and worry which they receive from professors because each man's prestige is linked to that of his department, and anything which threatens the prestige of the department is experienced as a threat to the individual's ego. There is seldom any feeling expressed that the replacement must be a pal, a "good buddy," to the members of the department, or personally charming; but he must be a reliable member of the peer group. If he is this, he may also be almost anything else he chooses.

So the poker game of personnel is haunted by uncertainty and anxiety. We have several instances where this anxiety about the process has so mounted within departments that even nontenured appointments are put on a short-term basis in order to assure that there will be no problem of disposal, should the replacement turn out to be a bogie-man. Thus we find the title of "acting assistant professor" in increasing vogue at certain major universities. The reader is asked to consider, if he will, the level of anxiety which makes a two-year contract seem too long, so that junior staff must be hired on an "acting" basis in order to shorten their tenure to one academic year at a time. We even have one case of an acting instructorship.

Signing and Sealing

An examination of the techniques of offering also reveals situational stresses at work. In general, candidates do not delay acceptance of offers very long. Universities, on the other hand, are apt to withhold final word until the last possible moment, presumably in case a better candidate appears or something unseemly is learned about the one in hand. It is much easier for a candidate to make up his mind than it is for the institution. (He knows more about the institution than it knows about him.) . . .

In general, the candidate tends to abandon his hesitations at an earlier point in the sequence of events, whereas the department is often undecided up to the moment an offer is made, and even beyond. *The immediate outcome of the academic personnel process, in the typical case, is a happy candidate and a worried department* . . .

Despite their general reluctance to reach a final decision, universities tend to make initial offers rather early in the process in order to get candidates to commit themselves. The offers are often extremely discreet in their wording and detail. A very common proceeding, for example, is to ask the candidate to accept the position before the university has offered it:

"I sent the nomination to the Dean, briefed him on what he wanted. The Dean recommended him to the Vice-President, the Vice-President to the President, and the President approved the nomination, so I called him to tell him so. I had, prior to that time, secured a letter from him saying that he would accept the position under the conditions stated if it were offered. That's S.O.P.—we always do that."

The candidate in this case, is ethically bound to accept the position and not to seek others while waiting. The university is not bound to make an offer, and the failure to do so can always be attributed to higher officials whom the candidate does not know. All questions of ethics aside, this procedure is a vestige of the buyer's market of an earlier era, and it can impose real handicaps on departments forced to operate in the seller's market of today.

SEVEN
TALKING AND
BECOMING: A
VIEW OF
ORGANIZATIONAL
SOCIALIZATION
Peter K. Manning

One of the enduring interests of sociologists is the study and analysis of the process by which people become actors upon a social stage. In order to provide a contrast to "socialized man," introductory readers and/or texts in sociology usually include sections on social isolation to manifest the results or effects of the absence or severe restriction of social contacts (see Park and Burgess, 1924:Chapter 4, 226–273). The fields of socialization, human development, and family life are studied by a wide range of social scientists. Adult socialization, although seen for some reason as less problematic, is also receiving more attention of late (Brim and Wheeler, 1966). Works that examine adult socialization are few and suggest that further work can be done.

Source: Reprinted from Jack D. Douglas, editor, *Understanding Everyday Life* (Chicago: Aldine Publishing Company, 1970). Copyright © 1970 by Aldine Publishing Company. Reprinted by permission of the author and Aldine Publishing Company. Slightly edited to delete typographical errors and awkward sentence construction. Since the publication of this paper in late 1970, a series of exciting developments in natural language analysis has made available a range of precise analytic procedures. [Cf. David Sudnow, ed., *Studies in Social Interaction* (New York: Free Press, 1972); Aaron Cicourel, *Cognitive Sociology* (Harmondsworth: Penguin, 1973); J.M. Atkinson and D.R. Watson, eds., *Ethnographics* (London: Martin-Robertson, 1974); and Emanuel A. Schlegloff and Harvey Sacks, "Opening Up Closings", *Semiotica* IV (1973): 289–327.]

The specific focus here is the development of means to study adult socialization in the context of organizations. Organizational socialization[1] is the process by which an individual, from both the individual and the organizational perspectives, becomes a part of the organization. It begins to take place, we assume, whenever an individual associates with others "under" a common symbolic label referring to that association (Bittner, 1965).[2]

The study of organizational socialization is conventionally assumed to involve at least two dimensions: the social role(s) and the organization as a social structure (the set of "slots" into which persons who play roles in the organization are to fit). However, when these conventions have been closely examined, some suggestive gaps and shortcomings in explanation have appeared. This chapter seeks to identify some of the shortcomings of organizational theory and sociological views of roles in order to address the problem we have called organizational socialization. The first part of the chapter will address the former notions; the second part will address organizational socialization.

Organizational Structure

The sociologist's concern in doing sociology is with making action social, that is, creating tales, stories, reports, accounts, articles, monographs, and essays that make social action reportable, accountable, publishable, and judicable for his purposes and for those of other sociologists. Sociological attempts to understand concerted action among organization members is usually dated from the work of Max Weber.[3]

Weber began by creating a model of social life within bureaucracies that held true whenever, and insofar as, efficiency (formal rationality) was the criterion for action. As a distribution of authority that made the outcome of command predictable, the organization existed for Weber in the pure form as linkage between command and compliance. The literal meaning of the formal rules for which the organization was assembled as a model were taken as describing the actual behavior occurring. Variations from the normatively ordered scheme of behaviors were accounted for by irrational, nonrational, informal, or otherwise foreign behavior deriving from normative conflicts, ignorance, or strains.

Selznick, in *TVA and the Grass Roots* (1966), turns the Weberian theory into a formal theory that is ideally possible but practically unattainable. Formal theories are seen as normative idealizations, as descriptions of organizations based on the assumption that actors follow only the sociological scheme.

Bureaucracy as an administrative system constantly faces external and internal forces that threaten to create tension that will permanently destroy the equilibrium necessary for organizational survival. For Selznick, as for Weber, organizations are seen in the formal sense, but for Selznick, they are additionally seen as adaptive and as schemes. "Schemes" refer here to the notion that an organizational view is always *someone's view.* Selznick locates the source of this scheme in the managerial echelon. It is seen by Selznick as a practical theory in use by managers in their interpretation of the course of organizational events.

Informal or irrational forces in the organization are those that are not included in the managerial view but nonetheless must be dealt with in some day-to-day coping or managing basis; the tension between the ideal and the actual requires somebody's (usually the manager's) constant attention if the organization is to survive.

Organizational socialization is not solely a structural problem. Organizational maps should be distinguished from actual, typical, or "normatively organized" behavior. Some sociologists have concerned themselves with "actors' theories" or perspectives that are rooted in the experience of lower participants rather than in the experience of managers. For example, there are the works of Becker et al (1961), Goffman (1961a), Roth (1963), and others of the "Chicago school." These works suggest that by taking the perspective of the lower participants within an organization one attends to other nonmanagerial practical theories, in this case the problems of work arising out of viewing organizational contingencies through the "worker's eyes."[4]

Bittner argues that the literal meanings of any scheme cannot be attained in practice. Even if schemes for making action social and meaningful are located in the social structure (as Mannheim urged) and assuming that actors are implicated in the scheme (cast by the sociologist in orderly interaction), to ask these actors to act in accord with the lexical meanings of social rules is to ask much of them. Not only are they asked to understand, define, clarify, choose among, compare, and contrast rules, they are asked to understand them as the sociologist would or does (Garfinkel, 1967: Chapter 8).

The actor's operations in concert with the scheme are described as if they met the requirements of rationality without a discussion of rationality itself as a problematic attainment of the theorist and the actor (Garfinkel, 1967:Chapter 8). Instead of giving attention to the requirements of actors in social life that make "rationality" manifest, the sociologist makes use of a scheme that seizes upon actions that are taken as pointing to rational grounds for action, choice, or commitment. That is, sociologists use the scheme to organize actors' behavior within an organization rather than ask how actors defer to, manage, reject, or apply a symbolic framework to the objects that make up their daily environments.

Rules, the central source of order in organizations according to organizational theorists, are not, indeed cannot be, understood in their literal form. General rules, such as laws pertaining to juveniles that are the ostensive basis for assigning cases to the delinquent or nondelinquent category, are applied to specific cases by juvenile officers, judges, etc., *on the grounds of their situated activity.* In one public defender's office, Sudnow described how cases of child molesting or burglary were assigned to legal categories on the basis of a conception held by the organization's members of what constituted a "normal crime" (Sudnow, 1965). Thus, although general rules may be invoked to explain the assignation of a case, close attention to the working of an organization will reveal devices used to match general rules with specific instances. In effect then, the meaning of the rules resides in the practical procedures by which they are administered (Sudnow, 1967). Rules within organizations, like grammatical rules and rules of logic, take on an indexical quality, that is, they can be understood only contextually, as practical problems that themselves arise out of the association of those people, facing those problems, in those periods of time (Garfinkel, 1967:Chapter 1;Bar-Hillel, 1954).[5]

It is just these contingencies of rule applications that are for members fundamental, normal, taken for granted, and that have been bypassed by theorists constructing organized life from without. Selznick and Weber, as well as many others, draw upon the contextual resources actors have generated *in situ* in order to proceed to their describing and accounting work. Bittner (1965:244–255) has succinctly summarized criticism of this sort.

When one lifts the mantle of protection from the unstated presupposition surrounding the terms of Weber's theory of bureaucracy, one is confronted with facts of a particular sort. These facts are not sociological data, or even theoretically defensible hypotheses. Instead, one is confronted with the rich and ambiguous body of background information that normally competent members of a society take for granted as commonly known. In its normal functioning this information furnishes the tacit foundation for all that is explicitly known and provides the matrix for all deliberate considerations without being itself deliberately considered. While its content can be raised to the level of analysis, this typically does not occur. Rather, the information enters into that commonplace and practical orientation to reality which members in society regard as 'natural' when attending to their daily affairs. Since the explicit terms of the theory are embedded in this common-sense orientation, they cannot be understood without tacit reference to it. If, however, the theorist must be persuaded about the meaning of the terms in some prior and unexplicated way, then there exists collusion between him and those about whom he theorizes. We call this unexplicated understanding collusive because it is a hidden resource, the use of which cannot be controlled adequately.

These sociologists' views of action contain what Bittner usefully calls a "short-circuiting of social theory." Although he views action from the point of view of the actor, Weber fails to recognize and explicate the underlying common-sense presuppositions of his own theory. That is, he assumes what actors have to create as an everyday task: social order. Or, to formulate the critique in another fashion: theoretical statements are made about X (organizational behavior) at the same time that knowledge of X (how people behave in organizations) is taken as proof that the theoretical statements made about X are adequate. The concept short-circuits theory by building upon what organizationally situated actors assume when they use the concept. To understand what rationality means, one must understand what is taken for granted within organizations in which rationality is said to be found.

To understand organizational behavior, and in this case organizational socialization, one must deal with the relativity of models for making behavior social. Bittner, following Kenneth Burke (1965), suggests some exaggerations (meta-schemes) by which organizations can be studied which are informed by the presumptive mistakes of Weber and his interpreters.

1. The sociologist can proceed to investigate formal organizations assuming that the unexplicated common-sense meanings of the terms used are adequate definitions for the purposes of his investigations. In this case, he uses what he proposes to study as a resource for the study.

2. The sociologist can tag terms with a more or less arbitrary meaning by defining them operationally, what Torgerson (1958) aptly calls measurement by *fiat*. In this case the relationships between the object observed and the terms used to describe it are defined by the procedures used. Interest in the actor's perspective is

either abandoned, or some handy version of it is adopted.

3. The sociologist can decide that the meaning of a concept and all the terms and determinations that are subsumed under it must be discovered by studying their use in action by persons who are socially sanctioned as competent to use them. (Listing paraphrased from Bittner, 1965.)

We propose that the construction of organized social action remain in the hands of the actor, while the sociologist seeks to report the way in which the actor manages the problems that face him in organizations. How he manages them is seen in the *devices* he uses to make them consistent, repetitive, normal, and natural. By means of his linguistic behaviors the actor selects things which through naming become social objects. That is, they have a potential for action when they are named, counted, assessed, and ordered. The fashioning of order takes place as objects at hand become named as part, in the context of, or standing for, order. The *primary rule for the study of organizations from a phenomenological point of view is that one must study the ways in which terms of discourse are assigned to real objects and events by normally competent persons in ordinary situations* (Bittner, 1965). Garfinkel, and others, suggest the title "ethnomethodology" for this study of stable procedures by which actors relate common-sense constraints to objects in the world. Ethnomethodologists insist that substituting schemes that point out objects as if they had a constitutive meaning is not preferred to studying the ways in which objects come under the control of various schemes.

A study of an organization must then begin with the study of its use by actors. Becoming a socially sanctioned member of an organization, by implication, involves displaying, adhering to, and being sanctioned for use of an ordering scheme or subschemes.

We will assume that this information can be obtained by close attention to the linguistic devices employed by members to discuss their problems. We will also assume that attention should be paid to the setting in which these devices are called upon and to the rules that govern their use. Organization being partially accounted for, our attention shifts to roles, conventionally assumed to be things that must be learned.

Roles and Role Learning

One "traditional" view of role, usually associated with Linton and Parsons, begins with role as a given in a system of social relationships. The aim is typically to proceed to the task of understanding human action by making the assumption that people are people-in-roles. Goffman (1961b) perceptively argues that this formulation, although there is a "dynamic dimension" (role in contrast to status), is based upon an "as if" assumption. Actors' performances are seen as behaviors they would engage in if they were to act solely with reference to the normative demands made of persons occupying their positions in a social system. *Position* is taken to explain behavior, other things being equal. Offenbacher (1967) labels this assumption a " 'black box' type of causal explanation" in which abstractions, that is, rights and duties, are fed at one end only to come out the other end as observed behaviors. Variations from the as if assumption are accounted for with reference to normatively induced strains, stresses, or role conflicts. Abstracted to this level, as Goffman shows: (1) Sociologists are in danger of taking the normatively structured expectations of an abstractly created social system as the reality of human behavior. (2) They may assume that the knowledge about a category (doctor, lawyer, sociologist, or any other structural profile with its attributes) informs us of the nature of interaction in which members of that category engage (Goffman, 1961b).

This traditional conceptualization, in spite of the ostensive actor-relevant nature of it, suffers additionally from short-circuiting. Briefly, as sketched above, short-circuiting takes place whenever an object is described without a separation being made between the description of the action by those implicated in the action and those describing it as a practical, professional task (Bittner, 1965; Sacks, 1963).

This use of "role" draws upon actors' common-sense knowledge as both an object and a resource. To some it appears as a reasonable way to proceed. Many articles are scattered with references that are the scholarly equivalent to "you know what I mean when I say that." A recent monograph on role contains a statement of these assumptions that dismisses them as relatively unimportant problems.

If one were simply to array all the terms introduced into the literature of role theory, one would confront a sizable glossary of overlapping, vague and imprecise terms. Nevertheless, we have assumed that the central terms of role theory are sufficiently known and communicable among social scientists to overcome whatever obscurities their usage in this report may contain. . . . The priority which ought to be assigned to terminological affairs is contingent upon the stage of theory at which one begins to operate. At this stage in the development of role theory we see this as a low-priority

item. We could through rather simple linguistic conventions establish a delimited set of meanings to such central concepts as role,
status, expectations, visibility, power, etc. But such a set of definitions independent of a well-delineated theoretical scheme, would
shed little light on the crucial problem of the relationships among
the constituent terms (Preiss and Ehrlich, 1966: 163-164).

One paragraph later, however, it states:

From an operational standpoint, establishing hard criteria for the
identification of a role is perhaps the most elusive problem of role
theory. If we were to exhibit a series of behavior episodes before
a group of sociologists and social psychologists, we could probably
get rather high agreement in their selection of those episodes which
constituted role behavior. But if we asked them to specify the criteria
by which they selected some behaviors and excluded others, we
would probably discover that their decisions were more intuitive
than specifiable, and that they could achieve little common agreement on criteria. At this level most role theorists have converged,
regardless of orientation (Preiss and Ehrlich, 1966:164).

A set of analytic definitions suggested by Preiss and Ehrlich without
specified relationships between constituent terms would be relatively un-
dramatic, yet we do not have even that. This lexicon might establish the
sociologists' practical usage of the concept "role" as an organizing
scheme.[6] It might begin to clarify the meanings of "central terms of role
theory [that] are sufficiently known and communicable among social scientists to overcome whatever obscurities their usage . . . may contain." It
would move toward clarification of presumptive sociological schemes as
symbolic frameworks. The relationships between these schemes (of whatever clarity and logical precision) and the behavior to which they are
directed as explication is left in the mores of the profession. That it is a
matter of the mores, things assumed but not explained, is perhaps suggested by the statement above that competent observers deal with the
relationship between role as a concept and role behavior in an intuitive
fashion. The concept is in effect left to spin in the rich vortex of what
sociologists assume about what their work points to, stands for, or is a case
of.[7]

The study of organizational socialization calls for a modified conception of role that will remain with the actor, avoid measurement by fiat

(operationalism), and extricate the concept from some sociological mores. The study of role learning, that is, the use of the concept role to bring order into one's behavior, is based upon a setting (organization) that provides the context within which roles are assembled, maintained, or dissembled. The priority list for the sociologists with these aims is headed by the demand for a lexicon of indexical statements (statements that require a social context to provide their meaning) by which actors refer to their behaviors and attitudes. A lexicon of concepts and usages should then be followed with statements of the order of: Given the linguistic tags and descriptions of behavior, what are the situational, objective, and phenomenological factors that make such behavior meaningful and possible?

Social roles can be considered linguistically as situated vocabularies or rhetorics. As Mills (in Manis and Meltzer, 1967) writes, "Motives may be considered as typical vocabularies having ascertainable functions in delimited social situations." They are a shorthand means for the imputation of reasons for conduct. Lofland (1967:9–10) tenders a description of role as a linguistic device. Role can be used in

> designating the set of all those linguistic terms which themselves designate patterns of individual activity or physical characteristics, on the basis of which actors centrally organize the manner in which they organize their own action toward one another . . . Roles are *claimed* labels, from behind which people present themselves to others and partially in terms of which they conceive, gauge, and judge their past, current and projected action. And roles are *imputed* labels toward which and partially in terms of which, people likewise conceive, gauge and judge others' past, present and projected action.

A difficulty arising in this definition is that the lexicon of role terms and role imputations that might be built up following Lofland's suggestions would have varying degrees of applicability to the behaviors prescribed to them by actors.[8]

Further, the extent to which the terms themselves could be seen to refer to unseen meanings embedded in a cultural matrix is problematic. The classical works of this sort, begun by Goffman in his dissertation (1953), tend to break down at the point where interactional forms (ploys, collusions, teamwork, etc.) reference a host of meanings that can be understood only by understanding what is at stake or what is being managed.

In other words, the common-sense features of Anglo-American life, which Goffman admits are a resource in his writings, "fill in" for the reader as he goes along. It may be that the study Goffman made was as successful as it was because he understood the routine bases of action, had the ability to take them as normal and natural and mutually acceptable, and was able to furnish his own credentials as competent in this understanding. These resources allowed him to see through, and see the interactional forms as standing for, other intentions of actors' uses.[9]

We can perhaps bypass the problems we have suggested by making some further distinctions. We have introduced the indexical properties of role terms, noting that their situational properties, and suggesting that the common-sense base of the organization embeds role terms and role imputations. Furthermore, the process of role imputation, role naming, and role behavior has a common, repetitive, and expected quality. We can assume that the repetitive nature of situated social action leads to typification. Actors derive and use typifications of others' behaviors and motives. In the process they not only organize others' behaviors, they derive meaningful assessments of their own actions. Schutz (1962:60) describes the process.

> The world of everyday life is from the outset also a social and cultural world in which I am interrelated in manifold ways of interaction with fellow-men known to me in varying degrees of intimacy and anonymity. . . . Yet only on particular situations, and then only fragmentarily, can I experience the other's motives, goals, etc.— briefly, the subjective meanings they bestow upon their actions, in their uniqueness. I can, however, experience them in their typicality. In order to do so, I construct typical patterns of the actors' motives and ends, even of their attitudes and personalities, of which their actual conduct is just an instance or example. These typified patterns of others' behavior become, in turn, motives for my own action, and this leads to the phenomenon of self-typification.

We are led then to understand socialization by attention to the linguistic use of terms referring to organization, organizational life, and to role terms and imputations. The latter, we have suggested, take their meanings from the organizational context in which they have currency. That is, actors order their expectations in settings with reference to vocabularies (especially those referring to typical cases, typical roles, and typical organizational phenomenon, which are themselves features of the settings in which they are found). They cannot be seen simply in the relationship of sign to referent; but as expressions that are known by the style with which they are uttered (ironically, metaphorically, analogically, poetically, prosaically, etc.) (Garfinkel, 1967:31; Garfinkel and Sacks in McKinney and Tiryakian, 1970).

Organizations as Socializing Settings

We have suggested above in our discussions of role and organization that if we could describe and account for socialization as easily as Parsons (1951:205) does ("[Socialization is] the acquisition of the requisite orientations for satisfactory functioning in a role"), there would be no need for concern with either organizational structure or role learning, other than specifying the character of each. That is, specifying the character of role and structure and noting their equivalence. The second step would be to simply classify for the purposes at hand all those actors who were adequate or inadequate for the role-statuses outlined. However, features of organizational settings are not exhausted by structural characteristics. To ascribe to this view is analogous to believing that language behavior can be understood by a close study of a dictionary.[10]

Features of organized settings, on the contrary, can never be fully exhausted, because they have a reflexive quality. They are described by competent actors with language terms, nonverbal cues, and behaviors that themselves constitute part of the setting. Words themselves have an indexical quality by virtue of their use within a given setting. The qualities of organized and organizational life most at issues are those that are not raised to the conscious level, are assumed, are resources for managing and aligning action, are reciprocal among actors involved, are characteristic and natural, and are not exhausted by talking about them. In short, they are the *common-sense grounds of organizational life.*[11]

Characteristics of these grounds have been discussed by Schutz, Garfinkel, and others. An enumeration of them is but a passing bow in the direction of an enormous, yet unfinished, task. (1) These grounds have the character of reciprocity in that A assumes that B assumes things as he (A) does; that, given a change in position, B would assume that A assumes things as he does, and that the consequence of this would be ordered interaction. (2) They have the character of taking shape from the course of their own development. Things are seen as taking place within a context that orders both "things to come" and things that have passed but takes its own sense from a redefinition of both past and future as the " present" unfolds. A "film of continuity" binds together conversationalists so that "wait and see," "I thought so," and "you didn't mean that" can be employed to discount certain phrases and meanings while waiting for the "real" meaning to "come clear." Events are taken as pointing to the norms in the situation. Yet, these same events cannot be unequivocally assigned that status by nonmembers. (3) An *et cetera* quality resides in conversational flow. "You know what I mean" is not only a conversational device, it is taken as being literally, for the purposes at hand, true. (4) Normal forms of conversation are employed. That is, if mistakes, misunderstandings, embarrassments, and unclarities in conversation emerge (the features enumerated above vanish or are made to vanish), means for restoration are always present. Goffman (1956a, 1956b, 1957, 1961b) has suggested the existence of these aspects of orderly interaction. (5) Talk in settings is reflexive. "Organizational talk" is talk that is both a feature of the setting and itself descriptive of the setting. Conversation, for example, is a normal part of most work settings.[12] (6) Vocabularies present in a setting are made up of lists of actors' vocabularies. Cicourel uses Garfinkel's example of a library catalog, in which the titles used to index the books are a part of the things described (Books' titles). The role types described in prison research not only organize (presumably) the behavior there, their existence in use is a part of the necessary description of the prison itself (Sykes, 1956). Roles are to be found embedded in the language actors normally use to talk about them. A socialization language for a setting would include the language used to talk about actors' roles, vocabularies, normal usage, etc., as a sign of competence.

Organizations have these features in common, but vary in substance. This is a substance that is practically characteristic (that is, it makes a difference for the things that are done within the organization). Implicit is that these grounds are the fundamental basis for an orderly life. They cannot be bypassed by the new men, the recruits, because not only are they the basis for life within, they provide grounds for interpretation of the meaning of their behavior.

Susanne Langer (1951:238–239) provides a clear statement of the nature of the assumed taken-for-granted features of life which are problematic to the "newcomer."

> Yet, all these signs and abbreviated symbols have to be supported by a vast intellectual structure in order to function so smoothly that we are almost unaware of them; and this structure is composed of their full articulate forms and all their implicit relationships which may be exhumed from our stock of buried knowledge at any time. Because they do fit so neatly into the frame of our ultimate world picture we can think *with* them and do not have to think *about* them, but our full apprehension about them is really only suppressed.

> They wear a 'cap of invisibility' when, like good servants, they
> perform their tasks for our convenience without being *evident* in
> themselves. Though we ordinarily only see things with the economy
> of practical vision, we can look at them instead of through them, and
> then their suppressed forms and their unusual meanings emerge for
> us. It is just because there is a front of possible meanings in every
> familiar form, that the picture of reality holds together for us.

This is a well-stated description of the nature of common-sense knowledge: it is that type of experience taken for granted upon which significa-
tion, marking, indexing, and symbolization are based. It is an organization
of finite meanings. Strangers or new members of an organization are both
a part and not a part of the organization. They act within the limits of the
system but do not share the common-sense knowledge current among the
other members.

How sociologists make these grounds visible to themselves and others
should follow "actors' rules" for doing the same thing. How is it that this
task can be approached? The final section, prior to a methodological note,
addresses itself to the problem of discovering actors' rules as a means to
study organizational socialization.

Talking and Becoming

The gathering of an actors' dictionary or oral lexicon is a generally followed practice among anthropological fieldworkers, but in most cases the
"deep rules," which allow the linking of the lexicon with the flow of
conversation, which underlie continuity and provide clues to others' response, and which allow actors to talk about things not present in the
setting, remain as things known to anyone in the society (and perhaps also
to the fieldworker himself). The categories chosen, why they were chosen,
the sense of closure when words do not provide it, and the use of terms
that are normal to the setting, that is, uses of and referrals to role, all
provide a context within which the norms (or known standards of behavior)
take on significance. Explaining behavior in any organization without reference to the common-sense grounds by which it takes its form is analogous to analyzing a college student's choice of courses and curriculum by
means of the college catalog alone.

We have suggested that the ability of speakers and hearers to make
sense of conversation—when it is truncated, when "words fail," or when
people speak ironically (it isn't really this way, but I am telling you in this
way in order to impart some sense of what my tale means to me), or by

glossing (hitting the high spots, but you can fill in the rest), by synedoche (using a part to stand for the whole, or vice-versa), or by analogy (something else)—has reference to a source that clarifies the course of events. This source, however, is not equally distributed: sediments of experience in the organization, biographically accumulated knowledge, and situational constraints (can't say what I mean here because of the audience) introduce barriers to socialized, fully acceptable conversational understandings and, hence, to role imputations, typifications, normal events, and the rest. It is not enough to learn the language, as some fieldworkers have suggested (for example, in studies of the poolroom hustler, prisons, drug addicts, etc.), without attention to the rules that make adequate use of it possible. One of the standard suggestions for fieldwork is attention to the oral lexicon and its use, but it may be the very attention to the oral lexicon that allows the listener to absorb the means by which it is used. Some of the very contingencies in understanding (socialization) have been used, inadvertently, by workers to construct prospective schemes of the process. It is assumed by some that the operations by which conversations are maintained of their course—the et cetera clauses, the reflexive nature of talk, the wait and see nature of it—are available to all. In fact, the competent use of such devices is an index of the extent to which one can be considered a competent user, a member of the organization.

Although the ideal study of socialization (organizationally or otherwise) might seek general rules for the implementation of alternative usages, phrases, clauses, bits, or ways of talking, it is more likely initially that a denotative listing (glossary) is needed. Other studies provide some already assembled data on language. For example, Sykes's study of the New Jersey State Prison contains some important descriptions of what he calls argot roles or "a number of distinctive tags for distinctive social roles played by its members in response to the particular problems of imprisonment. It is these patterns of behavior, recognized and labelled by the inmates of the prison, which we have chosen to call argot roles" (Sykes, 1956:86). It is not clear whether these are role terms (self-designations) or role imputations (other designations), or an inductive analysis of the sociologist. There is no mention of the adequate use of these terms in the prison, nor of the relationships between situated usage and rules for their use in the organization. Although this could be done retrospectively, it would only be by way of a hypothesis that would require further information. Glossaries begin the task.

If there is an adequate and competent use of language in accord with some set of actors' rules, then there are logically cases of "inadequate use." Cicourel's recent work on socialization of children suggests a method developed by Harvey Sacks (1966). The term *contrastive analysis* is used to describe the technique. They suggest that, as before, the investigator utilize his own knowledge of the rules implicit in conversational episodes to make those rules explicit. A *device,* or term having two or more categories (e.g., "illness" can be categorized as "physical" or "mental" in our society), can be used to refer to a population of objects ("patients"). Devices and categories to which they are linked are repeatedly used in a given setting, and are therefore characteristic of that setting. Role, for example, can be used as a device to which categories known within the organization can be referred and can be seen to operate systematically. That is, actors' rules for the assigning of categories to a device are implicit in conversation and writing and can be developed inductively from the study of conversations.[13] Rules are seen to reside in the fact that members are able to describe and make accounts of settings by means of devices to which categories can be referred. Rules are the recognition among members that a device and a category cluster together in some fashion. The way in which the device and the category are linked is itself a source of a rich catalog. Rules, it would seem, refer to the ways in which markings, signifying, indexing, symbolizing, and so on take place.[14] In medical settings, the device "patient" is used to refer categories such as "crock," "alcoholic," and "malingerer," to certain populations encountered there. The grounds or basis of this referral relationship could be found by investigating the symptoms used to make the transition between categories and the device to which they refer. Sacks offers another example of the use of a device, sex, which can be paired with the two categories male and female.

These categories are recognized by actors as going together, but the difficulty in such a task appears in the construction of these relationships, since the investigator relies in large part on his own common-sense knowledge of the way actors do describing to make his own analysis. The way in which contrastive analysis is done is by building up sets of rules by which these pairings are made, such as the "consistency rule." The consistency rule reads: if a population is associated with a category and that category is referred to a device, then other members of the population can be classified as well by the use of that category or another. Other rules and their titles seem to be interminable, but the inductive nature of the work makes the building of categories and devices into rules an interesting pursuit. Uses of categories that are not linked in the same way to devices (referring "crock" to the device "pottery" rather than to "patient" would contrast with the setting— specific association of crock with patient, for example). Categories in sentences have a continuity that is part of what users rely upon; contravention of these conventions leads to confusion, clarification, etc. The assumption that everyone knows the referent of certain categories and the means by which they are linked to population, is the basis for normal use and, by contrast, abnormal use. Both the hearer and the listener are able to put together conversations by means of these induced rules of conversation.[15]

We can now return to the problem of indexical expressions. The discovery of meanings rooted in an organizational context and their connection with rules of use can be derived from glossaries associated with the competent use of words in the organization. The use of the category "headache," "broken leg," or "sore throat" may or may not be linked to the device "emergency," but understanding of the knowledge that makes this linkage possible is a sign of knowledge of what members of the emergency-room population mean when they utilize the category to refer to a person. The meanings that arise and have persistence in any organization have certain "unique" qualities, and these unique and practical matters give the organization the features that new people must become aware of. (But see footnote 8 above concerning the generality of the findings of this sort of work.)

In a sense, effective contrastive analysis requires ethnographic studies. Some of the recent work of Sudnow (1967) and Cavan (1965), as well as Garfinkel, make important use of concepts such as "standing patterns of behavior," "conventional usage," "normal troubles," and the like to describe the workings of particular organizations or types of organizations. (The use of types is itself a phenomenological question and probably both follows and accompanies the gathering of ethnographics.)

The context is in part described by the language used within it. It provides the special meanings that allow the linkage of device and category that is shared by hearer, speaker, and researcher. The researcher's job lies ahead: generating listings or oral lexicons, linking conditions for device, category, and population, and building rules of their use. Presumably this involves gathering information on the conditions under which rules obtain or fail to obtain. Rules should clarify discovered differences in usage among the "new" and "old" members of a group. Cicourel has adopted the use of contrastive analysis to create a developmental model of children's socialization. Contrastive analysis might be utilized also to study how rules develop over a time and how they are maintained as features of the setting over turnovers and change in population. It is the learning of these "members' rules" for the use of language that is the basis for becoming a member of the group. Talking is becoming.

A Recourse, a Method

Socialization again appears, unsolved, as a process in everyday life. Some of the things it is not, and how one should not study it, have been briefly indicated; some of the things it is sociologically have also been suggested. The process involves taking as apparent the matters in daily life that are not apparent; it associates actors with the use of schemes, terms (roles), linguistic labels, and lexicons; it facilitates an indexical understanding of this lexicon, in part by typification and normal usage.

Yet, the learning or acquisition of operative knowledge takes place, by actors' admissions, in the context of generated meanings. These are the objective or limiting factors within which the common-sense base flourishes. An organizational language will contain the information necessary for dealing with the problems of the organization. As these are faced, role terms, role imputations, and typifications arise and have with them sets of acceptable referents. A scheme accounting for the growth of argot roles within a prison could be constructed, but so far we have but the lexicon, not the basis for use (by whom and with what referent in accord with what rules of use).

Acquisition of the common-sense or routine grounds of organizational life is fundamental to the acquisition of the oral lexicon and the surface rules (norms of use, grammar, and syntax) for its use.[16] The base supplies a context in which the vocabularies typical to the organization are embedded. Culture "operates" in an unseen way, and making it seen is a practice of lay as well as professional recorders of social life.

Let us assume that we wish to examine organizations socially and sociologically. Let us assume that we wish to make it a process that is practical and useful. "Useful" here refers to sociologically useful in the sense of continued reference and cumulative possibilities.

The following are some programmatic suggestions:

1. Learning the natural language of the organization. This would involve fieldwork of a classical anthropological sort based on gathering an oral lexicon or glossary (a listing of words used in the context and with what referent).

    a. Paying special attention to those terms used to designate terms referring to roles
    b. Listing of the devices and categories and the rules for their use in the setting.

2. Developing a language, or a *metalanguage,* that would enable the researcher to talk about the language actors use to talk about their roles and the appropriate rules for its use within the setting.

3. Schematically attending to the naming function of members of the organization insofar as this power to order by naming is differentially distributed. In this sense, there is a parallel between studying adults' use of words and the way in which they interpret the meaning of children's use. The power to pass on to subordinates a set of meanings is critical; the way in which this process comes about is a phenomenological question.

4. Doing ethnographic studies of the organization in which socialization is to be studied. That is, how do actors describe to each other the scenes in which they find themselves; what are the ways they use to refer to their own actions and those of others; how are the problems they face of a daily nature handled and managed as a part of the life they lead in the organization?

Footnotes

[1] Vollmer (1967) uses the concept of organization socialization, but provides no definition of it in the paper. My original conceptualization was made in 1965, and there is little overlap in our foci or method.

[2] A distinction is often made between organizations whose stated goals are socialization for future social roles, those whose stated goals are resocialization, and those whose major interest is in some other output. The focus here is a generic one which seeks to explore organizational socialization in the context of any organization. It assumes that none of the stated goals of organizations can be achieved without actors' management of the practical problems of organizational life. It is likely that if one could analytically separate the *generic* from the organizationally *specific* one would find that the two "processes" are somehow simultaneous, and that adequate accounting for an actor or for one's self means "skill" in both dimensions.

[3] The following discussion is based on Bittner (1965).

[4] See detailed ethnographies of Donald Roy (1953, 1954, 1959-1960).

[5] It is misleading to assume that the situationally based qualities of meanings of organizational procedures or rules do not have systemic or generalizable features. Investigation of a single setting, or culture, or type of organization is an attempt to reveal features of the organization that are likely to occur in many

settings. Sudnow's (1967) study of death was an attempt not solely to understand "death work" within the hospital studied but to understand "Death and Dying as Social States of Affairs" (Chapter 4). Our basic assumption is that there is a taken-for-granted basis for everyday life that undergirds all attempts to constrain objects either coming under its jurisdiction or departing from it, and that this is a universal feature in most cultures. Therefore, the manifestation of operations by which this process takes place are taken as indices both of the common-sense realities of organizational life and of the universality of practices by which people handle their everyday organizational affairs.

[6] Suggested here is a "workers' dictionary," which would include definitions of the sociological use of role, examples of its use, mode of "testing," and an assessment of the utility of the concept. The Biddle and Thomas (1966) reader attempts this. The task suggested for consideration at the conclusion of this paper is an "actor's guide to the use of everyday role-terms," which would contain the practical use of words referring to role-oriented action within a given organization. If done completely, this would become an organizational or cultural ethnography. See Ladd (1957).

[7] One of the finest statements of the importance of distinguishing between the *cultural subject* (the object to be investigated, in this case role) and the *empirical categories* created by investigators is supplied by Karl Mannheim (in Kecskemeti, 1952:60). Accordingly, one would commit the gravest methodological error if one simply equated this cultural subject (which has been defined merely as a counterpart to an objective cultural generalization) with empirical collective subjects defined on the basis of anthropological categories, such as race or class. And for this reason no documentary interpretation of the kind we have in mind can be demolished by proving that the author of a work belongs by descent or in terms of status to a 'race' or 'class' other than the one whose 'spirit' was said to be exemplified by the work. Our formulation shows that we do not object to the investigation of race as a problem of cultural history, or of 'class' as a problem of cultural sociology; surely both topics designate problems which deserve to be solved; all we wanted to do was to point out certain methodological implications which apply to these lines of research. Inquiries of this sort employ two sets of concepts which the investigator must rigorously keep apart; on the one hand, a collective subject will be characterized in terms relating to the documentary interpretation of a cultural product, and on the other, we shall obtain collective subjects of a different sort by using the categories of sciences like anthropology or sociology which form their concepts in an altogether different fashion. (The concept of class, for instance, is defined in terms of an individual's role in this economic process of production, and that of race, in terms of purely biological relationships.) Between these two kinds of subject—the subject of collective spirit, derived from the interpretation of cultural objectifications, and the anthropological or sociological subject—the discrepancy due to their heterogeneous origin is so great that it seems absolutely imperative to

interpolate an intermediate field of concepts capable of mediating between these two extremes.

8 For example, roles delineated by respondents in cross-cultural research may have similarity to role concepts in American society but may refer to entirely different activities. The vocabulary of a social group may reference a set of possible behaviors, altered as the group-life situation of the users changes. A study of collegiate subculture or of urban blacks would probably reveal not only a set of new terms but a set of new behaviors associated with the old terms, e.g., "hip" is now applied to a group in a modified form, "hippies," and connotes retreatism, drug use, hedonism, and a quasiidealism. The root term derives from opium users who lay on their hips: hence, to be on the hip. In the late forties, jazz musicians used it to refer to someone who was sensitive to the latest things and knowledgeable. "Hippies" now has a pejorative connotation, and was in all probability generated from without and refers to behaviors having nothing to do with music, knowledge, or sensitivity per se (See Polsky, 1967:Chapter 4). The occupational studies done in Chicago in the twenties might be reinterpreted now within a framework that attends to change in the referent of role terms as well as changes in the terms themselves.

9 I would like to thank Paul Ray for suggesting several of the points in this and the two preceding paragraphs.

10 Some modern sociology seems to me to be analogous to the Galenic theory of medicine. It was only after actual autopsies began to be done in medicine that it became clear that Galenic theories could not be proven when actual body tissues were examined. In the same way, "structural sociology" has persisted in spite of its obvious glossing of social behavior.

11 This paragraph is based on Chapter 2 in Garfinkel's *Studies in Ethnomethodology* (1967), and additionally draws on Cicourel's work on acquisition of social structure.

12 Sociologists' practical work often attends to these features of the work setting, e.g., see the study by Miller and Form (1964:229–231) in which they divide conversations into "sociotechnical" and "social," an example of acceptance of a managerial symbolic framework into which talk is sorted.

13 Further examples of this linguistic analysis are found in the writings of Sacks (mimeo, no date) and of Schegloff (1968).

14 See Cicourel's (1964:212–215) discussion of these processes.

15 The preceding paragraphs are based upon Cicourel's description of Sacks's (in Garfinkel and Sacks', forthcoming) technique.

16 Cicourel has suggested this distinction between "deep rules," which we have

called common-sense or routine grounds of organizational life, and "surface rules," referring to specific norms of use; that is, grammar and syntax. A parallel distinction in regard to rules is found in Rawls (1955).

REFERENCES

BAR-HILLEL, YEHOSHUA
1954   "Indexical expressions."*Mind* 63: 359–379.

BECKER, HOWARD S., BLANCHE GEER, EVERETT HUGHES, AND ANSELM STRAUSS
1961   *Boys in White: Student Culture in a Medical School.* Chicago: University of Chicago Press.

BIDDLE, B.J., AND E. THOMAS, (EDS.)
1966   *Role Theory.* New York: Wiley and Sons.

BITTNER, EGON
1965   "The concept of organization." *Social Research* 32: 230–255.

BRIM, O., AND S. WHEELER
1966   *Socialization After Childhood.* New York: John Wiley and Sons.

BURKE, KENNETH
1965   *Permanence and Change.* 2nd edition, Indianapolis: Bobbs-Merrill.

CAVAN, SHERI
1965   *Liquor License.* Chicago: Aldine.

CICOUREL, AARON V.
1964   *Method and Measurement in Sociology.* New York: The Free Press.

GARFINKEL, HAROLD
1967   *Studies in Ethnomethodology.* Englewood Cliffs, N.J.: Prentice-Hall.

GARFINKEL, HAROLD, AND HARVEY SACKS, EDS.
forthcoming *Contributions to Ethnomethodology*. Bloomington: University of Indianna Press.

GOFFMAN, ERVING
1953   "Communication and conduct in an island community." Unpublished doctoral dissertation. University of Chicago.
1956a   "Embarassment and social organization." *American Journal of Sociology* 62: 264–271.
1956b   "The nature of deference and demeanor." *American Anthropologist* 58 (June): 473–502.
1957   "Alientation from interaction." *Human Relations* 10: 47–60
1961a   *Asylums*. Garden City: Doubleday-Anchor.
1961b   *Encounters*. Indianapolis: Bobbs-Merrill.

KECSKEMETI, PAUL, ED.
1952   *Essays in the Sociology of Knowledge*. New York: Oxford University Press.

LADD, JOHN
1957   *The Structure of a Moral Code*. Cambridge: Harvard University Press.

LANGER, SUSANNE
1951   *Philosophy in a New Key*. 2nd edition. New York: New American Library.

LOFLAND, JOHN
1967   "Role management: a programmatic statement." Mimeographed paper No. 30 of the Center For Research in Social Organization, University of Michigan.

MCKINNEY, JOHN C., AND EDWARD TIRYAKIAN, EDS.
1970   *Theoretical Sociology: Perspectives and Developments*. New York: Appleton-Century-Crofts.

MANIS, JEROME, AND BERNARD MELTZER, EDS.
1967   *Symbolic Interaction: A Reader in Social Psychology*. Boston: Allyn and Bacon.

MILLER, D., AND W. H. FORM
1964   *Industrial Sociology.* 2nd edition. New York: Harper.

OFFENBACHER, D.
1967   "Roles, norms and typifications in contemporary American society." Unpublished paper presented at the Annual Meeting of the American Sociological Association, San Francisco.

PARK, R. E., AND E.W. BURGESS
1924   *An Introduction to Sociology,* 2nd edition. Chicago: University of Chicago Press.

PARSONS, TALCOTT
1951   *The Social System.* New York: Free Press.

POLSKY, NORMAN
1967   *Hustlers, Beats and Others.* Chicago: Aldine.

PREISS, J., AND H. EHRLICH
1966   *An Examination of Role Theory.* Lincoln: University of Nebraska Press.

RAWLS, J.
1955   "Two concepts of rules." *Philosophical Review* 64:3–32.

ROTH, JULIUS
1963   *Timetables.* Indianapolis: Bobbs-Merrill.

ROY, DONALD F.
1953   "Work satisfaction and social reward in quota achievements." *American Sociological Review* 18:507–514.
1954   "Efficiency and 'the Fix': Informal intergroup relations in a piecework machine shop." *American Journal of Sociology* 60 (November): 255–266.
1959–1960 "Banana time—job satisfaction and informal interaction." *Human Organization* 18 (Winter): 158–168.

SACKS, HARVEY
1963   "Sociological secription." *Berkeley Journal of Sociology* 8:1–16

1966   "The search for help: No one to turn to." Unpublished doctoral dissertation. University of California at Berkeley.
n.d.   "An introduction to the study of conversation" First draft of an unpublished mimeographed paper.

SCHLEGLOFF, EMANUEL A.
1968   "Sequencing in conversational openings." *American Anthropologist* 70 (December): 1075-1095.

SCHUTZ, ALFRED J.
1962   *Collected Papers I: The Problem of Social Reality.* Edited by Maurice Natanson. The Hague: Martinus Nijhoff.

SELZNICK, PHILLIP
1966   *TVA and the Grass Roots.* (originally published in 1949). New York: Harper Torchbooks.

SUDNOW, DAVID
1965   "Normal crimes: Sociological features of the penal code in a public defender's office." *Social Problems* 12 (Winter): 255-272.
1967   *Passing On: The Social Organization of Dying.* Englewood Cliffs, N.J.: Prentice-Hall.

SYKES, G.
1956   *The Society of Captives.* Princeton: Princeton University Press.

TORGERSON, W.
1958   *Theory and Method of Scaling* New York: John Wiley and Sons.

VOLLMER, H.
1967   "Organizational socialization among scientists." Unpublished paper presented at the Annual Meeting of the American Sociological Association, San Francisco.

EIGHT ORGANIZATIONAL CAREERS: AN INTERACTIONIST PERSPECTIVE *

Ralph L. Blankenship

The aim of this paper is to present a theoretical perspective which places organizational careers in a crucial relationship to the symbolic order of an organization, and to its ongoing programs of joint action within itself, and with client-publics. The perspective assumes the functional priority of negotiation processes within organizations which allow members a greater degree of freedom to interact socially than would be found in the ideal-typical bureaucracy, military organization, or industrial organization.

Prior theoretical models of complex organizations[1] have consistently failed to recognize formally the functions of individual organizational members for social organization. Members are the keystone of the organizational situation. Only the member can perceive, understand, define, assess, interpret, and interact with the symbolic order. Only the member can select and negotiate common objectives. Only the member can enact the moral meanings of the organization in programmatic interactions with other members and with publics. Only a member can act, at all. The only reality adhering to the organization per se, or to its symbolic goals or its programs of action, is the social reality which is created when members symbolize these and treat them collectively as an organizational situation.

* The research on which this paper was written is supported in part by Public Health Service Research Grant MH 07346 from the National Institute of Mental Health.
Source: "Organizational Careers: An Interactionist Perspective" by Ralph L. Blankenship. The Sociological Quarterly, 14 (Winter 1973): 88–98.

When he *acts for the organization,* it becomes real to him and it is real in its effect on his action (Schutz, 1962; Berger and Luckman, 1966). The organization is nothing more than the interactions of its members within a commonly perceived organizational situation (Bittner, 1965; Manning, 1970).

A Model of the Organizational Situation

The organizational career is the basic structural form from which organizational situations derive their reality and their capacity for social action. An organizational situation is partly a complex network of crosscutting, over-lapping, competing, and complementary careers, each pursued by a particular member, each affected by the others. An organizational situation is like an arena in which members interact in order to construct and enact multiple personal and organizational careers (Strauss et al., 1963, 1964).

In order to enact his organizational career, the member intermediates between a symbolic order and a number of programs of joint action—defining the former in action, interpreting the latter in appropriate symbolic terms. The intermediating function of organizational careers is realized primarily through communication processes, principally in the form of negotiation of agreement.

The organization is a negotiated order in which action and symbolism are united by members' construction and enactment of careers within a commonly defined organizational situation. The interactive process thus described accounts for observable, routine organizational activity. Such activity is enacted and re-enacted with a degree of certainty and continuity determined by prior and present negotiation of agreement on the shape of the symbolic order, the career goals of the members, and the rationality and moral correctness of ongoing programs of action. Orderly change is accounted for as well; goals can be redefined to indicate different action programs and programs can be reinterpreted to reflect different symbolic goals. Only agreement is required, and even that can be partial and contingent.

The remainder of this paper will expand on the model above through elaboration and explication of two of its basic elements, the symbolic order and organizational careers.

The Symbolic Order as Goals

The symbolic order of an organization, like the values of a society, is an elusive object of study. It cannot be addressed directly. It can only be drawn by inference from partial and sometimes equivocal observations. In the perspective of this paper, its elusiveness is further enhanced by the existential character given to it. This paper is of too limited scope to resolve this difficulty. The symbolic order will be treated as goals.

It is helpful to distinguish between three levels of symbolic goals: (1) the general, abstract goals of the organization-as-a-whole; (2) the programmatic objectives of the several formal subdivisions and functional subgroupings of the organization, and; (3) the personal goals of particular personnel, including generalized career plans, internalized standards of performance, and concrete programmatic objectives.

The sum of these goals, the various acts which are constructed to attain them, and the perceptions of them held by members and interested non-members, indicate the symbolic order. The three levels of goals are interdependent. Each serves the other two and is, in part, a condition of the other two.

Organizational Goals

The general goal of all community mental health centers may be treated as community change through decentralization and broadening of mental health services, and the application of the general principles of community social psychiatry (Albee, 1959; Hobbs, 1964; Joint Commission, 1961; Knight and Davis 1964; Reidy, 1964; Glasscote et al., 1964; National Institute, 1964; Jarvis and Nelson, 1966). One particular mental health center, created as part of the program of building community-based mental health centers in a midwestern state, offered the following set of organizational goals . . . a somewhat less vague rendering of the general, national program goals.[2] Three major goals of the Kennedy Regional Center were: (1) the prevention of illness, (2) care for persons experiencing illness, and (3) the strengthening of community resources.

To specify these abstract goals, corollary goals of continuity of care for the ill person, the development and application of knowledge based on social and behavioral research to prevent and to treat a broad range of mental problems, interdisciplinary collaboration, and excellence of practice were developed. Creativity, spontaneity, innovativeness, eclecticism, and inquiry were presented an ancillary goals.

What can be learned from the elaborate set of goals above? The most striking characteristic of these goals is their utter abstractness. Organizational goals cannot function as determinants of direct action. Their primary function lies in their capacity to provide a repertoire of appropriate and acceptable meanings for actions taken. The symbolic order discloses the moral order of actions.

Programmatic Objectives

Under the general limits of organizational goals, programs of action are created and developed. Purposive interactions with a particular client-public are matched with particular organizational goals. Program goals, then, must specify a discrete population with which interaction is to occur, indicate the location of the interactions, and schedule them in time. For example, a program might prescribe interactions with pre-adolescent girls from a particular section of the city who frequent a certain recreation hall during certain evening hours of each Friday of the next twelve months. Programs fix upon a specific social object which is seen as a suitable means for the attainment of organizational goals.

Program goals do not deal with the question of why interactions with the selected social object would be morally desirable. Issues of legitimation can be met through deference to organizational goals. The infinite number of programs which might be planned to implement even a few general goals such as "prevention and care of mental problems" staggers the imagination. The limited number of programs actually staged, however, becomes the substantive definition of the organization's general goals.

Personal Goals as Careers

ORGANIZATIONAL CAREERS.   Personal careers motivate members to negotiate joint plans of action with their colleagues and to interact with client-publics. Such negotiations are conducted with reference to already-defined organizational symbols and goals, and within a context of ongoing plans of action and prior agreements. Efforts to enact personal careers are the primary acts which define, modify, and limit each of the other elements of the organizational situation.

This perspective does not hold that organizational goals and programs are simply functional "spin-offs" from selfish career efforts; nor would it be reasonable to posit that careers are simply the by-products of the symbolic order or of the concrete interactions with client-publics. Rather, the perspective maintains that careers, programs, and symbolic order interact, primarily through the medium of interpersonal negotiations, to produce what may be observed as the organizational situation in all its structural, symbolic, and processual aspects.

Careers offer the most viable object of organizational study (1) because careers offer both structural and symbolic materials, (2) because careers penetrate the other two elements of the organizational situation, and (3) because the negotiation of careers (see Glaser, 1964, 1968) is the primary social process involved in the social construction of the organization. Careers can be studied throughout the entire spectrum of organizational types. But the the study of careers is greatly aided by the general features found in colleges and similar organizations which offer fewer impediments to negotiation processes, and, in fact, depend upon negotiations as the modal process for goal selection and program development.

OBJECTIVE CAREERS AND SUBJECTIVE CAREERS.

Historically, the sociological concept of career owes much to Thomas and Znaniecki (1918) who reported regularities in the experiences of Polish peasant families that immigrated to American cities. Immigrants and their families passed through a succession of statuses in their socialization into the new situation. This early use of career included both objective status changes and the corresponding personal response—the definition of the situation. But little sense of process was given in this conception.

Many sociologists of the Chicago School used the concept in the above sense during the decades of the '20s and '30s (Becker, 1966). Lemert (1951, 1967) noted that careers in deviant behavior could not be adequately explained as a simple function of the actor, but required treatment as an emergent product of interactions between the actor and certain audiences. Following this, Becker (1963) and Scheff (1966) became the foremost articulators of labeling theory, a perspective which stresses interactional process and role-making in the construction of careers in deviance.

MORAL CAREERS AND THE STUDY OF THE SELF.

Goffman (1961) expanded our understanding of the subjective career by describing careers as consisting of three interdependent elements. In addition to the objective social status, there is a subjective aspect of the career which is expressed as financial reward, deference, privilege, and prestige. These forms are social reactions to and confirmations of the objective status. Beyond this external social dimension of the subjective career lies an internal, social, and physchological dimension—the moral career. The moral career is based on the reactions of the status holder to his self within the situation, leading to ongoing revisions and shifts in the conception of the self. Career studies can be direct studies of the self, if they focus on the moral career. Goffman states (1961:127):

One side is linked to internal matters . . . such as the image of self and felt identity; the other side concerns official position . . . and is part of a publicly accessible institutional complex. The concept of career, then, enables one to move back and forth between . . . the self and its significant society . . .

Career studies enable the study of the self with greater objectivity, but not at the cost of losing the subtle and shifting essence of everyday interactions. Goffman urges the study of the " . . . moral aspect of the career— that is, the regular sequence of changes that career entails in the person's self and his framework of imagery for judging himself and others" (Goffman, 1961:128).

The study of moral careers leads, Goffman added, to the study of work and to the study of identity. These aspects of human life are so intimately related that they can be described as embracing each other. The career of work is the primary career in our society, among careers of marriage, of parenthood, or of citizenship, for example. Work sets a man's identity and thereby it has a profound effect on his conception of self (Hughes, 1958:3–11). The precise characters of work, identity, and career are naturally obfuscated in everyday life due to their interrelatedness and interactiveness. It is therefore helpful to treat each of these concepts as interdependent aspects of the self, as a social object, among which the career is most readily accessible for direct study. Seen in this viewpoint[3] a personal career or an organizational career is more than a simple life history, for it may be directly linked to the larger body of sociological theory of the self (see Denzin, 1970).

An organization consists of multipile, interdependent, and overlapping moral orders within which the members interact in routines of everyday activity. It is essential to study the effects of the organizational situation on the selves of the members and their significant others. Social reactions to the organizational career are important. We must also consider that the reflexive self monitors, evaluates, and responds to the career. In this consideration, we come closest to Goffman's (1961) contribution in his conceptualization of the moral career. A career is of greatest sociological interest when it has become lodged in the self, which is a sacred, morally defined object.

CAREERS AS SACRED OBJECTS. Shifts in the career reshape the moral nature of the self and can signal strong defensive responses. If the self were held to be sacred (Durkheim, 1961:44–52), it must be protected from vulgarization and profanation. Such a need would function as a powerful motivator toward career enactment. What might pass superficially as aggrandizement could simply be defensive preparations against an uncertain future in which the self must always stand at risk.

Consider, for example, the case of a person whose downward career progression signals a sense of ultimate failure in the sacred obligation to protect the self and who imposes the death penalty—egoistic suicide (Durkheim, 1951). Altruism, in this perspective, would flow outward from the primary loyalty to self, to include primary loyalties with others. But the most venal of all sins would always be to permit the debasement, the disgrace of the self. Disgrace is imminent through the intimate interrelatedness of work, identity, and career as aspects of the self as a morally defined social object (Hughes, 1962, 1958).

Judgments of morality are not made in absolute or non-relative terms. Moral definitions of the self are constructed within moral hierarchies. Few social definitions are more repugnant than being subordinated to one whom you consider to be less morally worthy than yourself. Many recurring interactional routines are enacted for the simple purpose of defining and ritualizing the moral worth or lack of worth of certain organizational members (Goffman, 1961:1–125). Seen in this way, the study of a moral career within an organizational situation is always the study of a number of interrelated careers, and it is always political in character.

Careers and Organizational Context

Careers are increasingly enacted under organizational aegis. It is thus the more salient and necessary to ask how careers are shaped by organizational contexts, and how the organization is shaped in turn by the careers of its members.

BUREAUCRATIC CAREERS.   Weber suggested (Gerth and Mills, 1946:196–245) that career lines within bureaucracies are eufunctional, that is, they are constructed in a rationality relating to efficiency of production. Ordinary members are recruited, rewarded, and promoted in terms of universally applied criteria. Consequently, ordinary members are freed from institutional politics and entanglements which would decrease their functions as obedient subordinates, or would inhibit their issuance of commands. Loyalty is due to the organization. But as Blau (1955), Dalton (1959), and others have so firmly declared, bureaucrats do not remain impersonal in their relationships with each other. The organizational scheme does not require them to construct interpersonal relationships as a condition of career enactment. Yet they develop and maintain complex networks of interpersonal communication and influence through which they"humanize" their work setting. They may attempt thus to subvert the "formal," bureaucratic career-line structure in order to gain competitive advantage.

In practice, bureaucratic careers are determined in part by the official criteria for advancement, and in part by the subtleties of unsanctioned negotiations between members. As a part of a new member's socialization into the work role and into the organizational situation, he must develop understanding of the mechanisms, both official and unsanctioned, by which careers are enacted in that particular setting. When this understanding is internalized, it may be expressed through career aspirations, perceived functional career limits, and personal timetables (Dalton, 1951; Martin and Strauss, 1956:106; Roth, 1963). Or, as Becker (1952) found, one may take an unappealing work assignment with the understanding that it is a necessary step toward a favored position.

CAREERS AS ENACTMENT. Beyond the bureaucracy an organizational career is not necessarily linked to a conception of movement from one status to another. Although organizational situations permit and support individuals to act in ways which lead to their "becoming" something else (Manning, 1970), their functions for all members may not be the same. For some members, the organizational situation is important primarily because it permits them to continue being what they have already become. For example, while a novice attorney is concerned with the socialization process through which he will become a successful attorney, the successful attorney seeks the opportunity to enact excellence of practice. Similarly, the respected surgeon, on the staff of a prestigious medical center, may have already become what he wishes to be, and may seek only a viable supporting organization where he can play out his career as a leader in the medical community.

Organizations of this latter type would principally offer their members an enabling medium for enacting and maintaining statuses and identities. Such an organization could not demand strong expressive commitment from its members. It would summon a sense of instrumentality. Strong bonds of loyalty and sentiment among its members would be rare. Members would not subrogate their rights in favor of organizational goals, nor would they commit themselves to tenure which would extend beyond the certainty of usefulness of the organization for their personal career goals. Membership would be contingent—so long as it serves.

Consider the case of the large state-supported university and the persistent state of conflict which so often reduces its attractiveness as a setting for work. For its junior faculty, it affords a springboard from which careers can be launched. For its senior faculty, it provides a setting in which resources and facilities are available for broad research activity which may bring their promising careers into full bloom. But for faculties as a whole, personal careers are lodged in their professions-at-large, not in the particular university. So there is little incentive toward compromise and coordination in the competition for limited local resources and status.

Gouldner (1957; 1958) made a similar point about organizations which employ mostly experts and professionals. Their commonality with universities is that both organizations distribute authority along horizontal axes as expressed in collegial participation in decision-making. Centralized authority, with vertical lines of participation, as superiors and subordinates, tends to foster greater identification with the organization as the career locus. The horizontal status structure of collegial organizations precludes the growing organizational commitment which is a common concomitant of promotional advancement within an organizational hierarchy (Goffman, 1961:201; Grusky, 1966:489).

The organizational career in a collegial organization shows most clearly that all organizational careers consist of situated interactions between peers and significant others, of efforts toward enactment of the role of the worker, and of monitoring the reactions of one's social audiences. In McCall and Simmons' (1966) terms, the organizational career is expressed through ongoing presentations of self and identity within a setting of work, and through repeated appraisals of the kind and degree of role support forthcoming from audiences of colleagues and significant others.

ORGANIZATIONAL CAREER

AS BECOMING AND BEING. Consider the organizational career as a state of becoming and being (Strauss, 1959), as an existential modality which emerges from the ongoing interactions of: (1) expectations of self and others, (2) the immediate situation of work, (3) the member's actions, (4) the symbolizations and evaluations which others develop and communicate in response to those actions, which lead to, (5) modifications in the member's definition of his self in the situation.

The particular aspect of the situation which is always in question, in this perspective, is the member's right to continue to claim the status of the respected colleague. This right adheres permanently to his audience of colleagues. They may grant it to him only in the form of role support. They may confer the status upon him by reacting to his performance of it in a way which gives substance and credence to the claim. Or they may withhold approving responses and thereby deny the claimed status. The latter tactic would obligate the member to rework his claim before resubmitting it for collegial approval. If the collegial audience persists in with-holding role support in spite of the member's revisions, the member may be compelled to withdraw from the situation, either on the psychological level or physically. The organizational career is enacted by successfully maintaining the status of respected colleague through continual negotia-tion and re-negotiation of role support from an audience of peers and significant others [see Garfinkel (1956) for a statement of the conditions of degradation].

An organizational career normally requires some interaction with out-sider publics as well as with member-peers. But client-directed interactions may be relevant for the career only to the extent that those interactions enter into the negotiations for continuing role support. A career is not achieved solely through task-performance; a career is partly a conferred status, replete with ascriptive qualities. It is temporally defined, and ever up for renewal.

Review and Conclusions

The concept of career has come to be viewed as a composite of objective status elements, social reaction elements, and elements which refer to conceptions of self. In our society the self is largely defined in terms of work. Therefore, the organizations in which work is performed must be treated as partial determinants of both the objective aspects of career and the closely interrelated personal identity (Hughes, 1958; Strauss, 1959; Goffman, 1961).

Both bureaucracies and collegial organizations reveal the importance of negotiational process in career enactment, although the different social arrangements in the two types of organization lead to subversional negotiation in one, and more open negotiation in the other. In both types of organization, careers are constructed through the joint negotiation of roles and statuses, in which successful performances of role are rewarded through role support and continuance in colleagueship. Careers can re-veal both processes of becoming and of being, a distinction previously overlooked by many.

This paper presents a perspective on the organizational career which neither assigns undue ''reality'' to organizations and organizational struc-ture, nor does it deny the structural imagery employed by organizational members as they pursue their everyday actions (Denzin, 1969). By symbol-izing his own career within an organizational situation, the member is enabled to lend the reality of his and others' interactions to the organiza-tion. In this manner, we are enabled to account for the social reality of organizations without relinquishing the commitment we hold to the study of the self and of social interactions as the basic social units.

Footnotes

[1] Mouzelis (1968) provides an excellent survey of perspectives on organizations and bureaucracies. Wolin (1969) offers a way of viewing these perspectives by casting them in two lots. The first lot treats organizations as organismic phenomena which persist over time, independently of their members' mortal lives, and which display functional system characteristics resembling those of living organisms. This view accounts for change through an evolutionary analogy. An organization is purported to have observed characteristics because it underwent certain antecedent conditions of development; it endeavors to maintain present forms in spite of variable external conditions. Small changes may accrue over time, due to modification and accommodation. This view presents a passive image of members, generally denying their capacity to act except in forms and patterns determined by the system. The processes in which members choose between alternative courses of action, which might present functional equivalence, and the processes of implementation after choices are made, are only dimly revealed.

Wolin's (1969) second lot includes perspectives which view the organization as a rationalistic mechanism contrived by certain of its members in order to achieve certain specific outputs with maximal efficiency. Facets of organizational reality are explainable in terms of rationality and efficiency, with reference to the organizational goals. But irrationality and inefficiency arise when means are followed as petty ends and when members pursue personal or local goals in place of the organization's goals. The discovery of "informal" structure, and especially the discovery of significant reliance on "informal" means in everyday organizational life, has led to judgment of these perspectives as partial and somewhat inaccurate.

Undue emphasis on either the independent existence of the organization vis-à-vis its members, or on the organization's rationality with reference to certain goals, must be avoided. This may be achieved, in part, by setting case studies in organizations which have not yet become fully formed around selected goals and particular production systems.

[2] The empirical basis for the grounded theory (Glaser and Strauss, 1967) of organizational situations and of organizational careers is a longitudinal field study of a particular mental health center, identified in this paper only by the pseudonym, Kennedy Regional Center. The study covered four years of planning and development and was terminated after all program units were operating at capacity, and the initial planner-leader was replaced. A full report, including a topical life history of the organization's development and grounded theory chapters on the organizational situation and the process of its development, is contained in the author's unpublished doctoral dissertation (Blankenship, 1971). [Editor's note: this study is now published under the same title, by R and E Research Associates, San Francisco.]

[3] A different viewpoint is expressed in a paper by Robert Stebbins (1970). Two types of career are posited, distinguished on the basis of an objectivity-subjectivity factor. Of the objective type, two forms are found. The first form is distinguished by the sequence of events which constitute the life history of an individual. Second is the career as distinguished by a line or pattern of sequential experiences which pertain to a social category such as an occupation or a profession. The subjective career is distinguished by a predisposition toward particular actions in future situations, based on cognitive and conative residues from past and present experiences. In this writer's opinion, Stebbins' position strives to create a type of career to account for role, identity, and self. Stebbins loses theoretical parsimony with no apparent gain of either insight or power.

REFERENCES

ALBEE, GEORGE W.
1959   Mental Health Manpower Trends. New York: Basic Books.

BECKER, HOWARD S.
1966   "Introduction." Pp. v-xviii in Clifford R. Shaw, The Jack-roller. Chicago: University of Chicago Press.
1963   Outsiders. New York: The Free Press.
1952   "The career of the Chicago school teacher." American Journal of Sociology 57 (March) :470-477.

BERGER, PETER L. AND THOMAS LUCKMAN
1966   The Social Construction of Reality. Garden City, N.Y.: Doubleday.

BITTNER, E.
1965   "The concept of organization." Social Research 32 (Autumn) :239-255.

BLANKENSHIP, RALPH L.
1971   The Emerging Organization of a Community Mental Health Center. University of Illinois at Urbana-Champaign: Unpublished Ph.D. dissertation.

BLAU, PETER M.
1955   The Dynamics of Bureaucracy. Chicago: University of Chicago Press.

DALTON, MELVILLE
1959   Men Who Manage. New York: Wiley.
1951   "Informal factors in career achievement." American Journal of Sociology 56 (March) :407-415.

DENZIN, NORMAN K.
1970   The Research Act. Chicago: Aldine.
1969   "Symbolic interactionism and ethnomethodology: A con-

vergence of perspective." American Sociological Review
34 (December) :922-934.

DURKHEIM, EMILE
1961   The Elementary Forms of the Religious Life. New York: Collier Books.
1951   Suicide. John A. Spaulding and George Simpson (trans.). New York: The Free Press.

GARFINKEL, H.
1956   "Conditions of successful degradation ceremonies." The American Journal of Sociology 61 (March) :420-424.

GERTH, HANS H. AND C. WRIGHT MILLS
1946   From Max Weber: Essays in Sociology. New York: Oxford University Press.

GLASER, BARNEY G.
1968   Organizational Careers. (ed.). Chicago: Aldine.
1964   Organizational Scientists: Their Professional Careers. Indianapolis: Bobbs-Merrill.

GLASER, BARNEY G. AND ANSELM STRAUSS
1967   The Discovery of Grounded Theory. Chicago: Aldine.

GLASSCOTE, RAYMOND, DAVID SANDERS, H. M. FORSTENZER, AND A. R. FOLEY
1964   The Community Mental Health Center. Washington, D.C.: The Joint Information Service.

GOFFMAN, ERVING
1961   Asylums. Garden City, N.Y.: Doubleday.

GOULDNER, A. M.
1958   "Cosmopolitan and locals—II." Administrative Science Quarterly 2 (March) :444-480.
1957   "Cosmopolitans and locals—I." Administrative Science Quarterly 2 (December) :281-306.

GRUSKY, O.
1966   "Career mobility and organizational commitment." Ad-

ministrative Science Quarterly 10 (March) :489-490; 497-502.

HOBBS, N.
1964   "Mental health's third revolution." Journal of Orthopsychiatry 34 (October) :822-833.

HUGHES, EVERETT C.
1962   "Good men and dirty work." Social Problems 10 (March) :3-11.
1958   Men and Their Work. New York: The Free Press.

JARVIS, P. E. AND S. E. NELSON
1966   "The therapeutic community and new role for clinical psychologists." American Psychologist 21 (June) :524-529.

JOINT COMMISSION ON MENTAL ILLNESS AND HEALTH
1961   Action for Mental Health. New York: Wiley.

KNIGHT, JAMES A. AND WINBORN E. DAVIS
1964   Comprehensive Community Mental Health Clinic. Springfield, Ill.: Charles C Thomas.

LEMERT, EDWIN M.
1967   Human Deviance, Social Problems, and Social Control. Englewood Cliffs, N.J.: Prentice-Hall.
1951   Social Pathology. New York: McGraw-Hill.

MANNING PETER K.
1970   "Talking and becoming: a view of organizational socialization." Pp. 239-258 in Jack D. Douglas (ed.), Understanding Everyday Life. Chicago: Aldine.

MARTIN, N. H. AND A. STRAUSS
1956   "Patterns of mobility within industrial organizations." Journal of Business 29 (April) :101-110.

MCCALL, GEORGE J. AND J. L. SIMMONS
1966   Indentities and Interactions. New York: The Free Press.

MOUZELIS, NICOS P.
1968   Organization and Bureaucracy. Chicago: Aldine.

NATIONAL INSTITUTE OF MENTAL HEALTH
1964   The Comprehensive Community Mental Health Center. Washington, D.C.: U.S. Government Printing Office.

REIDY, JOHN P.
1964   Zone Mental Health Center. Springfield, Ill.: Charles C Thomas.

ROTH, JULIUS A.
1963   Timetables. Indianapolis: Bobbs-Merrill.

SCHEFF, THOMAS J.
1966   Being Mentally Ill. Chicago: Aldine.

SCHUTZ, ALFRED
1962   The Problem of Social Reality: Collected Papers I. The Hague: Martinus Nijhoff.

STEBBINS, R. A.
1970   "Career: the subjective approach." The Sociological Quarterly 11 (Winter) :32-49.

STRAUSS, ANSELM
1959   Mirrors and Masks. New York: The Free Press.

STRAUSS, ANSELM, LEONARD SCHATZMAN, RUE BUCHER, DANUTA EHRLICH, AND MELVIN SABSHIN
1964   Psychiatric Ideologies and Institutions. New York: The Free Press.
1963   "The hospital in its negotiated order." Pp. 147-169 in Eliot Freidson (ed.), The Hospital in Modern Society. New York: The Free Press.

THOMAS, WILLIAM I. AND FLORIAN ZNANIECKI
1918   The Polish Peasant in Europe and America. New York: Alfred A. Knopf.

WOLIN, SHELDON S.
1969   "A critique of organizational theories." Pp. 133-149 in Amitai Etzioni (ed.), A Sociological Reader in Complex Organizations, 2nd Edition. New York: Holt, Rinehart, and Winston.

CHAPTER THREE
PROCESS

INTRODUCTION:
NEGOTIATION AND CRISIS MANAGEMENT

In this chapter we are concerned with the things members do in organizational settings that make it possible for them to do their work.

Organizational activity is by definition joint activity. It is usually done by more than one person and it is meaningful for more than one person. But before several persons can engage in an activity jointly it is generally necessary for there to be some common agreement . . . about what to do, how and why it should be done, what each member's part shall be. Indeed, there must be an foundation of understandings, some very ambiguous and others very clear. This foundation constitutes of body of *taken-for-granted knowledge* that is created and shared by members.

To understand an organizational setting one must learn how agreements are created, maintained, and changed. The *negotiation of agreement* among members is a basic and necessary social process for members to make and to manage the everyday life of an organization.

A preliminary word of caution is in order, however. Some shared understandings about the situation *must* be there, but even the most structured understandings, bureaucratic regulations for example, are essentially *problematic*. An organization is not merely a set of rules, agreements, norms, and contracts. No reasonable effort at enforcing rules and contracts is sufficient to make them binding and final beyond the willingness of particular members to accept them within the context of a particular situation. In scientific language, we could state that *agreement is a necessary but not a sufficient condition for joint activity*, and further, that *the power of formal rules and contracts is contingent upon the maintenance of agreement among the parties*.

Order, defined by the rules, cannot be taken for granted by organizational members. As students of organizational settings, we must not credit the rules with more deterministic power than they deserve. Even the most thorough study of our nation's laws will not lead to an adequate understanding of crime or of the criminal experience. Due process by itself is a poor explanation of the criminal justice system.

NEGOTIATION AND ACTION

In the prime introduction to this book, the work of Anselm Strauss and his associates was described. Strauss, you will recall, described an organization as a negotiated order—a sum of all the negotiated understandings, agreements, rules, contracts, and joint plans of action existing at any point in time. In that view the "order" enables the everyday work of the organization to proceed. Negotiation, then, can be seen as the "work" that must be done to enable other work to be done. Negotiation has a special relationship to action.

Negotiation can be analyzed as a special case of the more general process of symbolic communication between self-conscious persons. The significant difference that distinguishes negotiation from other forms of communication is its relationship to action. But this difference is relative. Even when two persons exchange a nominal hello, it is conceivable that they have negotiated an agreement, a very general agreement to be sure, but still an agreement that further interaction may be pursued if either party wishes to do so. All symbolic communication, even the involuntary "ouch," depends on common and agreed upon understandings and can be expected to signal a certain kind of response from others within hearing. So if negotiation is to be treated as a form of communication that creates potential for joint action, that quality must be recognized as a matter of degree.

The kinds of action agreements that can be negotiated also vary widely in their specificity. A set of colleagues may meet and negotiate an agreement to order a new piece of office equipment from a certain vendor at a certain price and so on. But they may also negotiate an agreement to act in a highly generalized way, such as "becoming more involved" or "rethinking" a previous line of action.

To use sociological terms; the *functions* of some agreements are *manifest* (that is, they lead directly to action) while some others function in a *latent* manner (that is, they lead to action through an indirect and unintended series of effects). The analysis of agreements, the consideration of negotiated outcomes, is always *teleological*—the answers become known over time.

LIMITS ON NEGOTIATION

The limits of orgainzational negotiation are the same as those that constrain social interactions generally, although the unique features of each organizational situation must also be considered. *Time* is a limiting consideration. Future and past are beyond our reach and we can only negotiate with those with whom we share the present. Among that set, fewer yet share our *social space*. Age, sex, social status, vocation, and religion tend to define a limited social sphere within which we live our lives. While communication technology permits geographical space to be crossed, we cannot and certainly we do not cable or telephone persons with whom we have no common social relationship.

The nature of the *social relationship* between oneself and those with whom negotiations occur, limits its form and its content. A young working-class male would negotiate differently with other young working-class males, with old, working-class females, with old upper-class males and so on. The joint activities that are possible or likely with one cross-match might be out of the question for another. The *prior history* of negotiations with the other party is important. Even the *location* of the negotiation affects its form and content. We work out different deals in public situations from those that might be struck in situations where nobody can observe.

The context of an organization's existing *negotiated order* may direct or preclude certain negotiations. If a group of colleagues has already agreed on certain programs of action, any shift from that course would depend on the question of *power*. Like a physical object in motion, organizations tend to move in a "straight line" unless they are deflected. Within an organization, however, a great many sources of deflection can be identified. For example, men see things differently. For one man, an agreement may be taken as a total *commitment*. He would view no obstacle as too great to be overcome. Another might view the agreement as a guideline, a ruling to go by for the moment. Faced with a problem, his response would undoubtedly be different, more *expedient*.

Power and *influence* limit negotiations. These resources are distributed unevenly across the organizational membership. Powerful and influential members can project activities more freely than their lesser colleagues. Their opportunity to control the scarce organizational resources is much greater.

Organizational and personal economics cannot be taken for granted. If an organization has committed its budget, manpower, and workspace to certain projects, those economic resources are tied up and may not be easily diverted into new enterprises. And of course last year's budget is gone forever; next year's funds are equally beyond reach. Individuals also must conserve their personal resources, which are very limited. Each of us has one lifetime of indefinite duration to spend building a career. If we spend our time and energy wisely, success may accrue but if we drop unfinished projects to take up new ones, or if we commit ourselves to spend time on projects that draw no professional rewards, our personal resources are unretrievable.

Cultural limits on negotiations can be very binding. Certain medical research involving the interface of human, animal, and electromechanical components would be highly desirable to scientists involved in space medicine, for example. But the cultural milieu in America will not permit that kind of experimentation. If it were to be done at all, it would have to be secretly contracted, perhaps to an agency in some other country.

Another kind of cultural limit is presented in the form of *roles and traditions*. A prison warden, for instance, is a cultural role familiar to Americans. How many times have you seen the warden portrayed in drama or in comic skit? Often enough to recognize the existence of a stereotype, no doubt. Role expectations, shared by the wardens themselves, limit the range of styles any warden may adopt as his own without losing credibility, and probably losing his job as well. Equally as difficult as playing a stereotyped role in an innovative manner, is the problem of making a role where no traditional patterns exist. During the sixties, college students demanded a participative role in making decisions within their universities and professional schools. When they were granted a role, however, many discovered that they could not be effective since they had no idea of what to do. What followed was often a retreat to other more familiar roles . . . the junior administrator role or the student-radical role.

Order is created and maintained within organizations as members act on the basis of existing understandings and agreements. Action is limited by prior action. But at each step of the way some latitude exists and a variety of agreements is possible. An emerging pattern is created as a synthesis of prior agreements and actions; this is what is meant by order. However order is not to be taken for granted. It is the result of continuous interactional work on the part of members. Change, as well as order, emerges from the ongoing negotiations that characterize organizational life.

ORDER, CHANGE, AND CRISIS

Order and change are like two sides of a coin. If you observe a situation objectively from the vantage point of the present you might describe what you see as an order. Without a comparative dimension, all description and analysis must refer to order. Change, on the other hand, is a comparison of states of order, viewed in different points of time. Change is also potentially evaluative. Vested interests or ideological interests can operate to cause an observer to advocate further change, the cessation of further change or even the return to a previous order.

There is no reason, theoretically, why change cannot be controlled and made to operate in any direction chosen by an organizational body. Only the cessation is change is impossible. That would require both a constant environment and termination of basic social processes within the organizational situation. As long as members endeavor to enact careers within an organization, that alone would keep the situation changing.

Although change never ceases, there are times when it is accelerated by situations or events that call for unusually intensive negotiations. We will call these times *crises*. Some crises are created by changing conditions in the organization's environment. If market demands show a sharp rise or an unpredicted decline, new definitions of the situation are signalled, new agreements are needed leading to revisions of programs and purpose. Massive economic shifts such as the Great Depression affected organizations throughout the entire world. Over the long term, however, the less dramatic crises that come from everyday interactional processes are both more certain to occur and more marked in their effects.

Some common and recognizable organizational crises stem from the elements of which the organization is built, including its particular members, programs, understandings, and so forth. We may call these *contingency crises*, since they are likely but not certain to occur as a result of the combination of elements comprising the organizational situation.

Little can be done to protect an organization or its members from the effects of external crises, but contingency crises are subject to *contingency planning* . . . deciding in advance just how a particular situation that is likely to occur can be managed to limit its deleterious effects. An example is the case of the clinical psychologist with a commitment to behaviorism, who sets forth a detailed analysis of the possible range of controllable behaviors that might be encountered within a residential treatment setting, and then decides whether each behavior will be reinforced within a token system. Or consider the case of a military general preparing for a major battle.

In organizational settings, contingency crises generally fall into two classes—those stemming from *reliance on members* and those stemming from *uncertainty* about the environment and the future. Reliance on members leads to crises caused by: role reworking, human error, human mortality, interpersonal conflict, role conflict, interference from other careers and self-dislodging. Let us consider each of these in turn.

Reliance on Members

No organization reflects exactly what its originator or planner dreamed. Much of the deviation stems from the leader's inability to do everything himself. Instead, he must *delegate* many parts of the organizational program to others. The person who is appointed to a position in the organization is ordinarily given a general outline of his duties and options, sometimes more and sometimes less. Many positions offer severely limited options; that is, there may be few variations possible in how the job is done because of its simplicity, or perhaps because of social checks and balances. But even in what might appear to be a simple case of delegation, the role-holder can alter the existing order by merely doing his job his own way.

Members bring *purposes, goals, timetables* of their own into the organizational situation. Performance of a job must satisfy not only the requirements of the program, but of the member himself. Corruption of ideal schemes also occurs when some members manipulate other members to act in terms of special ends. The selection of members is very important as a means of avoiding the most serious effects of *role-reworking*. Persons are usually sought who are in close agreement with the leader, but appearances are often deceiving. Often a new member takes up his position, but then unexpected changes occur. Unpredictable interaction effects prevent complete effectiveness in planning against the contingencies of delegation and role-reworking.

It is part of being human to make *errors of judgment*. Oversights and erroneous estimates can lead to crises of all sorts. No one or no body of colleagues is infallible. Intelligence and experience only permits one to contemplate possible areas of error, as in the case of the protracted consideration of candidates for academic posts. But errors are still made; the university, for example, allows years and years of observation before granting a professor tenure.

On occasion, what appears to be error may later be seen as a smart move. An entrepreneur, for example, in need of capital might take a loan at an exhorbitant interest rate. At the critical beginning of a business venture this would appear to be a mistake. But if the venture survives and prospers, few men would cling to their initial judgment of the loan as an error.

Members are human, and humans are *mortal*. We are born, we live, and we die. We are prone to illness and to aging. Thus it is essential to provide for the replacement of members from time to time. Moreover, these same human frailties affect a member's family. Some provision must be made for the effects of others' death, disability, or infirmity on the member. Contingency planning against the crises of mortality includes in-service training, educational leave, sick leave, sabbatical programs, retirement programs, recruitment programs, taking-on of proteges, and a variety of schemes relating to succession.

According to many social theorists, *conflict* is a component of all social relationships. Some psychologists maintain that the persistent conflict between an individual and society is certain to lead to conflict within his own personality. Conflict then, both between members and within the personality of each member, is present as part of any organizational setting.

At times conflict is manifested as a perceived *conflict of interests* between the member and the organization as a whole. A member can come to see his self as debased or threatened by continued membership. If so, he may leave the organization. Short of that, he can shift his attention away from the organizational activities and draw upon other careers—that of club member, father, political figure—for the experiences and social rewards he needs to sustain his sense of well-being. His involvement in the organization can become as limited as ritualistic performance of his duties and, of course, taking his salary. Contingency planning against this crisis includes many schemes and programs that are intended to keep members' interests and to provide alternative ways to vent frustrations and hostilities that emerge. Periodic performance ratings, participation in decision making, competitive promotion systems, interdepartmental transfer options, bonuses, and incentive schemes are all attempts to keep members involved in the organizational situation. Industrial psychology has emerged as a clinical specialty—counselling with members is sometimes provided as an alternative to letting conflicts build up. Reportedly, a Japanese factory once offered frustrated workmen the option of using a meditation room or another room in which an effigy of their foreman could be flogged with long sticks.

In addition to their professional career, members also pursue careers as parents, as spouses, and in other roles. *Other careers* compete with professional and organizational careers. At times other careers interfere with the performance of professional and organizational activities. For example, a man who is ending his career as husband by divorce may be more prone to absenteeism and low performance levels. A member's careers are multiple, overlapping, and interdependent. Another way this problem is presented is in the matter of friendships, relationships, and cliques within the organization. Performance can be affected if a member is too involved in the affairs of his associates. Growing animosity between colleagues, as well as growing friendships, introduces conflicts. Bureaucracies prescribe impersonality between members, but collegial organizations seem especially prone to political problems. As the internal political situation shifts and changes, members are affected.

The last type of member-reliance crisis we will consider refers mainly to leaders who have acted as *entrepreneurs*. Entrepreneurs tend to build very personal organizations. Their own ideas about what things are important, what techniques are best, or what kind of members should be found tend to dominate. But projecting an enterprise is an arduous line of activity that takes great amounts of effort over a long time. Compromises must be made from time to time, and they, along with the shifts that occurs from all of the contingencies we have just listed, can result in an organization that is very far from the leader's initial ideal.

An example, familiar to academicians, is the case of the department head brought in to set up a new department or to straighten out a declining department. He must have some idea of what kind of a department he wants to build in order to give direction to recruitment and other matters. Success in large-scale change is almost certainly precluded by the residual characteristics of the parent organization, the university, and to the contingency factors already discussed. The typical experience presents a camelot phase, a period of growing problems, a rude awakening, an effort at purging the department, counterreactions, including charges of tyranny, and a long hard look at self and situation, followed by a "look around" for greener pastures.

Uncertainty in the Environment

Another source of contingency crises that lead to organizational negotiations is related to the unpredictability of outcomes. Some agreements, for instance, can be reversed later if they prove to have been wrong but others are irreversible. *Fateful decisions*, that is, decisions that prove in time to be points of major change and from which one cannot retreat occur often enough to explain some of the apparently endless deliberation over many decisions in professional settings. Leaving an academic position for a position in government, for example, is likely to mean the permanent closing of campus gates. The acceptance of a first academic position in an obscure college is likely to rule out future offers of more prestigious positions regardless of professional achievement. Not all fateful decisions are negative in outcome, but since many decisions bind members in future situations, deliberation is common.

In our view, the future is not strictly predetermined, but conditions and events do form as a result of historic precedents. Events are not linked across time in a simple causal chain. Influences often come from unexpected quarters. What I am arguing is that the future is *becoming* as a result of the actions we are taking today, but our power over future events and conditions is qualified—there must be some sort of "all things being equal" clause. Beyond our own human frailties, there is the domain of the social environment that cannot be controlled directly by any man or group of men. Designing a better buggy whip, even building a better buggy whip at a lower price, would not have stopped the ongoing flow of change as Western societies moved into the twentieth century. Declining birth rates, longer life spans for everybody, rising costs of living are all external *social trends* that can affect professional organizations, but little can be done to bring them under control.

Few have thought about the matter, but many organizations depend upon *failure* for their existence—police agencies, disaster agencies and health care agencies, to name a few. The goals of some organizations are assumed to be unattainable. But on occasion, a suprise is found . . . *success.* Things were going rather nicely for the newly formed Red Cross in 1917, until peace broke out and then the organization faced its greatest crisis. New reasons for continued existence were found, however, and the organization is still around. The discovery of a polio vaccine caused similar concern in a well-known research foundation, which faced its crisis by also finding new goals.

Career goals may be replaced occasionally, as well. When older patterns of service delivery came under criticism, many medical professionals found themselves taking another look at their career goals. In the process, some *new career patterns* were developed in which a psychiatrist, for example, split his time between direct service to the most serious patients in his practice, supervision of lesser-trained clinical staff in their work with less serious cases, and teaching others the necessary knowledge and skills that will permit the eventual expansion of manpower to meet society's needs.

In summary, the purpose of this chapter is to sketch a view of organizational process that stresses the action of members, and deliberately underplays the alternative perspective of systemic interchanges. In this view, an organization looks much more like a pickup team playing sandlot baseball than like a modern computer. This is not to deny rationality in organizations, only to put it in its proper place. Members interact within what they define as an organization. They accept that certain goals account for the existence of the organization, but they also have goals of their own—career goals. What they do is to partly find and partly make a role within the organization, largely through negotiating agreements with their colleagues and carrying out some agreed-upon activities. Some of the areas of negotiation can be anticipated by consideration of the ordinary and unique components of the organizational setting and the sources of uncertainty that abound in the environment. Many of the problems are recurrent. In managing recurrent problems and in meeting unique crises, members negotiate changes in the existent order. Crises occur frequently and, along with changes in the external environment, account for the ongoing process of organizational development.

OVERVIEW

This set of readings focuses on negotiation. Each essay considers a different aspect of negotiation, from its character as a dynamic process to its part in our most general understandings about our environment.

In the first essay negotiation is described as a dynamic interpersonal process of bargaining that can be understood by considering some strategies and principles used in making deals. The second essay shows more of the complexities that arise when the negotiation process is considered in the context of a particular collegial setting—in this case, a police agency. Rules abound as a result of external pressures, but the ongoing relationships between police officers and their superiors are based mainly on understandings and agreements that result from common, everyday experiences. Informally, the negotiated order surpasses and supersedes the formal and rational system of regulations.

The third essay extends the perspective on negotiation by considering the ongoing interplay between an organizational setting and its environment that influences the defining and setting of goals. When goals are not taken for granted, a question arises—how are goals created? The answer is given in terms of an interaction process; goals are negotiated by members. The final essay offers a more general perspective from which it appears that the environment itself must be considered as a negotiated reality, as a social phenomenon created by the interactions of members.

Before taking up the first essay, by Schelling, some background on the theory of conflict will be helpful. It is easy enough to recognize that conflict is inherent in bargaining situations. Each bargaining agent enters into the encounter with a desire to exercise power over the other, to cause the other to do something that he would not otherwise do. However, bargaining power is not the same as what we might ordinarily refer to as strength. An analogy to adversarial combat, wherein each party attempts to subdue the other by superior force, would be very inappropriate.

Conflict, unlike indifference, is a common part of all social relationships and can function to stabilize the relationship as long as each party recognizes his dependence on, that is, his interest in, the other's well-being. The goal of bargaining is to create an agreement by which each party willingly serves the others' interests in a reciprocal exchange of values. Conflicts of interest become stabilizing forces when reciprocity arises.

Bargaining power can be understood as the ability of an agent to induce the other to come to terms or, to say it another way, bargaining power is the ability to close the deal. Schelling begins with the assumption that deals can be brought to a close most effectively by establishing what he calls commitment. Commitment is closely tied with the notion of being bound to a position, which makes that position no longer negotiable. The first party to establish commitment enjoys an advantage as his position can be made final in place of the other's position. Therefore, the power to bind oneself is more important in bargaining than the power to bind the other, whether by superior strength or other means.

Commitment can be established by many structural and institutional tactics including the use of devices such as third parties and public declarations. For example, a third party who bargains for one of the principals can claim to be bound by a rigid set of limitations that produces a take-it-or-leave-it situation. Or, by making a public declaration of his position, the bargaining agent establishes an unbearable price to be paid for making concessions—the loss of public face.

Schelling maintains that threats, overt and implied, are often present in bargaining situations. If a party threatens to act if his position is not met, however, certain risks are created. He must be willing and able. It is very binding if he can demonstrate that he no longer has the power to not do what he threatens to do—the doomsday bomb for example. If he is found to be bluffing his bargaining power is totally lost.

In the second essay, Manning offers a look at the complexity of negotiating a stable order within an actual organizational setting that contains two sets of members who share a conflict of interests. Conventional analyses of police organization have stressed the traditional lines between superior and subordinate representing both military and bureaucratic virtues. Rules existed as a device by which the superior could ensure that his subordinates would not deviate from their duties as he defined and commanded them. Over time, rules emerged to ensure that senior officers did not shirk from their duties to enforce the other rules, and so on. This system made certain that the senior officers would dominate the lower members.

In Manning's paper an alternative view is given; the above description is treated as mere superficial appearances. Police officers hold that it is important to present a militaristic face to outsiders. But in the absence of outsiders, police organization is enacted as an interplay between the perspectives of the lower members (who stress that real police work is a matter of resolving unexpected situations as they are met "out there" in the community) and their administrator colleagues (who posit norms of reliability, accountability, and compliance with rules). Rules (which represent outcomes of prior mistakes, indiscretions, and embarrassments) and, most particularly, rules about rule infractions provide an interactional arena for the two opposing world views. The resulting conflict is moderated by a common base of police experience, which permits senior officers to "understand" rule infractions, and by efforts on the part of lower members to control information that would lead to confrontations.

Thus, police organizations are integrated in terms of rules, but the true meaning of rules requires knowledge of the network of understandings and taken-for-granted knowledge shared by the members; relations with the external environment often require punitive enforcement of the rules for the sake of appearances, but, in most cases, having reports of infractions in an officer's record is understood as "part of the job."

Next, Thompson's and McEwen's essay introduces an interest in policy and environmental relations. Goal-setting refers to a continuous and ongoing process of finding purpose and meaning, which is part of the everyday life of an organization. Thompson and McEwen view the process as change in response to both external changes and the outcomes of interactions among members. It is necessary to carry on negotiations through which the goals are continuously redefined and realigned within the changing situation. Goal-setting is a regular part of the everyday life of an organization.

For some organizations the questions of evaluating goals and products is easier than for others. Profit-making, as a goal leading to the manufacture and sale of shoes for example, is easier to appraise than an intangible goal with uncertain products, such as the goal of mental health which may lead to the operation of a hospital for the confinement and treatment of patients. In short, it is easier to choose between shoes and purses than between hospitals and community-based programs because the goals differ in terms of specificity and concreteness.

The essay continues, taking up environmental relations. An organizational environment imposes demands and sets limits on members' actions. Environmental controls are related to the complexity of an organization's social setting. This view draws on the earlier work of Emile Durkheim, a sociologist who was concerned with social control and social change; some additional background may be helpful.

Durkheim began by noting that societies grow. Growth leads to complexity, as in the case of a complex division of labor. If every citizen possesses only part of the skills and knowledge on which the welfare of the whole depends, every citizen must depend on other specialists to do what he cannot do for himself. Interdependence among a society's members raises a control problem, for even if a member violates the social norms he may still be valuable to the whole for the specialized functions he can perform. The solidarity of the whole can only be maintained by a system that restores the deviant member to his proper social role and restores orderly relations among the citizens. A restitutive social control system generally relies on the development of formal rules that prevail over personal desires for revenge and on the use of impersonal third parties such as the police and the courts to handle the problems as they arise.

Getting back to the essay, Thompson and McEwen posit that complexity, whether in the environment or within the organizational setting, leads to increasing reliance on legalistic forms of control. This tendency accounts for the increasing development of bureaucracy in Western society.

Competition and cooperation offer alternative modes of developing environmental relations. Competition over scarce resources such as clients, funds, members, and loyalties are seen as very important. But cooperative strategies, including bargaining, cooperation, cooptation, and coalition, are widely adopted to ensure stability and order.

To reflect for a moment on the meaning of this essay for our understanding of collegial organizations, consider the prevailing trend toward increasing complexity and legalistic relations within organizations and with their environments. Collegiality represents a reversal of the trend—a return to older and simpler relations. Collegial settings are really very different from their environments in this respect. Consequently, the members of collegial organizations relate to their fellow members according to one scheme of reality and to everybody who comprises their social environment according to a different scheme. This gives each set of relations a special meaning and leads to different patterns of expectations, tolerance, and reaction. Professionals relate to their colleagues in terms of primary group norms and to those in the larger environment in terms of impersonal, legalistic, universalistic, and specific norms.

In the concluding essay, Weick approaches the negotiation process from the broadest view of all—he suggests that the environment is itself largely a matter for negotiation. Much of our understanding of environmental influences on organisms, he argues, cannot be applied to human societies because unlike other life forms, humans do not merely react to their environment. Humans are active agents—they create their environment!

Following Alfred Schutz, the process of creating an environment is related to man's limited capacities of attention. We receive far more sensory inputs than we can possibly incorporate into our awareness, so some inputs are selected for attention and others, perhaps equally valid, are merely denied or ignored. We experience only a selective portion of our environment, yet that portion which we experience is all that we are aware of. What is not experienced cannot be learned. Nor can it be acted upon. We draw our lines of action from an environment that we ourselves have enacted.

Continuing, Weick shows that man's ability to plan action based on an enacted environment has important consequences in terms of finding meaning. To plan an action involves its assessment, its evaluation. But evaluations of action are based on outcomes. Plans and outcomes become the same thing. In other words, to say *I will do a thing* is to say *it is done.* Action is anticipated and meanings are anticipated outcomes of completed acts. Meaning is retrospective. I look back at what I have done and say it was good or it was bad.

Planning action is not done by a person totally alone. Part of the process of selection is the evaluation of plans of action in terms of individual meanings and the other part involves what Weick calls system meanings. Meanings are not only retrospective but are social as well. Finally, meanings are essentially related to concerns about *doing;* they are future-directed and have only secondary significance for the status quo.

In sum, this chapter presents organizational process as social interaction between members, especially in the form of negotiating action and meaning in the everyday life of organizational members.

NINE
AN ESSAY
ON BARGAINING
Thomas C. Schelling

This paper presents a tactical approach to the analysis of bargaining. The subject includes both explicit bargaining and the tacit kind in which adversaries watch and interpret each other's behavior, each aware that his own actions are being interpreted and anticipated, each acting with a view to the expectations that he creates. In economics the subject covers wage negotiations, tariff negotiations, competition where competitors are few, settlements out of court, and the real estate agent and his customer. Outside economics it ranges from the threat of massive retaliation to taking the right of way from a taxi.

Our concern will *not* be with the part of bargaining that consists of exploring for mutually profitable adjustments, and that might be called the "efficiency" aspect of bargaining. For example, can an insurance firm save money, and make a client happier, by offering a cash settlement rather than repairing the client's car; can an employer save money by granting a voluntary wage increase to employees who agree to take a substantial part of their wages in merchandise? Instead, we shall be concerned with what might be called the "distributional" aspect of bargaining: the situations in which more for one means less for the other. When the business is finally sold to the one interested buyer, what price does it go for? When two dynamite trucks meet on a road wide enough for one, who backs up?

These are situations that ultimately involve an element of pure bar-

Source: Abridged from "An Essay on Bargaining" by Thomas C. Schelling. *American Economic Review,* 46 (June 1956): 281–306. The author notes that this article also appears as Chapter 2 in *The Strategy of Conflict,* by Thomas C. Schelling. © 1960, Cambridge: Harvard University Press.

gaining—bargaining in which each party is guided mainly by his expectations of what the other will accept. But with each guided by expectations and knowing that the other is too, expectations become coumpounded. A bargain is struck when somebody makes a final, sufficient concession. Why does he condede? Because he thinks the other will not. "I must concede because he won't. He won't because he thinks I will. He thinks I will because he thinks I think he thinks so. . . . " There is some range of alternative outcomes in which any point is better for both sides than no agreement at all. To insist on any such point is pure bargaining, since one always *would* take less rather than reach no agreement at all, and since one always *can* recede if retreat proves necessary to agreement. Yet if both parties are aware of the limits to this range, *any* outcome is a point from which at least one party would have been willing to retreat and the other knows it! There is no resting place.

There is, however, an outcome; and if we cannot find it in the logic of the situation we may find it in the tactics employed. The purpose of this essay is to call attention to an important class of tactics, of a kind that is peculiarly appropriate to the logic of indeterminate situations. The essence of these tactics is some voluntary but irreversible sacrifice of freedom of choice. They rest on the paradox that the power to constrain an adversary many depend on the power to bind oneself; that, in bargaining, weakness is often strength, freedom may be freedom to capitulate, and to burn bridges behind one may suffice to undo an opponent.

Bargaining Power: the Power to Bind Oneself

"Bargaining power," "bargaining strength," "bargaining skill" suggest that the advantage goes to the powerful, the strong, or the skillful. It does, of course, if those qualities are defined to mean only that negotiations are won by those who win. But if the terms imply that it is an advantage to be more intelligent or more skilled in debate, or to have more financial resources, more physical strength, more military potency, or more ability to withstand losses, then the term does a disservice. These qualities are by no means universal advantages in bargaining situations; they often have a contrary value.

The sophisticated negotiator may find it difficult to seem as obstinate as a truly obstinate man. If a man knocks at a door and says that he will stab himself on the porch unless given $10, he is more likely to get the $10 if his eyes are bloodshot. The threat of mutual destruction cannot be used to deter an adversary who is too unintelligent to comprehend it or too weak to enforce his will on those he represents. The government that cannot control its balance of payments, or collect taxes, or muster the political unity to defend itself, may enjoy assistance that would be denied it if it could control its own resources. And, to cite an example familiar from economic theory, "price leadership" in oligopoly may be an unprofitable distinction evaded by the small firms and assumed perforce by the large one.

Bargaining power has also been described as the power to fool and bluff, "the ability to set the best price for yourself and fool the other man into thinking this was your maximum offer."[1] Fooling and bluffing are certainly involved; but there are two kinds of fooling. One is deceiving about the facts; a buyer may lie about his income or misrepresent the size of his family. The other is purely tactical. Suppose each knows everything about the other, and each knows what the other knows. What is there to fool about? The buyer may say that, though he'd really pay up to twenty and the seller knows it, he is firmly resolved as a tactical matter not to budge above sixteen. If the seller capitulates, was he fooled? Or was he convinced of the truth? Or did the buyer really not know what he would do next if the tactic failed? If the buyer really "feels" himself firmly resolved, and bases his resolve on the conviction that the seller will capitulate, and the seller does, the buyer may say afterwards that he was "not fooling." Whatever has occurred, it is not adequately conveyed by the notions of bluffing and fooling.

How does one person make another believe something? The answer depends importantly on the factual question, "Is it true?" It is easier to prove the truth of something that is true than of something false. To prove the truth about our health we can call on a reputable doctor; to prove the truth about our costs or income we may let the person look at books that have been audited by a reputable firm or the Bureau of Internal Revenue. But to persuade him of something false we may have no such convincing evidence.

When one wishes to persuade someone that he would not pay more than $16,000 for a house that is really worth $20,000 to him, what can he do to take advantage of the usually superior credibility of the truth over a false assertion? Answer: make it true. How can a buyer make it true? If he likes the house because it is near his business he might move his business, persuading the seller that the house is really now worth only $16,000 to him. This would be unprofitable; he is no better off than if he had paid the higher price.

But suppose the buyer could make an irrevocable and enforceable bet with some third party, duly recorded and certified, according to which he would pay for the house no more that $16,000, or forfeit $5,000. The seller has lost; the buyer need simply present the truth. Unless the seller is enraged and withholds the house in sheer spite, the situation has been rigged against him; the "objective" situation—the buyer's true incentive —has been voluntarily, conspicuously, and irreversibly changed. The seller can take it or leave it. This example demonstrates that if the buyer can accept an irrevocable commitment, in a way that is unambiguously visible to the seller, he can squeeze the range of indeterminacy down to the point most favorable to him. It also suggests, by its artificiality, that the tactic is one that may or may not be available; whether the buyer can find an effective device for commiting himself may depend on who he is, who the seller is, where they live, and a number of legal and institutional arrangements (including, in our artificial example, whether bets are legally enforceable).

If both men live in a culture where "cross my heart" is universally accepted as potent, all the buyer has to do is allege that he will pay no more than $16,000, using this invocation of penalty, and he wins—or at least he wins if the seller does not beat him to it by shouting "$19,000, cross my heart." If the buyer is an agent authorized by a board of directors to buy at $16,000 but not a cent more, and the directors cannot constitutionally meet again for several months and the buyer cannot exceed his authority, and if all this can be made known to the seller, then the buyer "wins"—if, again, the seller has not tied himself up with a commitment to $19,000. Or if the buyer can assert that he will pay no more than $16,000 so firmly that he would suffer intolerable loss of personal prestige or bargaining reputation by paying more, and if the fact of his paying more would necessarily be known, and if the seller appreciates all this, then a loud declaration by itself may provide the commitment. The device, of course, is a needless surrender of flexibility unless it can be made fully evident and understandable to the seller.

Incidentally, some of the more contractual kinds of commitments are not as effective as they at first seem. In the example of the self-inflicted penalty through the bet, it remains possible for the seller to seek out the third party and offer a modest sum in consideration of the latter's releasing the buyer from the bet, threatening to sell the house for $16,000 if the release is not forthcoming. The effect of the bet—as of most such contractual commitments—is to shift the locus and personnel of the negotiation, in the hope that the third party will be less available for negotiation or less subject to an incentive to concede. To put it differently, a *contractual* commitment is usually the assumption of a contingent "transfer cost," not a "real cost"; and if all interested parties can be brought into the negotiation the range of indeterminacy remains as it was. But if the third party were available only at substantial transportation cost, to that extent a truly irrevocable commitment would have been assumed. (If bets were made with a number of people, the "real costs" of bringing them into the negotiation might be made prohibitive.)[2]

The most interesting parts of our topic concern whether and how commitments can be taken; but it is worth while to consider briefly a model in which practical problems are absent—a world in which absolute commitments are freely available. Consider a culture in which "cross my heart" is universally recognized as absolutely binding. Any offer accompanied by this invocation is a final offer, and is so recognized. If each party knows the other's true reservation price, the object is to be first with a firm offer. Complete responsibility for the outcome then rests with the other, who can take it or leave it as he chooses (and who chooses to take it). Bargaining is all over; the commitment (i.e., the first offer) wins.

Interpose some communication difficulty. They must bargain by letter; the invocation becomes effective when signed but cannot be known to the other until its arrival. Now when one party writes such a letter the other may already have signed his own, or may yet do so before the letter of the first arrives. There is then no sale; both are bound to incompatible positions. Each must now recognize this possibility of stalemate, and take into account the likelihood that the other already has, or will have, signed his own commitment.

An asymmetry in communication may well favor the one who is (and is known to be) unavailable for the receipt of messages, for he is the one who cannot be deterred from his own commitment by receipt of the other's. (On the other hand, if the one who cannot communicate can feign ignorance of his own inability, the other too may be deterred from his own commitment by fear of the first's unwitting commitment.) If the commitments depend not just on words but on special forms or ceremonies, ignorance of the other party's commitment ceremonies may be an advantage if the ignorance is fully appreciated, since it makes the other aware that only his own restraint can avert stalemate.

Suppose only part of the population belongs to the cult in which "cross my heart" is (or is believed to be) absolutely binding. If everyone knows (and is known to know) everyone else's affiliation, those belonging to this particular cult have the advantage. They can commit themselves, the others cannot. If the buyer says "$16,000, cross my heart" his offer is final; if the seller says "$19,000" he is (and is known to be) only "bargaining."

If each does not know the other's true reservation price there is an initial stage in which each tries to discover the other's and misrepresent his own, as in ordinary bargaining. But the process of discovery and revelation becomes quickly merged with the process of creating and discovering commitments; the commitments permanently change, for all practical purposes, the "true" reservation prices. If one party has, and the other has not, the belief in a binding ceremony, the latter pursues the "ordinary" bargaining technique of *asserting* his reservation price, while the former proceeds to *make* his.

The foregoing discussion has tried to suggest both the plausibility and the logic of self-commitment. Some examples may suggest the relevance of the tactic, although an observer can seldom distinguish with confidence the consciously logical, the intuitive, or the inadvertent, use of a visible tactic. First, it has not been uncommon for union officials to stir up excitement and determination on the part of the membership during or prior to a wage negotiation. If the union is going to insist on $2 and expects the management to counter with $1.60, an effort is made to persuade the membership not only that the management could pay $2 but even perhaps that the negotiators themselves are incompetent if they fail to obtain close to $2. The purpose—or, rather, a plausible purpose suggested by our analysis—is to make clear to the management that the negotiators could not accept less than $2 *even if they wished to* because they no longer control the members or because they would lose their own positions if they tried. In other words, the negotiators reduce the scope of their own authority, and confront the management with the threat of a strike that the union itself cannot avert, even though it was the union's own action that eliminated its power to prevent the strike.

Something similar occurs when the United States government negotiates with other governments on, say, the uses to which foreign assistance will be put, or tariff reduction. If the executive branch is free to negotiate the best arrangement it can, it may be unable to make any position stick and may end by conceding controversial points because its partners know, or believe obstinately, that the United States would rather concede than terminate the negotiations. But if the executive branch negotiates under legislative authority, with its position constrained by law, and it is evident that Congress will not be reconvened to change the law within the necessary time period, then the executive branch has a firm position that is visible to its negotiating partners.

When national representatives go to international negotiations knowing that there is a wide range of potential agreement within which the outcome will depend on bargaining, they seem often to create a bargaining position by public statements, statements calculated to arouse a public opinion that permits no concessions to be made. If a binding public opinion can be cultivated, and made evident to the other side, the initial position can thereby be made visibly "final."

These examples have certain characteristics in common. First, they clearly depend not only on incurring a commitment but on communicating it persuasively to the other party. Second, it is by no means easy to establish the commitment, nor is it entirely clear to either of the parties concerned just how strong the commitment is. Third, similar activity may be available to the parties on both sides. Fourth, the possibility of commitment, though perhaps available to both sides, is by no means equally available; the ability of a democratic government to get itself tied by public opinion may be different from the ability of a totalitarian government to incur such a commitment. Fifth, they all run the risk of establishing an immovable position that goes beyond the ability of the other to concede, and thereby provoke the likelihood of stalemate or breakdown.

Institutional and Structural Characteristics of the Negotiation

Some institutional and structural characteristics of bargaining situations may make the commitment tactic easy or difficult to use, or make it more available to one party than the other, or affect the likelihood of simultaneous commitment or stalemate.

USE OF A BARGAINING AGENT.   The use of a bargaining agent affects the power of commitment in at least two ways. First, the agent may be given instructions that are difficult or impossible to change, such instructions (and their inflexibility) being visible to the opposite party. The principle applies in distinguishing the legislative from the executive branch, or the management from the board of directors, as well as to a messenger-carried offer when the bargaining process has a time limit and the principal has interposed sufficient distance between himself and his messenger to make further communication evidently impossible before the time runs out.

Second, an "agent" may be brought in as a principal in his own right, with an incentive structure of his own that differs from his principal's. This device is involved in automobile insurance; the private citizen, in settling out of court, cannot threaten suit as effectively as the insurance company since the latter is more conspicuously obliged to carry out such threats to maintain its own reputation for subsequent accidents.[3]

SECRECY VS. PUBLICITY.   A potent means of commitment, and sometimes the only means, is the pledge of one's reputation. If national representatives can arrange to be charged with appeasement for every small concession, they place concession visibly beyond their own reach. If a union with other plants to deal with can arrange to make any retreat dramatically visible, it places its bargaining reputation in jeopardy and thereby becomes visibly incapable of serious compromise. (The same convenient jeopardy is the basis for the universally exploited defense, "If I did it for you I'd have to do it for everyone else.") But to commit in this fashion publicity is required. Both the initial offer and the final outcome would have to be known; and if secrecy surrounds either point, or if the outcome is inherently not observable, the device is unavailable. If one party has a "public" and the other has not, the latter may try to neutralize his disadvantage by excluding the relevant public; or if both parties fear the potentialities for stalemate in the simultaneous use of this tactic, they may try to enforce an agreement on secrecy.

INTERSECTING NEGOTIATIONS. If a union is simultaneously engaged, or will shortly be engaged, in many negotiations while the management has no other plants and deals with no other unions, the management cannot convincingly stake its bargaining reputation while the union can. The advantage goes to the party that can persuasively point to an array of other negotiations in which its own position would be prejudiced if it made a concession in this one. (The "reputation value" of the bargain may be less related to the outcome than to the firmness with which some initial bargaining position is adhered to.) Defense against this tactic may involve, among other things, both misinterpretation of the other party's position and an effort to make the eventual outcome incommensurable with the initial positions. If the subjects under negotiation can be enlarged in the process of negotiation, or the wage figure replaced by fringe benefits that cannot be reduced to a wage equivalent, an "out" is provided to the party that has committed itself; and the availability of this "out" weakens the commitment itself, to the disadvantage of the committed party.

CONTINUOUS NEGOTIATIONS. A special case of interrelated negotiations occurs when the same two parties are to negotiate other topics, simultaneously or in the future. The logic of this case is more subtle; to persuade the other that one cannot afford to recede, one says in effect, "If I conceded to you here, you would revise your estimate of me in our other negotiations; to protect my reputation with you I must stand firm." The second party is simultaneously the "third party" to whom one's bargaining reputation can be pledged. This situation occurs in the threat of local resistance to local aggression. The party threatening achieves its

commitment, and hence the credibility of its threat, not by referring to what it would gain from carrying out the threat in this particular instance but by pointing to the long-run value of a fulfilled threat in enhancing the credibility of future threats.

THE RESTRICTIVE AGENDA. When there are two objects to negotiate, the decision to negotiate them simultaneously or in separate forums or at separate times is by no means neutral to the outcome, particularly when there is a latent extortionate threat that can be exploited only if it can be attached to some more ordinary, legitimate, bargaining situation. The protection against extortion depends on refusal, unavailability, or inability, to negotiate. But if the object of the extortionate threat can be brought onto the agenda with the other topic, the latent threat becomes effective.

Tariff bargaining is an example. If reciprocal tariffs on cheese and automobiles are to be negotiated, one party may alter the outcome by threatening a purely punitive change in some other tariff. But if the bargaining representatives of the threatened party are confined to the cheese-automobile agenda, and have no instructions that permit them even to take cognizance of other commodities, or if there are ground rules that forbid mention of other tariffs while cheese and automobiles remain unsettled, this extortionate weapon must await another opportunity. If the threat that would be brought to the conference table is one that cannot stand publicity, publicity itself may prevent its effective communication.

THE POSSIBILITY OF COMPENSATION. As   Fellner has pointed out, agreement may be dependent on some means of redistributing costs or gains.[4] If duopolists, for example, divide markets in a way that maximizes their combined profits, some initial accrual of profits is thereby determined; any other division of the profits requires that one firm be able to compensate the other. If the fact of compensation would be evidence of illegal collusion, or if the motive for compensation would be misunderstood by the stockholders, or if the two do not sufficiently trust each other, some less optimum level of *joint* profits may be required in order that the initial accrual of profits to the two firms be in closer accordance with an agreed division of gains between them.

When agreement must be reached on something that is inherently a one-man act, any division of the cost depends on compensation. The "agenda" assumes particular importance in these cases, since a principal means of compensation is a concession on some other object. If two simultaneous negotiations can be brought into a contingent relationship with each other, a means of compensation is available. If they are kept separate, each remains an indivisible object.

It may be the advantage of one party to keep a bargain isolated, and to the other to join it to some second bargain. If there are two projects, each with a cost of three, and each with a value of two to A and a value of four to B, and each is inherently a "one-man" project in its execution, and if compensation is institutionally impossible, B will be forced to pay the entire cost of each as long as the two projects are kept separate. He cannot usefully threaten nonperformance, since A has no incentive to carry out either project by himself. But if B can link the projects together, offering to carry out one while A carries out the other, and can effectively threaten to abandon both unless A carries out one of them, A is left an option with a gain of four and a cost of three, which he takes, and B cuts his cost in half.

An important limitation of economic problems, as prototypes of bargaining situations, is that they tend disproportionately to involve divisible objects and compensable activities. If a drainage ditch in the back of one house will protect both houses; and if it costs $1,000 and is worth $800 to each home-owner; neither would undertake it separately, but we nevertheless usually assume that they will get together and see that this project worth $1,600 to the two of them gets carried out. But if it costs 10 hours a week to be scoutmaster, and each considers it worth 8 hours of his time to have a scout troop but one man must do the whole job, it is far from certain that the neighbors will reach a deal according to which one puts 10 hours on the job and the other pays him cash or does 5 hours' gardening for him. When two cars meet on a narrow road, the ensuing deadlock is aggravated by the absence of a custom of bidding to pay for the right of way. Parliamentary deadlocks occur when logrolling is impracticable. Measures that require unanimous agreement can often be initiated only if several are bundled together.[5]

THE MECHANICS OF NEGOTIATION. A number of other characteristics deserve mention, although we shall not work out their implications. Is there a penalty on the conveyance of false information? Is there a penalty on called bluffs, i.e., can one put forth an offer and withdraw it after it has been accepted? Is there a penalty on hiring an agent who pretends to be an interested party and makes insincere offers, simply to test the position of the other party? Can all interested parties be recognized? Is there a time limit on the bargaining? Does the bargaining take the particular structure of an auction, a Dutch auction, a sealed bid system, or some other formal arrangement? Is there a *status quo,* so that unavaila-

bility for negotiation can win the *status quo* for the party that prefers it? Is renegotiation possible in case of stalemate? What are the costs of stalemate? Can compliance with the agreement be observed? What, in general, are the means of communication, and are any of them susceptible of being put out of order by one party or the other? If there are several items to negotiate, are they negotiated in one comprehensive negotiation, separately in a particular order so that each piece is finished before the next is taken up, or simultaneously through different agents or under different rules.

The importance of many of these structural questions becomes evident when one reflects on parliamentary technique. Rules that permit a president to veto an appropriation bill only in its entirety, or that require each amendment to be voted before the original act is voted on, or a priority system accorded to different kinds of motions, substantially alter the incentives that are brought to bear on each action. One who might be pressured into choosing second best is relieved of his vulnerability if he can vote earlier to eliminate that possibility, thereby leaving only first and third choices about which his preference is known to be so strong that no threat will be made.

PRINCIPLES AND PRECEDENTS.   To be convincing, commitments usually have to be qualitative rather than quantitative, and to rest on some rationale. It may be difficult to conceive of a really firm commitment to $2.07½; why not $2.02¼? The numerical scale is too continuous to provide good resting places, except at nice round numbers like $2.00. But a commitment to the *principle* of "profit sharing," "cost-of-living increases," or any other basis for a numerical calculation that comes out at $2.07½, may provide a foothold for a commitment. Furthermore, one may create something of a commitment by putting the principles and precedents themselves in jeopardy. If in the past one has successfully maintained the principle of, say, nonrecognition of governments imposed by force, and elects to nail his demands to that principle in the present negotiation, he not only adduces precedent behind his claim but risks the principle itself. Having pledged it, he may persuade his adversary that he would accept stalemate rather than capitulate and discredit the principle.

CASUISTRY.   If one reaches the point where concession is advisable, he has to recognize two effects: it puts him closer to his opponent's position, and it affects his opponent's estimate of his firmness. Concession not only may be construed as capitulation, it may mark a prior commitment as a fraud, and make the adversary skeptical of any new pretense at commitment. One, therefore, needs an "excuse" for accommodating his opponent, preferably a rationalized reinterpretation of the original commitment, one that is persuasive to the adversary himself.

More interesting is the use of casuistry to release an opponent from a commitment. If one can demonstrate to an opponent that the latter is not committed, or that he has miscalculated his commitment, one may in fact undo or revise the opponent's commitment. Or if one can confuse the opponent's commitment, so that his constituents or principals or audience cannot exactly identify compliance with the commitment—show that "productivity" is ambiguous, or that "proportionate contributions" has several meanings—one may undo it or lower its value. In these cases it is to the opponent's disadvantage that this commitment be successfully refuted by argument. But when the opponent has resolved to make a moderate concession one may help him by proving that he *can* make a moderate concession consistent with his former position, and that if he does there are no grounds for believing it to reflect on his original principles. One must seek, in other words, a rationalization by which to deny himself too great a reward from his opponent's concession, otherwise the concession will not be made.[6]

The Threat

When one threatens to fight if attacked or to cut his price if his competitor does, the threat is no more than a communication of one's own incentives, designed to impress on the other the automatic consequences of his act. And, incidentally, if its succeeds in deterring, it benefits both parties.

But more than communication is involved when one threatens an act that he would have no incentive to perform but that is designed to deter through its promise of mutual harm. To threaten massive retaliation against small encroachments is of this nature, as is the threat to bump a car that does not yield the right of way or to call a costly strike if the wage rate is not raised a few cents. The distinctive feature of this threat is that the threatener has no incentive to carry it out either before the event or after. He does have an incentive to bind himself to fulfill the threat, if he thinks the threat may be successful, because the threat and not its fulfillment gains the end; and fulfillment is not required if the threat succeeds. The more certain the contingent fulfillment is, the less likely is actual fulfillment. But the threat's efficacy depends on the credulity of the other party, and the threat is ineffectual unless the threatener can rearrange or display his own incentives so as to demonstrate that he would, *ex post,* have an incentive to carry it out.[7]

We are back again at the commitment. How can one commit himself in advance to an act that he would in fact prefer not to carry out in the event, in order that his commitment may deter the other party?One can of course bluff, to persuade the other falsely that the costs or damages to the threatener would be minor or negative. More interesting, the one making the threat may pretend that he himself erroneously believes his own costs to be small, and therefore would mistakenly go ahead and fulfill the threat. Or perhaps he can pretend a revenge motivation so strong as to overcome the prospect of self-damage; but this option is probably most readily available to the truly revengeful. Otherwise he must find a way to commit himself.

One may try to stake his reputation on fulfillment, in a manner that impresses the threatened person. One may even stake his reputation *with the threatened person himself,* on grounds that it would be worth the costs and pains to give a lesson to the latter if he fails to heed the threat. Or one may try to arrange a legal commitment, perhaps through contracting with a third party.[8] Or if one can turn the whole business over to an agent whose salary (or business reputation) depends on carrying out the threat but who is unalterably relieved of any responsibility for the further costs, one may shift the incentive.

The commitment problem is nicely illustrated by the legal doctrine of the "last clear chance" which recognizes that, in the events that led up to an accident, there was some point at which the accident became inevitable as a result of prior actions, and that the abilities of the two parties to prevent it may not have expired at the same time. In bargaining, the commitment is a device to leave the last clear chance to decide the outcome with the other party, in a manner that he fully appreciates; it is to relinquish further initiative, having rigged the incentives so that the other party must choose in one's favor. If one driver speeds up so that he cannot stop, and the other realizes it, the latter has to yield. A legislative rider at the end of a session leaves the President the last clear chance to pass the bill. This doctrine helps to understand some of those cases in which bargaining "strength" inheres in what is weakness by other standards. When a person—or a country—has lost the power to help himself, or the power to avert mutual damage, the other interested party has no choice but to assume the cost or responsibility. "Coercive deficiency" is the term Arthur Smithies uses to describe the tactic of deliberately exhausting one's annual budgetary allowance so early in the year that the need for more funds is irresistibly urgent.[9]

A related tactic is maneuvering into a *status quo* from which one can be dislodged only by an overt act, an act that precipitates mutual damage because the maneuvering party has relinquished the power to retreat. If one carries explosives visibly on his person, in a manner that makes destruction obviously inevitable for himself and for any assailant, he may deter assault much more than if he retained any control over the explosives. If one commits a token force of troops that would be unable to escape, the commitment to full resistance is increased. Walter Lippmann has used the analogy of the plate glass window that helps to protect a jewelry store: anyone can break it easily enough, but not without creating an uproar.

Similar techniques may be available to the one threatened. His best defense, of course, is to carry out the act before the threat is made; in that case there is neither incentive nor commitment for retaliation. If he cannot hasten the act itself, he may commit himself to it; if the person to be threatened is already committed, the one who would threaten cannot deter with his threat, he can only make certain the mutually disastrous consequences that he threatens.[10] If the person to be threatened can arrange before the threat is made to share the risk with others (as suggested by the insurance solution to the right-of-way problem mentioned earlier) he may become so visibly unsusceptible to the threat as to dissuade the threatener. Or if by any other means he can either change or misrepresent his own incentives, to make it appear that he would gain in spite of threat fulfillment (or perhaps only that he thinks he would), the threatener may have to give up the threat as costly and fruitless; or if one can misrepresent himself as either unable to comprehend a threat, or too obstinate to heed it, he may deter the threat itself. Best of all may be *genuine* ignorance, obstinacy, or simple disbelief, since it may be more convincing to the prospective threatener; but of course if it fails to persuade him and he commits himself to the threat, both sides lose. Finally, both the threat and the commitment have to be communicated; if the threatened person can be unavailable for messages, or can destroy the communication channels, even though he does so in an obvious effort to avert threat, he may deter the threat itself.[11] But the time to show disbelief or obstinacy is before the threat is made, i.e., before the commitment is taken, not just before the threat is fulfilled; it does no good to be incredulous, or out of town, when the messenger arrives with the committed threat.

In threat situations, as in ordinary bargaining, commitments are not altogether clear; each party cannot exactly estimate the costs and values to the other side of the two related actions involved in the threat; the process of commitment may be a progressive one, the commitments acquiring their firmness by a sequence of actions. Communication is often neither entirely impossible nor entirely reliable; while certain evidence of one's commitment can be communicated directly, other evidence must travel by newspaper or hearsay, or be demonstrated by actions. In these cases the unhappy possibility of both acts occurring, as a result of simultaneous commitment, is increased. Furthermore, the recognition of this possibility of simultaneous commitment becomes itself a deterrent to the taking of commitments.[12]

In case a threat is made and fails to deter, there is a second stage prior to fulfillment in which *both* parties have an interest in undoing the commitment. The purpose of the threat is gone, its deterrence value is zero, and only the commitment exists to motivate fulfillment. This feature has, of course, an analogy with stalemate in ordinary bargaining, stalemate resulting from both parties getting committed to incompatible positions, or one party mistakenly committing himself to a position that the other truly would not accept. If there appears a possibility of undoing the commitment, *both* parties have an interest in doing so. How to undo it is a matter on which their interests diverge, since different ways of undoing it lead to different outcomes. Furthermore, "undoing" does not mean neglecting the commitment regardless of reputation; "undoing," if the commitment of reputation was real, means disconnecting the threat from one's reputation, perhaps one's own reputation with the threatened person himself. It is therefore a subtle and tenuous situation in which, though both have an interest in undoing the commitment, they may be quite unable to collaborate in undoing it.

Special care may be needed in defining the threat, both the act that is threatened against and the counter act that is threatened. The difficulty arises from the fact, just noted, that once the former has been done the incentive to perform the latter has disappeared. The credibility of the threat before the act depends on how visible to the threatened party is the ability of the threatening party to rationalize his way out of his commitment once it has failed its purpose. Any loopholes the threatening party leaves himself, if they are visible to the threatened party, weaken the visible commitment and hence reduce the credibility of the threat.

It is essential, therefore, for maximum credibility to leave as little room as possible for judgment or discretion in carrying out the threat. If one is committed to punish a certain type of behavior when it reaches certain limits, but the limits are not carefully and objectively defined, the party threatened will realize that when the time comes to decide whether the threat must be enforced or not, his interest and that of the threatening party will coincide in an attempt to avoid the mutually unpleasant consequences.

In order to make a threat precise, so that its terms are visible both to the threatened party and to any third parties whose reaction to the whole affair is of value to the adversaries, it may be necessary to introduce some arbitrary elements. The threat must involve overt acts rather than intentions; it must be attached to the visible deeds, not invisible ones; it may have to attach itself to certain ancillary actions that are of no consequence in themselves to the threatening party. It may, for example, have to put a penalty on the carrying of weapons rather than their use; on suspicious behavior rather than observed misdemeanors; on proximity to a crime rather than the crime itself. And, finally, the act of punishment must be one whose effect or influence is clearly discernible. [13]

In order that one be able to pledge his reputation behind a threat, there must be continuity between the present and subsequent issues that will arise. This need for continuity suggests a means of making the original threat more effective; if it can be decomposed into a series of consecutive smaller threats, there is an opportunity to demonstrate on the first few transgressions that the threat will be carried out on the rest. Even the first few become more plausible, since there is a more obvious incentive to fulfill them as a "lesson."

This principle is perhaps most relevant to acts that are inherently a matter of degree. In foreign aid programs the overt act of terminating assistance may be so obviously painful to both sides as not to be taken seriously by the recipient, but if each small misuse of funds is to be accompanied by a small reduction in assistance, never so large as to leave the recipient helpless nor to provoke a diplomatic breach, the willingness to carry it out will receive more credulity; or, if it does not at first, a few lessons may be persuasive without too much damage. [14]

The threatening party may not, of course, be able to divide the act into steps. (Both the act to be deterred and the punishment must be divisible.) But the principle at least suggests the unwisdom of defining aggression, or transgression, in terms of some critical degree or amount that will be deemed intolerable. When the act to be deterred is inherently a sequence of steps whose cumulative effect is what matters, a threat geared to the increments may be more credible than one that must be carried either all at once or not at all when some particular point has been reached. It may even be impossible to define a "critical point" with sufficient clarity to be persuasive.

To make the threatened acts divisible, the acts themselves may have to be modified. Parts of an act that cannot be decomposed may have to be left out; ancillary acts that go with the event, though of no interest in themselves, may be objects to which a threat can effectively be attached. For example, actions that are only preparatory to the main act, and by themselves do no damage, may be susceptible of chronological division and thus be effective objects of the threat. The man who would kick a dog should be threatened with modest punishment for each step toward the dog, even though his proximity is of no interest in itself.

Similar to decomposing a threat into a series is starting a threat with a punitive act that grows in severity with the passage of time. Where a threat of death by violence might not be credited, cutting off the food supply might bring submission. For moral or public relations purposes, this device may in fact leave the "last clear chance" to the other, whose demise is then blamed on his stubborness if the threat fails. But in any case the threatener gets his overt act out of the way while it is still preliminary and minor, rather than letting it stand as a final, dreadful, and visible obstacle to his resolution. And if the suffering party is the only one in a position to know, from moment to moment, how near to catastrophe they have progressed, his is the last clear chance in a real sense. Furthermore, the threatener may be embarrassed by his adversary's collapse but not by his discomfort; and the device may therefore transform a dangerous once-for-all threat into a less costly continuous one. Tenants are less easily removed by threat of forcible eviction than by simply shutting off the utilities.[15]

A piecemeal approach may also be used by the threatened person. If he cannot obviate the threat by hastening the entire act, he may hasten some initial stage that clearly commits him to eventual completion. Or, if his act is divisible while the threatener's retaliation comes only in the large economy size, performing it as a series of increments may deny the threatener the dramatic overt act that would trigger his response.

The Promise

Among the legal privileges of corporations, two that are mentioned in textbooks are the right to sue and the "right" to be sued. Who wants to be sued! But the right to be sued is the power to make a promise: to borrow money, to enter a contract, to do business with someone who might be damaged. If suit does arise the "right" seems a liability in retrospect; beforehand it was a prerequisite to doing business.

In brief, the right to be sued is the power to accept a commitment. In the commitments discussed up to this point, it was essential that one's adversary (or "partner," however we wish to describe him) not have the power to release one from the commitment; the commitment was, in effect, to some third party, real or fictitious. The promise is a commitment to the second party in the bargain, and is required whenever the final action of one or of each is outside the other's control. It is required whenever an agreement leaves any incentive to cheat.[16]

This need for promises is more than incidental; it has an institutional importance of its own. It is not always easy to make a convincing, self-

binding, promise. Both the kidnapper who would like to release his prisoner, and the prisoner, may search desperately for a way to commit the
latter against informing on his captor, without finding one. If the victim has
committed an act whose disclosure could lead to blackmail, he may con-
fess it; if not, he might commit one in the presence of his captor, to create
the bond that will ensure his silence. But these extreme possibilities illustrate how difficult, as well as important, it may be to assume a promise. If
the law will not enforce price agreements; or if the union is unable to
obligate itself to a no-strike pledge; or if a contractor has no assets to pay
damages if he loses a suit, and the law will not imprison debtors; or if there
is no "audience" to which one can pledge his reputation; it may not be
possible to strike a bargain, or at least the same bargain that would otherwise be struck.

Bargaining may have to concern itself with an "incentive" system as
well as the division of gains. Oligopolists may lobby for a "fair-trade" law;
or exchange shares or stocks. An agreement to stay out of each other's
market may require an agreement to redesign the products to be unsuitable in each other's area. Two countries that wish to agree not to make
military use of an island may have to destroy the usefulness of the island
itself. (In effect, a "third-party commitment" has to be assumed when an
effective "second-party commitment" cannot be devised.)[17]

Fulfillment is not always observable. If one sells his vote in a secret
election, or a government agrees to recommend an act to its parliament,
or an employee agrees not to steal from inventory, or a teacher agrees to
keep his political opinions out of class, or a country agrees to stimulate
exports "as much as possible," there is no reliable way to observe or
measure compliance. The observable outcome is subject to a number of
influences, only one of which is covered by the agreement. The bargain
may therefore have to be expressed in terms of something observable,
even though what is observable is not the intended object of the bargain.
One may have to pay the bribed voter if the election is won, not on how
he voted; to pay a salesman a commission on sales, rather than on skill and
effort; to reward policemen according to statistics on crime rather than on
attention to duty; or to punish all employees for the transgressions of one.
And where performance is a matter of degree, the bargain may have to
define arbitrary limits distinguishing performance from nonperformance;
a specified loss of inventory treated as evidence of theft; a specified increase in exports considered an "adequate" effort; specific samples of
performance taken as representative of total performance.[18]

The tactic of decomposition applies to promises as well as to threats.
What makes many agreements enforceable is only the recognition of

future opportunities for agreement that will be eliminated if mutual trust is not created and maintained, and whose value outweighs the momentary gain from cheating in the present instance. Each party must be confident that the other will not jeopardize future opportunities by destroying trust at the outset. This confidence does not always exist; and one of the purposes of piecemeal bargains is to cultivate the necessary mutual expectations. Neither may be willing to trust the other's prudence (or the other's confidence in the first's prudence, etc.) on a large issue. But if a number of preparatory bargains can be struck on a small scale, each may be willing to risk a small investment to create a tradition of trust. The purpose is to let each party demonstrate that he appreciates the need for trust and that he knows the other does too. So if a major issue has to be negotiated, it may be necessary to seek out and negotiate some minor items for "practice," to eastablish the necessary confidence in each other's awareness of the long-term value of good faith.

Even if the future will bring no recurrence, if may be possible to create the equivalence of continuity by dividing the bargaining issue into consecutive parts. If each party agrees to send a million dollars to the Red Cross on condition the other does, each may be tempted to cheat if the other contributes first, and each one's anticipation of the other's cheating will inhibit agreement. But if the contribution is divided into consecutive small contributions, each can try the other's good faith for a small price. Furthermore, since each can keep the other on short tether to the finish, no one ever need risk more than one small contribution at a time. Finally, this change in the incentive structure itself takes most of the risk out of the initial contribution; the value of established trust is made obviously visible to both.

Preparatory bargains serve another purpose. Bargaining can only occur when at least one party takes initiative in proposing a bargain. A deterrent to initiative is the information it yields, or may seem to yield, about one's eagerness. But if each has visible reason to expect the other to meet him half way, because of a history of successful bargaining, that very history provides protection against the inference of overeagerness.[19]

Footnotes

[1] J. N. Morgan, "Bilateral Monopoly and the Competitive Output," *Quart. Jour. Econ.*, Aug. 1949, LXIII, 376, n.6.

[2] Perhaps the "ideal" solution to the bilateral monopoly problem is as follows. One member of the pair shifts his marginal cost curve so that joint profits are now zero

at the output at which joint profits originally would have been maximized. He does this through an irrevocable sale-leaseback arrangement; he sells a royalty contract to some third party for a lump sum, the royalties so related to his output that joint costs exceed joint revenue at all other outputs. He cannot now afford to produce at any price or output except that price and output at which the entire original joint profits accrue to him; the other member of the bilateral monopoly sees the contract, appreciates the situation, and accepts his true minimum profits. The "winner" really gains the entire original profit via the lump sum for which he sold royalty rights; this profit does not affect his incentives because it is independent of what he produces. The third party pays the lump sum (minus a small discount for inducement) because he knows that the second party will have to capitulate and that therefore he will in fact get his contingent royalty. The hitch is that the royalty-rights buyer must not be available to the "losing member"; otherwise the latter can force him to renounce his royalty claim by threatening not to reach a bargain, thus restoring the original marginal cost situation. But we may imagine the development of institutions that specialize in royalty purchases, whose ultimate success depends on a reputation for never renegotiating, and whose incentives can thus not be appealed to in any single negotiation.

[3] The formal solution to the right-of-way problem in automobile traffic may be that the winner is the one who first becomes fully and visibly insured against all contingencies; since he then has no incentive to avoid accident, the other must yield and knows it. (The latter cannot counter in kind; no company will insure him now that the first is insured.) More seriously, the pooling of strike funds among unions reduces the visible incentive on each individual union to avoid a strike. As in the bilateral monopoly solution suggested earlier, there is a transfer of interest to a third party with a resulting visible shift in one's own incentive structure.

[4] W. Fellner, *Competition Among the Few* (New York, 1949), pp. 34-35, 191-97, 231-32, 234.

[5] Inclusion of a provision on the Saar in the "Paris Agreements" that ended the occupation of Western Germany may have reflected either this principle or the one in the preceding paragraph.

[6] In many textbook problems, such as bilateral monopoly between firms, the ends of the bargaining range are points of zero profits for one or the other party; and to settle for one's minimum position is no better than no settlement at all. But apart from certain buying and selling situations there are commonly limits on the range of acceptable outcomes, and the least favorable outcome that one is free to accept may be substantially superior to stalemate. In these cases one's overriding purpose may be to forestall any misguided commitment by the other party. If the truth is more demonstrable than a false position, a conservative initial position is indicated, as it is if any withdrawal from an initial "advanced" position would discredit any subsequent attempt to convey the truth. Actually, though a person does not commonly invite penalties on his own behavior, the existence

of an enforceable penalty on falsehood would be of assistance; if one can demonstrate, for example, his cost or income position by showing his income tax return, the penalties on fraud may enhance the value of this evidence.

Even the "pure" bilateral monopoly case becomes somewhat of this nature if the bargaining is conducted by agents or employees whose rewards are more dependent on *whether* agreement is reached than on how favorable the terms of the agreement are.

[7] Incidentally, the deterrent threat has some interesting quantitative characteristics, reflecting the general asymmetry between rewards and punishments. It is not necessary, for example, that the threat promise more damage to the party threatened than to the party carrying it out. The threat to smash an old car with a new one may succeed if believed, or to sue expensively for small damages, or to start a price war. Also, as far as the power to deter is concerned, there is no such thing as "too large" a threat; if it is large enough to succeed, it is not carried out anyway. A threat is only "too large" if its very size interferes with its credibility. Atomic destruction for small misdemeanors, like expensive incarceration for overtime parking, would be superfluous but not exhorbitant unless the threatened person considered it too awful to be real and ignored it.

[8] Mutual defense treaties among strong and weak nations might best be viewed in this light, i.e., not as undertaken to reassure the small nations nor in exchange for a *quid pro quo,* but rather as a device for surrendering an embarrassing freedom of choice.

[9] A. Smithies, *The Budgetary Process in the United States* (New York, 1955), pp. 40, 56. One solution is the short tether of an apportionment, process. See also T. C. Schelling, "American Foreign Assistance," *World Politics,* July 1955, VII, 609-25, regarding the same principle in foreign aid allocations.

[10] The system of supplying the police with traffic tickets that are numbered and incapable of erasures makes it possible for the officer, by writing in the license number of the car before speaking to the driver, to preclude the latter's threat. Some trucks carry signs that say, "Alarm and lock system not subject to the driver's control." The time lock on bank vaults serves much the same purpose, as does the mandatory secret ballot in elections. So does starting an invasion with a small advance force that, though too small and premature to win the objective, attaches too much "face" to the enterprise to permit withdrawal: the larger force can then be readied without fear of inviting a purely deterrent threat. At Yale the faculty is protected by a rule that denies instructors the power to change a course grade once it has been recorded.

[11] The racketeer cannot sell protection if he cannot find his customer at home; nor can the kidnapper expect any ransom if he cannot communicate with friends or relatives. Thus, as a perhaps impractical suggestion, a law that required the immediate confinement of all interested friends and relatives when a kidnapping occurred might make the prospects for ransom unprofitably dim. The rotation

of watchmen and policemen, or their assignment in random pairs, not only limits their exploitation of bribes but protects them from threats.

[12] It is a remarkable institutional fact that there is no simple, universal way for persons or nations to assume commitments of the kind we have been discussing. There are numerous ways they can try, but most of them are quite ambiguous, unsure, or only occasionally available. In the "cross-my-heart" society adverted to earlier, bargaining theory would reduce itself to game strategy and the mechanics of communication; but in most of the contemporary world the topic is mainly an empirical and institutional one of who can commit, how, and with what assurance of appreciation by the other side.

[13] During 1950, the Economic Cooperation Administration declared its intention to reward Marshall Plan countries that followed especially sound policies, and to penalize those that did not, through the device of larger or smaller aid allotments. But since the base figures had not been determined, and since their determination would ultimately involve judgment rather than formulas, there would be no way afterwards to see whether in fact the additions and subtractions were made, and the plan suffered from implausibility.

[14] Perhaps the common requirement for amortization of loans at frequent intervals, rather than in a lump sum at the end of the loan period, reflects an analogous principle, as does the custom of giving frequent examinations in a college course to avoid letting a student's failure hinge exclusively on a single grading decision after the course is finished.

[15] This seems to be the tactic that avoided an explosion and induced de Gaulle's forces to vacate a province they had occupied in Northern Italy in June 1945, after they had announced that any effort of their allies to dislodge them would be treated as a hostile act. See Harry S. Truman, *Year of Decisions* (New York, 1955), pp. 239–42; and Winston S. Churchill, *Triumph and Tragedy,* Vol. VI of *The Second World War* (Boston, 1953) pp. 566–68.

[16] The threat may seem to be a promise if the pledge behind it is only one's reputation with his adversary; but it is not a promise from which the second party can unilaterally release the threatener, since he cannot convincingly dissociate his own future estimate of the threatener from the latter's performance.

[17] In an earlier age, hostages were exchanged.

[18] Inability to assume an enforceable promise, like inability to perform the activity demanded, may protect one from an extortionate threat. The mandatory secret ballot is a nuisance to the voter who would like to sell his vote, but protection to the one who would fear coercion.

[19] Perhaps two adversaries who look forward to some large negotiated settlement would do well to keep avenues open for negotiation of minor issues. If, for example, the number of loose ends in dispute between East and West should narrow down so much that nothing remains to be negotiated but the "ultimate

issue" (some final, permanent disposition of all territories and armaments) the possibility of even opening negotiations on the latter might be jeopardized. Or, if the minor issues are not disposed of, but become so attached to the "big" issue that willingness to negotiate on them would be construed as overeagerness on the whole settlement, the possibility of preparatory bargains might disappear.

TEN
RULES, COLLEAGUES, AND SITUATIONALLY JUSTIFIED ACTIONS *
Peter K. Manning

Introduction

Formal organizations attempt to systematically reward participants who adhere to some set of stipulated goals or objectives; the organizations also use a public official imagery of their operations to both constrain members and to obtain deference from external audiences. However, organizations vary in their internal compliance structures and external environment.[1] Organizations operating in highly problematic environments (environments that engender public deference and expectations of diverse but effective intervention; e.g., the police, military, and to a lesser degree fire, ambulance, and emergency services of all types), have historically tended to develop rigid and quasi-military internal structures (McNamara, and Reiss and Bordua, in Bordua, ed., 1967, and Bittner, 1970). In such organizations, although the degree of dependency of lower participants on higher participants may fluctuate around the midpoint among organizations (Stinchcombe, 1965: 180–185), rules, especially disciplinary rules,

* Research funded by a General Research Support Grant from the College of Human Medicine and All University Research of Michigan State University. The data were gathered during my tenure as Visiting Research Scholar at University of London, Goldsmiths' College, London, 1972–73. I gratefully acknowledge the assistance provided by Chief Superintendent Stephen O'Brien, Chief Superintendent Benjamin Plunkett, Superintendent Angus Pattison and the many men who so willingly gave of their time and energy to facilitate my inquiries. Mike Chatterton and Maureen Cain were very helpful throughout my investigations. None of them is responsible for my conclusions.

are the primordial nexus around which colleague relationships are negotiated. The types of dependency and exchange that result are fundamentally different from organizations typically called "professional" or even
those with a high degree of flexibility and innovative potential. (Scott,
1966 and Wilensky, 1960). The aim of this paper is to explore some of
the commonsense or assumed grounds of organizational integration (Manning, 1970). An English police organization serves as a context or background against which to analyze the perspectives of the two principle
organizational segments. Those perspectives become most visible through
a study of the place of rules and rule-enforcement upon colleagueship
within this organization. The results of such a study have important consequences for the participants' view of the organization as an acting unit and
the boundaries of organizational reality.[2]

Method and Setting

The study from which these data are drawn was undertaken in July and
August 1973 in one of three subdivisional headquarters within one of the
23 divisions of the London Metropolitan police. Interviews, observation,
and records were gathered.[3]

The subdivision studied ("Thameside") was bordered on one side by the
Thames, on one side by one of the "home counties," and on the other sides
by metropolitan London. Once a lively industrial and military center, the
area declined in size following the end of World War II and is now a quiet
lower middle and middle class community that includes riverside, docks,
several large commons, numerous public housing developments, and
residential dwellings.

Police work on the subdivision is varied, but tends toward "order
maintenance" (Banton, 1964). The clearance rate for crime allegations is
considered to be one of the highest in the London metropolitan police
area. The chief superintendent sets the style of law enforcement to a
considerable degree and is "community minded" rather than "crime
minded," an emphasis compatible with the career concerns and age of the
men on the station. The average age is 38.5, and it has been 4½ years
since a new probationer reported to this subdivision. The age and experience of the men, with this policy emphasis, contributes to the general
feeling of satisfaction and high morale that characterizes the station.

The Commonsense Reality of Policing

Policemen on this subdivision are bound by a set of implicit and unexplicated understandings that might be called the "commonsense reality of

policing"—what everyone knows and takes for granted—and the skills that a policeman must acquire in order to be viewed as a competent member of the force. Three aspects of this organizational reality are the shared assumptions about the nature of police work, the occupational culture, and task dependency.

All London policeman share a *base-line of experience* as a lower participant because they enter the organization at the same point. Practical experience forms the basis for a conviction that policing is to a certain extent, situationally justified ("You can't police by the book") and lacks certainty and clarity ("You never know what to expect next"—"A policeman has seen everything"). Although this experiential foundation of police work is seldom discussed as a basis of agreement, it is implicitly accepted and recognized as essential to occupational competence. Policemen understand that people (especially "civvies," i.e., the public) who lack this work experience cannot understand "what it is like being a policeman." Further, it is understood that: (1) all decisions, whether "on the ground" (on patrol), or in the station, whether by patrolmen or senior officers, are made situationally, are based on commonsense and require discretion. They cannot be made on the basis of an abstract theory of policing, the law, or police regulations. (2) That both internal and external sources offer competing definitions of rules is a reality of police work. Ample collective experience supports the belief that different segments of the public make different demands on the police Senior officers and men can recall having used more than one interpretation of a law, depending on the situation. They have seen courts reverse previous positions and make illegal what was once legal. Policemen have argued, often in self-defense, over the meanings of many disciplinary rules and legal statutes.

At the center of the occupational culture of policing (Manning, 1971; 1972) are features of the role considered to be *core skills, cognitions,* and *affect.* They collectively serve as the defining characteristics of the "good practitioner" and "good police work." Among the uniformed English policemen who were interviewed, administrative policemen (above the rank of sergeant) and others agreed that the following were aspects of "good police work":[4] a cool emotional tone, properly executed tactics (in order to obtain and maintain control over interaction), properly applied skills, and a fair and open-minded view of given encounters with the public. If these conditions obtain, then policemen feel that they can bring off a clear closure or termination based on agreement or at least minimal dissensus, and they remain able to control the level and direction of effort. That is, they feel able to exercise a level of conscientious withdrawal of efficiency if need be to protect a definition of good police work derived from the implicit rules of the occupational culture.

A third basis for collective action as well as tension and misunderstanding is a set of ties growing from *task dependence.* The extensive nature of this web of solidarity binding together police constables (PCs) and senior officers, intermediate and immediate supervisors, is well documented. With regard to the constable's dependency on senior officers, matters of formal discipline, promotion and evaluation of performance, transfers, accomodation, general welfare, and other informal and formal rewards are most important. Constables also depend on their intermediate and immediate superiors (sergeants and inspectors) for support in extralegal situations (e.g., domestic disputes), good progress reports, recommendations for formal rewards congenial working conditions, and backing in disputes with senior officers. Senior officers depend on the men below them for information, restraint and discretion in "easing" behavior (drinking, sleeping on the job, accepting favors), legal infringements, and for striving for a level of work efficiency (Cain, 1973: 181). Although situational and problematic, these exchange networks that channel information, gifts, nonverbal affirmations, and written data between organizational segments constitute an important determinant of the internal morphology of the organization.

Organizational Segments

These potentially binding funds of shared experience (assumptions, occupational culture, and task dependence) are simultaneously a basis of organizational integration *and* a source of shared misunderstandings. The ambiguous basis for organizational action and the means by which it is accomplished (rules) creates the context within which the two principle organizational segments interact. One's perspective on these shared assumptions dervies directly from one's position in the organizational structure.

Senior officers (ranks above sergeant, including in this subdivision inspectors, chief inspectors, superintendent, and chief superintendent) see their connection to the organization through the ideology of scientific police administration. This view justifies their life style, mobility aspirations, and, most importantly, their identification with the respectable and propertied middle classes whom they define as their target audience. Their world is organized from a seemingly natural acceptance of the legitimacy of their position within the organization, a justification of this position through an identification with the traditions of upholding the law and providing protection for British citizens, and a perceived consensus on their role provided from their target audience. Positing a *consensual other* seems to be a significant part of the police ideology articulated by the administrative strata:

> Policemen need to believe in a largely consensual populace whose values and standards they represent and enforce. It is by reference to this that they legitimate their activities. They are intermediaries who bring forth for punishment whom 'most people' deem to deserve it. (Cain, 1973:69)

Since senior officers are not required to appear in court, deal with face-to-face problems of justice, or to do "real police work," they are paradoxically insulated against the stigma of policing while they are denied a degree of credibility from those they supervise. That is, once senior officers accept administrative posts they are deprived of direct contact with social groups and persons who are seen as representatives of evil and are thus permitted to move symbolically closer to the socially sacred and traditional values of English society. On the other hand, senior officers are deprived of the legitimacy within the organization that is granted by constables to officers who maintain even an intermittent contact with the men and with activities defined by policemen as containing the essence of the entire enterprise.

Police constables cannot draw upon a formalized ideology of policing. For them, the legitimacy of police authority is unquestioned and assumed rather than discussed; obedience to senior officers is, however, contextual rather than entirely categorical. Constables simultaneously hold a view of senior officers as incompetent to serve in the positions they hold (e.g., "when you join a rat race, as you move up, there are fewer contenders . . . ") and an envious understanding that "somebody has to do it." The *ambivalence* of constables is manifest in two ways. There is a common belief that Chatterton (personal communication) has called "the myth of protecting the higher ups." Constables, recognizing there are no concrete rules governing policing, believe that it is "down to them" to prevent senior officers from embarrassing themselves. This is done in part by avoiding blatant displays of skyving or easing behavior,[5] by informally sanctioning policemen who are considered to be excessively lazy or self-serving, and by informally providing information to senior officers. (Since channels are rarely used "up the line" by patrolmen except in their written reports of incidents, senior officers are quite dependent on sergeants to fill them in on "what's happening downstairs" and to discretely avoid telling other things.)

The other manifestation of ambivalence bears on the conception of higher officers. They see senior officers as equivalent on "human terms" insofar as both constables and other ranks "are fathers and heads of families, property owners, and members of the community." Other named features of sergeants' role, for example, such as "more pay," "a little more knowledge of the law," were considered as embroidery upon the basic fact that they could "do the job" (the constables' job—real police work) but were "the same on other grounds." "One does not respect them [officers] because of rank only." If PCs view those above them in this way, they reason, then the men above should view PCs as individuals as well as policemen. Solidarity of policemen is seemingly required vis-à-vis outside groups where policeman and person are not separated; within the organization, however, it is not possible to respect an officer who does not see one as a person.[6]

It is quite possible the *stability and continuity of the authority of the organization required a reification of higher authority while personal face-to-face contacts made individualistic and situational judgments necessary.* Even in the absence of a general theory of policing, it was agreed that the administration was held responsible and publicly accountable for policy and operations. Policemen of all ranks see police work as logically requiring personalistic and particularistic decisions. However the police mandate in the context of the British political system required them to act collectively *as if* there were indeed a clear abstract legal and social mandate from which they derived goals and purposes.

Dilemmas of Organizational Action

Given these very different commitments, or social anchorages, within the organization, the dilemmas of organizational action are very real. Given the two segments and their perspectives on organizational action, and the structural features of police work (to be discussed), *rules can only function as resources for organizing and rationalizing a given contingency.* This characteristic of the work exercises important influences on the nature of colleagual relationships within the police organization. There are four fundamental reasons why police work is essentially situationally justified action. Let us explore these four structural conditions of police work.

First, knowledge is *asymmetrical:* all senior officers have served at least two years "on the ground" as constables, but with very few exceptions (none on this subdivision) constables have not served as senior officers. Senior officers continue to believe that they "understand" their men, and they are encouraged in this belief by exercising their legitimate capacity to reverse decisions taken by men on the street. Constables, on the other hand, deny this understanding, seeing most of their senior officers as out of touch, careerist, preoccupied with paper work, trivialities, and public relations. Second, the work is defined and justified "clinically" or tactically, rather than theoretically or even organizationally. *Police work is seen as individualistic, entrepreneurial, practical, face-to-face activity involving particular people and their problems.* As a consequence, only the everyday activities of the constable even approach the form and functions of "real police work." Paper work, court appearances, administrative tasks, or report writing (even routinely required occurrence booklets) are considered *ex post facto* glosses upon the real work on the ground. "Let's face it," one PC said to another as he gestured grandly out the window, "real policework is out there." Third, administrative tasks rarely permit dispensing of work within a clear, encapsulated episode, meeting the public directly in a law-enforcement capacity, or performing activities defined in line with "on the ground" standards of adequacy, competence, and level of effort. Since administrators do not and often cannot publicly define the decision-making rules by which police work should be carried out, and since the degree of discretion that is required is admittedly high, the administrator from the patrolman's perspective appears to be an accessory after the fact. From the administrator's point of view, on the other hand, the execution of policy, the efficient achievement of organization goals, and the maintenance of hierarchy and discipline are both required and a source of prestige and satisfaction. Fourth, although critical personal concerns, such as the nature of the work and the progress of an individual career, are located within the context of exchange between and mutual dependency of the ranks, implicit meanings are provided by the frames of *separate* experiences and individual biographies.

Conflicts between organizational segments over fundamental issues of policy and the degree of control of the organization over its members is *publicly* resolved in terms of the ideology of the higher strata. This rhetoric serves the important symbolic functions of defining publicly the limits of organizational action and providing terms of reference within which the outer boundaries of the organization's control over its participants are discussed. However, definitions implicit in the social world of lower participants (e.g., informally sanctioned discretionary practices and understandings) constantly *modify* and make *problematic* the imagery of bureaucratic authority displayed by the higher strata. In an important sense, the negotiation of organizational authority takes place *internally* rather than externally, particularly in the context of rules about the infraction of rules.

Negotiation and the Meaning of Rules

The principal arena in which the relationships between organizational segments are patterned is the domain of the enforcement of internal or *disciplinary rules* (Gouldner, 1954a, 1954b, and McNamara, in Bordua, ed., 1967).[7] Although rules can clarify particular procedures, they also provide for areas of discussion, negotiation, and uncertainty; each rule contains an indexical or contextual quality that makes it *defeasible* (Bittner, 1970:4).

Wilson writes: "The absence of agreed-upon standards for how the police should behave makes it hard for the patrolman in his opinion, to do his job properly; the presence of many procedural rules makes it easy to penalize him for doing it, in somebody's opinion, improperly." (Wilson, 1968:75) Only one aspect of rules will be discussed here. Uncertainties in the enforcement, interpretation, and consequences of disciplinary rules bearing primarily on the behavior of lower participants lead to forms of association which in turn modify the impact, and thus display the limits, of the power and authority of the administrative segment.

The seemingly inherent *uncertainties* manifest in the actual process of internal discipline within the subdivision reflect the tenuous multiplex relationships that obtain between senior officers and constables. First, and most importantly, there is a general feeling among PCs that one cannot predict when one will be sanctioned for a violation. The view is that there are so many regulations, covering so many aspects of the job, that routine work will intrinsically require violation of one or more of the rules listed in the 10,000-paragraph *General Orders*. It is considered purely a matter of chance or luck whether a rule will be invoked at a given time. One sergeant explained that the *General Orders* contained

> 140 years of fuck-ups. Every time something goes wrong, they make a rule about it. All the directions in the force flow from someone's mistake. You can't go 8 hours on the job without breaking the disciplinary code. For example, you have to sign [in CID] the duty book which places you specifically when you leave the station. Perhaps you return to the station at 3:00, but you chat, or have a cup of tea, and forget to book back in until 3:45 or 4. Then you forget what time you returned when you make out your weekly personal diary [a record of activities, expenses and evidence that must be turned in weekly to the Detective Inspector], and maybe put down 3 or 4, but in any case don't remember what time you

actually appeared, when you signed the duty book, or what time you entered when you did. But, no one cares until something goes wrong. The job goes wild on trivalities.

Two PCs and Sergeant A. were discussing the use of disciplinary reports by a notorious station sergeant, Sergeant B.:

A PC has been investigating a traffic accident and at a time when discipline was very strict, and where a specific refreshment time was assigned to each constable, and fairly carefully observed. He arrived after other constables on his relief had left the canteen. As he sat down for tea, the Sergeant entered and put him on report for exceeding his refreshment time. He did not ask the PC for details of the circumstances of his being there. The Sergeant asked for his book, entered the report, and made a note in his own book. It was later revealed when the Sergeant talked with the Chief Superintendent that he was in error. The incident was dropped. On another occasion Sergeant A [when a PC] was in the canteen and was asked for his book by Sergeant B who was going to put him on report for excessive refreshment time. Sergeant B didn't have a pen, used the PCs pen to write a report with an incorrect date and time. In this case, the charge was never carried to an investigation because of the error in the book.

Sergeant B was said "to put you on report and ask questions afterward." However, uncertainty also undercuts the authority of sergeants' disciplinary reports. A perception of dependent uncertainty among sergeants and PCs is heightened by the ways in which many apparently major violations of the disciplinary code reported to seniors by sergeants are handled:

One PC could not be raised on the personal radio while on patrol; his supervisor could not locate him for over two hours. Finally, the sergeant set out and found him drunk in his car parked on a side street. He put him on report. The chief superintendent called in the man charged and merely cautioned him, did not fine him or ask for further disciplinary action. Two weeks later, the same PC was on a small traffic patrol motorcycle [a "noddy"], and was shooting a .22. He thought he saw a rabbit walking on the sidewalk, took out his gun and shot the pet terrier of a citizen taking an evening stroll. Again, he was put on report and the chief superintendent cautioned him.

In this case, the expectations of the sergeant and the chief superintendent were not in conjunction; and as in many cases of disciplinary action, it could be said that the intention of the chief superintendent to give the man a second chance, and to "prove himself" was not well-understood by the sergeant in the case. (This is assuming that the sergeant did in fact desire to carry out the orders of the senior officer.) These kinds of situations demonstrate the importance of the *assumptions* in which orders are embedded, assumptions that to an important degree are rooted in the organizational position of the persons involved[8] Orders from senior officers to sergeants with regard to the enforcement of laws or the disciplinary code are like the orders given from senior officers to patrolmen in the form of general advisements, suggestions, or policy statements written in the parade book (a book containing useful information—e. g., "prisoner escaped; work to be done on Barclays' bank this weekend; child runaway from home on the section"—which officers are required to read when they come on duty.) The following appeared in the parade book: "The number of stops has increased, but I cannot believe there are not more to be made on this section" signed, Chief Inspector D. This note followed by a week an earlier "suggestion" written in the parade book asking PCs to increase the number of "stops" they made for investigatory purposes (odd-looking cars, persons on the street late at night). The first note had not been taken "seriously enough"; that is, it was not understood by constables. Since they turn in stops at the end of each duty turn, it is quite easy to check on their production rates. The second note was written in more threatening language in an attempt to decrease discretion. Similar dynamics of threat and then excess in applying negative sanctions occur when "disciplinary crackdowns" are mobilized by sergeants. From the point of view of the chief superintendent and superintendent, the enforcement of disciplinary rules by sergeants is always lax. When sergeants do periodically respond to ambiguous instructions from command officers (similar to the instructions regarding "stops"), for example, actually routinely enforce the disciplinary code, their actions are perceived by constables as unpredictably harsh, capricious and arbitrary. Thus, to *make sense of instructions,* one has to understand what "lies behind" instructions and to anticipate "what is really meant" by the person setting the task. To the degree that PCs are *unable* to make an "accurate" reading of formal or informal instructions they receive, they perceive themselves to be subject to enormous variations in enforcement practice. Stories concerning failure to understand the intentions of instructions are often told, and these "failures" as well as one's own delicts may be told in mixed groups of officers and constables by inspectors and sergeants who supervise the very men to whom they are talking.

Secondly, if a complaint is filed with the chief superintendent and an investigation initiated, there is uncertainty concerning the "side" that the investigatory officer will take—the "public's side" or the "policeman's side." [9] One CID man said, "the present state of mind in the force is roughly like that of the Jews in Nazi Germany in the late 'thirties. We fear knocks at the door at night and the like, and it has happened." An incident on the subdivision gave substance to the remark:

> Three policemen were sent to a fire in a local chemists' shop to supervise the protection of possible damaged goods, etc. After the fire, it was discovered that a large 25–30 cup tea boiler had "gone missing." The policemen suspected members of the fire brigade because they were not watched and moved freely in and out of the shop while attending the fire. The policemen, on the other hand, were under constant observation: two were outside, while one policeman was inside accompanying the owner. Subsequently, the three policemen were subject to an inconclusive investigation, and their homes were searched by other officers at the order of the chief superintendent. It was said that since one was usually given a pack of cigarettes or something anyway, taking goods was "more than the job was worth."

Another set of incidents illustrates the uncertainty with which police constables view the support of their senior officers. Police regulations state that no unauthorized passengers shall ride in police vehicles. In practical terms, this permits only prisoners or those under the authority of the policemen to ride. On the other hand, the public expects a wide range of generally willingly provided services from the police. Doing such services often leads to friendly thanks, a cup of tea, or sense of having accomplished a good piece of work (i. e., all the ends are tied up and the episode is closed). When a citizen requests a ride, the policeman feels that whether he refuses or offers a ride, he "cannot win."

> While driving a panda car, B encountered two girls standing on a street corner at about 2 a.m. He stopped and asked if he could help (a polite way of asking them what they were doing out at this time of night. Virtually everyone out after 12 or 1, depending on the area

of London, is stopped and questioned.). One of the girls explained that they had been at a party and that she had been subject to unwanted advances from a young man. They were afraid that he might make further advances, so they left the party on foot. The patrolman decided to give them a ride home. One girl saw her Dad on the corner; he asked if they were in trouble and the PC explained he was taking them home. He left the girls with the father. Three days after, correspondence was received from the father of one of the girls thanking the policeman for bringing his daughter home. The PC was called to the chief superintendent's office and given a lecture on the importance of following departmental regulations, and it was suggested that the only thing which prevented a disciplinary action (2 or 3 days' pay lost) against the PC was the fact that the girls made the allegation of rude and annoying behavior on the part of the boys at the party. The PC involved alleged that if he hadn't picked up the girls, and something happened to them, someone could ask, "Why didn't you take them home?"

On another occasion, the same policeman was involved in an accident investigation. The driver of one car was not injured, but could not drive home. The PC was asked to drive him home, but refused explaining that it was against departmental regulations. A letter was received from this driver complaining that the police did not provide a minimal public service in the form of transport home for a hapless accident victim. Since all correspondence must be shown to have been dealt with, the PC was again called into the chief superintendent's office and the matter was discussed.

Thirdly, PCs consider that there is a further set of uncertainties surrounding the *meaning of any given violation*. I asked one chief inspector what the ribbons on his tunic indicated. He pointed out that the last one was a police good conduct ribbon (or the equivalent) for "14 years of keeping out of trouble." PCs nearby said it was for "14 years of covering up mistakes or blaming them on someone else." The C.I. replied that "if you don't have any complaints after 14 years, you're in trouble! If they [a promotion board] look at a man with 14 years and he's got no 7's (investigations of complaints against him), they wonder what he's been doing." At a lunch with three detectives inspectors and a chief inspector, one of the senior detectives on the division, the chief inspector, laughed at one point and said, "The public expects you to police by the book, the guvs (administration) expect you to police by the book, but it can't be done. Given the fact you can't police by the book, if a bloke hasn't got a few investigations in his file, he's probably not doing his job." The implication here is that if you are active as a policeman, you will have complaints against you. Another chief inspector, now nearing retirement, said that when he served on promotion boards some members would inspect a man's dossier, see a "black mark" against him (a complaint), and conclude "as you would about any person with a criminal file (convicted or not), that he's 'bent' " (a criminal). The existence of such marks, he explained, affects promotion possibilities when names are sifted for a "short list" group [those included in the final group sent before a promotion board]. He further explained that a man's file can include items of which he is unaware, for example, a traffic patrolman's file can include complaint letters written to the Yard without his knowledge. Complaints are filed and listed anonymously, and it was said that they are sometimes sent in by one's colleagues at a station (a "poison pen" letter). These anecdotes suggest at least that a constable can reasonably suspect that items in his file are held against him, and this knowledge may be a source of a degree of realistic "paranoia." However, even if one is aware of the complaint, its investigation, and the outcome, one can never be precisely certain what it means. Other policemen are also warned, everyone talks about the complaint experience, the air is full of tales of mistaken and erroneous complaints, and "policing by the book" is not seen as a guaranteed means for obtaining a "clean record." *It all depends, they feel, on whether the "guys" will support you when questions are raised.*

Rules, Indeterminacy, and Colleagueship

What is most significant about police regulations is that they are soon stripped of moral coating. People in general are viewed as stupid, fallible, greedy, lustful, immoral, and hypocritical—such views provide policemen with resources for hours of stories and jokes. Man is seen as a translucent Machiavelli, easily uncovered by insightful probing or police action. Fellow policemen are viewed in much the same fashion. Rules and written records become for the most part a *tactical* means of defending oneself against accusation, and a basis for counterattack if necessary. In relations with the public, the police, sensitive to the needs and demands of the more powerful members of the community (Black, 1968; 1970), are virtually forced to adopt a strategic moral position in order to ritualize the appearance of consensus (Burns, 1953:660). Since rules are resources by which a number of outcomes can be rationalized, policemen are often caught between these demand conditions and personal morality.[10] Sometimes PCs must manipulate the paper reality—what the record shows—in order to achieve desired outcomes, and sometimes they must conspire with others in the same situation to alter the dynamics in a way that makes a given outcome highly probable. The reality of police work, given this high component of uncertainty, is at times defined as writing the proper paper (what Goffman, 1961, calls "paper reality") in order to construct the appearances (what one wants to show to superiors in order to protect himself), and at other times, it is seen as managing problematic interactions such that analogous outcomes are generated.

There are thus two types of situations in which relationships based on norms not shared by those in the dominant group are displayed or in which ambiguity of the supervision of the senior officers leads to collusion. Two types of colleague relationships emerge: a *vertical/situational clique* based on the need to manipulate a face-to-face situation involving both PCs and senior officers (including in this case sergeants); and *horizontal/-situational cliques* based on PC relationships.[11]

Vertical situational cliques result because situations are presented repeatedly that, if they were solved by the book, would be time-consuming, potentially embarrassing, and explosive for all concerned. These cliques most commonly were observed in the reserve room with a sergeant present with a compliment of PCs. An efficacious solution required trust between the persons involved. When one manipulates the situation rather than the written record, one enters into a collusion with others present. For example, an act of Parliament stipulates that all phone messages received at a station must be logged in writing. In practice, the enormous volume of calls could not possibly be completely logged.

> The manager of a local department store calls to report to the police that he is turning over to them the fact that a woman had her purse stolen in the store. He reports that she does not want to report it to the police (but he wants to protect himself against a later claim by her against him or the store). The sergeant volunteers to enter it in the lost property book (therefore it is not a crime, and will not require investigation or clearance). The call is not shown in the message book.

Calls out are not logged unless they close an episode ("keyholder notified and went to the scene"). Errors in calls to area cars, duplications in messages to a panda and an area car are not recorded. Inter-police calls are not logged.

Once a man wanted a car which was left on his lot investigated as stolen property. He tried to hand the key to the sergeant on duty. The sergeant refused it (policemen cannot accept gifts nor property without a written reason or justification). He suggested that, "if the key were left, and if they looked around later, it might be found and then they might try some cars in the area to ascertain if any of them belonged to the key." The lot attendant blinked, left the key, and walked out. A PC immediately said in a false tone of surprise: "Hey, Sarg, someone left a car key on the counter! What should we do?" None of this was recorded.

In acting as they did in these incidents, policemen were violating laws requiring a written record to be kept of all police communications and of police handling of property. They were acting in collusion not only against "the public interest," but by handling the matter informally, they prevent senior officers from monitoring performance by means of written records. Thus informal control substitutes for formal controls and cliques become an active force in procedural matters. A similar pattern is revealed in the conversations between sergeants and constables prior to writing a charge in the charge book. Various laws are discussed as covering the event, and related charges are discussed; procedural questions; especially with juveniles (there have been a number of recent changes in the juvenile rules), are discussed and a final polished version is entered. This informal conference makes the eventual countersigning by the sergeant a ritual affirmation rather than a formal means of social control. It is these discussions, the understandings that the men draw on when they engage in such negotiations as well as their typifications of "crimes like this one" (Sudnow's "normal crimes" concept), that permit another policeman to "see" or understand what has happened prior to the written record. Understandings of the meanings of written records that emerge from situational negotiation with sergeants or inspectors are frequently made possible by direct personal knowledge of the sergeants on the shift at the time.

There was one sergeant on the station who was not trusted by the men because he was said to be the chief superintendent's man ("his toady"). He was assigned paper work duties in the station and had little contact with the daily affairs in the reserve room. But other sergeants, because there was an excess of sergeants on the subdivision, were often looking for something to do and would take out the reserve area car on patrol. One sergeant became well known for obtaining this duty and became closely associated with men on this turn. On nights and weekends, especially Sundays, sergeants and at least two of the inspectors on the station would play pool in the basement or cards in the charge room with the men. Thus, when problematic cases of rule-violation occurred, these sergeants "didn't want to know," and were particularly critical of the station sergeant (Sergeant B. in the above anecdotes) who was known for harsh and unquestioning punishment.

If, however, one manipulates the written record to protect himself against superiors and sergeants, one typically must have the trust of a horizontal clique (what is sometimes called the "occupational subculture"; (Westley, 1970). Since rules are surrounded by uncertainty, when disciplinary action is taken it is always viewed as arbitrary; cynicism is expressed about all forms of supervision on the subdivision. "Supervisors do not enforce what they want to enforce, but what they are told to enforce." (One ranking member of Scotland Yard, when asked what he was doing at the moment said, "I'm doing what I'm told to do.") "It isn't the conviction or detection rate they are worried about any more," one Sergeant told me,

> I work more and more to cover the trivialities. I'm all right provided I appear to be doing something, provided it all looks all right, and that all the squares are filled so that supervisors could come around and say, "You did something right yesterday." So you only do as much as necessary to have others conclude that you're doing something. Provided that you give the impression that you're doing something no one can know differently. Carrying a piece of paper indicates work.

One virtually always manipulates the written record to protect oneself. As one detective sergeant put it, "We work against when one might go wrong. It comes down like a rocket" [is returned with a note from the legal department at the Yard]. Thus, when one manipulates the written record in a case, one has to have specific knowledge and *trust* of the others involved.

The manipulation of the rules that takes place among horizontal cliques, typically partners in an area car, crew in the reserve room, or a team of people working plain clothes, allows lower participants to decrease the uncertainty in rule-enforcement and to protect themselves so that things don't come back. Young policemen must learn these guiles, lest they be as vulnerable as one very successful detective inspector who was asked to do a favor for his "Skip" (supervising sergeant) while working as a TDC (Temporary Detective Constable):

> Because there was no transport available at the time on the station, he took his own car and was subsequently involved in a traffic accident. He was bustled back to a uniform and lost 5 day's pay. He pointed out that it was stupid, he should have covered himself. [How?] "I should have asked someone to book me off, or book myself off when I got back to the station so that I would be covered, i.e., be off duty (detectives have to write in the duty book where they are at any time they leave the station, what they are investigating, and the purpose of the visit, e.g., Manning, to 121 Blackhearth Park S.E. 3, in Re: Smith to obtain statements).

However, these collusions and situational clique formations did not seem to create major rifts within the organization, perhaps because "success" and competition for success, either in the occupational milieu or outside, was not a ubiquitous concern, and the segments of the organization were more often divided by rank than by orientations to success. Had the success milieu obtained, as Burns (1955) has described, it is likely that the growth of corruption, the conscientious withdrawal of efficiency, and attempts to alter the legal and social constraints on policing might have been commonly observed among these policemen.

Comment

The quasi-military structure of police organizations creates the potential for capricious authority to be employed to define proper and adequate work. This seems to flow from the uncertain organizational environment in which Anglo-American police organizations operate: the relationships between the publics served by the organization and organizationally tied actors are open, ambiguous, and problematic. Rules, in the context of police work, are also areas in which negotiations will typically occur (e.g., if arrests and charges are more highly valued than community order-maintenance, then greater uncertainty will surround questions of a "good pinch"—an arrest that will stick. Rules legitimate punishment and provide rationalizations for administrative action. The rules stipulate universal minimal performance (grounds for dismissal, acceptable days of leave). The most significant source of power, or, conversely, the area of perhaps least dependence of

lower participants upon senior officers, is that which devolves from variations in the enforcement practices themselves, what Weber has called "the
conscientious withdrawal of efficiency." This is seen in the common American phenomena of "Blue Flu" (calling in sick in large numbers), waves of
ticket enforcements, or refusal to enforce laws against some kinds of victim-
less crimes especially gambling, prostitution, and after-hours drinking. In
English police departments, these actions are unknown. Nevertheless,
rules stipulate an *area of autonomy* for lower participants. The very proliferation of rules within a police organization permits lower participants to
virtually always "work to rule." That is, they always have some rule as a
resource and protection insofar as certain stipulated areas are those within
which rules operate.

What might be investigated in future analyses of police organizations
is the extent to which *rules* are not stipulated solely for the use of administrators in line with the ideology of scientific police theory, but set a bargaining ground for organizational strata, bring them into contact to negotiate
the meanings of events, and thus to produce the basis for *justifications* of
organizational action that draws together segments into *acting units*. [12] The
acquiescence of lower participants to the rule negotiation process is itself
an important and significant indication of their acceptance of the
legitimacy of the organization. The ways in which these rules are negotiated are a most significant indicator of the limits of the organizational
situation. That is, rules set out the limits of the organization's power over
its various publics (a phenomenon, which as Hughes has pointed out,
expands and contracts over time) and its power over its members. The
degree to which a person is submerged within an organization (Burns,
1961; Goffman, 1961) is at least in part a function not only of rules, but
the ways in which they are applied to particular persons and situations.

The application of these rules in turn creates a set of perhaps temporary collusions, or flexible alliances that are a form of colleagueship well
suited to negate some of the more potentially repressive and distructive
consequences of highly elaborated, codified system of rules and rules
about rules. As McNamara notes, "police work does not consist of a standardized product or service. . . . Given that the individual problems presented to officers are unique and given the existence of a bureaucratic
structure, then one should expect to find that officers face many of the
problems generally faced by professionals who are employed by large
organizations." (McNamara, in Bordua, ed., 1967:185) "Professional" in
this context does not refer to elaborated codes, abstracted theories, or
formalized training procedures, but rather to the form of problem faced.
In the absence of the public affirmation of a mandate, and the structural

dilemmas of police work, cliques and flexible informal groups may have both the potential for corruption and malfeasance and for enabling a degree of coping with relatively unpredictable events in a routine fashion.

Footnotes

[1] Structural features of the police *mandate* in Anglo-American society, i.e., the virtual monopoly on the legitimate use of violence and the authority to intervene in private affairs, create socially patterned demands for maintaining viable means of controlling the politicality of police actions, insuring the use of legal means for coercing the civilian populace, and guaranteeing an approximation of universal criteria in application of the law. The police, however, do not possess what they consider to be adequate public confirmation of their *mandate*, and are subject to socially structured (e.g., class, race, age, and situational) variations in public definitions of acceptable modes and frequency of legal intervention (Reiss, 1971:2). [See the writings of Banton (1964); J. O. Wilson (1968); the essays in Bordua, ed. (1967); and Manning (1971).] Because they do not enjoy the solidity of mandate required to establish the necessary degree of autonomy from their environment, police organizations have accomodated to their threatening situation by developing strategies and tactics by which they expect to maximize (dramatize) the appearance of their own efficacy. In what follows I am deliberately avoiding the issue of cross-cultural comparison, i.e., the issue of generality of my findings. The emphasis upon scientific policing and the police theory is less pronounced in England than in the United States, but it appears to dominate the public statements of police administrators in both societies. To that extent, then, criticism based on actual functioning of police departments in either nation should bear on the relevance of police theory to everyday reality in either society. I believe that the basic problems of policing in Anglo-American society are endemic and structural, and that the present paper contains themes and data that could be generalized to American police departments. I am not making the claim here. At present, I am engaged in an organizational study in a medium-sized police department in the American Midwest that should provide data bearing on these questions.

[2] I draw here on writings of Burns (1958); Crozier (1964, 1971); Bittner (1965); Silverman (1971); and Blankenship (1973). See also Manning (1970, 1973, 1973a).

[3] Observational and focused interview techniques were employed. I took field notes while making home beats, while riding in area and panda cars, while sitting in the reserve room (the main information room of the station), canteen, in the office of the Criminal Investigation Division (CID or "Detectives") and in the office of the chief superintendent. I also gathered statistics and assisted reserve officers by collating phone and teleprinter messages received at the station. The hours of observation were spent as follows:

TABLE 1   HOURS OF OBSERVATION ON "THAMESIDE"
SUBDIVISION JUNE 13 THROUGH AUGUST 13, 1973[a]

"Early Turn" 6 A.M. – 2 P.M.	"Late Turn" 2 P.M. – 11P.M.	"Nights" 11 P.M. – 6 A.M.	
74 hours	89 hours	21 hours	
	Total hours		184

[a] Since the research problem did not require comparison of functions or differences in work load, crime reporting or the like, the distribution of time spent at the station, walking, or on patrol, is relatively unimportant. However, by varying the times at the station and the days of the week, I satisfied myself that there were regularities in behavior and attitude that were not specific to given reliefs or turns (men work in reliefs that are rotated through turns on a 5-week basis). The outlines of the English urban policing system are well described in Cain, 1973: Chapter 3. Although she studied a Midlands city, her description of the fundamental organization of policing is also accurate for "Thameside."
Focused interviews were conducted with 33 men [10 officers above the rank of sergeant; 9 sergeants and 14 police constables (PCs)] in an attempt to gather information on concepts of success and competence as well as acceptable work performance (the level and direction of effort and terms for variation from "acceptable normal behavior"). Eliciting techniques were used with 26 men (4 officers, 8 sergeants, 14 PCs) to generate data relevant to the latter issues. Five group interviews with officers were held in the officers' dining room of the subdivisional headquarters.

[4] "Real police work" as a concept has parallels in other occupations. To the policeman, these are considered the "core skills" of the occupation and the "characteristic professional acts." These concepts are found, respectively, in Harvey L. Smith, "Contingencies of Professional Differentiation," *American Journal of Sociology,* 63 (January 1958), 410–414; and Rue Bucher and Anselm Strauss, "Professions in Process," *American Journal of Sociology,* 66 (January 1961), 325–334. For an application of these concepts to medicine, especially in regard to associated political attitudes, see Peter K. Manning, "Occupational Types and Organized Medicine: Physicians' Attitudes Toward the American Medical Association" (unpublished Ph.D. dissertation, Duke University, 1966), especially Chapter 3.

[5] The policeman, not unlike members of other occupations, may elect to control the extent of effort applied in the course of work. Argot terms, such as skyving and easing, give evidence that what is expected in the way of effort on-the-job is an open question. Easing behavior, for example, may allow one to hold back effort, but still be prepared to deal with problems which may arise. Skyving goes further. Skyving implies actual avoidance of situations calling for effort. To park one's patrol car alongside the river, with the radio left on, is easing behavior.

To do the same with the radio turned off is skyving behavior. The subject is treated more fully in Cain (1973).

6 I do not fully understand the implications of this argument. Perhaps the symbolization of rank, which is displayed by the use of titles while in organizational role (which occurs always when addressing a person of higher rank in the presence of a member of the public or of another person of higher rank), projects the constraints of the classification of relationships as hierarchically ordered, impersonal, and categorical. On the other hand, senior officers including sergeants, often address those below them, especially constables, by first name. Superiors can individualize "rank inferiors," while at least in face-to-face address, inferiors can only symbolize linguistically categorical and hierarchical relationships. Behind their backs, the men will refer to senior officers by nicknames of by affectionate corruptions of their names, thus providing the undertone of individualization and egalitarianism that draws attention to the fundamental equality of policemen, and to those who have been constables. The same pattern of assymetrical exchange takes place in the lending of money.

7 Invoking of rules as a means of social control clearly is related to a number of structural properties of types of organizations. Cf. Rushing's useful paper, "Organizational Rules and Surveillance: Propositions in Comparative Organizational Analysis" *Administrative Science Quarterly,* 10(March 1966), 423–443. In this subdivision, the ratio of sergeants to police Constables was 6–7 to one; and there was an additional sergeant supervising the three subdivisions under the command of the subdivisional headquarters. Conflict within the organization was low; it was relatively small, the degree of differentiation of task was relatively low (criminal investigation division members, dog men, and traffic patrol were supervised by divisional command which in part overlapped with the chief superintendent of the subdivision), and the organization had been characterized for years by a low turnover rate. This sort of stable organization in a relatively "quiet" area perhaps makes this a limiting case for studies of police work. In the United States police organizations are large, the supervisory ratio is high, conflict is typical, and conflict with the public is the norm.

8 The following story illustrates what can happen when the unexplicated and nonverbal understandings which embed instructions are *not properly* or "accurately" read by a subordinate receiving orders from a senior officer:

A Chief Inspector was asked to go to the home of an Inspector who was just coming off duty and return him to the station. He suspected that it was because the man had been drinking on duty and the Superintendent wanted to have him on report. The C.I. went to his house and asked him to come to the station for a breathalyzer (used to determine the amount of alcohol in the blood; a test must be made initially to ascertain whether there is possible evidence for a blood sample to be drawn by the divisional surgeon and further analysis done). The C.I. administered the breathalyzer at the man's house and then took him in. The indication that a blood sample was needed was a green tinge in the sample vial. The vial of fluid was bright green. When the Chief Inspector took in the evidence, the Superintendent looked at it, said, "Well, that's all that's necessary," and had the C.I. take the Inspector home. No disciplinary charges were filed. The C.I. said the Superintendent "didn't want to know," i.e., he was unwilling to consider the evidence, and made the entire process into a ritual. (Presumably, either no report was written, or it was written stating that the investigation had been made and the Superintendent was satisfied that the man was not drunk on duty.)

Mike Chatterton, who has done extensive work in a large Midlands police department has commented extremely insightfully on this anecdote, and his remarks reveal what I take to be the *essence* of the problem of cross-rank communication, even though it occurred between members of the higher strata. Chatterton writes (personal communication): "In this particular case it could be argued (and this would increase the degree of uncertainty and support your point as it reveals the problem which men have in knowing what the bosses expect and in inferring what is at the back of their instructions) that the Chief Inspector *ought* to have known that the Superintendent would deal with the case in this way. As it was, he (the Chief Inspector) had not realized that it was not the Superintendent's intention to collect evidence to have the man charged with an offence. Had he correctly read the boss orders as intended to frighten the Inspector, give him a second chance, he would have furnished the Superintendent with evidence which would not have required him to make the embarrassing and, indeed, potentially incriminating decision he did."

My point here and in the above text is that the context of rule announcement and rule enforcement is one of implicit understanding; to the degree that one does not share this context, one is likely to see the actions and feelings of others as "random," "arbitrary" "capricious" or "stupid."

[9] The internal investigatory division of the Metropolitan Police, A-10, is feared within the force, and has grown in size and authority over the years, especially since the tenure of the present commissioner who is known as a "crusader" and "reformer." In late 1973, the commissioner was publically advocating the institutionalization of a public procedure for the investigation of public complaints against the police.

[10] Conflict between personal morality and the demands of social groups can be illustrated by two examples from fieldnotes. In both situations, the personal morality of the policemen involved differed from the actual outcomes of the case, and in each case the outcome favored the interests of the higher or more powerful classes. (The temporary refusal of the police to prosecute for petty theft was a pyrrhic victory because such cases were subsequently accepted from the factory by CID).

CID officers on a station in the subdivision were frequently asked to a toy factory to arrest and charge (as was the company policy) employees caught stealing the little cast metal scale model autos (the 50 ¢ Corgi/Matchbox type) the company manufactured. This was a fairly regular occurrence, and the young DCs were eager for an arrest and charge so cleanly and simply accomplished. These arrests were, however, a source of some discussion among the DCs, since the value of the item was small and the crime insignificant. They felt it a bit extreme to routinely arrest people for such a petty crime. However, they rationalized the practice as helping their careers, saying it "looked good on your record to have frequent arrests and convictions." A call was received by CID asking officers to come to the board room of the same factory to make an arrest. The officers learned that is was alleged that one of the managers had altered the production instructions in the plant, substituting inferior materials and selling the high quality metal specified for the casting of the cars. By so doing, he had accumulated and sold some 20,000 Pounds ($50,000) worth of metal. The Board of Directors of the company was meeting to decide whether to file a legal charge against this manager. The CID, as they sifted the facts, were convinced of his guilt. They waited outside the board room, were served dinner and drinks, but were finally informed by the Chairman of the Board that the company had decided not to prosecute. It was suspected by the police that since the manager held stock in the company, they had decided to drop the case to avoid public embarrassment and possible financial loss. Soon thereafter, the same company called to have an arrest made for stealing one of the 50¢ model cars, and they were informed they would have to proceed in the matter by private summons. That is, the police did not wish to take legal action, although the company could utilize its private resources to bring the matter to adjudication.

[11] A brief overview is provided by Miller and Form (1964:252–262). My discussion of cliques draws on Dalton's ideas (1959:57–67), but places these matters more in the context of situational adjustments rather than crisis management or of orientations toward mobility or success. See the elegant formulations of Burns (1953, 1955, 1958, 1960). Wilson (1968) writes: "One reason for the oft-noted tendency of patrolmen to form cliques, factions and fraternal associations is not so much to celebrate the virtues of ethnic solidarity, though the organizations be among ethnic lines, but to defend officers against what is to them arbitrary authority and "outside influence." The power of the administrator is to be checked because the administrator, if he is a strong man, is "out to get us," and, if he is a weak one, is "giving way before outside pressure." (73). This is a very insightful analysis, although in urban American departments race and ethnicity are apparently a more critical basis for cliques than in the department studied. Although there were a number of officers of Scottish descent, they did not form a clique, partially because they were spread out throughout the rank hierarchy of the subdivisional headquarters.

[12]   Ethnomethodologists (Cf. Manning, Wieder, Zimmerman, and Zimmerman and Wieder chapters in Douglas, ed., 1970) have argued that rules are a means by which social settings and situations are made accountable and coherent for participants, "The work of making and accepting such descriptions of conduct makes social settings appear as orderly for the participants, and it is this *sense and appearance* of order that rules in use, in fact, provide . . . " (Zimmerman and Wieder, p. 292). It is clear that greater emphasis must be placed upon the underlying and assumed organizational reality to which the rules are "referred" (what it takes to properly understand what is meant by an instruction or by the invocation of a rule) rather than to rules themselves as providing order. What is well captured in the above quotation is a necessary but not sufficient feature required for competent functioning and understanding within organizations. That is, people must be able to indicate to each that they "understand" by means of rules or other formal blueprints of action, but without the ability to understand what "lies behind" a rule and to communicate that understanding to others, the appearance of order is just that. It should be recalled that misunderstandings are so central a feature of everyday life that a sense of order may be "false" i.e., it may isolate a person outside the bounds of others' experience, and the invocation of rules is itself an indexical and therefore defeasible process.

REFERENCES

BANTON, M.
1964   The Policeman in the Community. New York: Basic Books.

BLACK, D. J.
1970   "The production of crime rates." American Sociological Review 35 (August): 733–748.
1968   "Police encounters and social organization." Unpublished Ph.D. dissertation, Department of Sociology, University of Michigan.

BITTNER, E.
1970   The Functions of the Police in Modern Society. Washington, D.C.: United States Government Printing Office.
1965   "The concept of organization." Social Research 32 (Winter): 230–255.

BLANKENSHIP, R.
1973   "Organizational careers." Sociological Quarterly 14 (Winter): 88–98.

REISS, A., AND D. BORDUA
1967   "Environment and organization: a perspective on the police." In D. J. Bordua (ed.), *The Police*. New York: John Wiley and Sons.

BURNS, T.
1961   "Micropolitics: mechanisms of institutional change." Administrative Science Quarterly 6 (December): 257–281.
1958   "Forms of conduct." American Journal of Sociology 64 (September): 137–151.
1955   "The Reference of conduct in small groups." Human Relations VIII (November): 467–486.
1953   "Friends, enemies, and the polite fiction." American Sociological Review 18 (December): 654–662.

CAIN, M.
1973   Society and the Policeman's Role. London: Routledge, Kegan Paul.

CROZIER, M.
1971   The World of the Office Worker. Chicago: University of Chicago Press.
1964   The Bureaucratic Phenomenon. Chicago: University of Chicago Press.

DALTON, M.
1959   Men Who Manage. New York: John Wiley and Sons.

GOFFMAN, E.
1961   Asylums. Chicago: Aldine.

GOULDNER, A. W.
1954a   Patterns of Industrial Bureaucracy. Glencoe: Free Press.
1954b   Wildcat Strike. Yellow Springs, Ohio: Antioch Press.

MANNING, PETER K.
1973a   "Dramatic aspects of policing: selected propositions." Unpublished paper.
1973   "Existential sociology." Sociological Quarterly 14 (Spring): 200–225.
1972   "Observing the police: deviants, respectables and the law." In J. D. Douglas (ed.), Research on Deviance. New York: Random House.
1971   "The police: mandate, strategies and tactics." In J. D. Douglas (ed.), Crime and Justice in American Society. Indianapolis, Indiana: Bobbs-Merrill.
1970   "Taking and becoming: a perspective on organizational socialization." In J. D. Douglas (ed.), Understanding Everyday Life. Chicago: Aldine.

MCNAMARA, J.
1967   "Uncertainties in police work: the relevance of police recruits' backgrounds and training." In D. J. Bordua (ed.), The Police. New York: John Wiley and Sons.

MILLER, D. C. AND W. H. FORM
1964   Industrial Sociology. 2nd ed. New York: Harper and Row.

REISS, A. J., JR.
1971   The Police and the Public. New Haven: Yale University Press.

SCOTT, R. W.
1966   "Professionals in bureaucratic organizations: areas of conflict." In H. Vollmer and D. Mills (eds.), Professionalization. Englewood Cliffs, N.J.: Prentice-Hall.

SILVERMAN, D.
1971   The Theory of Organizations. New York: Basic Books.

STINCHCOMBE, A.
1965   "Social structure and organizations." In J. March (ed.), Handbook of Organizations. Chicago: Rand McNally.

WESTLEY, W.
1970   Violence and the Police. Cambridge: MIT Press.

WILENSKY, H. L.
1960   "Work, careers and social integration." International Social Science Journal 12 (No. 4): 543–560.

WILSON, J. Q.
1968   Varieties of Police Behavior. Cambridge: Harvard University Press.

ZIMMERMAN, DON H., AND D. LAWRENCE WIEDER
1970   "Ethnomethodology and the problem of order: Comment on Denzin." In Jack D. Douglas (ed.), Understanding Everyday Life. Chicago: Aldine.

ELEVEN
ORGANIZATIONAL GOALS AND ENVIRONMENT: GOAL-SETTING AS AN INTERACTION PROCESS

James D. Thompson and
William J. McEwen

In the analysis of complex organizations the definition of organizational goals is commonly utilized as a standard for appraising organizational performance. In many such analyses the goals of the organization are often viewed as a constant. Thus a wide variety of data, such as official documents, work activity records, organizational output, or statements by organizational spokesmen, may provide the basis for the definition of goals. Once this definition has been accomplished, interest in goals as a dynamic aspect of organizational activity frequently ends.

It is possible, however, to view the setting of goals (i.e., major organizational purposes) not as a static element but as a necessary and recurring problem facing any organization, whether it is governmental, military, business, educational, medical, religious, or other type.

This perspective appears appropriate in developing the two major lines of the present analysis. The first of these is to emphasize the interdependence of complex organizations within the larger society and the consequences this has for organizational goal-setting. The second is to

Source: "Organizational Goals and Environment: Goal-Setting as an Interaction Process" by James D. Thompson and William J. McEwen. *American Sociological Review*, 23 (February 1958): 23–31.

emphasize the similarities of goal-setting *processes* in organizations with manifestly different goals. The present analysis is offered to supplement recent studies of organizational operations.[1]

It is postulated that goal-setting behavior is *purposive* but not necessarily *rational;* we assume that goals may be determined by accident, i.e., by blundering of members of the organization and, contrariwise, that the most calculated and careful determination of goals may be negated by developments outside the control of organization members. The goal-setting problem as discussed here is essentially determining a relationship of the organization to the larger society, which in turn becomes a question of what the society (or elements within it) wants done or can be persuaded to support.

Goals as Dynamic Variables

Because the setting of goals is essentially a problem of defining desired relationships between an organization and its environment, change in either requires review and perhaps alteration of goals. Even where the most abstract statement of goals remains constant, application requires redefinition or interpretation as changes occur in the organization, the environment, or both.

The corporation, for example, faces changing markets and develops staff specialists with responsibility for continuous study and projection of market changes and product appeal. The governmental agency, its legislative mandate notwithstanding, has need to reformulate or reinterpret its goals as other agencies are created and dissolved, as the population changes, or as non-governmental organizations appear to do the same job or to compete. The school and the university may have unchanging abstract goals but the clientele, the needs of pupils or students, and the techniques of teaching change and bring with them redefinition and reinterpretation of those objectives. The hospital has been faced with problems requiring an expansion of goals to include consideration of preventive medicine, public health practices, and the degree to which the hospital should extend its activities out into the community. The mental hospital and the prison are changing their objectives from primary emphasis on custody to a stress on therapy. Even the church alters its pragmatic objectives as changes in the society call for new forms of social ethics, and as government and organized philanthropy take over some of the activities formerly left to organized religion.[2]

Reappraisal of goals thus appears to be a recurrent problem for large organization, albeit a more constant problem in an unstable environment than in a stable one. Reappraisal of goals likewise appears to be more difficult as the "product" of the enterprise becomes less tangible and more difficult to measure objectively. The manufacturing firm has a relatively ready index of the acceptability of its product in sales figures; while poor sales may indicate inferior quality rather than public distaste for the commodity itself, sales totals frequently are supplemented by trade association statistics indicating the firm's "share of the market." Thus within a matter of weeks, a manufacturing firm may be able to reappraise its decision to enter the "widget" market and may therefore begin deciding how it can get out of that market with the least cost.

The governmental enterprise may have similar indicators of the acceptability of its goals if it is involved in producing an item such as electricity, but where its activity is oriented to a less tangible purpose such as maintaining favorable relations with foreign nations, the indices of effective operation are likely to be less precise and the vagaries more numerous. The degree to which a government satisfies its clientele may be reflected periodically in elections, but despite the claims of party officials, it seldom is clear just what the mandate of the people is with reference to any particular governmental enterprise. In addition, the public is not always steadfast in its mandate.

The university perhaps has even greater difficulties in evaluating its environmental situation through response to its output. Its range of "products" is enormous, extending from astronomers to zoologists. The test of a competent specialist is not always standardized and may be changing, and the university's success in turning out "educated" people is judged by many and often conflicting standards. The university's product is in process for four or more years and when it is placed on the "market" it can be only imperfectly judged. Vocational placement statistics may give some indication of the university's success in its objectives, but initial placement is no guarantee of performance at a later date. Furthermore, performance in an occupation is only one of several abilities that the university is supposed to produce in its students. Finally, any particular department of the university may find that its reputation lags far behind its performance. A "good" department may work for years before its reputation becomes "good" and a downhill department may coast for several years before the fact is realized by the professional world.

In sum, the goals of an organization, which determine the kinds of goods or services it produces and offers to the environment, often are subject to peculiar difficulties of reappraisal. Where the purpose calls for an easily identified, readily measured product, reappraisal and readjustment of goals may be accomplished rapidly. But as goals call for increasingly intangible, difficult-to-measure products, society finds it more difficult to determine and reflect its acceptability of that product, and the signals that indicate unacceptable goals are less effective and perhaps longer in coming.

Environmental Controls Over Goals

A continuing situation of necessary interaction between an organization and its environment introduces an element of environmental control into the organization. While the motives of personnel, including goal-setting officers, may be profits, prestige, votes, or the salvation of souls, their efforts must produce something useful or acceptable to at least a part of the organizational environment to win continued support.[3]

In the simpler society social control over productive activities may be exercised rather informally and directly through such means as gossip and ridicule. As a society becomes more complex and its productive activities more deliberately organized, social controls are increasingly exercised through such formal devices as contracts, legal codes, and governmental regulations. The stability of expectations provided by these devices is arrived at through interaction, and often through the exercise of power in interaction.

It is possible to conceive of a continuum of organizational power in environmental relations, ranging from the organization that dominates its environmental relations to one completely dominated by its environment. Few organizations approach either extreme. Certain gigantic industrial enterprises, such as the *Zaibatsu* in Japan or the old Standard Oil Trust in America, have approached the dominance-over-environment position at one time, but this position eventually brought about "countervailing powers."[4] Perhaps the nearest approximation to the completely powerless organization is the commuter transit system, which may be unable to cover its costs but nevertheless is regarded as a necessary utility and cannot get permission to quit business. Most complex organizations, falling somewhere between the extremes of the power continuum, must adopt strategies for coming to terms with their environments. This is not to imply that such strategies are necessarily chosen by rational or deliberate processes. An organization can survive so long as it adjusts to its situation; whether the process of adjustment is awkward or nimble becomes important in determining the organization's degree of prosperity.

However arrived at, strategies for dealing with the organizational environment may be broadly classified as either *competitive* or *co-operative*. Both appear to be important in a complex society—of the "free enterprise" type or other.[5] Both provide a measure of environmental control over organizations by providing for "outsiders" to enter into or limit organizational decision process.

The decision process may be viewed as a series of activities, conscious or not, culminating in a choice among alternatives. For purposes of this paper we view the decision-making process as consisting of the following activities:

1. Recognizing an occasion for decision, i.e., a need or an opportunity.

2. Analysis of the existing situation.

3. Identification of alternative courses of action.

4. Assessment of the probable consequences of each alternative.

5. Choice from among alternatives.[6]

The following discussion suggests that the potential power of an outsider increases the earlier he enters into the decision process,[7] and that competition and three sub-types of co-operative strategy—*bargaining, co-optation,* and *coalition*—differ in this respect. It is therefore possible to order these forms of interaction in terms of the degree to which they provide for environmental control over organizational goal-setting decisions.

COMPETITION. The term competition implies an element of rivalry. For present pruposes competition refers to that form or rivalry between two or more organizations which is mediated by a third party. In the case of the manufacturing firm the third party may be the customer, the supplier, the potential or present member of the labor force, or others. In the case of the governmental bureau, the third party through whom competition takes place may be the legislative committee, the budget bureau, or the chief executive, as well as potential clientele and potential members of the bureau.

The complexity of competition in a heterogeneous society is much greater than customary usage (with economic overtones) often suggests. Society judges the enterprise not only by the finished product but also in terms of the desirability of applying resources to that purpose. Even the organization that enjoys a product monopoly must compete for society's support. From the society it must obtain resources—personnel, finances, and materials—as well as customers or clientele. In the business sphere of a "free enterprise" economy this competition for resources and customers usually takes place in the market, but in times of crisis the society may exercise more direct controls, such as rationing or the establishment of priorities during a war. The monopoly competes with enterprises having different purposes or goals but using similar raw materials; it competes with many other enterprises, for human skills and loyalties, and it competes with many other activities for support in the money markets.

The university, customarily a non-profit organization, competes as eagerly as any business firm, although perhaps more subtly.[8] Virtually every university seeks, if not more students, better-qualified students. Publicly supported universities compete at annual budget sessions with other governmental enterprises for shares in tax revenues. Endowed universities must compete for gifts and bequests, not only with other universities but also with museums, charities, zoos, and similar non-profit enterprises. The American university is only one of many organizations competing for foundation support, and it competes with other universities and with other types of organizations for faculty.

The public school system, perhaps one of our most pervasive forms of near-monopoly, not only competes with other governmental units for funds and with different types of organizations for teachers, but current programs espoused by professional educators often compete in a very real way with a public conception of the nature of education, e.g., as the three R's, devoid of "frills."

The hospital may compete with the midwife, the faith-healer, the "quack" and the patent-medicine manufacturer, as well as with neighboring hospitals, despite the fact that general hospitals do not "advertise" and are not usually recognized as competitive.

Competition is thus a complicated network of relationships. It includes scrambling for resources as well as for customers or clients, and in a complex society it includes rivalry for potential members and their loyalties. In each case a third party makes a choice among alternatives, two or more organizations attempt to influence that choice through some type of "appeal" or offering, and choice by the third party is a "vote" of support for one of the competing organizations and a denial of support to the others involved.

Competition, then, is one process whereby the organization's choice of goals is partially controlled by the environment. It tends to prevent unilateral or arbitrary choice of organizational goals, or to correct such a choice if one is made. Competition for society's support is an important means of eliminating not only inefficient organizations but also those that seek to provide goods or services the environment is not willing to accept.

BARGAINING. The term bargaining, as used here, refers to the negotiation of an agreement for the exchange of goods or services between two or more oganizations. Even where fairly stable and dependable expectations have been built up with important elements of the organizational environment—with suppliers, distributors, legislators, workers and so on—the organization cannot assume that these relationships will continue. Periodic review of these relationships must be accomplished, and an important means for this is bargaining, whereby each organization, through negotiation, arrives at a decision about future behavior satisfactory to the others involved.

The need for periodic adjustment of relationships is demonstrated most dramatically in collective bargaining between labor and industrial management, in which the bases for continued support by organization members are reviewed.[9] But bargaining occurs in other important, if less dramatic, areas of organizational endeavor. The business firm must bargain with its agents or distributors, and while this may appear at times to be one-sided and hence not much of a bargain, still even a long-standing agency agreement may be severed by competitive offers unless the agent's level of satisfaction is maintained through periodic review.[10] Where suppliers are required to install new equipment to handle the peculiar demands of an organization, bargaining between the two is not unusual.

The university likewise must bargain.[11] It may compete for free or unrestricted funds, but often it must compromise that ideal by bargaining away the name of a building or of a library collection, or by the conferring of an honorary degree. Graduate students and faculty members may be given financial or other concessions through bargaining, in order to prevent their loss to other institutions.

The governmental organization may also find bargaining expedient.[12] The police department, for example, may overlook certain violations of statutes in order to gain the support of minor violators who have channels of information not otherwise open to department members. Concessions to those who "turn state's evidence" are not unusual. Similarly a department of state may forego or postpone recognition of a foreign power in order to gain support for other aspects of its policy, and a governmental agency may relinquish certain activities in order to gain budget bureau approval of more important goals.

While bargaining may focus on resources rather than explicitly on goals, the fact remains that it is improbable that a goal can be effective unless it is at least partially implemented. To the extent that bargaining sets limits on the amount of resources available or the ways they may be employed, it effectively sets limits on choice of goals. Hence bargaining, like competition, results in environmental control over organizational goals and reduces the probability of arbitrary, unilateral goal-setting.

Unlike competition, however, bargaining involes direct interaction with other organizations in the environment, rather than with a third party. Bargaining appears, therefore, to invade the actual decision process. To the extent that the second party's support is necessary he is in a position to exercise a veto over final choice of alternative goals, and hence takes part in the decision.

CO-OPTATION.   Co-optation has been defined as the process of absorbing new elements into the leadership or policy-determining structure of an organization as a means of averting threats to its stability or existence.[13] Co-optation makes still further inroads on the process of deciding goals; not only must the final choice be acceptable to the co-opted party or organization, but to the extent that co-optation is effective it places the representative of an "outsider" in a position to determine the occasion for a goal decision, to participate in analyzing the existing situation, to suggest alternatives, and to take part in the deliberation of consequences.

The term co-optation has only recently been given currency in this country, but the phenomenon it describes is neither new nor unimportant. The acceptance on a corporation's board of directors of representatives of banks or other financial institutions is a time-honored custom among firms that have large financial obligations or that may in the future want access to financial resources. The state university may find it expedient (if not mandatory) to place legislators on its board of trustees, and the endowed college may find that whereas the honorary degree brings forth a token gift, membership on the board may result in a more substantial bequest. The local medical society often plays a decisive role in hospital goal-setting, since the support of professional medical practitioners is urgently necessary for the hospital.

From the standpoint of society, however, co-optation is more than an expediency. By giving a potential supporter a position of power and often of responsibility in the organization, the organization gains his awareness and understanding of the problems it faces. A business advisory council may be an effective educational device for a government, and a White House conference on education may mobilize "grass roots" support in a thousand localities, both by focussing attention on the problem area and by giving key people a sense of participation in goal deliberation.

Moreover, by providing overlapping memberships, co-optation is an important social device for increasing the likelihood that organizations related to one another in complicated ways will in fact find compatible goals. By thus reducing the possibilities of antithetical actions by two or more organizations, co-optation aids in the integration of the heterogeneous parts of a complex society. By the same token, co-optation further limits the opportunity for one organization to choose its goals arbitrarily or unilaterally.

COALITION. As used there, the term coalition refers, to a combination of two or more organizations for a common purpose. Coalition appears to be the ultimate or extreme form of environmental conditioning of organizational goals.[14] A coalition may be unstable, but to the extent that it is operative, two or more organizations act as one with respect to certain goals. Coalition is a means widely used when two or more enterprises wish to pursue a goal calling for more support, especially for more resources, than any one of them is able to marshall unaided. American business firms frequently resort to coalition for purposes of research or product promotion and for the construction of such gigantic facilities as dams or atomic reactors.[15]

Coalition is not uncommon among educational organizations. Universities have established joint operations in such areas as nuclear research, archaeological research, and even social science research. Many smaller colleges have banded together for fund-raising purposes. The consolidation of public school districts is another form of coalition (if not merger), and the fact that it does represent a sharing or "invasion" of goal-setting power is reflected in some of the bitter resistance to consolidation in tradition-oriented localities.

Coalition requires a commitment for joint decision of future activities and thus places limits on unilateral or arbitrary decisions. Furthermore, inability of an organization to find partners in a coalition venture automatically prevents pursuit of that objective, and is therefore also a form of social control. If the collective judgment is that a proposal is unworkable, a possible disaster may be escaped and unproductive allocation of resources avoided.

Development of Environmental Support

Environmental control is not a one-way process limited to consequences for the organization of action in its environment. Those subject to control are also part of the large society and hence are also agents of social control. The enterprise that competes is not only influenced in its goal-setting by what the competitor and the third party may do, but also exerts influence over both. Bargaining likewise is a form of mutual, two-way influence; co-optation affects the co-opted as well as the co-opting party; and coalition clearly sets limits on both parties.

Goals appear to grow out of interaction, both within the organization and between the organization and its environment. While every enterprise must find sufficient support for its goals, it may wield initiative in this. The difference between effective and ineffective organizations may well lie in the initiative exercised by those in the organization who are responsible for goal-setting.

The ability of an administrator to win support for an objective may be as vital as his ability to foresee the utility of a new idea. And his role as a "seller" of ideas may be as important to society as to his organization, for as society becomes increasingly specialized and heterogeneous, the importance of new objectives may be more readily seen by specialized segments than by the general society. It was not public clamor that originated revisions in public school curricula and training methods; the impetus came largely from professional specialists in or on the periphery of education.[16] The shift in focus from custody to therapy in mental hospitals derives largely from the urgings of professionals, and the same can be said of our prisons.[17] In both cases the public anger, aroused by crusaders and muck-rakers, might have been soothed by more humane methods of custody. Current attempts to revitalize the liberal arts curricula of our colleges, universities, and technical institutes have developed more in response to the activities of professional specialists than from public urging.[18] Commercial aviation, likewise, was "sold" the hard way, with support being based on subsidy for a considerable period before the importance of such transportation was apparent to the larger public.[19]

In each of these examples the goal-setters saw their ideas become widely accepted only after strenuous efforts to win support through education of important elements of the environment. Present currents in some medical quarters to shift emphasis from treatment of the sick to maintenance of health through preventive medicine and public health programs likewise have to be "sold" to a society schooled in an older concept.[20]

The activities involved in winning support for organizational goals thus are not confined to communication within the organization, however important this is. The need to justify organization goals, to explain the social functions of the organization, is seen daily in all types of "public relations" activities, ranging from luncheon club speeches to house organs. It is part of an educational requirement in a complicated society where devious interdependence hides many of the functions of organized, specialized activities.

Goal-setting and Strategy

We have suggested that it is improbable that an organization can continue indefinitely if its goals are formulated arbitrarily, without cognizance of its relations to the environment. One of the requirements for survival appears to be ability to learn about the environment accurately enough and quickly enough to permit organizational adjustments in time to avoid extinction. In a more positive vein, it becomes important for an organization to judge the amount and sources of support that can be mobilized for a goal, and to arrive at a strategy for their mobilization.

Competition, bargaining, co-optation, and coalition constitute procedures for gaining support from the organizational environment; the selection of one or more of these is a strategic problem. It is here that the element of rationality appears to become exceedingly important, for in the order treated above, these relational processes represent increasingly "costly" methods of gaining support in terms of decision-making power. The organization that adopts a strategy of competition when co-optation is called for may lose all opportunity to realize its goals, or may finally turn to co-optation or coalition at a higher "cost" than would have been necessary originally. On the other hand, an organization may lose part of its integrity, and therefore some of its potentiality, if it unnecessarily shares power in exchange for support. Hence the establishment *in the appropriate form* of interaction with the many relevant parts of its environment can be a major organizational consideration in a complex society.

This means, in effect, that the organization must be able to estimate the position of other relevant organizations and their willingness to enter into or alter relationships. Often, too, these matters must be determined or estimated without revealing one's own weaknesses, or even one's ultimate strength. It is necessary or advantageous, in other words, to have the consent or acquiescence of the other party, if a new relationship is to be established or an existing relationship altered. For this purpose organization administrators often engage in what might be termed a *sounding out process.*[21]

The sounding out process can be illustrated by the problem of the boss with amorous designs on his secretary in an organization that taboos such relations. He must find some means of determining her willingness to alter the relationship, but he must do so without risking rebuff, for a showdown might come at the cost of his dignity or his office reputation, at the cost of losing her secretarial services, or in the extreme case at the cost of losing his own position. The "sophisticated" procedure is to create an ambiguous situation in which the secretary is forced to respond in one of two ways: (1) to ignore or tactfully counter, thereby clearly channeling the relationship back into an already existing pattern, or (2) to respond in a similarly ambiguous vein (if not in a positive one) indicating a receptiveness to further advances. It is important in the sounding out process that the situation be ambiguous for two reasons: (1) the secretary must not be able to "pin down" the boss with evidence if she rejects the idea, and (2) the situation must be far enough removed from normal to be noticeable to the secretary. The ambiguity of sounding out has the further advantage to the participants that neither party alone is clearly responsible for initiating the change.

The situation described above illustrates a process that seems to explain many organizational as well as personal inter-action situations. In moving from one relationship to another between two or more organizations it is often necessary to leave a well defined situation and proceed through a period of deliberate ambiguity, to arrive at a new clear-cut relationship. In interaction over goal-setting problems, sounding out sometimes is done through a form of double-talk, wherein the parties refer to "hypothetical" enterprises and "hypothetical" situations, or in "diplomatic" language, which often serves the same purpose. In other cases, and perhaps more frequently, sounding out is done through the good offices of a third party. This occurs, apparently, where there has been no relationship in the past, or at the stage of negotiations where the parties have indicated intentions but are not willing to state their positions frankly. Here it becomes useful at times to find a discrete go-between who can be trusted with full information and who will seek an arrangement suitable to both parties.

Conclusion

In the complex modern society desired goals often require complex organizations. At the same time the desirability of goals and the appropriate division of labor among large organizations is less self-evident than in simpler, more homogeneous society. Purpose becomes a question to be decided rather than an obvious matter.

To the extent that behavior of organization members is oriented to questions of goals or purposes, a science of organization must attempt to understand and explain that behavior. We have suggested one classification scheme, based on decision-making, as potentially useful in analyzing organizational-environmental interaction with respect to goal-setting and we have attempted to illustrate some aspects of its utility. It is hoped that the suggested scheme encompasses questions of rationality or irrationality without presuming either.

Argument by example, however, is at best only a starting point for scientific understanding and for the collection of evidence. Two factors make organizational goal-setting in a complex society a "big" research topic: the multiplicity of large organizations of diverse type and the necessity of studying them in diachronic perspective. We hope that our discussion will encourage critical thinking and the sharing of observations about the subject.

Footnotes

[1] Among recent materials that treat organizational goal-setting are Kenneth E. Boulding, *The Organizational Revolution*, New York: Harper and Brothers, 1953; Robert A. Dahl and Charles E. Lindblom, *Politics, Economics, and Welfare*, New York: Harper and Brothers, 1953; and John K. Galbraith, *American Capitalism: The Concept of Countervailing Power*, Boston: Houghton Mifflin, 1952.

[2] For pertinent studies of various organizational types see Burton R. Clark, *Adult Education in Transition*, Berkely and Los Angeles: University of California Press, 1956; Temple Burling, Edith M. Lentz, and Robert N. Wilson, *The Give and Take in Hospitals*, New York: G. P. Putnam's Sons, 1956, especially pp. 3-10; Lloyd E. Ohlin, *Sociology and the Field of Corrections*, New York: Russell Sage Foundation, 1956, pp 13-18; Liston Pope, *Millhands and Preachers*, New Haven: Yale University Press, 1942; Charles Y. Glock and Benjamin B. Ringer, "Church Policy and the Attitudes of Ministers and Parishioners on Social Issues," *American Sociological Review*, 21 (April, 1956), pp. 148-156. For a similar analysis in the field of philanthropy, see J. R. Seeley, B. H. Junker, R. W. Jones, Jr., and others, *Community Chest: A Case Study in Philanthropy*, Toronto: University of Toronto Press, 1957, especially Chapters 2 and 5.

[3] This statement would seem to exclude antisocial organizations, such as crime syndicates. A detailed analysis of such organizations would be useful for many purposes; meanwhile it would appear necessary for them to acquire a clientele, suppliers, and others, in spite of the fact that their methods at times may be somewhat unique.

[4] For the *Zaibatsu* case see Japan Council, *The Control of Industry in Japan*, Tokyo: Institute of Political and Economic Research, 1953; and Edwin O. Reischauer, *The United States and Japan*, Cambridge: Harvard University Press, 1954, pp. 87-97.

⁵ For evidence on Russia see David Granick, *Management of the Industrial Firm in the U.S.S.R.,* New York: Columbia University Press, 1954; and Joseph S. Berliner, "Informal Organization of the Soviet Firm," *Quarterly Journal of Economics,* 66 (August, 1952), pp. 353-365.

⁶ This particular breakdown is taken from Edward H. Litchfield, "Notes on a General Theory of Administration," *Administrative Science Quarterly,* 1 (June, 1956), pp. 3-29. We are also indebted to Robert Tannenbaum and Fred Massarik who, by breaking the decision-making process into three steps, show that subordinates can take part in the "manager's decision" even when the manager makes the final choice. See "Participation by Subordinates in the Managerial Decision-Making Process," *Canadian Journal of Economics and Political Science,* 16 (August, 1949), pp. 410-418.

⁷ Robert K. Merton makes a similar point regarding the role of the intellectual in public bureaucracy. See his *Social Theory and Social Structure,* Glencoe: The Free Press, 1949, Chapter VI.

⁸ See Logan Wilson, *The Academic Man,* New York: Oxford University Press, 1942, especially Chapter IX. Also see Warren G. Bennis, "The Effect on Academic Goods of Their Market," *American Journal of Sociology,* 62 (July, 1956), pp. 28-33.

⁹ For an account of this on a daily basis see Melville Dalton, "Unofficial Union-Management Relations," *American Sociological Review,* 15 (October, 1950), pp 611-619.

¹⁰ See Valentine F. Ridgway, "Administration of Manufacturer-Dealer Systems," *Administrative Science Quarterly,* 1 (March, 1957), pp 464-483.

¹¹ Wilson, *op. cit.,* Chapters VII and VIII.

¹² For an interesting study of governmental bargaining see William J. Gore, "Administrative Decision-Making in Federal Field Offices," *Public Administration Review,* 16 (Autumn, 1956), pp. 281-291.

¹³ Philip Selznick, *TVA and the Grass Roots,* Berkeley and Los Angeles: University of California Press, 1949.

¹⁴ Coalition may involve joint action toward only limited aspects of the goals of each member. It may involve the complete commitment of each member for a specific period of time or indefinitely. In either case the ultimate power to withdraw is retained by the members. We thus distinguish coalition from merger, in which two or more organizations are fused permanently. In merger one or all of the original parts may lose their identity. Goal-setting in such a situation, of course, is no longer subject to inter-organizational constraints among the components.

¹⁵ See "The Joint Venture Is an Effective Approach to Major Engineering Pro-

jects," *New York Times,* July 14, 1957, Section 3, p. 1 F.

16 See Robert S. and Helen Merrell Lynd, *Middletown in Transition,* New York: Harcourt Brace, 1937, Chapter VI.

17 Milton Greenblatt, Richard H. York, and Esther Lucille Brown, *From Custodial to Therapeutic Patient Care in Mental Hospitals,* New York: Russell Sage Foundation, 1955, Chapter 1, and Ohlin, *loc. cit.*

18 For one example, see the Report of the Harvard Committee, *General Education in a Free Society,* Cambridge: Harvard University Press, 1945.

19 America's civil air transport industry began in 1926 and eight years later carried 500,000 passengers. Yet it was testified in 1934 that half of the $120 million invested in airlines had been lost in spite of subsidies. See Jerome C. Hunsaker, *Aeronautics at the Mid-Century,* New Haven: Yale University Press, 1952, pp. 37-38. The case of Billy Mitchell was, of course, the landmark in the selling of military aviation.

20 Ray E. Trussell, *Hunterdon Medical Center,* Cambridge: Harvard University Press (for the Commonwealth Fund), 1956, Chapter 3.

21 This section on the sounding out process is a modified version of a paper by James D. Thompson, William J. McEwen, and Frederick L. Bates, "Sounding Out as a Relating Process," read at the annual meeting of the Eastern Sociological Society, April, 1957.

TWELVE
THE ENACTED
ENVIRONMENT
Karl E. Weick

Although one of the central propositions in any evolutionary theory concerns the continuing press of the environment on the organism, the precise nature of this environment is never made explicit. This lack of clarity is especially troublesome when we begin to think of human organizations within an evolutionary framework. If we review the preceding amendments, it soon becomes clear that they have something to do with the ways in which environments are discussed. It has been mentioned that variations retain some orderliness, that information is the commodity processed in human systems, and that information retained by the actor may then constrain his subsequent actions. These subtle features of human organizing are difficult to fit into the gross portraits of the environment which are associated with evolutionary theory. We need a more explicit statement of what constitutes the environment of an organization, and we need to be certain that this portrait is consistent with what is known about the ways in which human beings function.

Instead of discussing the "external environment," we will discuss the "enacted environment." The phrase "enacted environment" preserves the crucial distinctions that we wish to make, the most important being that the human *creates* the environment to which the system then adapts. The human actor does not *react* to an environment, he *enacts* it. It is this enacted environment, and nothing else, that is worked upon by the processes of organizing.

The concept of an enacted environment derives from a number of sources, including Mead (1956), Allport (1967), Skinner (1963, 1966),

Source: "The Enacted Environment," from *The Social Psychology of Organizing* by Karl E. Weick, © 1969, Reading, Mass.: Addison-Wesley Publishing Company.

Bem (1965, 1967), Garfinkel (1967), Schachter (1967), and especially Schutz (1967), whose concepts comprise the bulk of this discussion.

To understand the crucial features of an enacted environment, one must cultivate an exquisite sensitivity to time. The chapter in which Schutz develops the most important portions of his analysis is entitled, "Meaningful Lived Experience." The importance of this title resides in the fact that it is phrased in the past tense: the meaningful experience is lived; it is not living or to be lived. This is the most crucial feature of the enacted environment. Stated bluntly, we can know what we've done only after we've done it. Only by doing is it possible for us to discover what we have done. One can also state this in stimulus-response language: only when a response has been completed does the stimulus become defined.

To understand these statements is to understand time. Time exists in two distinct forms, as pure duration and as discrete segments with spatiotemporal properties. Pure duration can be described in any one of a number of ways, the most useful being a stream of experience. Note that experience is stated in the singular, not the plural. To talk about experiences implies discrete, separate contents, and pure duration does not have this property. Pure duration is a "coming-to-be and passing-away that has no contours, no boundaries, and no differentiations" (Schutz, 1967, p. 47). The reader may object that his experience seldom has this quality of continual flowing, merging, and melting of phases into phases. In fact, experience as we know it has the quality of discreteness, separateness, the quality of being bounded and distinct. But the only way we get this impression is by stepping outside the stream of experience and directing attention to it. It is only possible to direct attention to what has already passed; it is impossible to direct attention to what is yet to come. All knowing and meaning arise from reflection, from a backward glance. The workings of the reflective glance can be glimpsed in the following quotation:

> When, by my act of reflection, I turn my attention to my living experience, I am no longer taking up my position within the stream of pure duration, I am no longer simply living within that flow. The experiences are apprehended, distinguished, brought into relief, marked out from one another; the experiences which were constituted as phases within the flow of duration now become objects of attention as constituted experiences. What had first been constituted as a phase now stands out as a full-blown experience, no matter whether the Act of attention is one of reflection or of reproduction. . . . *For the Act of attention*—and this is of major importance for the study of meaning—presupposes an elapsed, passed-away

experience—in short, one that is already in the past.[1]

Given this concept of time, several properties of an enacted environment now become apparent. First, the creation of meaning is an attentional process, but it is attention to that which has already occurred. Second, since the attention is directed backward from a specific point in time (a specific here and now), whatever is occurring at the moment will influence what the person discovers when he glances backward. A complete formulation of meaning that preserves these features is "here, now, and thus." Attention is directed backward from a given point in time (here and now), and whatever past experiences it fixes on are the meaningful objects (thus). Third, the quotation from Schutz makes it apparent that memory processes, whether they be retention or reconstruction, influence meaning. Fourth, we can now see why it is that only when a response occurs does the stimulus become defined. The reason is that we cannot know the beginning phase. An action can become an object of attention only *after* it has occurred. While it is occurring, it cannot be noticed.

To be certain that the reader understands the nature of reflective meaning, we will cite an excerpt from Mead (1956) which demonstrates the same point: "We are conscious always of what we have done, never of doing it. We are always conscious directly only of sensory processes, never of motor processes; hence we are conscious of motor processes only through sensory processes, which are their resultants" (p. 136). Actions are known only when they have been completed.

The next question that must be faced is what to do with the fact that people seem to plan and to guide their actions according to their plans. If everything is retrospective, what are we to do with plans? Schutz's answer to this is imaginative, though difficult to summarize. Basically, his argument is that when one thinks about the future, this thinking is not done in the future tense, but rather in the future perfect tense. If asked what I plan to do, I might say, "I will write a memo to the president requesting a budget increase." Schutz's argument is that what I'm really saying is, "I shall have written a memo to the president requesting a budget increase." I think of the future action as if it had already been completed. My statement contains *both* future and past time. Even though a plan appears to be something oriented solely to the future, in fact it also has about it the quality of an act that has already been accomplished. The *meaning* of the actions that are instrumental to the completion of the act can be discovered because they are viewed as if they had already occurred. We have said that meaning is established retrospectively. Thinking in the future perfect tense retains this requirement. The actions gain meaning because attention is directed to them as if they had already occurred.

Note, in addition, that the meaning of the actions is determined by the projected act as a whole (Schutz refers to this as the project). What this means is that the actor visualizes the completed act, not the component actions that will bring about completion. It is only when the realization of this future act is imagined that it is possible for means to be selected. Mead (1956) says the same thing when he remarks, "in general, one sees things which will enable the ongoing activity to be carried out" (p. 137). A similar argument is found in Slack (1955) and in Barnard (1938, p. 36).

To see precisely how Schutz portrays this property of anticipated acts, the reader should study the following quotation:

> [T]he actor projects his action as if it were already over and done with and lying in the past. It is a full-blown, actualized event, which the actor pictures and assigns to its place in the order of experience given to him at the moment of projection. Strangely enough, therefore, because it is pictured as completed, the planned act bears the temporal character of pastness. . . . The fact that it is thus pictured as if it were simultaneously past and future can be taken care of by saying that it is thought of in the future perfect tense.[2]

To the original point about retrospective meaning has been added the fact that meanings which seem to be prospective are in fact also retrospective. It becomes apparent also that any action can take on a variety of meanings. The meaning depends on the project in which the action is embedded. But note another crucial variable. The meaning of an action will also change depending on the span of the project. To return to the memo-writing example, the meaning of my making marks on a paper (actions that accomplish the act of getting a budget increase) changes if my project becomes getting a promotion rather than getting a budget increase. It could be that I am trying to increase a budget so that the president will regard me as an ambitious employee who should be promoted. In this case, the meaning of the action of writing changes. Note the problems this creates for the observer who tries to explain whether an actor has reached his goal and, if so, how. The observer's judgment of where an act begins and ends will always be arbitrary. This could be dubbed the "woodcutter's warning to myopic researchers." "When one is watching a woodcutter it will make a great deal of difference whether we try to analyze 'objectively' the individual blows of the axe or whether we simply ask the man what he is doing and find that he is working for a lumber company" (Schutz, 1967, p. 62).

While we have sketched out some idea of the process by which meaning in general is established, we have yet to indicate how specific meanings arise. The clue to this lies in the nature of the act of attention. Think of the reflective act as a cone of light that spreads backward from a particular present. This light will give definition and contours to portions of lived experience. Since the cone starts in the present, whatever the ego's attitude or mood is at that moment, the identical mood will carry over to the backward glance. The attitude of the ego toward ongoing activity determines its attitude toward the past. Thus, "*the meaning* of a lived experience undergoes modifications depending on the particular kind of attention the Ego gives to that lived experience" (1967, p. 73). The meaning, in other words, is the kind of attention directed to the past. The kind of attention and the meaning of that which is attended to *are one and the same thing.* Since a backward act of attention emanates from a here and now, the attitude that exists in that here and now will determine the kind of attention, which in turn determines what is singled out and given definition. The reader must avoid any tendency to say that meaning is "attached" to the experience that is singled out. This is precisely what meaning is not. Meaning is not something apart from attention, something that exists alongside or above the act of attention for eventual attachment. Instead, the meaning of anything *is* the way it is attended to and nothing else.

To understand this point, one need only assume that the predominant orientation of the human actor is pragmatic (e.g., Mills, 1966; Watzlawick, Beavin, and Jackson, 1967; Schutz, 1967; Mead, 1956). Any here and now may be described as a pragmatic here and now; a here and now in which some projects are visualized, some are underway, and some have just been completed. Any reflective act originates in a here and now where projects are underway and where pragmatic attitudes are uppermost. Since the attitude to life is a pragmatic one, attention is pragmatically conditioned. Whatever items are singled out of the flow of experience for closer attention will take on whatever meaning is implicit in the pragmatic reflective glance. Whatever is now, at the present moment, underway will determine the meaning of everything that has already been accomplished. Meanings, in other words, shift as a function of the projects underway in a here and now. Restated loosely, the present interests of the actor determine the meaning of his lived experiences. A here and now that slips into the past may be attended to or ignored. If attended to, the meaning of that former here and now will be determined by the interests in the immediate here and now. The crucial point is that the meaning is retrospective and is determined by the mode of attention directed to the lived experience.

It is possible to illustrate the preceding points by a phenomenon that Garfinkel (1968) labels "Ed Rose's Function." This phenomenon is based on the following sequence of events. When Ed Rose (a sociologist) visits a strange city and is being driven by his host from the airport to a motel, Rose looks out the car window and at some random moment says, "My, that's changed." In response to this senseless statement, Rose's host usually makes some sensible reply such as "yes, it burned down," "there is some new urban renewal work going on," "the heat plays funny tricks out here," etc. Having heard his host's answer, Rose then is able to discover the meaning of what he said in the first place. Only by hearing the response does Rose discover what the stimulus was. This example illustrates retrospective meaning. Rose refers to something that has already elapsed by the time his host replies. The host is able to make a meaningful statement because he can refer to something that has already occurred, not something that will occur. More importantly, the meaning of Rose's statement resides solely in what the host attends to and singles out of the flow of appearances passing by Rose's window. And this attending itself is pragmatically conditioned. Whatever the host's interests or projects are at that particular moment, they will provide the meaning of that to which the attention is directed. This is so because attention originates in that same here and now where projects are underway. As outside observers, we can't say for certain precisely what project the host was engaged in that led him to single out a site "where something burned down." To speculate about the content of this project in the absence of the host's own report would be to defy the "woodcutter's warning." It is sufficient to state that we would expect to find some linkage between the host's attitude toward the here and now, and the noticing of the burned-out structure.

In this example, Rose could discover what he had said only after he had said it. Even though here a second party provided the backward glance, reflective meaning could just as easily have been provided by the actor himself. Having said, "My, that's changed," Rose could just as easily have sorted back through his own previous knowledge. Whatever he singled out would have been the meaning of his response (e.g., his reflective glance might highlight the item, "Oh, that's the phrase I use whenever I want to play games with my colleagues").

Given this simplified version of only a small portion of Schutz, we have a sufficient number of tools to make more explicit what is meant by an enacted environment. Whenever there are human actors in a collectivity, we can assume that each is immersed in an ongoing flow of experience. Once lived, this experience is *potentially* available for attention, although most of it remains unnoticed. If the actor removes himself from the ongoing stream and gazes reflectively at that which has already passed, then it is possible for his experience to be changed into separable, well-defined experiences, the meaning of which will be determined by whatever his attitude is at that moment toward his ongoing activities. His attitude determines the kind of attention that will be directed backward, and this mode of attention is the meaning that the experiences will have.

We assume that this is the basic manner in which variation occurs within human evolutionary systems. Variation does retain some orderliness. The sequence whereby some portions of the elapsed experience are made meaningful can be viewed as a removing of some of the equivocality that is inherent in a flow of experience. Variation does not produce equivocality; rather, it is the primitive stage at which some equivocality is removed from the ongoing experience—removed by the reflective glance which singles out and defines more sharply some portion or portions of the past experience. *It is these primitive meanings, these bits of enacted information, that constitute the informational input for subsequent processes of selection and retention.* For a human organization, the variation process could be renamed the *enactment* process.

It may appear at first glance that all the equivocality possible is removed in this initial phase, and that there is nothing but unequivocal information passed along to subsequent processes. That this assumption is incorrect can be seen from several vantage points. First, remember that time is continually passing, projects are changing, interests are being modified. Selection occurs in a later here and now than does enactment. A meaning that arises in the enactment phase and seems obvious may become problematic when viewed from a later moment in time. The meaning of the enacted information is not fixed, but fluid. It is fluid precisely because its interpretation varies as a function of the temporal distance from which it is viewed (Schutz, 1967, p. 74). Second, any enacted meaning can exist in one of three forms. The reflective glance can fixate either on the completed deed, on the stages by which the deed was accomplished, or on both (Schutz, 1967, p. 71). This means that the information which is passed along can consist of statements about ends, means, or ends plus means. Since organizational members typically have to justify their actions to supervisors, means plus ends are probably the principal contents that are fed into the selection process. Third, any specific interpretation that emerges from a reflective glance never tells it all. There is always surplus meaning. Portions of the stream of experience which went unnoticed at the moment of the reflective glance can still be noticed on some future occasion. "No lived experience can be exhausted by a single interpretive scheme" (Schutz, 1967, p. 85). Now one may question whether this potential multiplicity of meanings is passed along to the group or retained in the head of the actor who makes the interpretation. After all, it is *his* lived experience, and in this sense it is absolutely private (Bridgman, 1959). But though the lived experience, in all its variety, may not be transmitted at a given moment in time, it still remains to shade the meanings given to all the actor's subsequent experiences; it can be reconstituted and rearranged. Eventually, then, sizable portions of this lived experience probably do get transmitted to the group selection process.

Another crucial point is implied in this discussion. Up until the information reaches the selection process, it is pragmatically conditioned by the interests of the *individual* actor. His interests, and his interests alone, determine the meaning. But when this information is passed along to the selection process, collective rather than individual pragmatics control the establishment of meaning. This being the case, it is likely that different components of the imput will be attended to, in different ways, with the eventual establishment of different meanings. Stated in another way, information that is unequivocal for the individual can be equivocal and problematic for the system. The first time the system "intercepts" the individual informational inputs is when the selection process is applied to the input. This should not be read as positing anything like a group mind. Instead, selection consists of criteria built up from collective action, criteria that maintain collective action, and the implications of any given individual input for the functioning of the collective structure necessarily are different than they are for the individual. Selfish acts preserve the individual but destroy the collectivity. The same actions can be more or less equivocal depending on the aggregate level from which they are retrospectively viewed.

From still another standpoint we can see that enactment produces equivocal inputs for selection. While it is true that enactment refers to the constituting of an environment by actors, it also remains true that actors live in situations. These situations are continuously changing even if the actor takes account of them only occasionally. Now it is probable that in human organization the environment impinges on the variation process and *not on the selection process.* Though it is never made explicit in evolutionary theory, if a theorist drew a box labeled "ecological change," and had to connect it to either variation, selection, or retention, he would probably attach it to selection. His argument would be that selection is biased by environmental changes, and it produces the fit of the organism to the environment. But we have already seen that selection and adaptation do *not* seem to fit quite as closely as has been assumed. They are, in fact, separable, as is demonstrated by the phenomenon of superstitious behavior. Our proposal, then, is that ecological change affects actions directly, rather than selection. Its impact on the human organization arises from the control it gains over the actions that are emitted. And it is these actions, under the control of ecological changes, that are the raw material out of which primitive meanings are created and passed along. This means that one determinant of action and meanings in the enactment process is *not* present in the selection process. Since the determinants of the enactment process are thus more diverse than those of the selection process, any output from enactment will be equivocal relative to selection.

As a final point, it has been noted that the selection process is analogous to a decision center in organizations. This means that selection is the hub into which inputs are fed from diverse sets of actors. Enactment as a process is only loosely structured, and this means that the diversity of its outputs can be substantial. It is the function of the selection process to sort these equivocal outputs and make them less equivocal. The enactment process is more concerned with doing and less concerned with questions of "why am I doing this?" or "what are the implications for the system?" These questions are answered in the selection process. In other works, enactment is less constrained than are the other processes. The only major constraint it operates under is that of making interpretable those actions that have already occurred. Remember that we are trying to preserve within the enactment process the basic properties of the variation mechanism in evolutionary theory. The variation mechanism constitutes the prototypic instance which we are trying to refine into something consistent with the properties of human actors. Although we have made it more orderly, our version of the variation process is still a way of producing many diverse variations.

Footnotes

[1] From A. Schutz, *The Phenomenology of the Social World,* trans. G. Walsh and F. Lehnert (Evanston, Ill.: Northwestern Univ. Press, 1967), p. 51. Reprinted by permission.

[2] From A. Schutz, *op. cit.,* p. 61. Reprinted by permission.

REFERENCES

ALLPORT, F. H.
1967   "A theory of enestruence (event-structure theory): report of progress."*American Psychologist* 22:1—24.

BARNARD, G. I.
1938   *The Functions of the Executive.* Cambridge: Harvard University Press.

BEM, D. J.
1965   "An experimental analysis of self-persuasion." *Journal of Experimental Social Psychology* 1:199–218.
1967   "Self-perception: the dependent variable of human performance." *Organizational Behavior and Human Performance* 2:105–121.

BRIDGMAN, P. W.
1959   *The Way Things Are.* Cambridge: Harvard University Press.

GARFINKEL, H.
1967   *Studies in Ethnomethodology.* Englewood Cliffs, N. J.: Prentice-Hall.
1968   "Ethnomethodology and everyday life." Talk presented at The Ohio State University, April.

MEAD, G. H.
1956   *Social Psychology* (ed. A. Strauss). Chicago: University of Chicago Press.

MILLS, C. W.
1966   *Sociology and Pragmatism.* New York: Oxford

SCHACTER, S.
1967   "Cognitive effects on bodily functioning: studies of obesity and eating." In D. C. Glass (ed.), *Neurophysiology and*

Emotion. New York: Rockefeller University Press.

SCHUTZ, A.
1967   *The Phenomenology of the Social World.* Evanston: Northwestern University Press.

SKINNER, B. F.
1963   "Behaviorism at fifty." *Science* 140: 951–958.
1966   "The phylogeny and ontogeny of behavior." *Science* 153: 1205–1213.

SLACK, C. W.
1955   "Feedback theory and the reflex arc concept." *Psychological Review* 62: 263–267.

WATZLAWICK, P., JANET BEAVIN, AND D. D. JACKSON
1967   *Pragmatics of Human Communication.* New York: Norton.

CHAPTER FOUR

CONTROL

INTRODUCTION:
ORGANIZATIONAL POWER
AND STRUCTURE

PROCESS AND STRUCTURE

In the beginning of this book two questions were raised: "What is an organization?" and, "Why do professionals organize?" Many theories were raised and rejected in favor of a member-directed perspective that focused on social interactions and meanings. A picture was drawn, showing organizations of professionals constructing situations within which to perform activities and develop careers. The view showed mainly the processual aspects of organizational activity, while the products of negotiation and other interactions were underplayed.

At this point you may ask, "Is that all there really is to an organization . . . ordinary people becoming professionals and becoming members and everyone trying to decide on the shape and meaning of their situation?" The answer is a qualified yes. That's all there is if you strip away layer after layer of secondary phenomena until you reveal the primordial level; the rudest, the crudest, the most primitive and the simplest form of organization is just that and no more. But no organizational situation can be found in that form because these very simple processes produce social organization—the secondary phenomena which we call organizational structure, or power. Our task is to understand organizations, so we cannot permit ourselves to become infatuated with the systems of production, the coordinated programs of joint activity, the elaborate and rational schemes by which individuals become interlocked in the pursuit of purposes of the whole. Important as these are, they are still derivations from the more basic social process, and they are meaningful as manifestations of power. Beginning with the primordial processes, through a process of development, organizational structure is generated, leading to the kinds of organizational settings we see every day.

In this essay we will take the viewpoint of Hydebrand (1973), Crozier (1964), Nadel (1963), Coser (1955), and many others who posit that the central concept for understanding social structure is power—the questions of how resources and actions are controlled in organizational settings, and by whom.

Power, the capacity to control the actions of others, is organizational structure in a very basic form. It is concern about questions of power that leads members to develop stable schemes of order, by which their own interests can be secured. For the purposes of this essay, the terms organizational power and organizational structure will be used interchangeably. It should be clear from this that structure is considered as essentially social —none of the physical imagery evoked by the term is intended.

Conventional theory about social structure has argued that an organization is a social system, social systems have certain functional needs which must be met for reasons of survival, and the needs account for the development of structure that is merely an orderly arrangement for meeting a system's needs. We will not accept that viewpoint, mainly because it implies or attributes consciousness to the system and assumes that members' actions are system-directed—caused by the system.

An alternative model explains social structure differently. An organization is a social system that is essentially a scheme for controlling members' actions. The social system is social structure, not the cause of social structure, and its essence is power.

Although power is recognized as a central concept that can help in understanding how organizations become organized, few social scientists have yet brought power to the foreground and treated it fully. Other concepts, including leadership, authority, interests, compliance, conflict and concensus, which deal with some aspects of power, have received much more attention. These latter concepts gain theoretical meaning to the social scientist when they are conceptualized as commonsense understandings of power.

In the preceding chapter much attention was given to the process of negotiation, especially as that process leads to the creation of agreement and permits plans of action to emerge. So we have already considered the interplay between process and organizational structure. The baseline of taken-for-granted knowledge that members share is structure, and further development proceeds from this structure.

CONFLICT AND AGREEMENT

Making such a point of agreement may seem too one-sided, since conflict and disagreement also exist in every organizational setting and also function as a basis for organizing. Conflict gives rise to the negotiation of agreement, even if the agreement is to engage in further conflict.

Conflict is not to be confused with the absence of agreement; they are not polar conceptions, but different social relationships that can both be present in the same situation. They do not cancel each other out. Conflict can exist in states of active disagreement, passive neutrality, and active agreement. We must think of organizational power in terms of both conflict and agreement.

Until recently there was much heated debate about whether conflict or consensus was the basis for social organization. A summary of the debate may be helpful, to understand these concepts better.

Organizations are built up of members who are interlocked within many cross-cutting and often conflicting small groups. From the study of groups, we know that even the very small ones are essentially unstable. As a result, they tend to break up into smaller and more stable parts. A three-person group, for example, tends to reform into a two-person and a one-person group. A two-person group is the most stable. Holding groups together (integrating the social structure) is a continuous problem in social life. Organizational members have to face it in doing their work every day.

Consensus or a generalized state of agreement among the members of a group is sought to achieve social integration. But the tendency of groups to break apart would suggest that consensus is adversely affected by something that is endemic to group life. Some social theorists posited that there were two opposing forces—integration and differentiation—that pulled in opposite directions (Smelser, 1968). Consensus was identified with the integrative force. It pulled the members together. Conflict was identified with the differentiative force. It pulled members apart. Like darkness and light, good and evil, man's destiny presumably lay in the outcome of a dramatic confrontation. Would the group survive or perish?

Dahrendorf (1959:161–162) has noted that the consensus–conflict dilemma led to advocacy on the parts of many social scientists. Those who chose the consensus side always seemed to stress the rational, the functional and the efficiency aspects of groups; those who chose the conflict side were more likely to stress irrationality, dysfunctionality, and inefficiency. The structuralists argued that conflict was wasteful of resources and led to the decline of system and order. Conflict theorists in turn characterized their counterparts as reactionary, overly dedicated to the existing order, and unconcerned about how it might be improved.

More recently it is agreed that the debate raised false issues (Silverman, 1971) for each of the viewpoints implies the existence of the other, and both are important aspects of organizational settings, which arise from the same basic social process.

Power Struggles in Organizations

The preceding section sets a highly abstract theoretical background for the consideration of power struggles in organizational settings. Many case studies of organizations ranging from industrial settings (Gouldner, 1954) to voluntary associations (Gusfield, 1966) have observed that a great deal of time and energy is consumed in power struggles, which can be short-lived episodes but often recur over and over as part of the ongoing course of everyday organizational life. Our position here is that power struggles require both high agreement and high conflict levels and that these elements must converge or be focused, either on issues and means, on rules, or on goals.

In this discussion, agreement does not imply consensus of opinion about the desired outcome, but indicates a state of consensus concerning the salience, urgency, or importance of staging interactions in which some perceived problem is centrally involved. Agreement of this sort is essential to achieve mobilization of members to bring about a resolution, that is, to create a new definition of the situation. Conflict, on the other hand, implies a difference of opinions over the shape of the desired outcome. When both agreement and conflict are high, the consequence may be the effective mobilization of members into partisan coalitions that confront opposing groups in an effort to impose a desired outcome. In Figure 1 a paradigm of interactional situations is presented.

FIGURE 1   A PARADIGM OF INTERACTIONAL SITUATIONS

	Conflict					
	High (Change-Producing)			Low (Not Change-Producing)		
Agreement	Focus on Goals	Focus on Rules	Focus on Issues/ Means	Focus on Goals	Focus on Rules	Focus on Issues/ Means
High (Active Form)	a	b	c	d	e	f
Low (Latent Form)	g	h	i	j	k	l

The morphology presented in Figure 1 permits us to consider the differential meanings of conflict and agreement matches that bear on different levels of organizational structure. Each morphon implies different forms of interactions and different potential for internal organizational change. First, let us consider the conflict/agreement matches.

1. High conflict–high agreement: this match is typical of confrontations and active power struggles—the various parties commit themselves to a win or lose course of interactions in an effort to impose a preferred outcome.

2. Low conflict–low agreement: this match suggests indifference, a condition in which potential interaction can be regarded as too unimportant or irrelevant to serve as a basis for action; interests are not perceived or are regarded as petty and inconsequential.

Morphons a, b, and c are most likely to produce confrontations, coalition-forming, and struggle, while j, k, and l are least likely to lead to significant interactions. Two cross-matches also exist.

3. High conflict–low agreement: this set of situations may be regarded as "sleeping dogs" in the sense that the potential for mobilization exists, lacking only change in the perceived importance of the matter; a critical episode could cause this situation to become salient, resulting in its transformation to morphon 1, above.

4. Low conflict–high agreement: situations of this sort offer members a vehicle for the expression of group solidarity through apparently spontaneous, although possibly ritualistic, collective responses; at a committee meeting, for example, the vote to approve the minutes of a previous meeting, is likely to signal a unanimous vote.

Generally, we can posit that high agreement is associated with high probability of interaction while low agreement is associated with latency and passivity. Also, high conflict is associated with high probability of change while low conflict is more likely to reaffirm existing conditions. Let us consider the change factor further.

We may begin with the assumption that goals and rules are abstractions that function primarily as justifications or explanations for action, rather than causes of action. Issues and disputes over rather specific courses of action are the most common basis for dispute in everyday organizational life. By this, we mean to say that professors rarely argue about the goals of the university or the principle of academic freedom unless they are spurred by something like the refusal to grant a colleague a promotion, a raise, or a leave of absence.

The question of whether a colleague should be promoted or not is an issue, but if the question cannot be resolved at that level the issue may become a question of rules—how should promotion decisions be made. The latter question calls the relationship between faculty and administrators to the foreground. Questions resolved at the issue level are not likely to result in changing the organization but if the question is escalated to the higher level of rules, the potential for change is greater. A hierarchy of control operates such that the higher the level of focus, the more likely interactions will lead to organizational change.

As a consequence, a powerful coalition of members may opt to raise the level of interaction, when a satisfactory resolution is blocked, in order to force the opposing party to come to terms. To be successful, the coalition must be sufficiently powerful to support its play if the opposing party calls for a showdown. The risk of losing power results in a conservative attitude toward the use of the escalation strategy. In unionized industry the workers are sufficiently powerful to use the strategy effectively. But in most collegial organizations, the interest group consists of a loosely organized coalition of members who are formed on a tentative and fragile basis which centers around a specific issue. Escalation often results in fragmentation of the coalition and so most collegial confrontations are issue-focused and remain so.

The comparison of industrial and collegial settings can be characterized as a difference between collective behavior (see Blankenship, 1976) —spontaneous, episodic, and issue-focused—and collective bargaining— institutionalized, formal, and rule-focused. Both settings are prone to disturbances over specific issues and means, however, the disturbances are less likely to produce change in collegial settings because of the absence of permanent organization among membership, thus the differential in professional power versus administrative power. Power struggles are nevertheless a common feature of everyday collegial experience. Let us now turn our attention to the more stable power structures.

AUTHORITY, LEADERSHIP, AND COMPLIANCE

Power and Authority

Relationships between powerful agents and those under their control take many forms. Some forms require more effort than others, and are less effective as well. It is natural, therefore, to transform one's power into the most efficient forms. In part, this transformation of power accounts for authority. Weber's statement on authority is classic and still stands as the best on the subject (Gerth and Mills, 1946).

The simplest but most inefficient form of power is force and violence. In this case, a powerful agent uses pain and injury or the threat of pain and injury to control others. Force is inefficient because the victim complies against his will. At the first opportunity he will probably revert to his own course of action. If the victim could be made to want to comply, that is, if some reason could be given why compliance would be good for the victim, less attention would be needed to ensure continued compliance, and the compliant performance might be improved as a further benefit.

Weber conceived a form of power that could achieve that purpose —authority—which we may understand as power plus a feeling on the parts of the subordinate persons that obedience is *right*. The sense of rightness is the result of legitimation, a condition in which power is identified with socially valued institutions and ideals. Powerful men can become more powerful by legitimating their rule—convincing others that their rule is ordained by some greater power that the people already accept and acknowledge.

Weber observed that the least stable (but most flexible) authority was charisma, a form in which a man seems to his followers to be as one with their values and ideals. Charisma and religious movements make a compatible pair as shown by the historical prevalence of religious reformers and their groups of devoted disciples.

Charismatic authority is short-lived. It can be destroyed if unsaintly traits are uncovered and, more importantly, it cannot be passed on when the leader dies. A leader can resolve these and other problems by assuming a traditional status; perhaps he can become a priest. In the areas of secular charismatic leaders, the appropriate statuses might be king, caesar, emperor, or father. All traditional leaders have the same authority because traditional authority is independent of the person—it depends on the status. Any status-holder can do whatever the respective role demands, including controlling those persons in inferior statuses. However, traditional authority roles suffer from sluggishness; often one must be born to them and they are not very adaptable to changing conditions. In modern western society we have almost completely switched to a third form—legalistic authority.

Under a system of legalistic authority, the stability of tradition and the flexibility of charisma are combined; rules must be obeyed by everybody but they can be changed or new ones made to adapt to changes in the environment. The bureaucracy, discussed in Chapter 1, is an organizational type that draws its efficiency from reliance on a set of comprehensive and universalistic rules which outline a division of labor, channels of command and responsibility, programs of activity, and so forth. The power of an office is independent of the member who holds it and the criteria of eligibility for the office are also objective. No aspect of organizational activity is exempt from rational regulation and no member of the organization, not even the most powerful officeholder, is above the rules. Legalistic authority is objective, comprehensive, and impersonal. It can be used by any qualified man for any purpose.

Over time, Weber continued, legalistic authority is becoming more widespread and, as rule by law is more fully accepted, legalistic authority is displacing charisma and tradition as the basic form of legitimate power in society. Reflecting on this trend, we would tend to agree with Mills (1956) who, writing about American society, declared that the class in society that has access to the uppermost offices in the military, governmental, and industrial bureaucracies can use its massive power for any purpose that seems fit from its point of view. Our increasing reliance on systems of control based on rules has led to the rise of an American power elite.

Authority and Interests

If we take Weber and Mills seriously, the American work situation has become a highly sophisticated control system with serious implications for our total way of life. This conclusion is very close to the position of Dahrendorf (1959) who posited that our American society has become modeled after modern industry. In an industrial society every relationship, whether worker and supervisor or father and son, is constructed on a basis of differential authority, which raises the questions of which party can rightfully control the other and how many of the others' activities are subject to his control. What this has meant in everyday terms is a decline in feelings of community and commonality among the population. Competition and control have become overriding concerns and cooperation is generally ignored as a way of resolving conflicts.

Perhaps Dahrendorf's position is clarified most by considering his views on interests. First, let us consider the term itself: interest is conceptually related to matters of economics, as when one has an interest in a business, meaning a right or share of ownership and a claim for benefit and profit. A social interest is more broadly defined, being understood as a social relationship with something that can affect you, either to your advantage or your disadvantage. When people are aware of a social interest they are likely to take action that will protect or prosecute their cause for their personal benefit. We can think of many possible kinds of interests, as suggested by common phrases including public interest, personal interest, special interest, and disinterested party. But considering that the public interest is mute and truly disinterested parties do not get involved in disputes, our experience is probably limited to issues raised by personal and special interests.

Dahrendorf's position, to return, is that the differential authority structure which typifies our social relationships is a source of conflict because it generates two different interests, causing each party to become actively opposed to the other. The interest of the powerful party is in the preservation of the status quo because he draws unequal benefits under it. The interest of the exploited party is in change, since his fair share of the benefits is denied him under the existing order. The heat and turmoil of labor–management relations can be found in every major social institution —church, family, government, education, and so on.

A very brief survey of organizational research reveals that in a wide variety of settings, workers have been able to subvert the rules and systems of control imposed by their superiors and have asserted controls of their own making.

Roethlisberger and Dickson (1939) studied employees in an electrical equipment manufacturing firm. Reportedly, the researchers entered the field under the general influence of scientific management theory. They assumed that workers responded to organizational conditions as isolated individuals, motivated primarily by rational self-interest. Out of their studies they developed human relations, a managerial viewpoint that recognized the power of informal work-groups—the power to limit a worker's productivity, the power to set and maintain group output levels, and the power to make life unbearable for those who resist (cf. Homans, 1950).

Mayo (1945), Whyte (1969), Roy (1952; 1960), and many others added to our knowledge about the role of work groups in staff–line conflict. Staff–line conflict is what results when managerial interests and worker interests clash. For example, workers were subject to periodic visits by efficiency men who retimed each job. How a job was timed was important to both parties. For management it was a matter of efficiency and the maximization of profit; for the worker it was a matter of being free to work at a comfortable pace for a baseline payrate or being able to work harder for a bonus payrate. It also became a matter of winning or losing in a contest of wit and strategy. The payoff was power.

Dalton produced a major study of intergroup relations, but his study dealt with executives and managers (1959). Dalton reported that cliques (informal groups of managers and executives that are developed to realize some fairly specific ends) continuously formed, dissolved, and re-formed in response to the ebb and flow of issues and crises within the organization. In their struggles power was gained and lost and some cliques emerged in advantaged positions that bore little relationship to the objective organizational scheme. Cliques, not offices, controlled the resources and actions of members. Cliques held power.

In sum, Dahrendorf noted that authority differentials have affected American life, but in a dialectic switch, much evidence suggests that the exploited workers have found diverse means of offsetting the imbalance of power. The resulting view of American industry shows two powerful elements, both very conscious of their interests, engaging in ongoing conflict as a way of life.

Compliance

Etzioni (1961) has found that how an organization controls its members is a useful and informative way of classifying and comparing organizational settings. He identified three compliance models based on coercive power, utilitarian power, and social power.

Coercive organizational settings rely on crude control devices such as force and violence, or the threat of harm and injury in response to noncompliance. The modern prison is typical of this type of setting. An undesirable result of coercion is the development of alienation within the membership. Alienated members do not respond to gentler forms of control because they do not see any interest in common with the organization. Their lack of commitment to the goals of the whole is usually accompanied by feelings of isolation, thus coercive control does not lend itself to the development of small groups to offset the power of the whole. Individualistic responses are the usual thing.

Utilitarian power is reliant on the ability to manipulate material rewards for compliant actions. History has shown that large numbers of men are willing to comply to another's will if the price is right. Most business organizations use utilitarian power to control their work force of wage earners. The capitalist system is based on the willingness of men to treat their labor as a commodity that can exchange in a marketplace. Marx was one of the first to point to the alienation that arises when workers are separated from the fruits of their labor. And utilitarian power generates little in the way of commitment to the organization, since the worker is encouraged to sell his labor to the highest bidder. In recent years American industries have tried many ways to off-set these disadvantages, which lead to shoddy workmanship and high rates of absenteeism and turnover. Offering stock options, allowing participation in decision making, and enlarging jobs to cover a larger portion of the production process are among the efforts made to improve control of workers under this form of power.

The third compliance model is the least alienating, produces the greatest member commitment to the goals of the whole, and relies most on the members' being convinced that they should comply. This model is based on social power and it is typical of the organization with many professionals as members. Social power may be focused in an office, in a man, or in a combination of the two; the same is true of coercive and utilitarian power. However, social power may also be held by a body of peers or by an abstract collectivity such as a profession. In this important way, the control of professionals as colleagues is very different.

Power in Collegial Settings

Moving from bureaucracies and industrial firms to organizations of professionals the picture changes slightly. Etzioni has commented on the interplay of administrative authority and professional authority (1964: 75–93). He stressed that staff–line conflicts do not develop in professional organizations as they do in more vertically organized settings. In part this is due to the special role of knowledge (he defines professions as being different in that five or more years of specialized training is needed to learn the body of knowledge). In order to understand professional acts, one must be himself a professional. Administrators are frequently chosen by the collegial body from among their own ranks. They may serve as first-among-equals, often bearing the title of chairman, or they may have the additional powers of a head. The former type is preferred because of the advantages both sides gain from the constituent–representative relationship. A head is more reliant on legalistic authority, which makes him less dependent on the collegial body and less easily controlled.

When the day-by-day logistics of running the organization become too technical, it is common for a nonprofessional manager to be hired to take over those administrative tasks that do not bear directly on the performance of professional acts. In such cases, hospitals for example, professional members will be kept in charge of professional departments, surgery, obstetrics, etc. Thus, for the nonprofessional members, the primary authority is administrative, but for the professional members, the professional authority prevails. The professionals retain power over their activities and their peers. The result is a social structure in which vertical lines of authority and control are underdeveloped and lateral networks of peer influence, including coalitions and cliques, abound.

Professionals are simultaneously members in particular organizations and in their respective professions. Some members value their organizations membership over the membership in their profession and rely on local rewards to support themselves from day to day and to sustain their work identity. For others, the organization is merely a landing field from which they launch flights into the far reaches of their profession (Gouldner, 1957–58). Their need for the organization is perceived strictly in terms of its support for their professional activity, and they look to the professional college beyond their place of employment to provide the recognition and identity by which they are sustained. The latter, the cosmopolitan professional, is most difficult to control and his presence is a constant source of uncertainty to his local colleagues.

In summary, this introduction presents power as organizational structure that emerges naturally as an outcome of the basic process of defining the situation. Conflict and agreement are both basic social structures in the sense that they motivate and facilitate further rationalization of the setting. Authority was seen as a device used by leaders to secure greater power; the greatest power is possible under legalistic authority but that power is limited by the power of work groups and cliques. Three models of compliance have been developed in modern organizations based on coercive, utilitarian, and social power. The latter is most typical of collegial settings and, except for the development of administrative and professional conflict, these settings present great homogeneity and solidarity.

The readings in this chapter consider more intensively the nature of power in organizations, the variations typical of collegial settings, and the effects of client relationships on the administrative-profession power differential.

REFERENCES

BLANKENSHIP, RALPH L.
1976   "Collective behavior in organizational settings."*Sociology of Work and Occupations 3 (May), 2:151-168.*

COSER, LEWIS A.
1955   *The Functions of Social Conflict.* New York: The Free Press of Glencoe.

CROZIER, MICHEL
1964   *The Bureaucratic Phenomenon.* Chicago: The University of Chicago Press.

DAHRENDORF, RALF
1959   *Class and Class Conflict in Industrial Society.* Stanford: Stanford University Press.

DALTON, MELVILLE
1959   *Men Who Manage.* New York: John Wiley and Sons.

ETZIONI, AMITAI
1961   *A Comparative Analysis of Complex Organizations.* New York: The Free Press.
1964   *Modern Organizations.* Englewood Cliffs, N. J.: Prentice-Hall.

GERTH, H. H., AND C. WRIGHT MILLS
1946   *From Max Weber.* New York: Oxford University Press.

GOULDNER, ALVIN W.
1954   *Patterns of Industrial Bureaucracy.* Glencoe, Ill.: Free Press.
1957-58 "Cosmopolitans and locals, I and II." *Administrative Science Quarterly* 2, 281-306, and 444-80.
1965   *Wildcat Strike.* New York: Harper and Row.

GUSFIELD, JOSEPH
1966   *Symbolic Crusade, Status Politics and the American Tem-
       perence Movement.* Urbana: University of Illinois Press.

HOMANS, GEORGE
1950   *The Human Group.* New York: Harcourt-Brace.

HYDEBRAND, WOLF (ED.)
1973   *Comparative Organizations: The Results of Empirical Re-
       search.* Englewood Cliffs, N.J.: Prentice-Hall.

MAYO, ELTON
1945   *The Social Problems of an Industrial Society.* Boston: Har-
       vard University Press.

MILLS, C. WRIGHT
1956   *The Power Elite.* New York: Oxford University Press.

NADEL, S. F.
1963   *The Theory of Social Structure.* London: Cohen and West.

ROETHLISBERGER, FRITZ J., AND WILLIAM J. DICKSON
1939   *Management and the Worker.* Cambridge: Harvard Uni-
       versity Press.

ROY, DONALD F.
1952   "Quota restriction and gold-bricking in a machine shop."
       American Journal of Sociology 57 (March): 430-37.
1960   "Banana time: job satisfaction and informal interaction." *Hu-
       man Organization* 18:158-68.

SILVERMAN, DAVID
1971   *The Theory of Organizations.* New York: Basic Books.

SMELSER, NEIL J.
1968   "Toward a general theory of social change," in *Essays in
       Sociological Explanation.* Englewood Cliffs, N.J.: Prentice-
       Hall, pp. 192-280.

WHYTE, WILLIAM F.
  1969   *Organizational Behavior: Theory and Application.* Home-
          wood, Ill.: Richard D. Irwin.

OVERVIEW

Power, according to Michael Crozier, was dealt with badly by social theorists for a variety of reasons. Only during the last decade or so have we seen the beginnings of adequate conceptualizations of power and control in organizations. An adequate perspective on power in organizational settings must face the significance of rationality in the pursuit of goals, and it must simultaneously face the significance of reliance on human members —the technical and the human aspects of organizational situations.

The Crozier essay proceeds by considering the dependence of power on the availability of options. Rationality implies the reduction of options to the one best way. Thus rationality and power do not go well together. In the conflict it is power, and not rationality, that generally prevails. Reality does not permit the reduction of very many situations to the single option of the one best way. When two parties face each other in confrontations, some uncertainty as to the option each will take is always present. Uncertainty affects the balance of power. In general, the greater the party's options, the greater his power. In a confrontation, the party whose actions are most limited has the least power.

In the main part of his essay, Crozier offers a probabilistic viewpoint on power in which rationality is a main tool used in power relationships, working in the reduction of uncertainty. In the power struggle between administrators and experts, the administrators rely on the development of rules (rationality) to check the power of uncertainty held by those who control specialized knowledge. Organizational structures emerge through which dependence relationships are protected and the achievement of formally sanctioned goals is ensured.

In the next selection, Bidwell and Vreeland introduce another dimension to the power struggle—the effects of the form of the relationship, that of the professional as well as the organization, with the client. In brief, this article proposes that the relative power of the professional vis-à-vis the administrator is greater when the client contracts with an individual professional for professional services to be delivered on organizational premises, preferably on a cash-and-carry basis. If a client enters into a more complex contract for a wider set of services, it is likely that the contract will be with the organization and not with the individual professional. The delivery of professional services recedes in importance and, with it, the power of the professional.

The question of power is then related to a question of whether the professional member serves *his* clients on organizational premises or whether he serves the organization's clients. Thus, a physician has greater power as one partner in a small clinic than as a staff member of a large hospital. A psychologist has greater power as a member of the staff of a child-guidance clinic than as part of the staff of a public school system.

Rue Bucher offers an excellent account of the social and political underlife of an academic setting in her essay on social process and power in a medical school. A critical governance structure, the departmental head, is found to offer a variety of styles ranging from the colleague to the chief. In some areas, the head is more tightly bound to the will of the powerful members of the department, but in areas of less vital interest he has wide ranging powers and some autonomy. When faced with issues that seem to touch upon faculty interests, however, the head is likely to be confronted by coalitions of members who mobilize to press their particular position.

The question of when a head may disregard the advice of his members appears to be related to the power and prestige of the coalitions an issue generates. Rarely does a head act so quickly after the introduction of an issue that coalitions do not have time to form and be heard. In this manner, few instances occur in which a head goes against the will of his more powerful members on issues that they define as important. Bucher includes an extensive section in her essay which examines the various bases for power found in medical schools.

The final essay in this chapter is intended to develop a unified perspective on power and control, but it is also intended to function as a synthesis and summary of the entire perspective on colleagues in organization. A model of organizational situations is outlined. It stresses joint enactment of organizational activity within a commonly understood situation. The enacted organizational situation is strongly reliant on individual members who are motivated by personal career goals. As a result, there are recurring crises in which individualistic actions must be brought into accord with the collective interest. Controlling a member, in this case a leader, is achieved through the power of the peer group to define the individual as deviant and to exclude him from the rewards of the member-role.

The process by which members exert collegial control is illustrated through the presentation of a crisis stemming from the exercise of unilateral power by a head, in contrast to his pledge of collegial status to the professional membership. In the case study, a model of control for collegial situations is implied. The model serves to demonstrate that power struggles are a means of constructing social organization.

THIRTEEN
POWER AND
UNCERTAINTY
Michel Crozier

Power as the New Central
Problem of the Theory of Organization

Power is a very difficult problem with which to deal in the theory of organization. It refers to a kind of relationship that is neither unidimensional nor predictable like the kind of stimulus-response relationship which social psychologists found so rewarding to study when they began to use scientific methods for understanding organizational behavior. Moreover, the use of power carries a distinct value connotation, so that ideological, as well as methodological, reasons have been working simultaneously to cause researchers to avoid facing the issue.

The consequences of this kind of approach have been serious. Communication problems, problems of work motivation, and problems of morale had been widely discussed and seriously studied in theory, empirically, and even through experiments. However, only a few years ago, the positive analysis of power relations did not seem to have progressed much since the days of Machiavelli and Marx. A brief review of the place that power problems have had in the development of modern organizational theory will give us a clearer perspective of their implications for the present and enable us to understand better the general framework within which our data must be discussed.

The early rationalistic theory of organization tended to ignore the problem of power altogether. Its mechanistic model did not allow for relationships as complex as those which power fosters. Its promoters, on

Source: Abridged from *The Bureaucratic Phenomenon* by Michael Crozier. © 1964 by The University of Chicago Press, Chicago, Illinois 60637. Reprinted by permission of the author and the publisher.

the other hand, were fighting for a radical departure from the remnants of an aristocratic past too much concerned with the methods of ruling and controlling subordinate groups. They believed mankind had to shift from the government of men to the administration of things, as their precursor Saint-Simon had claimed; and they felt they were achieving their aims by emphasizing financial stimuli and technical controls instead of human leadership. The delusion that they had suppressed power relationships prevented them from understanding the true nature of their own actions, which nevertheless had direct consequences on the power structure of modern organizations.

Early twentieth-century Marxists, although they viewed all contemporary problems of the capitalist world through the spectacles of power dialectics, also found themselves in the same predicament when dealing with the future. They felt that, when ownership relationships had been eliminated, an administration of things similar to the one Western industrialists were proposing would take care of all power problems. Lenin's famous definition of socialism, "Soviets plus electrification," was a terse statement characteristic of the same desire to escape the power problems of modern bureaucracies that was driving organizers and industrialists of the West.

Power problems were not squarely faced by the sociologists, social psychologists, and philosophers of the thirties and forties, whose "human relations approach" nevertheless made it possible to challenge more fundamentally the rationale of the classical theory.[1] This was true for the *interactionists*[2] as well as for the early *Lewinians.*[3]

To be sure, by directing devastating attacks against the mechanistic model of behavior upon which the classical theory rested, and by making it obvious to everyone that the human factor was a determinant, the *interactionists* were preparing the way for an understanding of power relationships. If one accepts the concept that human behavior cannot be directed by simple financial stimuli alone, that *sentiments* have an impact on *activities,* one must soon also admit that the allocation of power and the system of power arrangements have a decisive influence over the kind of adjustment people are able to make within an organization, and over the practical results and the efficiency of that organization.

Most interactionists, however, have tended to shy away from discussing such matters. They have preferred to study interactions in their most physical aspect, without taking into account the hierarchical system of domination.[4] They can explain the emergence of spontaneous leadership,[5] but not the impact of an authority imposed from the top down and of the concomitant struggle for power. Finally, one can view their attempts at understanding sentiments and activities by measuring interactions as another stimulus–response approach, as simplistic in several aspects as the mechanistic model they had rightly criticized.[6] Moreover, the very imperfection of the instrument prevents analysis of the extent to which technical rationality may be shaped and determined by the human factor. It thus tends to reinforce the hold of mechanistic factors in decision-making.

At a deeper level, their avoidance of power problems seems to be linked with a conservative philosophy. According to this, as Clark Kerr has pointed out, human relations problems can be understood and solved without accepting dissatisfaction, antagonisms, and group conflicts as the price an open society has to pay for progress.[7]

Lewinians have not escaped power problems so simply. Their long-continued ignorance of the sociological and organizational aspects of leadership, however, has made it difficult for them to understand the struggles, the peculiar alignments, and the kind of bargaining engendered by the impact of power. They wanted to understand what makes an organization efficient, but at first they did not anticipate going beyond their demonstration of the superiority of permissive leadership and their rather naïve search for the best way of converting people to it. Research results, however, while contributing in a decisive way to our knowledge of the way organizations operate, have not validated their assumptions.[8] It was demonstrated, for example, that it was the supervisors who enjoyed more popularity with their subordinates who were apt to be those who had more influence within the organization—not the most permissive ones.[9] The main experimental project conducted by the Michigan Survey Research Center in an insurance company had mixed results; the authoritarian system of leadership appeared to be as successful as the "permissive" one.[10] Careful investigations, by Floyd Mann at the University of Michigan[11] and by Fleishman, Harris, and Burtt at Ohio State,[12] of the net results of human relations training, then demonstrated conclusively that it had been a conspicuous failure. As many people had suspected, it was useless for changing people's attitudes outside of their own work and power structure surroundings. Floyd Mann and his associates devised new ways of intervention, taking into account the organizational structure. But even their feedback techniques fell short of integrating the problems of power —to whose importance their own researches testified.

The logic of those cumulative experiences and the critical discussion they caused were not without results. During the last five years especially, power problems have come to the forefront on the study of organizational behavior. Social psychologists such as Robert Khan and Arnold Tannenbaum, small group psychologists such as Dorwin Cartwright, J. P. R. French, and associates, sociologists with a more anthropological bias such as Melville Dalton and Norman Martin are conducting researches on the problems of control and power.[13]

Approaches to this new field, however, still seem to be awkward and groping, as if the factors which prevent people from dealing with power problems were still active when the investigators finally chose to study them.

The shyness and escapism we have described seem to be associated with the rejection of the human relations approach by the strict rationalist, and, at the opposite pole, by ignorance about all rational problems on the part of the strict "human relations" proponent. If one believes that co-ordination, conformity to orders, and the will to produce can be brought about with only economic and financial incentives—i.e., if the world of human relations is ignored altogether—then power problems need not be taken seriously. But the exact reverse is operating within the human relations approach. If one believes that a perfect equation between satisfaction and productivity can be achieved under permissive leadership, one does not have to study power; one has only to fight to accelerate its withering away.

A realistic appraisal of power relationships and power problems, however, can be made only when one has realized that there are no shortcuts. One must face at the same time the problem of the rational achievement of goals and that of the human means.[14] But even if one accepts both approaches as necessary, one can still see them as completely separate, pretending, implicitly at least, that they do not interfere. This is more or less the conventional contemporary view of two independent worlds which must be studied independently—the rational and technical world, under the primacy of goal-setting and goal-achieving; and the world of personnel, morale, and human organization.

Only with the recent developments of neo-rationalism and of the decision-making approach has it been possible to go beyond this lip-service integration and to understand how each set of determinants establishes the limits of the other sets' possibilities of application. The classic rationalists did not consider the members of an organization as human beings, but just as other cogs in the machine. For them, workers were only hands. The human relations approach has shown how incomplete such a rational was. It has also made it possible to consider workers as creatures of feeling, who are moved by the impact of the so-called rational decisions taken above them, and will react to them. A human being, however, does not have only a hand and a heart. He has also a head, which means that he is free to decide and to play his own game. This is what almost all proponents of the human relations theories, as well as their early rationalist opponents, tend to forget. This explains their failure and the hostility they have met among workers, in spite of their positive contributions and their most excellent intentions. By ignoring the subordinates' claims to freedom they immediately created among them fears of being manipulated. [15]

Neo-rationalist or strategic analysis methods have been used, until now, mostly for understanding decision-making at the managerial level. But they can have an even greater impact if they are used for understanding subordinates' behavior. Subordinates can be considered as free agents who can discuss their own problems and bargain about them, who do not only submit to a power structure but also participate in that structure. Of course, their degree of freedom is not very great, and their conduct, when viewed from outside, may seem to a large extent to be determined by non-rational motivations. But one must never forget that to them it is rational, i.e., adaptive.

March and Simon, among others, have put the problem in the proper light, with their concept of bounded rationality and their analysis of the different sets of factors that limit rationality. Such an approach allows us to deal with the problems of power in a more realistic fashion. It enables us to consider, at the same time, the rationality of each agent or of each group of agents, and the influence of the human relations factors that limit their rationality. [16]

The Role of Power Within an Organizational System

We should like to attempt to understand in more formal terms how power is likely to appear in a rational system of organization.

Let us take, to begin, Robert Dahl's[17] definition of power: *the power of a person A over a person B is the ability of A to obtain that B do something he would not have done otherwise.* It seems clear that a perfect rational system, such as was imagined by the exponent of the classical or of the Marxist theory, does not allow power relationships to develop in the normal course of the functioning of an organization. In such a system, we believe, there is only one rational choice to be made by each protagonist in a collective endeavor. Provided that goals are given, there is only *one best way* at each level to achieve the assigned task, and one best way also to arrange the hierarchical levels and to assign the necessary tasks. If there were actually only one best way to do things, individuals could not maintain any leeway in accomplishing their tasks and in making decisions about other people's tasks. Their behavior, therefore, would be entirely predictable, and they could, in turn, predict and rely on the behavior of all the other protagonists. One can say that they would simultaneously be bound as regards their own possibilities of action and free from any kind of personal dependence. Someone who has only one course of action available cannot ingratiate himself with the organization or with any individual within the organization. He does not have any possibility of bargaining. Power relationships could not develop in a context where no one could change the behavior of anyone else.

But contrary to the hopes of the industrialists and progressivists of the twenties, the very progress of rationality in the field of organization has shown how deceptive such beliefs in the *one best way* were. Power relationships and discretion in human interaction cannot be suppressed with rationalization; and the failure of classical rationalists does not stem from the resistance of an earlier power-ridden social order.[18]

Reality, in fact, appears extremely different from the perfect administration of things. Even in such a privileged case as the Monopoly, where it would be possible to simplify and rationalize to the extreme by cutting ties with the environment, strategical analysis makes it possible to discover that power can neither be suppressed nor ignored. It stems from the impossibility of eliminating uncertainty in the context of bounded rationality which is ours.[19]

In such a context, the power of A over B depends on A's ability to predict B's behavior and on the uncertainty of B about A's behavior. As long as the requirements of action create situations of uncertainty, the individuals who have to face them have power over those who are affected by the results of their choice.[20]

At present, a complete reversal of earlier conceptions about rationality can be discerned. The greater confidence effected by the progress of knowledge, the possibilities of mastering the environment that it implies, have not tended to reinforce the rigidity of the decision-making process. They seem, on the contrary, to have obliged organizations to discard completely the very notion of *one best way*. The most advanced organizations, because they now feel capable of integrating areas of uncertainty in their economic calculus, are beginning to understand that the illusion of perfect rationality has too long persisted, weakening the possibilities of action by insisting on rigorous logic and immediate coherence. Substituting the notion of program for the notion of operational process, introducing the theory of probability at lower and lower levels, reasoning on global systems, and integrating more and more variables without separating ends and means, they are experiencing a deep and irreversible change. The crucial point of this change consists, for us, in recognizing—first, implicitly, then more and more consciously—that man cannot look for the one best way and has not actually even searched for it. The philosophy of the one best way has been only a way of protecting oneself against the difficulty of having to choose, a scientist's substitute for the traditional ideologies upon which rested the legitimacy of the rulers' decision.[21] Man has never been able to search for the *optimum* solution. He has always had to be content with solutions merely *satisfactory* in regard to a few particularistic criteria of which he was aware.[22]

The reasoning on uncertainty that makes it possible to use the theory of probability in decision-making opens, at the same time, new ways to take into account all the affective reactions that are brought about by the power and dependence relationships around areas of uncertainty. Research in this domain, we feel, will be decisive for all future progress in the field, since it is there and there only that the world of rationality and the world of affectivity will be integrated.

THE PROBLEM OF THE SUPERVISOR–SUBORDINATE RELATIONSHIP
Let us take, as an example, an organization that has been completely rationalized in the classical sense that it has undergone scientific work organization. If the task assignment is such that neither the superior nor the subordinate has any kind of initiative, in relation not only to the processing of the task, but also to its amount and quality, which are rewarded independently on an automatic basis—i.e., if the supervisor does not personally control any important variable affecting his subordinates' behavior, he cannot obtain from them increases of their output or better the quality of their production. But if the supervisor has some leeway, if he can tolerate a breach of rules, a distortion of the work process that might make it easier to accomplish the task, his subordinates who want or need such tolerance will be dependent on him on that account. Supervisors will thus have at their disposal some kind of influence which is ultimately power that they will be able to utilize to attain their own personal ends.

We can thus envisage two complementary sorts of discretion within an organization. The first one ccmes from the uncertainty of the task itself, and the second from the rules that have been devised to make it more rational and more predictable. As long as some uncertainty remains about carrying out the task, the most menial subordinate retains some slight discretion. And, in a way, as long as a human being is preferred to an automatic machine there will be some uncertainty. On the other hand, the rules that limit the discretion of the subordinate to a minimum can and will be used by the supervisor for preserving an area of discretion and the possibility of bargaining.[23]

To the impossibility of suppressing completely the discretion of the subordinate, therefore, there corresponds the persistence of personal discretion in the interpretation and application of the rules. Thus pressure can be applied to force the subordinates to use their discretion for the benefit of the organization.

The battle between subordinates and supervisors involves a permanent basic strategy. Subordinates try to increase their amount of discretion and utilize it to oblige higher-ups to pay more for their co-operation.[24] Conversely, they exert pressure for new rules limiting the power of the supervisors; but they try, at the same time, to profit, whenever possible, from whatever discretion the supervisors have kept. Supervisors apply pressure symmetrically on both fronts, rationalization and bargaining, to gain as much co-operation as they can for what cannot be rationalized. Both sides must use double-talk. Officially, each supports the rules, and puts as much pressure as possible on the other side to oblige the latter to obey these rules, while it is fighting to preserve its own area of freedom and making covert deals in defiance of the same rules it is promoting.[25]

We would like to uphold the view, finally, that workers who have been restricted by scientific work-organization to a completely stereotyped task use every available means to regain enough unpredictability in their behavior to enhance their low bargaining power. Also, their struggle for making out is one of the essential elements of their strategy.

The Influence of Power Relationships on Organizational Structure

If we admit, according to our hypothesis, the importance of the link between the predictability of behavior and bargaining power, we must consider the impact of such relationships within an organization and the way that the necessity of handling them shapes organizational structure.

The possibility of prediction stems not only from the objective conditions of the task, but also, sometimes to a major extent, from the way information is distributed. The whole system of roles is so arranged that people are given information, the possibility of prediction, and therefore control, precisely because of their position within the hierarchical pattern.

This situation, in which certain individuals control variables unpredictable to other people, has an only partially objective foundation. It is man made and socially created, but it is nevertheless not arbitrary. It is the indirect result of the power struggle within the organization.

Were it to take place without any check, the power struggle would bring paralyzing conflicts and unbearable situations. It is thus necessary that a hierarchical order and an institutional structure impose discipline on the different individuals and groups, and arbitrate between their claims. But this power—which, of course, cannot be absolute—must bargain and compromise with all the people whose co-operation is indispensable at each level. It must, therefore, also dispose of an independent bargaining power. To be sure, it can use the influence of ideology, the ideas of the "common good" and of the "general interest," and it will do this. But this is insufficient, as the managers of socialistic communities have experienced time and again.[26] Its major means of action, finally, can only be the manipulation of information or at least the strict regulation of access to information.

Two kinds of power will develop out of these situations. First will evolve the power of the expert, i.e., the power an individual will have over the people affected by his actions, through his ability to cope with a source of relevant uncertainty. Second, there will emerge the power necessary to check the power of the expert. As we have stated earlier, every member of an organization is an expert in his own way, though his expertise might be extremely humble. He will, therefore, exercise some power upon other persons whose success depends, to a certain extent, on his own decision.[27]

As a matter of fact, one could thus generalize to the whole structure of an organization, the peculiar strategy of the supervisor–subordinate relationships analyzed earlier. We should like to suggest that studies be made on the repartition of roles and on formal regulations within an organization of the basis of such assumptions.

No organization can function, indeed, without imposing some check on the bargaining power of its own members. Thus certain individuals must be given enough freedom of action to be able to adjust conflicting claims and to impose decisions about general development—in other words, to improve the game they are playing against their environment. In order to obtain this necessary freedom of action, the *manager* will have to have power over his subordinates, formal power to make decisions as a last recourse, and informal power to bargain with each individual and each group to persuade them to accept his decisions.

To achieve his aims, the manager has two sets of conflicting weapons: rationalization and rule-making on one side; and the power to make exceptions and to ignore the rules on the other. His own strategy will be to find the best combination of both weapons, according to the objectives of the unit of which he is in charge and to the degree to which members of the unit are interested in these objectives. Proliferation of the rules curtails his own power. Too many exceptions to the rules reduce his ability to check other people's power. Formal structure and informal relationships should not be opposed. They interpenetrate and complete each other. If one wants to understand them, one must study them together, along with the system of power relationships that helps integrate them.

The Evolution of Power Relationships Systems

Comparing the competing claims of the different individuals and groups within an organization, one can state that, in the long run, power will tend to be closely related to the kind of uncertainty upon which depends the life of the organization. Even the managerial role is often associated with this kind of power—witness the successive rise of managerial control by financial experts, production specialists, or budget analysts, according to the most important kind of difficulties organizations have had to solve to survive. As soon as the progress of scientific management or of economic stabilization has made one kind of difficulty liable, at least to a certain degree, to rational prediction, the power of the group whose role it is to cope with this kind of difficulty, and of the people who represent it, will tend to decrease. It should be rewarding to analyze such recurrent trends in order to throw more light on a problem that is often discussed, but very rarely on the basis of power relationships—the problem of the power of the expert in those societies in which accelerated change has become a permanent feature of life.

Technocracy is still a constant cause of fear, at least in Europe, as well as a sort of fascination. Many intelligent observers[28] feel that because of the complexities of our technical age, certain groups of people, technical experts or managers, through their role as technicians of organizational life, are coming to hold more and more power in society as a whole, and that these technocrats will form the new ruling class or the new feudal order of our era.

Such a belief is not validated by a careful analysis of modern decision-making. It derives from a misunderstanding of the situation created by technical and scientific progress. The invasion of all domains by rationality, of course, gives power to the expert who is an agent of this progress. But the expert's success is constantly self-defeating. The rationalization process gives him power, but the end results of rationalization curtail his power. As soon as a field is well covered, as soon as the first intuitions and innovations can be translated into rules and programs, the expert's power disappears.

As a matter of fact, experts have power only on the front line of progress—which means they have a constantly shifting and fragile power. We should like to argue even that it can be less and less consolidated in modern times, inasmuch as more and more rationalized processes can be operated by non-experts. Of course, experts will fight to prevent the rationalization of their own tricks of the trade. But contrary to the common belief, the accelerated rate of change that characterizes our period makes it more difficult for them to resist rationalization. Their bargaining power as individuals in constantly diminishing.[29]

The Primacy of Organizational Goals and the Limits of the Power Struggle

We started with the mechanistic model of a rational system of organization and tried to show that such a model did not make it possible to understand and to place properly the kind of power relationships people are directly experiencing everywhere. To this model, we have opposed a "strategic" model relying solely on these same power relationships which it seems impossible to ignore. With this new model we can understand, at the same time, the power of the experts and pseudo-experts and the necessity of imposing a managerial authority to check their powers.

But even if we accept the usefulness of such a model, we must now ask ourselves to what extent it is sufficient. In order to achieve its own goals, an organization must elaborate a hierarchical structure to prevent the power struggle from becoming an intolerable burden. Can it do so only through a process of blackmail and bargaining and a pyramid of dependence relationships? Is such a conceptual system not so much a caricature of reality as the perfect rational system of classical theory? Are there other ways and other kinds of influence to control and limit the power struggle?

If we took into account only power relationships in the narrow sense, it would be difficult to understand how modern organizations could reasonably function. Melville Dalton, in the otherwise remarkable book we have already quoted, has fallen into such an error.[30] He is so haunted by the fear of being misled by the formal structure and the formal definitions of the roles that, in his analysis of the ways managers really behave, he reports only irregularities, back-door deals, and subtle blackmail. Dalton's description is extremely suggestive and should be welcomed as a real landmark in our understanding of the managers' role, but he forgets the rational side of the organization and the series of social controls that prevent people from taking too much advantage of their own strategic situation. No organization could survive if it were run solely by individual and clique back-door deals. For example, let us examine his analysis of the meeting as a façade necessary for presenting several partners with the opportunity of communicating informally, for starting the two-way funnel, and for preparing and carrying out private undercover deals. This may appear to be true in extreme cases; but even then, people must play the game of co-operation in order to maintain a good strategic position. They therefore have to pay a price which is a not inconsistent check on their bargaining possibilities. Finally, one may also conclude that, even in such extreme cases, the undercover relationships of the formal meeting are manipulated in a constructive way by the organization, since the participants are forced to express themselves in the language, and through a formal setup of co-operation.[31]

The same problem appears, although in a simpler context, in the Industrial Monopoly. If one were to follow to its extrme the logic of our analysis of the dependence relationships in the Monopoly, one could easily conclude that the maintenance men can do exactly as they please in the shop, and that the director and assistant directors are completely paralyzed except in case of large-scale transformations. Yet maintenance men observe certain aspects of discipline, always keep decorum as regards work, and, finally, care competently for the machines. They introduce certain whims in their way of giving service to the people in the shop, but nevertheless, they do provide the service. Directors may be severely restricted in their possibilities of taking initiative, but they are not totally paralyzed. They have, as we have already seen, indirect kinds of influence; and a change of director can bring substantial differences to a plant.

One should not translate, therefore, the logic of the struggle into an overly black-and-white picture. Even so simple a strategy as the one of the production workers, or of the maintenance men, or of the lower supervisors at the shop level cannot be reduced to win-or-lose considerations. Other forces are operating which insure the minimum of consensus and organizational commitment that prevent people from extracting too much from, or from being too much exploited in, their reciprocal deals.

What are these forces? Let us analyze them in the simple case of the Monopoly before trying to raise the problem of more complex systems. Four main factors apparently must be reckoned with in the Monopoly: the necessity for the members of the different groups to live together; the fact that the existence of each group's privileges depends to quite a large extent on the existence of other groups' privileges; the general consensus among all groups about keeping certain minimum standards of efficiency; and, finally, the very stability of group relationships.

The existence of the first factor is obvious. But it does not receive all the attention it merits. If all the participants in the power game know that they will have to live with each other, whatever the results of their quarrels, a minimum of harmony and good fellowship must be maintained, whatever the opposition of roles. And this harmony can be achieved only if the other fellow's feelings are not too much hurt, according to the conventions of the culture of which they are members.[32] This is a very powerful, although usually ignored, cultural restraint. Because of this restraint, feelings and the expression of feeling may be used as weapon in the power struggle. We have pointed out already that the dependence of the production workers upon the maintenance men cannot exceed what is considered acceptable in present-day France, and that production workers are very skilful at using the pressure of cultural norms to put their maintenance men on the defensive. We can generalize very well from this example. The members of an organization who can complain of some unfairness in regard to current norms will never fail to utilize their feelings of frustration for very rational goals. They know that their partners are vulnerable and cannot bear difficult interpersonal relationships for very long. Expressing true or half-simulated feelings will thus have a direct impact in bargaining. Certainly, if the roles of the protagonists permit avoidance techniques, some cold and guarded relationships are possible. This can be observed between lower supervisors and maintenance men. But the necessity to play the avoidance game is also a check upon the exaction of too heavy a price from the situation.

The second powerful force at work, the awareness of the interdependence of all privileges, is widely diffused among the different groups. No one would say it openly, but it is quite clear that every member of each of the participant groups, is convinced that their privileges depend to quite an extent on the privileges of the other groups and that an attack upon another group can endanger the whole system and, indirectly, the special interests of the attacking group. We have discussed the alliance of the production and maintenance workers and the mutual restraints resulting from this alliance. But this is only part of the picture. There is solidarity, not only between allied groups, but also between enemies. This was almost openly acknowledged during our experiment when the results of the survey were communicated to the different groups. Comments by the attacking groups, to our surprise, were directed at minimizing the sharpness of the attack. Far from capitalizing on the weaknesses of the attacked group as revealed by the survey, they tried to ignore them, as if fearful of upsetting the status quo.

One has to take into account, of course, the fact that the employees of the Monopoly feel, at least to a certain extent, that they occupy an especially advantageous position.[33] Because of this position, they may consider that they have something in common to defend, for which they must sacrifice some of their own claims against their partners. But what about organizations that do not enjoy special privileges? We may hypothesize, of course, that conflicts will go much further and that they will be less manageable. We must, however, take care to re-examine the definition of privileges. The sheer violence of a competitive world may transform survival into a common privilege and an acceptable goal, at least within certain limits. One may even argue that the privileges obtained in the non-competitive world of public administration are necessary to offset the absence of such a unifying force.[34]

The third factor, the general agreement of all groups about what constitutes a reasonable degree of efficiency, operates along the same lines. Maintenance men are definitely featherbedding. However, they are on the defensive, because of what is considered, generally and in the Monopoly, as a fair day's work. Certainly such a notion is elastic. However, one should not neglect the pressures that can be put on a group because their contribution does not fit the general pattern of our industrial civilization. This pressure is well utilized by management, with the backing of other groups, to set limits to such a group's special claims.

Within the Monopoly, the *Direction Générale* was able to induce the maintenance men to service three machines instead of two. Maintenance men resisted for a long time, but their position was relatively weak because it was too well known that they had very little work to do. Generally, one may say that the norms concerning interpersonal relationships, the aims of an organization, and the contribution to be expected from its members are very powerful forces, shaping the field of bargaining and restraining the full use of its own power by each group.

At the same time, the organization can manipulate the need of each individual to realize and to actualize himself. All the members of an organization are influenced by and attracted to the kind of collective and constructive achievement it is capable of offering them. These feelings expressing the individual's subjection to the norms of efficiency of his society, upon which these norms in turn are founded, give a great deal of power to the people who can mobilize them within the organization—especially, of course, to management.

The last factor, the stability of intergroup relationships, is peculiar to the Monopoly, although its actual implications may be wide. In the

Monopoly, as we have shown, the general position of all the groups is relatively frozen and the individuals themselves cannot pass from one group to another. This long-time commitment reinforces group solidarity and the power struggle. However, viewed from another angle, it is a powerful stabilizer which tends to regulate the equilibrium of conflict.

Let us try to be more precise. It could be concluded, from a too rapid reading of our analysis of the power relationships, that such a situation cannot last forever, that it is in the process of deteriorating. This is not the case. The equilibrium we have described is a conflictive equilibrium, but a very stable one. Groups bargain to defend their own privileges in a changing world, and they are fearful that their partners will gain some points over them if they are put off guard. But as a matter of fact, they know their risk is not too great; they are not by any means engaged in a life-and-death struggle; theirs is a war of position. This is another decisive factor in the power struggle and in bargaining. Groups know they cannot get rid of their partners, that they will have to live with them and compromise with them—if not forever, then at least for the foreseeable future. This stability has direct and important consequences on individual motivations and behavior. No one in any group expects to change affiliation or could be lured away from his basic group solidarity—not only for personal egalitarian purposes, but even for bettering the functioning of the whole. Let us imagine, for example, what the outcome of the game would be if the Monopoly were a private organization and people could transfer from one category and one occupation to another without difficulties. Certain technical engineers would use the temporary strength of their group to succeed personally in becoming managers. But they would be appointed only insofar as they could be expected to rationalize at least the maintenance field; and they would do this, thus curtailing the power of their own group and putting an end to the struggle we have analyzed.

The Monopoly situation can, therefore, be characterized as an unusually stable equilibrium—a special case within the general context of dynamic relationships characteristic of our industrial civilization. It is extremely interesting from a methodological point of view, because the elimination of all sources of uncertainty but one makes it a sort of laboratory medium in which to explore the mechanism of power relationships. The stable equilibrium we were able to describe may be considered as a useful slow-motion process of group bargaining.

Let us now try to state more clearly the differences from this case that are brought about by the usual context of dynamic relationships. Two main features of organization seem significant to us in this respect. First, there are usually several competing sources of uncertainty within the same organization. Second, groups are not normally permanent. They may disappear or change substantially in the near future; still more frequently, for a number of individuals, membership in a group is likely to be temporary.

The outcome of such influences is the development of much more complex bargaining systems where several groups are competing, each one with its own possibilities of applying pressure, and where fights between groups are held in check by the consideration, by individual group members, of their own selfish interests. The power of management is likely, of course, to benefit from this double complication of the simple pattern, since its function of adjusting conflicting claims will have more importance and since it will be able to influence key individuals within the groups. A most important angle to consider is the role which the sheer survival of the organization will often play as a paramount source of uncertainty; this will still further reinforce the position of management.[35]

What are the possible consequences of the existence of such traits? In conclusion, the three following hypotheses are presented about the sort of power relationships and the sort of social controls that will accompany them in the usual context of dynamic equilibria:

1.   The more complex and dynamic the system of power relationships and of bargaining, the more likely are social controls to be directly and consciously enforced by management instead of being left to the operation of the indirect forces of the milieu (although the existence of these same forces remains essential for management's ability to operate).

2.   The limits that management consciously fixes for the development of the power struggle are usually much narrower than the natural limits set by the pressures of the milieu. Factional quarrels and group bargaining are not allowed overt expression so easily as in organizations where power relationships are stable and simple.

3.   The dynamic equilibrium system is much more favorable to change, since the pressure to eliminate uncertainty, in the instrumental domain, will not be held in check by the resistance of well-entrenched groups.

Anticipating the discussion in the next chapter, we now turn to the external conditions of such processes. It seems perfectly clear, at first glance, that public administration, being less under pressure for survival, stands a much better chance of eliminating the over-all source of uncertainty, and thus more difficulties, to maintain the managerial power. It will give, therefore, undue importance to the remaining areas of uncertainty, protect the experts who are in charge of them, and allow them to stabilize the power struggle and develop stationary equilibria that favor them.

Such an opposition between public administration and private organization, however, is not so clear-cut as it may seem. In many cases private organizations are as well protected as public agencies. Under conditions of stable technology and stable markets, the private ones may have to face less uncertainty than a public agency, which exists under the pressure of an active political system. If it were possible to make a precise comparison of the French nationalized railroads organization (SNCF) with the American private railroad companies, one would most probably find a greater number of protected sectors for the workers, the supervisors, and the executives in the average American private company than in the French bureaucratic nationalized corporation.

Then, within otherwise dynamic systems of organization, one may often find stationary equilibriums in one or more protected sectors that have grown, at least temporarily, apart from the main bargaining system.

Gouldner's study, *Patterns of Industrial Bureaucracy*[36] and Selznick's *TVA and the Grass Roots,*[37] present two cases paradoxically opposed in this respect. Stationary equilibrium is the principal feature of a sector of a private organization, while a much more fluid system of relationships is characteristic of the public agency.

In Gouldner's case, miners control all sources of uncertainty at the work level in the mine.[38] Not only do they alone have to face the material risks involved in this activity, but the amount of work and the results of production depend directly on their decisions. Decisions must be made on the spot by the individual miner or by the team of coworkers. They do not depend on the foremen and on the maintenance men; but the whole of the organization depends on the miners' work, which cannot be controlled under present circumstances. They have been able, therefore, to maintain the stationary equilibrium they are enjoying because of the position of strength they occupy, since it has become extremely difficult to recruit people for this hazardous lower-class occupation.[39] As a result, they hold in check the power of all other groups and enjoy a very rewarding situation in a context otherwise completely rationalized, where their own behavior is the major source of uncertainty.[40]

The case of the TVA, as analyzed by Selznick, presents a much more complex relationship. Although this is a public corporation, several sources of uncertainty are competing, and management uses this complexity to increase its freedom of action. It has slowly elaborated a complex process of co-optation that allows it to pick up people in the different pressure groups and to have them participate in managerial problems. The fight for survival, finally, although appearing only covertly, is extremely important. It accounts for the development of a special kind of social control, the ideological allegiance of the members of the organization. These two examples will make it possible for us to understand better the case of the Clerical Agency, a curious mixture where we find at the same time traits of stationary equilibrium and other traits more characteristic of organizations under the impact of the struggle for survival. There is no actual fear about survival, of course, but the only source of uncertainty —instead of being, as in the Monopoly, within the production system— comes from the outside. The amount of work and the possibility of achieving the aims of the organization according to the rules depend on the behavior of the customers. The success of the organization itself, if it does not depend on the fluctuations of the free market, is still subject to the sanctions of government and Parliament. Management, finally, as we have shown, has been able to shift directly to the employees' shoulders the pressure of the public in a completely impersonal way. One finds, therefore, at the same time in the Agency, the bureaucratic protection that stems from centralization and from the distance central power has created around itself, and, second, a very strong hierarchical pressure that is exerted without the usual recourse to humiliating personal dependencies. In this respect, the Clerical Agency appears to offer the paradoxical example of an impersonal system of organization which has been able to eliminate the usual power dependencies but must rely instead on a rigid and authoritarian system of hierarchical social relations. Such a system can survive only because of the very deep and anachronistic dichotomy between managers and managed and the acceptance, partial at least, of their inferior social position by the subordinates. It is reproducing, forty years later, the paradox and contradictions of scientific work organization.

Footnotes

[1] Borrowing their arguments against Taylorism from the anticapitalist reformers of the time, they kept the same naive approach as the Taylorians about their own constructive propositions.

[2] We use the term "interactionist" to designate the Harvard School of the thirties (Elton Mayo, T. N. Whitehead, Fritz Roethlisberger, Elliot Chapple, Conrad Arensberg, William Foote Whyte). See W. F. Whyte, "An Interaction Approach to the Theory of Organization," in Mason Haire, *Modern Organization Theory*

(New York: Wiley, 1959), pp. 154-82.

[3] At least before 1955.

[4] This is what can de deduced from the classical restatement of George Homans in his book, *The Human Group* (New York: Harcourt, Brace, 1950).

[5] The most illumination piece of research on that account is still W. F. Whyte, *Street Corner Society* (Chicago: University of Chicago Press, 1943).

[6] This is still the impression one gets after reading the 1960 presentation of W.F. Whyte in Mason Haire, *loc. cit.*

[7] Clark Kerr and Lloyd Fisher, "Plant Society, The Elite and the Aborigines," in *Common Frontiers in the Social Sciences* (Glencoe, Ill.: The Free Press, 1957).

[8] For a discussion of these results with a very convincing reassertion of the permissiveness philosophy see Rensis Likert, *New Patterns of Management* (new York: McGraw-Hill, 1961).

[9] Donald Pelz, "Influence, a Key to Effective Leadership," *Personnel,* III (1952), 3.

[10] See Nancy C. Morse and Everett C. Reimer, "Experimental Change of a Major Organizational Variable," *Journal of Abnormal and Social Psychology,* Vol. LII (1955); and Rensis Likert, "Measuring Organizational Performance," *Harvard Business Review,* March, 1958, pp. 41–50.

[11] Floyd Mann, "Studying and Creating Change: A Means of Understanding Social Organization," in *Human Relations in the Industrial Setting* (New York: Harper, 1957), pp. 146–67.

[12] E. A. Fleishman, E. F. Harris, and H. E. Burtt, *Leadership and Supervision in Industry: An Evaluation of a Supervisory Training Program* (Columbus: Ohio State University, 1955).

[13] See, e.g., Arnold Tannenbaum and Robert Kahn in Dorwin Cartwright (ed.), *Participation in Local unions* (Evanston: Row Peterson, 1958); W. Lloyd Warner and Norman Martin, *Industrial Man* (New York: Harper, 1959); Melville Dalton, *Men Who Manage* (New York: Wiley, 1960); Michel Crozier, "De l'étude des relations humaines à l'étude des relations de pouvoir," *Sociologie du Travail,* I (1961), 80–83. Author's note: written in 1964.

[14] Talcott Parsons has pointed out that power, as the development of the decision process, must become the central problem of organization theory. Talcott Parsons, *Structure and Process in Modern Societies* (Glencoe, Ill.: The Free Press, 1960), pp. 41–43.

[15] We personally participated in the diffusion of these fears ten years ago. See Michel Crozier, "Human Engineering," *les Temps Modernes,* July, 1951.

[16] James March and Herbert A. Simon, *Organizations* (New York: Wiley, 1958). We shall use, quite often in this section, the contribution of these authors, which we believe will stand as decisive. Let us say, however, that their attempt at integrating the two approaches (human relations and neo-rationalism) does not seem very satisfactory to us.

[17] Robert Dahl, "The Concept of Power," *Behavioral Science,* II (July, 1957), 201-15.

[18] In practice, the *one best way* philosophy was used to provide the managers, whose job it was to discover and elaborate this sole rational solution, with the kind of absolute power that was necessary to break down the habits and privileges of all other groups. And this is one of the most striking paradoxes of recent social history: the fight of the pioneers of scientific work organization, as well as the fight of the Bolsheviks for substituting the administration of things for the government of men, ended very often with an increase of the dichotomy between managers and managed.

[19] There may be many examples to confirm this analysis of power relationships. We have analyzed, for example, the case of a few experts in a public agency, whose job has been rationalized in such a way that it has become pretty much routine, in contrast with a much simpler but more exposed job where the unpredictable reactions of the public might endanger the reputation of the whole department. The holder of this last job, who can partially control this variable and whose influence preponderant for his colleagues' success, has much more bargaining power than they have and their influence is subject to his influence, whereas he is not to theirs.

[20] One should be precise and specify *relevant* uncertainty, although the notion of relevance is vague and subject to change according to the objectives of the organization and to the progress of knowledge. People and organizations will care only about what they can recognize as affecting them and, in turn, what is possibly within their control. When there are no possibilities of control, power can be claimed by no one—although it may be argued that, in a more diffuse way, the necessity of submitting to leadership will be greater in a situation of true uncertainty, as certain experiments on the advantages, under conditions of duress, of the centrality system over more democratic circular systems and the role of the leader among small primitive groups on the verge of starvation seem to have proved. See for example Harold J. Leavitt, "Some Effects of Certain Communication Patterns of Group Performance," *Journal of Abnormal and Social Psychology,* XLVI (1951), 28–50; and Claude Levi-Strauss, *Tristes Tropiques* (Paris: Plon, 1958), pp. 325–339. This notion of uncertainty has been also used recently by an American political scientist, Herbert Kaufmann, in an interdisciplinary report on administrative theory ("Why Organizations Behave As They Do: An Outline of a Theory"). Kaufmann analyzed only organizations' global behavior, but his conclusions are similar to ours.

21 The collapse of the illusions that formed the rationale of scientific work organization, and still form that of the present Soviet organizational system, makes it possible to transform the role and situation of the managers that can now be more easily stripped of any mystic connotation. Indeed, the taboos that once surrounded power relationships are beginning to disappear, and one will be more and more able to analyze them rationally without having to question the whole organizational system.

22 See March and Simon's pertinent demonstration, *op. cit.*

23 This can be seen in Alvin Gouldner's description of the way supervisors use disciplinary rules in their relationships with their subordinates. Alvin Gouldner. *Patterns of Industrial Bureaucracy* (Glencoe, Ill.: The Free Press, 1954), especially pp. 172–74.

24 In so doing, they must be very careful not to expose themselves to the risk of furthering rationalization; this is why their pressure is usually indirect.

25 There is an important distinction to be made between rules prescribing the ways in which the task must be performed and rules prescribing the way people should be chosen, trained, and promoted for various jobs. Subordinates fight rationalization in the first area and want it in the second, and supervisory personnel do just the reverse; but there is such a great link between both sets of rules that, by and large, ambiguity remains.

26 See, for example, a long series of articles by Robert Valette in *Communauté,* the magazine of the French federation of "Communautés de Travail," during 1957 and 1958.

27 Workers affected to the most routine jobs have some power over their supervisors, inasmuch as they jeopardize supervisors' plans and imperil their careers, by slowing down, loafing, and just being careless.

28 See for example of course, James Burnham, *The Managerial Revolution* (Bloomington, Ind.: Indiana University Press, 1960) and among a very abundant French literature, the discussions of the symposium organized by Georges Gurvich, *Industrialisation et technocratie: Travaux de la première semaine sociologique"* (Paris: Armand Colin, 1949); Jacques Ellul, *La Technique ou l'enjeu du siècle* (Paris, Armand Colin, 1954); Nora Mitrani, "Attitudes et symboles techno-bureaucratiques," *Cahiers internationaux de sociologie,* XXIV, 148. For a more realistic discussion, see Jean Meynaud, *Technocratie et politique* (Lausanne, 1960), and the discussions of the Fifth Congress of the International Political Science Association around the report of Roger Gregoire, "Les Problèmes de la technocratie et le rôle des experts" (Paris, 1961).

29 The medical profession, which may be considered as one of the best examples of a group of experts whose role and influence within modern society have remained extremely strong, still does not offer to modern physicians the comparative remunerations and authority their predecessors enjoyed. Yet the public

is much more resentful of its privileges and much more critical of its income than before.

[30] Dalton, *op. cit.*

[31] *Ibid.,* pp 220–40.

[32] The capacity of individuals and groups to tolerate conflicts and overt or covert expressions of hostility constitutes, as we shall see later, a very important element for understanding power relationships and the kind of bureaucratic system that can develop within a given culture.

[33] There are, of course, differences. For certain groups, though not for others, this is a very advantageous position. The latter, however, are those whose role is to identify more with the whole organization, and those whose stock-in-trade in the bargaining relationship is in reference to the common whole (i.e., the supervisors and director).

[34] One must notice, however, that the moderating pressure that comes from the different groups' awareness of the interdependence of their privileges is only a very imperfect force of integration. It is "conservative" and its regulating functions operate within extremely wide limits. Reinhard Bendix has underlined this force in his comparison of Western and Soviet kinds of organizations (*Work and Authority,* p. 247).

[35] The history of the Industrial Monopoly provides a good illustration of this. Much of the rationalization process that decisively curtailed the power of the managers and of the supervisors was achieved when workers were able, after a ten-year struggle, to impose the adoption of a carefully written seniority code. Their success, it may be argued with good reason, may have been due to the fact that the supervisors' power of intervention in the allocation of jobs was nothing more than a man-made source of uncertainty. This power, wielded by the supervisors and, through them, by the director, was not in any respect necessary to allow them to cope with other sources of uncertainty in the production, the selling, or the personnel problems of the organization, since all other elements of their activity were stable and easily predictable.

[36] Gouldner, *op. cit.*

[37] Philip Selznick, *TVA and the Grass Roots (Berkeley: University of California Press, 1949).*

[38] The organization described by Gouldner is dominated by the opposition between the mine and the surface plant. In the mine, men are their own bosses, while the surface workers face a completely rationalized organizational system.

[39] A much higher degree of rationalization has been in operation for a long time in most coal mines in the Western world, but social and economic conditions are quite different from this small gypsum plant in the U.S. See the discussion about the system of organization in the English mines, Eric Trist and E. L. Bamforth,

''Some Social and Psychological Consequences of the Longwall Method of Coal Getting,'' *Human Relations,* IV (1951), 3–38.

[40] Miners enjoy a particularly favorable position, inasmuch as their freedom of action contrasts directly with the complete predictability of behavior of the surface workers, who have not been able to oppose rationalization.

FOURTEEN AUTHORITY AND CONTROL IN CLIENT-SERVING ORGANIZATIONS *
Charles E. Bidwell and
Rebecca S. Vreeland

Formal organizations, as well as individual practitioners, are important agents of professional service. Yet, despite the attention which has been given to the relations between clients and free professionals, relations between clients and client-serving organizations largely remain to be explored.[1] Since the form of the professional-client relationship has significant effects on the behavior of the free professional, presumably it has an equally marked impact upon the structures and activities of client-serving organizations. Our purpose here is to suggest what some of these effects may be.

We have chosen to analyze effects upon authority structures and control within the staff, assuming that these structures have a central, strategic position vis-à-vis other attributes of organization.[2] We shall attend especially to the effects of variations in the form of the organization–client relationship. The analysis begun here could be extended profitably to a number of other organizational characteristics.

* This paper derives from some of the work being done in the Harvard Student Study, a longitudinal investigation of undergraduate life, supported by the National Institute of Mental Health, under Grant No. 3M—9151, and by a grant from the Hazen Foundation.
Source: "Authority and Control in Client-Serving Organizations" by Charles E. Bidwell and Rebecca S. Vreeland. *The Sociological Quarterly*, 4 (Summer 1963): 231–242.

The Organization–Client Relationship

The model of the dyadic professional-client relationship is applicable with certain modifications to the organization–client relationship. This model depicts face-to-face interaction which is affectively neutral and functionally specific.[3] The professional commands specialized esoteric skills; the client needs the services these skills make possible. Between them the specific service to be rendered and the fee to be paid are agreed upon; that is, they consummate a utilitarian contract.[4]

But the client is in no position adequately to evaluate the professional's competence. His choice among available professionals usually is based upon general reputation and fragmentary information. Consequently the client must put himself in the hands of the professional, and the latter's willingness to add the former to his clientele is contingent upon this act. In other words, a normative contract also is consummated, the client, within the service relationship, subordinating himself on the basis of trust, to the professional. If for the client the normative contract is an expression of trust, for the professional it is the assumption of responsibility for the client's welfare. This responsibility is dual—to the client himself and, through the professional community, to the larger society. The normative contract, therefore, distinguishes clients from customers, who must observe the principle of *caveat emptor.*

When an organization becomes the serving agent, face-to-face interaction occurs between the client and members of the professional staff, who employ both their skills and the resources owned by the organization. The utilitarian contract occurs between the client and the organization rather than the individual professionals.

But the level and form of the normative contract varies. It may occur at either the staff or the organizational level. Moreover, the organization–client relationship may be either functionally specific or diffuse. These variations in the normative contract give rise to three types of client-serving organizations.

NONINDUCTING ORGANIZATIONS These are organizations such as the law firm or social service agency. The normative contract is located at the staff level. That is, while the client buys a service from the organization, he puts himself in the hands only of the professionals who provide it. Strictly speaking, the client is a customer of the organization, a client of certain of the staff. The client's participation in the organization is functionally specific and limited to his interaction with these professionals. He is not inducted as a member of the organization, and its authority structure does not extend to him. He is subordinate only to the moral authority of the staff members as professionals.

Professional responsibility, but not client trust, is in part diffused at the organizational level. The professional staff incur the dual responsibility for client welfare, but also are responsible to the organization. The organization in turn is responsible to the client and to the environing society for his welfare.

INDUCTING ORGANIZATIONS Inducting organizations, such as schools or hospitals, consummate the normative as well as the utilitarian contract at the organizational level. Their clients are inducted into the organization as client-members, subordinate in the authority structure to the professional cadre. The client-members put themselves in the hands of the organization rather than of its professional staff as individuals, for the client-member is in no better position to evaluate the competence of a client-serving organization than he is of a free professional. Indeed he is often less informed because the means of service are more differentiated and complex. In inducting organizations, the organization's responsibility for client welfare is reciprocated by the trust the client-member places in the organization itself.

THE ASSOCIATIONAL SUBTYPE Among these inducting organizations, the normative contract remains functionally specific. Day schools and commuter colleges are inducting organizations of this kind. The scope of the client-member role is defined narrowly as the pattern of activity required in face-to-face interaction with the professional staff.[5] The client-member role here is a segment of the client-member's life space.

That is, in associational inducting organizations the utilitarian contract is an agreement to exchange *only* professional services for a fee. Neither his organizational participation nor the organization's authority pervades his total personality.

THE COMMUNAL SUBTYPE These inducting organizations—for example hospitals and residential schools and colleges—approximate total environments for their client-members. Face-to-face interaction with the professional staff defines only one sector of the client-member role.

The utilitarian contracts between these organizations and their client-members are agreements to provide not only professional services for a fee but also a wide range of auxiliary services for fixed charges (or charges hidden in the fee or absorbed by subsidies from other sources). Residential colleges, for instance, provide food and lodging and typically a variety of extracurricular activities and counselling services for their students.

The normative contract in inducting organizations of this type is diffuse. Although the auxiliary services which are provided for the client-members usually do not themselves require professional skills, they are defined as ancillary to, and thus inextricably linked with, the organization's central professional activity. Hospital food services, for instance, are usually viewed as therapeutic, and college dormitories often are seen as at least potentially educational. Consequently the trust-responsibility bond between the client-member and the communal inducting organization must be diffuse. When, for instance, a student contracts for a dormitory room, he also agrees, perhaps implicitly, to abide by the rules of dormitory life and to accept the authority of the dormitory heads and residents. The hospital patient must eat what doctor and dietician prescribe.

Consequently, the client-members of communal inducting organizations participate in these organizations as total personalities and the scope of organizational authority is co-extensive with this participation.

Authority Structures and Problems of Control

Client-serving organizations must control the activities of both their staff members and clients. Although each area of control presents significant problems for the analysis of these organizations, the present discussion is limited to the control of staff behavior. We shall consider how authority over staff performance is variously allocated among staff roles in each of the three types of client-serving organizations and results in distinctive authority structures. We shall also examine some of the problems of staff control generated by these structures.

While differences among client-serving organizations arising from their characteristic relations with clients in themselves affect the distribution of authority among the staff, this distribution also is affected by the power of the professional cadres. We therefore approach authority structures as an interaction effect of variations in this power and in organizational type.

The power of the professional cadres may be viewed as an outcome of their bargaining positions in the environing society and of the normative contract. In general the bargaining positions of professionals depend upon the extent of social demand for their services and the criticalness of these services.[6] Thus doctors or lawyers are in a stronger position than teachers or social workers. Moreover, client-serving organizations seek a mandate from the society on the basis of their professional activities, and with this mandate, they attempt to legitimate their claims to resources and support apart from the competitive criteria of the economic market. The organization's mandate depends heavily upon the mandates of the professions represented in its staff, and the scope and strength of these mandates in turn are a function of the profession's bargaining position. Finally, the stronger the profession's bargaining position, the stronger and better organized the professional community tends to be, exercising close control over the supply of professionals and effective enforcement of the demands of its members.

While differences of bargaining positions thus lead to variations in the power of professional cadres within client-serving organizations, the normative contract sets a floor under this power. Relative to the organization, professional personnel therefore always are in a comparatively powerful position. As we have seen, the normative contract, whether it occurs at the staff or organization level, renders the organization responsible for client welfare. This responsibility opens the organization to supervision by professional associations and government agencies. Witness the triads of law firm-client-bar association or hospital-patient-medical society and public health department. Through their joint memberships in the organization and the professional community, the professional staff are in a key position to modify or intensify intervention by professional and governmental agencies. In this way, a client-serving organization is dependent upon its professional staff, whatever their bargaining strength.

What kinds of authority do client-serving organizations use to control the activities of their professionals? The possible alternatives are to employ financial or solidary incentives.[7] Perhaps the central problem of control in client-serving organizations is the necessary autonomy of the professionals which arises from their monopoly of expertise and the relative inaccessibility of their activities to direction by others. While the organization can indirectly control professional performance, for example, by the placement of the professional in the flow of work or by the allocation of resources, central decisions about the kind and quality of professional activities are made individually by the professional. This tendency to autonomy is, of course, increased by occupational ideologies which stress freedom from interference. To maintain sufficient quality to meet client welfare responsibilities and to maximize goal attainment, the professional must be brought to identify himself strongly with the organization.

Therefore solidary incentives centered upon professional values and commitments are necessarily the principal means of control in client-serving organizations.[8] The solidary incentive to which professionals will respond is colleague esteem. Consequently authority in these organizations must be in some way collegial. Moreover, the organization must identify its goals with the values and aims of the profession. Under these circumstances, adequate organizational performance is also competent professional performance, and it brings the rewards of colleague acceptance. In other words, the professional staff are controlled by the blending of occupational social controls and organizational authority.

From this analysis, it follows that the management of client-serving organizations will either be vested in the hands of the professional cadre, with administrative roles occurring as variants of professional ones, or maintain colleagueship among professionals and administrators, although their organizational roles are distinct. In the latter case administrators probably will be recruited from the professional ranks.

AUTHORITY AND CONTROL IN NONINDUCTING ORGANIZATIONS

When the client-serving organization is noninducting, the tasks of administration center upon the management of professional activities and the maintenance of relations with the external society. Under these circumstances, two kinds of authority structure are probable, according to the power of the professional cadre.

Pure Collegial Authority.

This structure should occur when the professionals are relatively strong, and indeed it is most common in legal firms and medical clinics. In this structure the distinction between the administrative and professional cadres is blurred. The combined professional-administrative hierarchy may be ordered according to professional seniority or according to the principle of *primus inter pares.*

Here the professional staff operate with broad autonomy in their interactions with clients. Control is primarily informal, exercised as the situation requires. Rules of procedure are few, centered more upon organization maintenance than upon professional tasks. Management of environmental relationships is diffused throughout the professional staff, although perhaps an especial responsibility of the senior men.

These structures are subject especially to two sources of strain. Strains may arise from power plays by individuals who seek to maximize their collegial advantage. Strains may also mirror tensions and uncertainties within the professional community over the domains and status of specialties and other subgroups.[9] The extent to which these strains can be contained will rest largely upon the integration of the professional community itself and the extent to which the organization has become identified with it.

Hierarchic authority.

This authority structure should occur when the professionals are relatively weak and may be observed in such noninducting organizations as social service agencies. Here there is a distinct separation between subordinate professionals and superordinate administrators, who represent the goals and demands of the organization in contrast to the personal or occupational interests of the professionals. The administrators manage the professionals' activities and handle external relations. The professional tasks are given a more narrow "technical" definition and typically are subject to specific rules of procedure.

The administrators usually are drawn from the professional cadre, but cease active practice upon assuming their new roles. Their professional identity gives them access to solidary occupational incentives, although diminished by their occupational defection. In view of the weaker position of the professionals, these incentives likely will suffice. This identity also makes it possible for the administrators to mediate effectively between the organization and professional and governmental regulators.

However, the asymmetrical normative contracts in noninducting organizations, in which client trust reposes in the professionals rather than in the organization, heightens organizational dependency upon its professionals and thus limits administrative control. If for no other reason than the risk of losing substantial numbers of clients, the administrator cannot afford to alienate his professional subordinates. The hierarchic authority structure, then, is prone to administrator-professional strains, as the latter seek to extend their own authority. At the same time there is a strong tendency for occupational social controls and organizational authority to become divorced, because of the subordination of the professional staff, so that financial incentives become predominant and the professional effectively withdraws from the organization. The professional then is likely to pursue his own and not the organization's interests. The problem of control in these structures is to maintain staff identification without undermining administrative authority.

AUTHORITY AND CONTROL
IN INDUCTING ORGANIZATIONS   The existence of a client-membership introduces new service functions. The complexity of these functions obviously varies with the scope of the normative contract. But even in associational inducting organizations, record-keeping will proba-

bly become more elaborate, client-members must be processed in and out of the organization, and the possibility of interactions among client-members, as well as with the professionals, may give rise to disciplinary tasks of a nonprofessional nature. In communal inducting organizations, these auxiliary functions further expand and typically include provision of residential facilities, health services, and leisure activities. The resulting authority structures are a mixture of segmental differentiation with either collegial or hierarchical arrangements.

Let us consider first communal inducting organizations. Auxiliary services require their own staff. In communal organizations, the auxiliary cadre will be larger and more differentiated and its power relatively greater than in their associational counterparts. When the professionals also are relatively powerful, the professional and auxiliary cadres are likely to be completely separate, as in hospitals where both the medical director and the hospital administrator report directly to the board of trustees. Here one finds the collegial professional structure preserved within a larger authority structure, employing segregation as a means for controlling conflicts between the interests of professional and auxiliary personnel.[10]

When the professionals are relatively weak, the auxiliary staff more probably will be only partially separate from the professional one. Both will be subordinate to a top administrator, drawn however from the professional group. Hierarchical structure is imposed upon segmental differentiation. This is the typical authority structure of residential colleges, for example. One of the functions of the administrator in these client-serving organizations is to mediate conflicts of interest between the professional and auxiliary staffs.

Collegial authority does not seem to occur in associational inducting organizations, probably because critical—that is, dangerous and complex —services require communal participation by client-members. Thus authority in these organizations, e.g., day schools, is hierarchically structured. But in associational inducting organizations, the auxiliary cadre, because they are relatively weak, are not in a position seriously to challenge the interests of the professionals or claim a co-ordinate position. Therefore segmental differentiation tends to be minimal, with auxiliary roles attached to the office of the top administrator or subordinated to the professional staff, at least to its senior members. Both structures may be observed in school systems, where a business manager works in the superintendent's office and counsellors work under school principals.

In inducting organizations, either communal or associational, the professionals' power is lessened since the normative contract is symmetrical, i.e., occurs at the organizational level. Even when client-members initially are recruited through individual professionals, as in private hospitals, once in the organization they come under the authority of auxiliary as well as professional personnel. The professionals no longer can claim sole competence vis-à-vis the client-membership. Conflicts of interest between professionals and auxiliary staff now may center upon the boundaries and exercise of their respective domains of authority over client-members.

If the professional and auxiliary staffs are completely separated, these strains may seriously lower the organization's effectiveness in the absence of a competent court of appeal. The more likely criterion for resolution is the comparative social status of the competing occupational groups. This situation is evanescent and shifting, liable to recurrent, never-resolved, organizational strains. If there is a top administrator, the problem is his. Given his professional identification he is likely to resolve such conflicts in favor of his former colleagues. In so doing, he risks alienating the auxiliary staff, but this is not as serious as alienating the professionals. As a result, these conflicts probably will be resolved by compromises which preserve the essential perquisites of the professional cadre.

In both associational and communal inducting organizations, auxiliary staff are likely to become professionalized. Many auxiliary roles involve face-to-face interaction with client-members and either require, or are defined as requiring, the skills of a professional group, e.g., social service in hospitals and counselling and guidance in schools. As an inducting organization recruits substantial numbers of professionally trained person into these roles, it comes to contain multiple professional cadres which perform functions different in content but not in form. It follows that the power of these newer professional cadres will be considerably enhanced vis-à-vis the older professionals and the organization. Differences in the power of these groups in the organization will now be based upon their bargaining positions and upon their claims to status according to the centrality of their contributions to goal attainment.

In communal inducting organizations, when the professional and auxiliary staffs are completely separated, one of two adaptations is likely. If the older professionals continue to be more powerful, one would expect them to assimilate the new professional group, although at a subordinate level. The collegial element of the authority structure would then be partially destroyed with the professional ranks now differentiated into two strata. One stratum would provide the older, and purportedly more central, services and would preserve collegiality. The other stratum would provide the newly professionalized services and be subordinate to the collegial stratum. Under these circumstances we should expect the new professionals to continue to press for more equal status. But if the older professionals do not maintain a clear power advantage, multiple separate professional staffs should develop—a situation prone to conflict and instability as each group maneuvers for advantage.

If the professional and auxiliary staffs of a communal inducting organization are united in a top administrator, the professionalization of auxiliary roles generates strong pressure for the establishment of multiple professional staff groups, each perhaps with its own chief, but all still responsible to a single administrative head. The possibilities for conflicts of interest are obvious. The criteria for their resolution are the power positions of these staff groups and their claim to central functions. The top administrator, however, cannot go too far in recognizing the claims of certain of these groups without endangering the organization by alienating the others. A series of uneasy compromises is likely to result which satisfy no one and give rise to further strains. The professional origin of the top administrator now becomes a central concern for the professional cadres, as it provides an additional resource in the struggle for advantage. Accession to this role consequently is a further source of intense struggle and may well give rise to deep and enduring cleavages between the professional groups.

If we turn to associational inducting organizations, the effect of professionalization of auxiliary roles is to move these organizations toward this same pattern. The auxiliary staff first should become larger and more differentiated and press increasingly for a co-ordinate position with the older professionals. When their power becomes sufficiently great, multiple professional staffs, with separate administrative hierarchies united in the top administrator will emerge. School counselling services, for example, have displayed this process. Consequently conflicts and control problems like those just discussed will be observed. They are unlikely to be as severe, however, since the associational participation of client-members in these organizations limits the costs of auxiliary services and tends to diminish their importance.

A Concluding Note

The different authority structures which we have discussed have often been described by students of organizations. But the approach taken in this paper suggests how their variety can be accounted for systematically. It also has allowed us to predict some of the distinctive problems of organizational control which each engenders. These predications await verification. If the organization-client relationship does appear to be a fruitful starting-point for studying client-serving organizations, the analysis begun here might well be extended to other attributes of these organizations.

Footnotes

1 For analyses of the relations of free professionals and clients, see especially the work of Everett Hughes and his students; Talcott Parsons, "The Professions and Social Structure," *Essays in Sociological Theory* (Glencoe, Ill.: The Free Press, 1954),pp. 34–49; and A. M. Carr-Saunders and P. A. Wilson, *The Professions* (Oxford: The Clarendon Press, 1933). The general problem with which we here are concerned has also interested Amitai Etzioni (*A Comparative Analysis of Complex Organizations* [New York: The Free Press of Glencoe, 1961]), and Peter Blau and W. R. Scott (*Formal Organizations* [San Francisco: Chandler Publishing Co., 1962] especially pp. 27–58, 81–85, 167–93). It has been most insightfully addressed by Erving Goffman in "The Medical Model and Mental Hospitalization," *Asylums* (Garden City: Doubleday Anchor Books, 1961), pp. 323–88.

2 Cf. Etzioni, op. cit., pp. 3–22.

3 Cf. Parsons, *op. cit.;* Carr-Saunders and Wilson, *op. cit.*

4 For the distinction between utilitarian and normative contracts discussed in somewhat different terms, see Talcott Parsons, "The Mental Hospital as a Type of Organization," in *The Patient and the Mental Hospital,* ed. by Milton Greenblatt *et al.* (Glencoe, Ill.: The Free Press, 1957), pp. 113–17.

5 This statement is subject to many exceptions which result from attempts by associational inducting organizations to capture increasing amounts of client-member participation and thus to approach the communal extreme. The extensive extracurricula of some commuter colleges or day schools are examples of this.

6 Cf. Edward Gross, "Sociological Aspects of Professional Salaries," *Educational Record,* 41:130-37 (1960).

7 Cf. Peter B. Clark and James Q. Wilson, "Incentive Systems: A Theory of Organizations," *Administrative Science Quarterly,* 6:129-66 (1961).

8 In this analysis we are ignoring, for the sake of simplicity, modifications of authority and control which will occur when, as in hospitals, the professional staff retain the status of free practitioners. This question is well worth pursuing within the frame set here.

9 Cf. Rue Bucher and Anselm Strauss, "Professions in Process," *American Journal of Sociology,* 66:325-34 (1961).

10 See Eugene Litwak, "Models of Bureaucracy which Permit Conflict," *American Journal of Sociology,* 67:177-84 (1961).

FIFTEEN
FACULTY POLITICS
AND POWER
Rue Bucher

Let us now confront the problem of how this organization runs. How the organization "runs" is essentially a process question, and we shall see that process and power are closely intertwined. In the following pages, I will attempt to demonstrate the utility of regarding this medical school as a *political* organization; in order to describe and understand the flow of events in the organization, it is necessary to use political concepts. Power is the most important such concept, but it also requires the use of related concepts, such as negotiation and persuasion. Authority as a concept has relatively little heuristic value in this setting. Questions might be raised about the proper definition of the terms "power" and "authority". Many sagacious writers have attempted to clarify these two concepts, but when one comes to apply the various distinctions to this kind of organization, categorization becomes more clouded than clarified. My own approach has been to postpone sharp definitions of my terms and concentrate on the empirical situation in the expectation that definitions appropriate to the setting will emerge from analysis of the data.

Process and power will be examined at all levels and in the various arenas of the organization. I would like it understood that while the major focus is upon process, I am not saying that normative elements are of lesser importance. Quite the contrary. Concepts such as professional identity and faculty perspectives are normative in character; they constitute the givens of the situation at a point in time. There are other normative elements that have not yet been introduced but which will appear as we go

Source: "Social Process and Power in a Medical School" by M. Rue Bucher, in *Power in Organizations,* edited by Mayer Zald. © 1970, by Vanderbilt University Press, Nashville, Tennessee 37203.

into the analysis of the political process in the medical school—elements such as university statutes and proper manners, for example, gentlemanliness and ceremony. In any case, process and power operate differently in different arenas but can be discerned in all areas of institutional life.

The Department

A close analysis of the workings of a department within the medical school would recognize the series of arenas internal to the department and the numerous nonacademic personnel whose work is critical to the functioning of the department. For the purposes of this essay, however, I will confine discussion to the academic actors in the situation and touch upon some of the recurrent situations which bring them into political interaction.

Of the academic actors, the department head in his relations with faculty is of the greatest moment in our inquiry. Some faculty might maintain that the following excerpt is based upon their department.

> When the collegiate type is fully developed, such bodies, in principle or in fiction, meet with the lord in the chair and all important matters are elucidated from all points of view in the papers of the respective experts and their assistants and by the reasoned votes of the other members. The matter is then settled by a resolution, which the lord will sanction or reject by an edict. This kind of collegiate body is the typical form in which the ruler, increasingly turns into a "dilettante," at the same time exploits expert knowledge and—what frequently remains unnoticed—seeks to fend off the overpowering weight of expert knowledge and to maintain his dominant position in the face of experts. He keeps one expert in check by others and by such cumbersome procedures he seeks personally to gain a comprehensive picture as well as the certainty that nobody prompts him to arbitrary decisions (Gerth and Mills, 1958).

The university statutes define the responsibilities and prerogatives of department heads. Few of the faculty have consulted the statutes. In my data, covering a five-year period, the few instances in which the statutes were consulted were mainly situations in which dusting off the statutes served the argument of a party in a dispute. In two bristling instances, the problem was a conflict between the head of a department and his faculty, in which faculty were attempting to check arbitrary decision-making on the part of the head. It behooves us, thus, to consider what the statutes have to say.

In brief, the statutes state that the department head has the responsibility for determining the goals of the department and for seing that they are achieved. In the same section is a paragraph which says that the department head cannot abridge the autonomy of faculty. (By not quoting, I am giving my own interpretation of these provisions.) These provisions give considerable latitude, and indeed, department heads play their roles with distinctive styles. However, there are some patterned differences between the clinical departments and the basic-science departments in the behavior of department heads and the response of their faculty.

The major difference between clinical and basic-science department heads is that the office of head has been admixed with the medical concept of "the chief" in the clinical departments. Authority appears in this organization only in those situations where some person defines himself as a chief, and he is so defined by others. The extent to which department heads are chiefs varies among the clinical departments. "Chiefmanship" is relatively weak in medicine and psychiatry and strongest in the surgical specialties. One can recognize that there is a chief in the background of the following vignette:

> One of the full-time junior faculty in surgery was on rounds with medical students. The students questioned him about certain procedures being used for preparing patients for surgery. The faculty member acknowledged that there are different "philosophies" about pre-operative preparation but Dr. X says . . . and that's the way we do it in this department.

The chief is not a chief just because he occupies an office. On the basis of the data gathered so far, it appears that a person is accorded the appellation of chief because of his undisputed *clinical* competence. For example, one faculty member, a surgeon, proudly called his department head "an operating chief." A man of international research reputation, he was revered by this faculty member because he kept his hand in and was still able to help his staff when they ran into difficulties. In another telling instance, a new department head in one of the surgical specialties informed me that he had devoted his first two months in the department to proving that he was better than any of his staff. A chief, then, speaks with the weight of authority, an authority which seems closer to charismatic than any other type.

At one of the first meetings of the faculty of the college which I attended, an imposing senior faculty member of a clinical department rose and presented a discourse upon department heads as "robber barons" who divide up the spoils among themselves. The term "robber baron" has been repeated in other situations. It would appear safe for us to conclude that both heads and their faculties consider the position of department head a seat of power. Further evidence will suggest that they may be the most powerful figures in the organization.

Department heads are sitting upon several sources of power, sources which are critical to the careers of the faculty: (1) The head prepares the budget, which is submitted to the dean, and allocates the available funds within the department; (2) the head allocates the space of the department; and (3) the head recommends and supports faculty members for promotion. All the indications are that the heads zealously guard these prerogatives. For example, one head who was departing for a full year of sabbatical leave fully commended the affairs of the department to an acting head, but announced that he would return for the preparation of the departmental budget and the recommendation of promotions.

Some prerogatives of the head seem to be more zealously guarded than others, though. The data so far indicate that heads are particularly close-lipped, even secretive, about the departmental budget. It remains a task for further data-collecting to ascertain whether or not heads consult with any of their faculty on the budget. Faculty talk to the head about their own needs, but it appears that they have no idea of the eventual priorities built into the budget. By contrast, many heads do consult with their faculty about promotions. This is more general among the basic-science departments. Courtesy dictates that the head consult with those faculty at and above the level of a prospective promotion. The observance of this courtesy by clinical heads is more spotty.

Control of these three prerogatives would appear to make the head very powerful indeed, but there are a number of checks and balances in the system. To begin with, these prerogatives are not the only sources of power in the organization. I still have much to learn about this, but it appears clear to me now that the *assessed stature* of a man, whether head or faculty, is very important. Stature can cover a lot of qualities; nonetheless its very ambiguity makes it appropriate here because the faculty who are continuously assessing each other are usually not explicit or clear about what they are responding to when assigning a colleague to a given level or type or stature. From listening to a large number of assessments of each other on the part of faculty, I would say that any one or more of the following qualities may enter into an assessment: the quality of a person's research; whether or not he appears to be "smart," or clear-thinking;

whether he is a decent human being (not just a "nice guy," which does not always procure respect); whether he has good judgment; and whether he "pulls his load." In addition, faculty take into account the reputations which colleagues have outside the department, either as researchers or effective participants in organization politics.

Any and all of the above qualities are quite fateful for the collegial group, particularly for the tenure faculty who have to live with each other for a long time. If a colleague fails to pull his load, someone else will have to pick it up. If his judgment is bad, he cannot be trusted to certain assignments for fear he will hurt the department. If he is an "operator" or vindictive, one must look to protecting himself. If he is stupid, the group must put up with a boor. If his research is mediocre or bad, he will not contribute to enhancing the reputation of the department or of his colleagues who are identified with the department. As we might expect, few faculty members are assessed as paragons of all the above virtues; however there are, unfortunately, those who are assessed as "dead wood," virtually a total loss to the department. Most people are judged as being good at some things and not so good at others. Thus, there can be different types of stature, or a man can have more stature in some situations than others. Stature is situationally specific. Also, the assessments can change: Faculty members can come to know each other better and decide that they were mistaken in their earlier assessments. Faculty can be perceived as "developing," too, with consequent reassessment of stature.

The major consequence of assessed stature is that it affects a person's ability to negotiate and persuade successfully, and it is primarily through negotiation and persuasion that the decisions that carry forward the work of the organization are made. This is true both within departments and between departments. Before proceeding to examine how this works within departments, though, we need another analytic distinction: namely, whether or not faculty are negotiating individually or as part of a coalition.

Some things are usually negotiated individually between faculty member and department head. These are precisely those things which are usually connected to the head's sources of power: the salary of the faculty member, the amount and quality of space he can command, and his promotions. It may be that as long as a faculty member considers himself successful in negotiating these rewards, he will prefer to keep the discourse on a one-to-one basis. It is to the head's interests to keep these negotiations on an individual basis. In these negotiations, both parties are operating on the basis of assessments of stature. The head has his notions about the value of this faculty member, but he is assessing how the faculty member assesses himself and how the faculty member assesses his stature as head. The faculty member likewise has his own self-assessment, an assessment of the head's stature, his perceptions of how the head regards him, and finally, judgments about what the head is in a position to give him.

I will leave the reader to work out the likely consequences of variations in these complex mutual assessments. It should be added, though, that this interaction can properly be called negotiation because what is at issue is not just what will be given to the faculty member, but what he is to give in return. This might be called the *academic bargain,* in which the head undertakes to supply certain necessities (or luxuries, depending upon point of view) in return for certain services. These services include the amount and kind of work which the faculty member will undertake for the department. They might also include the faculty member's avowal to publish more papers.

Another factor which enters into the negotiation between individual faculty member and head is how visible the consequences are to others in the department. Most visible to others are amount of space and other resources, amount of work they are performing for the department, and whether or not they are publishing. This places constraints upon both head and faculty member. The head has the problem of deciding how far he can support a "fair-haired boy" without bringing on a rebellion. He can also, though, negotiate with the rest of the faculty to attempt to gain their support for inequalities which might be demonstrated as in the department's best interests. This works in reverse when the head wishes to remove some "dead wood." He then has to ascertain whether or not his staff will fight for the principle of tenure or whether they will support him in cutting back the man's space or refusing a salary increase. The faculty member's problem is to avoid a miscalculation about how far the head will go. This could have disastrous results, such as forcing him to resign when he has had no intention of doing so. When the faculty member is not succeeding in improving his position with respect to the visible rewards, he has to face whether or not the embarrassment is sufficient to warrant his resignation.

Now let us examine the situation of collective negotiation within the department. I have already indicated that a group of colleagues can band together to confront the head on the behalf of one or more colleagues whom they deem are not receiving fair treatment. Most of the time the group becomes involved in negotiations around the more generalized aspects of the head's prerogatives, such as salary levels within the department and general priorities in the use of departmental space. There can also be general faculty discussion of criteria for promotion. These are major policy issues within the departments. Salary levels may be negotiable only within limits, limits which neither the head nor his faculty can much affect. Questions of criteria for promotion, though, touch upon such basic issues as the mission of the department and what kinds of persons they wish to attract and keep within the department. Questions of space-utilization equally involve issues of departmental mission and priorities. Faculty may not wish to discuss these things specifically with relation to themselves in the context of the collectivity, but the general policies which are derived from these areas have great consequences for the individual faculty members, who thus have considerable interest in the discussion of such issues.

An important point must be made here about which faculty are likely to engage in policy discussions with the head, either in a dyad or in the collegial group. The real questions are who are colleagues and who are valued advisors. The former of these questions takes on some unique properties in a medical school which has a large part-time and voluntary faculty in addition to a core of full-time faculty. The segmentalization between full-time and voluntary faculty is a major backdrop to the resolution of who participates in policy formation. For all the segmentalization that exists between departmental colleagues, between colleagues in different departments, and between the basic scientists and clinicians, one situation persistently unites them all: a confrontation between full-time faculty and part-time or voluntary faculty. In these situations it apparently comes home to the full-time faculty that they do share some basic values and would be equally vulnerable to the consequences should the local medical society prevail. (The town-and-gown conflict which characterizes the relations of academic physicians to those in private practice and represented by the AMA and local societies could be the subject for study in itself.)

The question which the full-time faculty members pose might be paraphrased as follows: Considering my stake in the institution, whom do I want to have any say in my fate? The answer is quite consistent. They do not wish those who do not have a similar stake to have anything to do with it. There are a few part-time men in clinical departments who are sufficiently esteemed by their full-time colleagues to be considered one of them when it comes to policy issues. (I have separated part-time and voluntary because there is considerable difference between the commitment of a man who devotes fifty or seventy percent of his time to the school for that percentage of a salary and one who voluntarily devotes two mornings for several months or even less.) Aside from excluding the nonfull-time faculty from policy, there is considerable variation among the departments in who, among the full-time faculty, constitute a collegium. However the lines are drawn in a department, though, the faculty in the inner circle tend to protect jealously each other's right to be there, whether or not they agree on issues or esteem one another.

At the same time it must be said that both heads and full-time faculty have their moments of guilt about the part-time and voluntary faculty. They need these people for the clinical teaching program, they use them with little or no monetary reward, and they occasionally call on them to come and vote at general faculty meetings for issues of import to the department. In the larger clinical departments it is patently impossible to carry out genuine committee-like deliberations in the context of a meeting of the full departmental faculty. The compromise which is usually taken is to hold an *affaire,* during which a report of what has been going on in the department is given and the nonfull-time faculty is given an opportunity to respond. Since the nonfull-time faculty have had no opportunity to organize among themselves in response to issues, these meetings have not produced any checking or reversal of the policies originating among the full-time faculty and the head.

The department head is enjoined by the statutes to listen to a departmental advisory group; he is not enjoined to follow their advice. It appears that department heads rarely proceed against faculty advice (a) when there is unity or near unity among the faculty, and (b) when the matter at issue is one about which the faculty have strong feelings. I witnessed a department meeting at which most of the faculty did not support the head in his intentions, but the problem under review was relatively remote from the department and did not threaten any vital interests of members of the department. Under these circumstances, the head announced that he would vote his own convictions at the executive committee of the college but would make it clear there that he was expressing his own opinions and not those of his department. In the instances in which faculty were attempting to check arbitrariness on the part of the head, there was a high degree of unity among the faculty and passionate feeling. Until further data prove me wrong, I would contend that a department head cannot, without grave consequences, engage in actions which his faculty considers an abuse of power. It seems that under those conditions the faculty unites quickly and pushes for a confrontation, which is successful.

Most of the time, though, the departmental faculty is not united but rather is divided into coalitions. Some coalitions persist through the years. The persistent coalitions reflect the continuing splits in professional identity within the department. They also tend to be activated around persisting, unresolved issues. For example, in one department meeting, a junior faculty member rose and asked about the current status of a proposal that would have involved a drastic reorganization of clinical services. The present organization of services reflects the professional identity of the head and a number of the senior faculty. A debate ensued, which the head concluded by saying that they had failed to convince him. They had also failed to convince a sufficient number of the senior faculty.

Most coalitions are shifting alliances, depending upon the issues. As issues come up, faculty within the department who are concerned shop around seeking out those who might be allies in relation to the particular issue. The most sought-after potential allies are those with the greatest assessed stature, since it is they who are most likely to persuade the department head and other faculty. It is quite possible that many issues are resolved without ever coming up for discussion at a meeting. One or more faculty may visit the head succeed in persuading him to their point of view. Sometimes, after a number of faculty caucuses, a delegation may be sent. In any case, if the faculty are serious about an issue, they are likely to prepare carefully before a faculty meeting, lining up allies and strengthening their arguments through discussion in caucuses. If an issue is introduced into a meeting "cold," it is rare that any decision is taken. It either drops by the wayside or is postponed.

A strong coalition is one which includes some of the most esteemed faculty. Sheer superiority of numbers does not seem to have the same impact. Much depends upon who the members of a coalition are. If the coalition includes esteemed persons from more than one persistent coalition, it probably can carry the department. If different coalitions confront each other and neither succeeds in winning over additional strength, the debate remains inconclusive. The department head then can either attempt to persuade the parties into some measure of consensus, or he can simply proceed to act upon his own judgment.

I do not have sufficient data to construct any hypothesis about the conditions under which the allies in a losing faction become disaffected. It may be so rare that I can never collect enough instances of it. If serious disaffection occurs only infrequently, it is probably because the tendency for coalitions to shift prevents lines from hardening unduly. It is my impression that disaffection is most often expressed by the junior faculty. In their case it tends to be explicitly tied to the fact that they have not had access to the councils in which decisions were made, or if they did they had no influence. In this sense there is a decided "establishment" phenomenon within departments of this medical school.

We have delineated a number of sources of power within departments of the medical school. We have seen that the exercise of power is a complex and fluid process, not solely located in the office of department head. Indeed, the preponderance of power at any one point in time may shift among the collectivity. Furthermore, power is exercised, not by the use of commands, but through the processes of persuasion and negotiation. Or, as one faculty member whose assessed stature is quite high put it, "If they want the faculty to do something, they have to convince them."

Interdepartmental Arenas and the Administrative Process

If department heads are robber barons who divide up the spoils, they do not all share equally. It is not just that smaller departments require fewer of the spoils. Some department heads are considerably more powerful than others. The size of the department, and the extent to which it is designated an important, or major, department, are clear contributors to the power of department heads. For reasons which doubtless have to do with deeply ingrained professional values in medicine, the chairman of the department of internal medicine tends to be among the most powerful, if not the most powerful, of heads in the school of medicine, followed by the head of the department of surgery. In this school, internal medicine is the largest department, and psychiatry, not surgery, is the next largest. I cannot judge now whether the head of psychiatry is more powerful than the head of surgery, but the power which the head of psychiatry has accrued is not a consequence of the size of his department, which is only grudgingly being acknowledged as a major department. He has achieved influence through the assessment which other department heads and administration have made of his performance. (As an interesting sidelight, the head of the department of medicine had been the chairman of the search committee that chose this head of psychiatry. The head of psychiatry is now chairman of the search committee that is seeking a replacement for the retiring head of medicine.) A newly appointed head of a major department can *ipso facto* expect that he will have the ear of the dean and the other department heads. However, he is being carefully observed, and a collective assessment of his stature begins to form.

The process of assessing the stature of a colleague is the same in interdepartmental arenas as within departments, except that there is some shift in the weight given to the various qualities attributed to the assessed one. The qualities which I summarize under the rubrics of "Is he a decent human being?" and "Does he have good judgment?" become further differentiated and come more to the forefront. A man can coast for some time on a brilliant research reputation, but if he comes to be assessed as a "bastard"—out to get all the spoils for himself and giving no one else any credit for claims to the spoils—his glamour pales; people may even begin to set up situations hoping to force the man into resigning. Or a potential Nobel Laureate may turn out to have no perceptiveness about other people and no political judgment. (The terms which are actually used are more pungent, but the reader can probably supply them for himself.)

The major point is that a department can—with whatever pain— accommodate the brilliant scientist who has no aptitude for handling the other aspects of academic life. But this combination of attributes is barely, if at all, tolerable with a department head in the interdepartmental arenas. It is not even much more tolerable from faculty members in committees. Department heads can probably become the victims of a bad assessment of stature outside the department more easily than their faculty, and then the department comes to suffer from this assessment too. I should hasten to add, though, that there does seem to be, in most situations, a genuine undercurrent of justice and good will on the academic scene, so that departments saddled with "difficult" heads do not suffer significant cuts in budget. (At least not in this school.) The price which departments pay for an ineffective head, then, is not so much that his budgets are cut, but that when he is speaking in an interdepartmental arena about issues which are of some interest to the department, his remarks may be discounted. This too should be qualified, again with a nod to the sense of collegial justice which usually prevails: If the head's remarks are interpreted as bearing directly upon what the department must have to carry on its work, people do listen carefully. After all, their aim is not to destroy Discipline X in the school.

There is, then, out of twenty heads of departments, a relatively small group of highly respected men who, when they rise to speak, are taken seriously. The men in this category who are heads of major departments are probably more influential, but there are also men who are heads of minor departments who have acquired considerable stature. In addition, there is an even smaller number of faculty members who receive an attentive audience. How this comes about will be discussed further on. Here let me just say that, over and above the virtues already discussed as entering into the assessment of a person's stature, there is the quality of articulateness. Articulateness is not often explicitly commended, but it seems to me that it is a sine qua non of effectiveness in interdepartmental arenas.

I have in effect been saying that the ability of those with high assessed stature to persuade and negotiate successfully is a form of power. Now is the time to take into consideration the relationship between extensiveness of role-set and assessed stature. There is the tendency of those higher up in the academic hierarchy to have a more extensive role-set, and department heads in particular tend to interact with a broad spectrum of persons within the organization. Does participation in an extensive network of relationships both inside and outside the departments constitute in itself a source of power? The data suggest that extensiveness of role-set is a necessary but not sufficient condition for power, and that assessed stature is the more critical variable. There are persons highly regarded within their departments, who thereby have an effect upon the formation of departmental policies; but however this may reverberate in interdepartmental politics, the direct influence of the particular man has been local. There are also faculty members of stature with extensive relations outside the department, and these tend to be among the powers of the institution. It is unlikely, except with department heads, that a person can have an extensive role-set without rating high in stature. The respective influence of these variables, assessed stature and role-set, is highlighted if one casts them into a fourfold table, as in Table I.

TABLE 1   THE RELATIONSHIP BETWEEN EXTENSIVENESS OF ROLE-SET, ASSESSED STATURE, AND POWER

| | Assessed Stature | |
Role-Set	High	Low
Wide	Much and extensive power	Little or no power
Narrow	Narrow but effective power	Little or no power

Clearly, assessed stature is the most powerful variable, but its influence is limited by extensiveness of role-set. These variables are so intertwined, however, that both are necessary conditions in the development of power. Participation in a number of arenas multiplies the assessments being made of a person. If those assessments are positive, a faculty power is in the making. If the assessments are negative, the role-set of a person does not expand.

Turning now to deans, two contradictory attitudes about deans are evident among the faculty. The first might be paraphrased: "Deans? Who needs them?" This attitude relegates deans to a housekeeping position: they certainly do not contribute anything of importance. The second attitude may be evinced by the same person who expressed the former:

faculty tend to attribute more power to the dean than he possesses. The question of just how much power the dean actually possesses may be unanswerable; however, this probably is the wrong way to ask the question. Does he possess as much power as the faculty thinks he has, or does he possess the power which he thinks is his? I am not being facetious. We could pose the same questions of any of the offices that have been scrutinized in this essay. The outer boundaries of prerogatives and potential influence melt away at the edges, but this is particularly evident with so visible an office as the deanship.

A major problem of empirical study of high offices is the difficulty of getting a sufficient sample for comparative study.[1] There are a lot more department heads than deans, and in five years there has been opportunity to observe how more than one head has approached a particular department. In five years, there has been one turnover of the deanship, with the latest incumbent still new in office. It was abundantly clear, early in his incumbency, that his approach to the deanship is quite different from that of the former incumbent. The previous dean indicated in all of his public behavior that he regarded himself as a mediator, a servant of the faculty. He was esteemed for his zeal in protecting the academic rights of faculty, but at the same time, he apparently never saw himself as influencing the course of faculty opinion in the development of issues. The new incumbent has a far more active conception of the deanship.

One immediate and highly visible indication of the different conceptions of the office held by the former dean and those of the new dean is the sheer size of the administrative office. The previous dean got along with one associate and one assistant dean and a few secretaries. The present dean has an "executive associate" dean, an associate dean, two assistant deans, and an "assistant to" the dean. The latter office is beginning to shape into a combination of a "systems analysis" and business-manager position. Incumbents of these new offices have found themselves increasingly busy. It is not that they have unearthed business left untended in the previous administration, but that they are discovering things which they define as requiring attention that were not previously under consideration.

The dean himself has made some bold strokes, mainly in response to a major reorganization of the college, which is projected as a means of coping with a doubling of student enrollment. Otherwise, he is moving with some caution, probing the potentialities of the office. One of his problems was that he was an internal candidate and assumed office already having some enemies, so that he has to be particularly careful in some areas while moving ahead in others. I have no doubt that he will be much more interested than I in discovering the type and range of power which he can command. Questioned about it, he agrees with me that the faculty tend to attribute greater power to him than he thinks he possesses. But then he proceeds to list his sources of power, which are much like those of the department head. He controls the budget of the college, he can allocate space among contending claims, and he has certain powers of appointment. (These were not listed by him in this interview situation but were discovered in other interview and observational situations.) The dean appoints the search committees which recommend candidates for head-ships. He can also appoint various ad hoc and "task force" committees charged with formulating policy to come back into the administrative structure. He also, in the semifarcical mode in which people will toy with the fringes of the expected, pointed out that the institution would grind to a halt if he stopped signing forms. This, it appears to me, highlights the problems surrounding the structural sources of power in this kind of organ-ization. Department heads, too, could grind many things to a halt if they chose not to sign forms. But both heads and the dean rarely balk at affixing their signatures. It is a power which must be very carefully exercised. Whether it is signing forms or allocating space and budgets, flagrant abuse of power can have disastrous repercussions for the institution—and the persons concerned.

Perhaps the greatest potential source of power which the dean has flows from the expansion of the office which he has instituted. Department heads and faculty who are active in interdepartmental arenas chalk up two additional sources of power, namely knowledge about what is going on elsewhere in the institution and contacts with people in other arenas. The dean has the greatest potentiality of being "on top" of things, particularly utilizing his expanded administrative officers. He is in a better position than others in the institution to (a) spot problems, and (b) gather information upon which to base policy. It is the business of those in the dean's office to concern themselves with a variety of institutional problems, while others on the faculty concern themselves only with selected problems.

The dean does not proceed in policy areas without advice. There is an institutionalized forum which he does utilize. The executive committee of the college elects a subcommittee to serve as the dean's advisory com-mittee. He also utilizes his own associate and assistant deans separately and in a forum. In addition, there appears to be a select group of heads and faculty who may be consulted. My information is understandably limited in these areas, but my impression is that these groups are used not so much for communication, but as testing boards—although it is difficult to draw a line between these functions. There is no doubt, however, that the dean's actions are influenced by these sources. What action is avilable for him is another question. A lot of problems can be handled by a phone call or luncheon with the right people, but for important policy issues, the dean is constrained to go through channels, and those channels are the committee structure of the college.

I have previously made a distinction between "standing committees" of the college and various ad hoc-type committees appointed by the dean. Figure 1 is provided to give the reader a visual guide to the committee structure of this institution.* The "executive" committee of the college is a standing committee, but its membership is not derived through the same processes as other standing committees. Department heads are automatically members of the executive committee, deans are automatically ex officio members unless elected by faculty, and there are sixteen members elected at large from and by the faculty at annual meetings of the whole faculty. The executive committee is the channel through which the recommendations of other committees, both standing and ad hoc committees, are funneled before the recommendations go to the faculty for approval. Policy issues may originate in any of the standing or ad hoc

FIGURE 1   THE MEDICAL SCHOOL COMMITTEE STRUCTURE

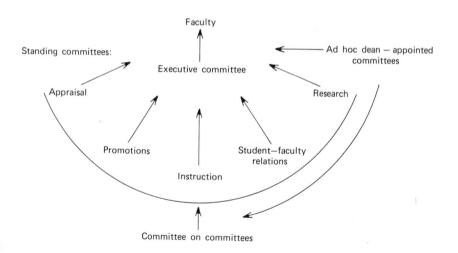

* Not all of the standing committees are included here. The object is to portray the relationships and flow of policy among the various types of committees.

committees. They may be placed before a committee by faculty or administration. It should be noted that the recommendations of the dean-appointed ad hoc committees can go directly to the executive committee for action, bypassing the standing committees. Decisions taken at the executive committee meetings are presented to the faculty either at regular, twice-a-year, general faculty meetings, or general faculty meetings called for special, more urgent problems.

Faculty members have told me that their department heads influence committee appointments. It may be that department heads can influence the dean's appointments to the ad hoc committees. Indeed, the dean may solicit advice from both heads and faculty concerning the appropriate makeup of a committee. However, I have not yet found any solid evidence that department heads influence the committee on committees' nominations to the standing committees. To the contrary, nominations of faculty to major committees flow from collective assessments of the stature of particular faculty members on the part of the members of the committee on committees.

The major evidence I have consists of an examination of who among the faculty has served on standing committees over a period of time. So far I have accumulated these data over a four-year period and can extend them for another four years with additional effort. I have not yet done all the possible permutations with these data that might be revealing. A relatively superficial screening seems to reveal quite enough. There is a definite "establishment" phenomenon. The same names appear again and again among the rosters of committee appointees. To analyze this phenomenon further, however, some additional distinctions are in order.

One distinction is whether the committee is charged with what are regarded as major issues. The "instruction" committee, charged with educational policy, is clearly a major committee. There are other major committees which carry on functions deemed highly significant but which are not the major seats of policy decisions affecting their activities. Then there are, overlapping with the last category, committees which are "working" committees, like the admissions committee, the committee which administers examinations, etc. Working committees do really put in a great amount of time on nonpolicy tasks, although their work is supposed to implement policies.

When one examines the roster of committee memberships, it is immediately obvious that junior faculty are underrepresented. Not only that, but with several conspicuous exceptions assistant professors are found only in the "working" committees. Looking at those persons who were members of three or more committees of the college, there are twenty people, twelve of whom are heads of departments. Focusing upon the major policy-making committees, aside from the executive committee of which department heads are automatically members, twenty-five names appear throughout the four-year period, nine of them department heads, sixteen general faculty members. So, again, we come down to a small number of persons who are participating in the making of policy. An important comparative point here is that these persons do not, as in governmental politics, depend upon their constituents for re-election. It is as if the members of Congress determine whether or not their colleagues will return.

While these facts might serve to give the lie to the value of collegial democracy in academic institutions, I would like to point out that the same processes of assessment of stature are operating in the committee arena as anywhere else. What is added particularly in this arena is a "willingness to serve." There is a decided process of induction of faculty members into positions of responsibility. If they have proven themselves in lesser assignments, they are made chairmen of minor committees and given assignments to major committees. There is no evidence that an establishment orientation—devotion to the status quo—is a prerequisite for rising in the committee structure. Quite the opposite. Those younger faculty members who have risen most quickly into major committee responsibilities have all been fervently outspoken and highly critical of the status quo. Persons with demonstrated courage and conviction tend to be snapped up quickly. In addition, if a man is known to feel strongly for or against something, the usual practice is to appoint him to the committee that will primarily deliberate the issue, so that his viewpoint will be expressed.

I would like to underscore that I do not believe that there is anything devious or deliberate in terms of power moves entailed in appointment to these standing committees. I am convinced that the appointments are a function of (a) a person's demonstrable willingness to serve, and (b) the emerging collective assessment of his stature, as he serves in various capacities. The faculty members concerned feel caught up in a system. There is, simply, a lot of work to be done. The issue is who is willing to do it, and how adequate is he? How persons perform in the lesser committee roles become grounds for considering them for more important assignments.

The various ad hoc committees appointed by the dean are even more "establishment" composed than others. It is a "blue ribbon" system. Persons are appointed who not only have proved themselves to be judicious but who have a constituency: faculty members in general will regard them as representing a viewpoint. Again, it is the same small group of people, reshuffled to meet another task. But it serves, for the most part. The work gets done, and, in the case of a well-chosen committee, faculty members can heave a sigh of satisfaction that someone will be representing their interests.

One might expect that the persons who go the whole road and enter into the smaller circle which is deliberating policy might be those whose professional identity comes to be predominantly associated with the school —the cosmopolitans-*versus*-locals hypothesis. That hypothesis does not hold in this institution. It should not be assumed that department heads are "locals." They differ in their readiness to move to other, greener, or more challenging pastures. Faculty members who move into the interdepartmental arenas also differ in their "local" orientation. Some of the most respected persons in the committee arena are also acknowledged as having cosmopolitan reputations. The dour evaluation of some of the leading faculty members in the institution is that the "good people are bled dry."

While the committee structure provides the forums through which the decision-making process is enacted, committee meetings are not the only place in which important discussions take place. When there are issues defined by the participants as important, a lively political process can go on outside of meetings. As in the departments, people seek out allies. In particular, department heads call upon other heads and sound them out on the issue, looking for support in the executive committee. It may even be that the head who initiates the call is really interested in reaching a faculty member in the other's department; or he may be interested in ascertaining whether the position taken by a faculty member in a committee reflects the ideas of others in the department, with the head being considered most important. Faculty members on a committee also may caucus, attempting to hew out a recommendation acceptable to those present and constructing arguments which may bring in additional support at the meetings.

Faculty members who have been caught up in the committee structure tend to become quite impatient about it. To them, the life and guts of the institution are in the work that they are autonomously carrying out in the departmental arenas. But grumble as they will, they miss a committee meeting with some trepidation: you never know what might come up. The significance of committees comes through in the following vignette, which I have abstracted from more detailed notes.

I was having lunch with a relatively new department head. He had succeeded in recruiting a number of bright new men only to see them being swallowed up in the committee system. "That isn't what

I brought them here for," says he. I ask, naively, but can't you use some of the part-time people for this committee work? "God no! They don't have to live with what they do!"

I have placed such stress upon the committee arena because once a recommendation has survived the committee structure and is placed before the faculty, it almost always gains faculty approval. One reason for this is that by the time a recommendation reaches the general faculty, the rough edges have usually been smoothed. It is quite unusual for a proposal to emerge from a committee over the strong opposition of some of its members. A majority vote is not enough. In the two conspicuous instances in my data in which a proposal was pushed through the proposal had to go back to the relevant committees for compromise later.[2] Thus, most of the opposition to an idea is worked through in the committee forums, or else the proposal dies.

The other reason that faculty approval looks like rubber-stamping is that it takes considerable prior organizations of a determined opposition to stop a proposal in a general faculty meeting. Over the years, I had asked faculty if they could remember any cases of a proposal's being defeated in a general faculty meeting. No such data came forth. It clearly is a rare phenomenon, but just last year it happened, and I was a very unhappy participant-observer in the controversy—a really blazing controversy. Normally, faculty meetings bring out one- to two-hundred people. In this instance, at least one third of the faculty—400 to 500 people—appeared. The departments were bringing in every body they could. There had been extensive discussion throughout the school, and several people came with prepared counterproposals which had already been shown to colleagues. By a close vote, the opposition succeeded in blocking the proposal. In "rehashes" after this stormy session, some persons who were in favor of the defeated motion expressed the notion that it would have been worse for the school if it had been a close vote in the other direction.

I have been analyzing a highly complex nonbureaucratic organization, namely the academic organization of a medical school. Perhaps its most distinctive feature is that all of its offices are occupied by professionals, and most important of all, a diverse collection of professionals. It is this latter attribute, the diversity of professionals, which gives rise to another major feature of the organization—the inevitability of conflict—as persons of differing professional identities define differing lines of policy as desirable or undesirable. As decision-making proceeds in this organization, it has seemed most appropriate to analyze it as a political organization.

Going back to the questions about power which were raised earlier, it does appear as if power is a far more meaningful concept than authority in this type of organization. If one takes authority to apply to those situations in which the subordinates experience an *obligation* to obey, on whatever basis, traces of authority were found only in some of the clinical departments, mainly surgery departments. In those instances, the type of authority manifested was closer to charismatic authority than any other.

Sources of power in this organization for the most part are familiar from studies of other organizations. Control of necessities for the advancement of a professional's career—such as salary, space, and promotions—were lodged in the offices of department heads and the dean. Insofar as we define power as involving the actual or potential use of negative sanctions, these were the *offices* in which power is located. However, one other potent source of power was discovered, namely *assessed stature*. Assessed stature works independently of office. Persons who are not department heads or deans can have great influence by virtue of the stature attributed to them by colleagues. Conversely, the powers that office conveys to heads and deans can be eroded by a collective low assessment of the incumbent's stature.

It is important that, although there were offices in this organization which offered the possibilities of invoking negative sanctions, they were rarely invoked and probably not often threatened. Instead, persons of power proceeded to manifest their power through processes of persuasion and negotiation. In this sense there is very little difference between the influence of particularly highly esteemed faculty members and heads of departments in the power arenas.

The major contribution of this study to an understanding of power in organizations is to direct attention to situations in which power is not securely located in particular offices. Power is diffuse, but the locus and balance of power shift. The balance shifts, not just with the incumbents of offices, but as power blocs among faculty are activated and dispersed.

In this organization, then, it can be concluded that the balance of power shifts in response to (a) the flow of issues to which faculty differentially respond, and (b) the flow of different kinds of professionals through the organization.

Footnotes

[1] It is difficult to do so by the methods used in this study. Demerath, *et al.* (1967) have studied university presidents by questionnaire and interview methods.

[2] Using cross-cultural data, F. J. Bailey (1965) discusses this phenomenon of committees which strive for consensus. He proposes some hypotheses to account for why some types of committees will push for unanimity while others will accept a majority vote. My own hypotheses differ from his. I think a majority vote is not enough because (a) faculty have to live with the decisions, and (b) the object of the game is to avoid damaging any sectors of the organization.

REFERENCES

BAILEY, F. J.
1965   "Decisions by Consensus in Councils and Committees." In Political Systems and the Distribution of Power. New York: Oxford University Press.

BARZUN, JACQUES.
1968   The American University. New York: Harper and Row.

BENNIS, WARREN G.
1966   Changing Organizations. New York: McGraw-Hill Book Company.

BLAU, PETER M.
1964   Exchange and Power in Social Life. New York: John Wiley and Sons, Inc.

BUCHER, RUE.
1962   "Pathology: A Study of Social Movements in a Profession." Social Problems 10:40–51.

BUCHER, RUE, AND JOAN STELLING.
1969   "Characteristics of Professional Organizations." Journal of Health and Social Behavior 10 (March): 3–15.

DALTON, MELVILLE.
1959   Men Who Manage. New York: John Wiley.

DEMERATH, NICHOLAS J., RICHARD W. STEPHENS, AND R. ROBB TAYLOR.
1967   Power, Presidents, and Professors. New York: Basic Books, Inc.

GERTH, H. H., AND C. WRIGHT MILLS (TRANS. & EDS.).
1958   From Max Weber: Essays in Sociology. New York: Oxford University Press (Galaxy).

GLASER, BARNEY G., AND ANSELM STRAUSS.
1967   The Discovery of Grounded Theory. Chicago: The Aldine
Publishing Company.

JENCKS, CHRISTOPHER, AND DAVID RIESMAN.
1968   The Academic Revolution. Garden City, New York: Doubleday and Co., Inc.

STRAUSS, ANSELM L., LEONARD SCHATZMAN, RUE BUCHER,
DANUTA EHRLICH, AND MELVIN SABSHIN.
1964   Psychiatric Ideologies and Institutions. New York: The Free
Press of Glencoe.

SIXTEEN
TOWARD A THEORY
OF COLLEGIAL
POWER AND
CONTROL *
Ralph L. Blankenship

There is a long and honored tradition placing the study of power and control at the center of organizational theory. Yet we would agree with Crozier (1964) that value commitments within American sociology have greatly retarded the development of adequate conceptualizations of these common elements of organizational reality. The familiar typology of organizations qua compliance systems (Etzioni, 1975) has stimulated interest, leading to the conduct of a considerable number of empirical studies. However, the research findings refer mainly to bureaucracies or other hierarchical systems. Incredibly, we know the least about those very types of organizations within which most sociologists function as members. The present study is responsive to the need for more theory about power and control processes in collegial organizations—not contemplated by the theory of hierarchical organizations. Generally, the research question may be stated: how can a college of equals achieve organizational integration without resort to systematic inequality?

The purpose of this paper is therefore primarily generative, to produce grounded models of explanation. Secondly, since the paper deals with the confluence of careers, interests, power, crisis, communication, and collective behavior, its purpose is also integrative. The intent of this paper

* The research on which this paper is written was supported in part by Public Health Service Research Grant MH 07346 from the National Institute of Mental Health.

is to present a schematic model of enacted organizational situations and a related process model of collegial control, through the intensive analysis of case materials on organizational crises viewed from the social constructionist perspective.

The data are from a field study of a community mental health center, conducted over a four-year span by a team of six sociologists (Blankenship, 1976). Field work generated a broad set of materials which were treated in the general analytic mode of constant-comparison method (Denzin, 1970; McCall and Simmons, 1969; Glaser and Strauss, 1967). In accord with the generative purpose, strategic sampling was followed, permitting the subsequent collection of focussed data referring to emerging conceptualizations and propositions.

The paper will proceed with a description of the research setting. In order, a theoretical perspective, an account of a crisis episode, and an analytic discussion will then follow.

With the backing of President John F. Kennedy, a vigorous political battle between traditional medical interests and advocates of newer perspectives on mental problems resulted in a radical break with the past system of providing mental health services through state and federal hospitals (Mechanic, 1969; 59–60; Leifer, 1966 see also: Joint Commission, 1961; Kennedy, 1963). One state pioneered in the community mental health movement by creating a new system of comprehensive, community mental health centers, located *within* their respective *catchment areas,* to offset some adverse effects of isolated "asylums." One center was located on the campus of a state university in order to facilitate its *special mission* of joint research and manpower training, in addition to service. The setting of the study is the "special case" Mental Health Center, in its unique setting.

From its beginning, over a two-year period the center grew to a membership of 135 to 150 persons; it had occupied permanent quarters after a long delay, and instituted outpatient (extramural—EM) and consulting services to its catchment area. Residential (intramural—IM) services were expanding gradually to a total of 60 children. Two of three IM cottages were involved in joint research projects with university faculty.

In line with the community mental health mandate for innovation, the superintendent-planner developed an organizational schema that broke with the established mental hospital model. In the older state mental hospitals, medical interests had dominated. The center was built upon two self-contained functional units integrated through committees of persons whose interests interlocked around common matters such as patient careers, policy making and program development. The superintendent's role was administrator plus consultant on matters of program and program policy. The EM clinician, a generic role filled by psychologists, social workers, educators, nurses, pediatricians, and psychiatrists, functioned in the style of a private physician. He could use the staff and facilities of IM Services as a setting for *his* practice without surrendering control and responsibility (continuity of care). He was to be a peer to all other EM clinicians and to administrators—"two tracks to the top." Consultation between clinicians of different levels of training and experience was the approved means to overcome limitations of individual knowledge or expertise. Figure 1 represents the schema as it appeared at the time of the study.

With the exception of the business services unit, (1) authority was lodged at the staff level with first responsibility for action, (2) members had access to each other without passing through intervening layers of command, and (3) matters of policy or program could be raised by a wide range of members. Collegiality and the *avoidance of hierarchy*, then, were the essence of the center's organizational schema. It is helpful to conceptualize such a collegial organization as an enacted organizational situation (Weick, 1969). The theoretical perspective below will elaborate on this theme.

In seeking to account for collegial interaction, we are led to identify a cline along a continuum from rationalistic bureaucracy to collective behavior. A plausible point of departure is the open system model.

Katz and Kahn (1966; 453–454) stress that human organizations present no physical linkages or tangible structures, only the indirect suggestion of structure indicated by *interactions* of members. Secondly, human organizations are totally dependent on *persons* as members to *enact* organizational *performances.*

However, Bittner (1965), Silverman (1971), and others warn that the analogy of human organizations to systems introduces the risk of reification of the concept to create a level of superordinate reality, akin to a Durkheimian social fact. A more sound premise is to posit that the organization *is* the interactions of its members. The "interactional arena" approaches this position. An organization of professionals can be viewed as a negotiated order, a situation defined through the ongoing social process of negotiation and bargaining (Schatzman and Strauss, 1966; Strauss, et.al., 1963, 1964; Bucher and Stelling, 1969; Bucher, 1970). Ephemeral though the conceptualization may be, it neither misplaces the level of social reality nor denies the primary inputs of members. But an arena model does understate the outcomes of conflicts that constrain an individual's freedom. The struggle over independence and control in organizations can be quite pronounced. Crozier (1964) sums up the dilemma,

FIGURE 1   ORGANIZATIONAL SCHEMA OF THE MENTAL HEALTH CENTER

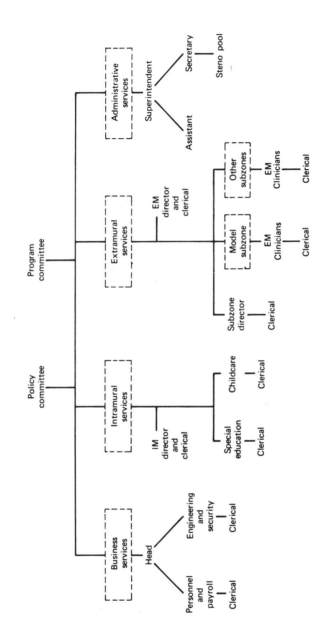

but his analysis emerges as a justification of bureaucracy and legalistic control systems. His work offers little explanation of alternatives—what solution may appear when bureaucracy doesn't? Careers may be a key.

The organizational career in a work-centered society motivates members to enact organizational performances. It also offers control potentials (Blankenship, 1973; Glaser, 1968). In the collegial situation, the college of peers holds the collective power to confer membership status or to deny it. Freidson and Rhea (1963; also Freidson, 1972) note the virtual absence of formal controls in a medical clinic, but report that "talking to" members whose actions fall outside of the group norms is sufficient to maintain standards. Individual power to act is controlled by collective power to deny support (McCall and Simmons, 1966). At this juncture, a formal definition can be presented:

> The enacted organizational situation is the interactions of members, with each other and with members of the social environment, the material products of these interactions, the meanings, careers, systems, and selves thus constructed, and the projections of interactions to come.

FIGURE 2   SCHEMATIC MODEL OF ENACTED ORGANIZATIONAL SITUATION, IN COLLEGIAL ORGANIZATIONS

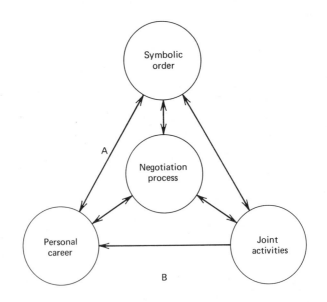

In the enacted organizational situation (see Figure 2), a set of relationships exists between persons, activities and symbols; interactions, and specifically negotiations, offer the common link. All of the relationships are mutual, except A and B. It is assumed that changes in the symbolic order (Turner and Killian, 1957) or in systems of joint activity can directly influence a member; it is further assumed that a member cannot exert reciprocal change except by the negotiation of agreement with others. However, the source of changes in the SO and JA aspects of organizations is the individual member. What he cannot do alone, he can routinely achieve with others.

In stressing social interaction, the model raises the clear riskiness of unilateral action. What happens in collegial organizations when a single member acts to force a change in the symbolic order or in systems of joint activity, as perhaps by administrative fiat? The answer lies in the conduciveness of the situation to collective negotiation. A form of collective behavior may be signaled as a control mechanism. Collectively, the situation can be redefined, or an existing understanding reaffirmed, *around the deviant member.* The experience of being excluded by the company of one's peers places social pressure on the deviant, leading either to his withdrawal or to an effort to collaborate and thereby remain. Collaboration does not exclude eventual withdrawal, but may precede it as a face-saving device for all parties' benefit. This process will be revealed in the case materials following. A model of collegial control will then be developed.[1]

Exposition

Crises are useful to the researcher since, by raising action from the level of the routine to the level of the problematic, they may reveal the very common meanings that underlie everyday activities. When everyday meanings collapse, structures and processes that are not visible during interludes of calm can be scanned. A model crisis episode, chosen as the best representative of its kind, will be presented to reveal the fullness of the perspective. Other episodes were documented and analyzed and became lodged in the perspective, however, the writer chose the intensive treatment of a unitary episode over the awareness of variability offered through comparison.

Certain key persons played conspicuous parts in the *steno pool crisis.* First in order of appearance is Dr. Martin, who designed the center and served as its first superintendent. Mr. Wilson, his assistant, Miss Jones, his secretary, and Mr. Green, his business manager, jointly planned the steno pool. Mr. Bates was the administrator of EM services; his staff was most directly affected by the pool and he fought to preserve the main features of the older system of personal secretaries. A number of secretaries were involved, but Mary and Sharon were most prominent. Sharon's bosses, Dr. Bailey and Dr. Victor, contributed strongly to the collective definition of the episode in its larger meaning to the organization. Mary's boss, Mr. Nader, was appointed to a new post directly under Martin, and given authority to settle the issue.

Superintendent Martin detected a flaw in the routine handling of typing, due to the decentralized structure of the center. To increase efficiency, he commanded the formation of a steno pool but the manner in which it was staffed posed a threat to the collegial status of the EM clinician and threatened to stratify the center staff along clinician–administrator lines. Martin's command was taken as reneging on his collegial status and resorting to legalistic authority. In response, the EM staff negotiated an opposing defintion of the situation in which their *right* to participate in making decisions was reaffirmed. Through work stoppage, collusive discussion, character distortion, and face-to-face confrontation by key clinicians and others, Dr. Martin was induced to appoint a group leader to resolve the crisis. The group leader restored former secretarial positions and hired new girls to staff the steno pool. He was later promoted to associate superintendent in charge of day-to-day operation of the center, while Martin prepared for resignation.

Near the end of the episode, Mr. Wilson was asked to run down the course of the crisis:

Wilson: Well, for several months the term steno pool has been used, but it was mainly used in the Committee. Martin did not communicate, even to this policy group, who and what would be involved. When he interviewed Miss Jones for the first time, in July, he mentioned to her that there would be a steno pool and in all probability she would be the supervisor. He had asked Mr. Green to draw up a plan for setting up this steno pool, which he did, and now, this also was not distributed any further. Martin has a copy of it, and he is the only one who has. I cannot guarantee that Martin ever read the plan. As soon as Miss Jones came on, she wasn't really that busy. Martin wasn't here that much and hadn't yet trained her to do his work independently. So he put to her, let's get this going, and she wanted to. So she and I talked the details of space and telephone lines over with Mr. Green, presented it to Martin and he went along with it. Miss Jones was at a great disadvantage. She had the assignment of implementing and supervising a steno pool, yet she had no idea what the implications were. I told her this was going to be a big mess —people were going to be really mad about it and there would be a lot of problems. On the morning of the Committee meeting, she said, well, Martin wants to discuss it at the meeting today but something came up in his schedule and he won't have time to do a rough draft of a memo. I said okay, I'll write a memo and sign his name—if he wants to distribute it—okay! It just said that, effective immediately, there will be a steno pool, and named the four girls to be put into the steno pool, and that the next morning, at 8:30, Miss Jones would meet with the secretaries for the details. So this was handed to Martin before the meeting, he saw what it said and at the meeting he handed it out. As the meeting was coming to an end, well, Mr. Green said, do you want to talk about the steno pool or should we pass this memo around and Martin said yes. So it went to the Committee members and everybody pretty much accepted it for what it was except for Mr. Bates. He gave arguments against it, but Mr. Green said, well, Dr. Martin put out the memo and this is what it is—there is no use arguing with it. Martin also replied, I have signed my name to it and this is what it is! So, the next morning, at 8:30, the other people, just poor, ignorant secretaries, you know, got pushed into a room and told what the memo said. It was a shock to them. So that's how it came about.

What follows may be more readily understood in reference to a preliminary model of collective negotiation, based on older models of collective behavior:

Collective control among colleagues is expressed as the negotiation of an understanding that (1) defines the deviant's behavior as inappropriate, (2) assesses the moral meaning of the deviant in the situation, and (3) prescribes necessary conditions and actions to be taken. We would agree that collective behavior has supplanted the usual communications channels when:

1. Colleagues talk mainly to each other, instead of to the deviant about the problem and its remediation

2. Time is collapsed into a comparatively short span, within which a great deal of information is exchanged, evaluated, and defined in terms of urgency and corrective action

3. The topic of the deviance displaces other concerns including ordinary activities such as work and recreation

4. The set of conditions or actions decided upon are different and apart from those that routinely control members.

We generally accept Smelser's (1968; 1963) position that collective episodes emerge through time, become progressively more specific, and remain subject to social control intervention even in final stages of development. The substance of the model is indicated in the events and flow of the crisis.

Mary was sought out by the research team to offer her account. She noted that a rumor without detail had circulated two or three weeks before the announcement, but the first concrete indication of the change was on Wednesday morning, September 27. Upon her arrival, she was told by Mr. Bates that a steno pool operation would be instituted beginning on Monday, October 2. The staff of the pool would be mainly the personal secretaries to the model subzone's senior EM clinicians, including three girls who had been supervised by Mary. Mr. Bates defended the change on organizational grounds and directed her to attend the 8:30 meeting with Miss Jones and Mr. Green. Mary observed that the meeting with Jones was calm except for her own statements in opposition. At the end of the meeting, she added, Kay threatened to quit rather than join the pool. Following the meeting, the girls met privately and vocalized their discontent.

Miss Jones observed a shift from relative calm, during the 8:30 meeting, to increasingly strong emotions:

Jones: At the very beginning they went along with me, and immediately after the meeting was over . . . the actual realization of it just hit them full force. I mean there was a complete turnabout Wednesday afternoon. They were for it in the morning at the meeting, and against it in the afternoon.

Interviewer: What took place? Did they start thinking about it?

Jones: Thinking about it—talking about it, indicating that they would lose their individuality if they went into a pool, and that a steno pool was so low that they didn't want to be involved in it! Because they would lose their status, I guess you would call it.

Sharon, a secretary among those designated to join the pool; revealed a substantive shift in the secretaries perceptions:

Sharon: I thought maybe this would be a fairly good idea and then after the meeting I got to thinking, I went to college for eighteen months—why waste it being in the steno pool? I had the training to be an executive secretary, not to say that I am good, but I am trying and this is what I was hired for—to be a secretary. After I got thinking about it, it irritated me because I was *taken away* from a particular job that I *had signed for* and *put* into the steno pool.
I felt that I had everything taken away from me—that I was no longer anything or anybody.

From the secretaries, concern spread to the EM clinicians:

Dr. Bailey: One day last week my secretary called me at home and said, she was all upset. She said that she was hired for one type of thing and now she was going to be forced into something else. Miss Jones had called them in and said, look, ah, we are going to have a steno pool and all the typists will be in this pool, not only from the model subzone, but also intramural, and this and that and so forth. So I said well, that's a nice thing—you know—nobody has told me . . . Apparently, Miss Jones said to the secretaries, well, I want you to tell your boss, the people to whom you are responsible, about this, you know.

Dr. Bailey responded strongly; but the issues were once again transformed in terms of his clinician's interests:

Dr. Bailey: Well, the secretaries didn't take to this too much, and you can imagine that the professional staff was not too pleased with this method of communication, much less the fact that it had been done *without any involvement.* So, *this was the basic issue.* I mean, I had never expressed myself personally to anybody because, number one, nobody asked me, and number two, I would have sent somebody a memo if I had thought it was really being seriously considered. So, I think the feeling, there was and still is a lot of feelings about this, seems to me, well, *the thing is symptomatic* of what people are concerned about.
. . . this Martin is making decisions *like a state hospital* superintendent, at least, this is my personal perception of it and I think it is the perception of other people, as far as I can gather.

By late afternoon, Mr. Wilson was at the point of breaking under the pressure of complaints from the staff; he sought out Superintendent Martin:

Mr. Wilson: Well, I play the role of a sounding board. Like, engineers come to me if they are complaining about something. When I went near the EM offices, you know, they would start. talking about—you know, even the professionals kept telling me things that is wrong about the center. And I just told them, why don't you all try to work together a report and I'll submit it to Dr. Martin. I said I don't know what he'll do with it, but I think that is the best way. Then that afternoon, I was pretty upset cause I was getting it from all directions—the same thing over and over again. Martin was in that afternoon and he wasn't doing anything and so I went in and I said—Dr. Martin, and I told him how all hell had broken loose and he—knew it! He didn't really care! And would you be so kind as to go up there and say, okay gang, let's have it, and listen to what they have to say and talk to them. And he said, if I went up there I'd fire the lot of them! So I told him how I'd been getting it and suggested that they send me into him and he said —well, that is what you should have done.

On Thursday, the disagreement continued, but an agreeable resolution was taking form:

Mr. Wilson: The girl who had been working for Dr. Victor and Dr. Bailey has been the loudest one and caused others to be more upset. I mean, she was going to quit. We had another meeting with them to try to shut them up. We asked if they had any other ideas as to what they would like to do about it. I presented to them the idea that they *all stay where they were,* but give them the responsibility of coming up with a solution for handling peak loads, and, maybe, *have the steno pool at the same time.* However, this, you know . . . I'm quite sure that they are all now trying you know, looking for new jobs.

Communication channels from calmer times seemed to fail. Just as Mr. Wilson got little satisfaction from Martin, Mary reported that a telephone call to her vacationing boss only convinced her that administrators stick together and don't really care about their workers' problems. Mr. Bates met with Martin several times between Wednesday and Friday but made little headway on his promise to his staff to salvage the old secretarial system. However, the deadlock began to loosen when two EM clinicians confronted Martin with the group's views. Dr. Victor met first with Mr. Wilson:

Mr. Wilson: Dr. Victor had asked to talk to me, and at that point he asked me if I *thought Dr. Martin would be interested* in hearing from him—how he felt things were happening —that the steno pool could be secondary, but really illustrating other problems.

Interviewer: And did he get an appointment?

Wilson: Yes, he did. They talked for an hour and a half.

Dr. Victor stressed his concern about prior commitments, that "when he came here he was told that the idea was to push forth, in program, push forth quality, clinical service, including showing people that you knew what you were doing before going out to do a lot of consultation and development of community resources and all that." Dr. Victor *charged* that certain administrative decisons, including the steno pool, were counterproductive *in terms of the center's goals* and strategies.

Dr. Bailey, a consultant during the planning phase of the center, accused Martin of placing central philosophical issues in jeopardy:

Dr. Bailey: My feeling is that one of the main components of the original program was to design a center so that people could have the *responsibility* for what they are best equipped to do, being right there on the spot, whether in regard to a clinical case *or a program or in regard to how a thing operates*. They ought to have something to say about it. There was general agreement as reflected in the planning document that we wanted to change from the normal way that state hospitals operate. Our intent was to do something more sensible.

Dr. Bailey acted as spokesman in reaffirming the demand for collegial participation, against the challenge of administrative power:

Dr. Bailey: The others requested that I make the point clear to Martin that it is the secretarial pool of *clinical* secretaries. That the administrators weren't hurt by it. You see, the other point that the original program was trying to change from the way outfits like this one usually operate, is to have *equivalent prestige and salary* and whatnot for clinical persons as well as for administrators. Now, the *administrators are being rewarded* by this change. I mean, they retain their personal secretaries. I thought of this right in the middle of talking to Martin, on Monday.

The issues of the steno pool crisis became fused with other organizational affairs, lending credibility to the claim for broader meaning. The ultimate definition of the problem emerged as a question of Martin's power against that of the professional staff, and of the conditions limiting each:

Dr. Bailey: Now, another thing we talked about—that he had appointed me to chair a committee to write up a policy manual. We came up with a report to him in June. Well, *there hasn't been word one* from him to anybody, that I know of! At least, not to me as chairman. At any rate, you see, much of the staff doesn't feel that they have any route to make suggestions about change. As I said to him, he had knowledge that the staff didn't want this. He is in a position to be able to *make the decision anyway.* I don't object to his having that kind of authority, but it seems *incumbent upon him* either to say or write, look, I know you all don't want this, but there are overwhelming considerations. *This is why we have to do it.* You know, there was not only the lack of this, but also the message about it came through the channels that I mentioned to you.

The broader meanings given to the crisis included negative definitions of Martin's personal character. Duplicity was either implied, or pointed out in detail. "Everybody's upset except the boss." "I don't see him as a person who needs to dictate to others, but there is something about him that is at variance—that he is truly more authoritarian." "He really likes all of this!" "He knew it! He really didn't care!"

On Monday, Martin telephoned Mr. Nader at his home and set up a luncheon meeting for the following day. Before the meeting, Mr. Nader circulated around the offices, talking to as many staff as he could, "getting their ideas, opinions, and attitudes." The committee met after lunch, and Mr. Nader was made an official assistant to Martin, charged with "revisiting the steno pool." In the meeting, Martin interpreted the preceding events:

Martin: As a result of changes, we had a juicy explosion. I did expect vigorous response to the change, but did not expect it to be quite the experience that it was. What was learned is that we do have *a problem of communication* between the Superintendent and major program groupings. Also present is the problem of communication horizontally between the three groups. *It is my responsibility.*
By *listening to people,* it shook me up enough to realize that I did not take the time. *We need to fit together* program components.

Remember when we were at the 4th Street offices—at that point, we were setting goals. We had that kind of communication, person-to-person and group-to-group. But it becomes more difficult as this organization expands. Perhaps I made a wrong decision in this matter. But *the steno pool is only an example.* It is *necessary to involve people* through participation. There is a deliberate compartmentalization. This represents a problem of interface, of articulation. The administrative services has to *work for* the organization. One more complication which is a *hazard to integration* is the policy of bringing on board people who might be characterized as prima donas. They have a *drive toward individuality and creativity.* This was overlooked. This could have been handled in a different manner, *at the peer level.*

Martin's comments pointed to basic problems, but his solution was for greater responsibility to be assumed *by others.* The crisis clarified Martin's intention toward withdrawal. Nader's appointment accelerated the course of delegation:

Interviewer: Am I correct, that the resolution of the steno pool crisis has your top priority, now?

Mr. Nader: No, it don't have top priority. It has equal priority with some other things. Everything has top priority. (Laughter).

Interviewer: What are some of the other things?

Mr. Nader: Well, getting kids in here. That has to be top priority. And setting up relations with other centers—we are the research and development center for the state, you know. We'll be servicing some children for other centers. I will be communicating with a number of people. Then there is the whole business of the new Mental

Health Code. It may have some effect on admissions policy as well as treatment programs. Guardianship, commitment, all that. We don't want to have the Sheriff delivering kids to our door. And some guidelines must be set down for the division of services between the disturbed and the retarded.

The formal resolution of the crisis followed lines developed by the group in collective negotiation; Mr. Nader's leadership was essentially symbolic.

Sharon summed up the crisis and its resolution as the episode appeared from the viewpoint of the secretaries.

Sharon: I was bound and determined that I was going to fight it! I wanted to work for Dr. Bailey and I wanted to work for Dr. Victor and they had said that they wanted me. They fought for me. They wrote memos, they talked to Dr. Martin himself—they sent memos to the staff, they had staff meetings. They still came in and gave me their work even though I was in the steno pool. I think they felt that I was really trying to do the best for them, even though I had only been there a short while and I felt that they needed a secretary. I think they fought very hard to try to get me back, all the secretaries back to their people. Yesterday we were called in and they said that we had our jobs back, that they were hiring girls for the pool. . . .

Martin's last year as superintendent was characterized by progressive phasing out—a steady shift of attention, time, and interest to the university setting, where he moved full-time after his resignation. Mr. Nader was named to succeed him as Superintendent of the Center.

Analysis

Few studies of crises and their effects on organizations can be found, but Hermann (1963) affords a beginning. Of fourteen propositions reported, three seem most applicable to the crises observed during the field study of the center.

FIGURE 3   CRISIS AND WITHDRAWAL: THE HERMANN MODEL Figure 3 represents propositions 1, 3, and 13.

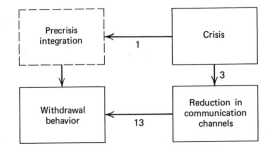

Proposition 1 indicates that *when precrisis integration is weak, a crisis leads to withdrawal behavior.* Proposition 3 indicates that *a crisis leads to a reduction in communication channels.* Proposition 13 indicates that *a reduction in communication channels leads to withdrawal behavior.* Hermann's textual examples indicate concern with hierarchical organizations. According to Hermann, withdrawal behavior is dysfunctional, a contingency that would limit the viability of the organization.

FIGURE 4   COLLEGIAL CONTROL IN ENACTED ORGANIZATIONAL SITUATIONS

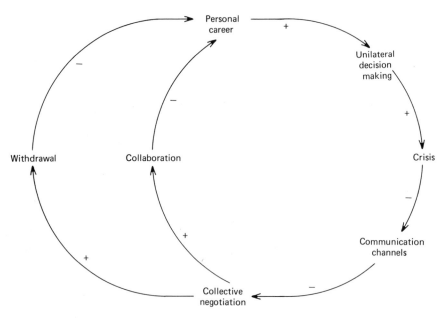

In the collegial organization, withdrawal may be seen as a corrective mechanism in the interplay between individual power and collective power. In Figure 4, both withdrawal and collaboration, reintegration of a dissident colleague, can check the amplification tendency (Maruyama, 1963) of individualism.

Figure 4 shows that *when the importance of the personal career increases, unilateral decision making also increases, leading to more control crises. Crises reduce communication channels, forcing colleagues to create collective negotiations and leading to withdrawal or to submission, either of which reduces the importance of the personal career. When the importance of the personal career decreases, there is less unilateral decision making and crises subside. Communication channels then expand and collective negotiation becomes unnecessary, requiring less withdrawal and submission, which restores viableness to personal careers.*

By taking the preliminary position that organization is problematic rather than given, Martin's decision to "act like a superintendent" may be rendered somewhat more understandable. Consider that in a bureaucracy, members often find it necessary to use the "informal structure" to achieve some purpose. Martin was merely responding to his organizational situation in the same fashion, by using the formal structure. Both formal and informal structure may be seen as problematic. It is helpful to conceptualize authority roles in organizations in terms of latent roles (Gouldner, 1957; Becker and Geer, 1960). A bureaucrat may act primarily on the basis of legalistic authority, yet hold *potential* authority on an interpersonal level. Within the center schema, Martin acted primarily in his mediator role, yet he held *potential* authority through his office. All types of organization may be subject to recurring authority crises resulting from inappropriate choices of authority bases for action in particular situations. Collective negotiation may be seen as one form of control mechanism that may operate when hierarchical or legalistic mechanisms are not present.

The center schema was especially conducive to collective reactions to legalistic authority for other reasons. Bidwell and Vreeland (1963) have dealt with the relatedness of authority structures and problems of control. They posit that *an authority structure is created as an interaction effect of the relative power (expertise and competitive demand) of the professional cadres and the structural differences generated by the relationship to clients (whether the client is inducted into the organization or not)*. Given this position, it follows clearly that the center's authority structure was highly uncertain at the time of the steno pool episode.

Martin's organizational schema denied members' conventional and familiar professional roles and relationships, but called instead for organization along generic functional lines, within which the various professions were set to interact as peers. Power was thereby made highly problematic. To some extent, prior conceptualizations of status differentials were useful in mapping the EM ground, and to some extent new roles were made along lines given within particular situations. One overall result of the generic-functional schema was to increase members' concern about status and power differentials along the professional/administrator cleavage. The second element in the authority structure, relationship to clients, was equally uncertain because the responsibility for directing residential treatment was given to EM clinicians. This device to achieve continuity of treatment required interlocking EM with the ancillary IM staff needed to conduct residential care and defining the relative power and authority of each. It also required clarification of client contracts for treatment and related services; in outpatient treatment, the client dealt almost exclusively with the EM clinician, but the contract for residential care was complex and unresolved, involving far more demands from other parties. This second aspect of the power structure was not affected directly by the steno pool crisis, which dealt primarily with the power of EM professional members and administrators. However, this reassertion of the integrity of the professional college, and demonstration of collective power strengthened the EM position in the negotiations with IM staff which followed later.

On a more general level it is common to treat change as the outcome of dynamic interplay between different forces that separate men and forces that draw men together. Although power plays in bureaucracies may be dysfunctional, the present study presents a view of the power play as a means of defining and constructing viable organizational situations, where hierarchical means are not present. The power of expertise and the power necessary to check expertise, in Crozier's terms, may be treated as dual expressions of the same factor—the basic conflict process leading to the construction of social reality.

Footnotes

[1] See also, Blankenship, 1976a, 1976b.

REFERENCES

BECKER, HOWARD S., AND BLANCHE GEER
1960   "Latent culture: A note on the theory of latent social roles," *Administrative Science Quarterly,* 5, 2 (September): 304–313.

BIDWELL, CHARLES E., AND REBECCA S. VREELAND
1963   "Authority and control in client-serving organizations," *The Sociological Quarterly,* 4, 3 (Summer): 231–242.

BITTNER, EGON
1965   "The concept of organization," *Social Research,* 32 (Autumn): 239–255.

BLANKENSHIP, RALPH L.
1973   "Organizational careers: An interactionist perspective," *The Sociological Quarterly,* 14, 1 (Winter): 88–98.
1976a   *The Emerging Organization of a Community Mental Health Center.* San Francisco: R and E Research Associates.
1976b   "Collective behavior in organizational settings," *Sociology of Work and Organizations 3 (May), 2:151-168.*

BUCHER, RUE
1970   "Social process and power in a medical school," in Mayer Zald (ed.), *Power in Organizations.* Nashville: Vanderbilt.

BUCHER, RUE, AND JOAN STELLING
1969   "Characteristics of professional organizations," *Journal of Health and Social Behavior,* 10 (March): 3–15.

CROZIER, MICHEL
1964   *The Bureaucratic Phenomenon.* Chicago: The University of Chicago Press.

DALTON, MELVILLE
1959   *Men Who Manage.* New York: Wiley.

DENZIN, NORMAN K.
1970   *The Research Act.* Chicago: Aldine.

ETZIONI, AMITAI
1975   *A Comparative Analysis of Complex Organizations.* New York: The Free Press

FREIDSON, ELIOT
1972   *Profession of Medicine.* New York: Dodd, Mead.

FREIDSON, ELIOT, AND BUFORD RHEA
1963   "Processes of control in a company equals" *Social Problems,* 11 (Fall): 110–131.

GLASER, BARNEY G. (ED.)
1968   *Organizational Careers.* Chicago: Aldine.

GLASER, BARNEY G., AND ANSELM STRAUSS
1967   *The Discovery of Grounded Theory.* Chicago: Aldine.

GOULDNER, ALVIN M.
1957   "Cosmopolitans and locals: Toward an analysis of latent social roles—I," *Administrative Science Quarterly,* 2:281–306.

HERMANN, CHARLES F.
1963   "Some consequences of crisis which limit the viability of organizations," *Administrative Science Quarterly,* 8 (June): 61–82.

JOINT COMMISSION ON MENTAL ILLNESS AND HEALTH
1961   *Action for Mental Health.* New York: Wiley.

KATZ, DANIEL, AND ROBERT KAHN
1966   *The Social Psychology of Organizations.* New York: Wiley.

KENNEDY, JOHN F.
1963   "Mental health and mental retardation—message from the President of the United States," House Document No. 58, Washington, D.C.: *Congressional Record—House* (February): 1744–1749.

LEIFER, RONALD
1966 "Community psychiatry and social power," *Social Problems* 14:16–22.

LOFLAND, JOHN
1969 *Analyzing Social Settings.* Belmont: Wadsworth.

MCCALL, GEORGE J., AND J. L. SIMMONS (EDS.)
1969 *Issues in Participant Observation.* Menlo Park, California: Addison-Wesley.
1966 *Identities and Interactions.* New York: The Free Press.

MARUYAMA, M.
1963 "The second cybernetics: Deviation—amplifying mutual causal processes," *American Scientist,* 51:164–179.

MECHANIC, DAVID
1969 *Mental Health and Social Policy.* Englewood Cliffs, N.J.: Prentice-Hall.

SILVERMAN, DAVID
1971 *The Theory of Organization.* New York: Basic Books.

SCHATZMAN, LEONARD, AND ANSELM STRAUSS
1966 "A sociology of psychiatry: A perspective and some organizing foci," *Social Problems,* 14:3–16.

SMELSER, NEIL
1968 "Toward a general theory of social change," in *Essays in Sociological Explanation.* Englewood Cliffs, N. J.: Prentice-Hall.
1963 *Theory of Collective Behavior.* Englewood Cliffs, N.J.: Prentice-Hall.

STRAUSS, ANSELM, LEONARD SCHATZMAN, RUE BUCHER, DANUTA EHRLICH, AND MELVIN SABSHIN
1964 *Psychiatric Ideologies and Institutions.* New York: The Free Press.
1963 "The hospital in its negotiated order," in Eliot Freidson (ed.), *The Hospital in Modern Society.* New York: The Free Press: 147–169.

TURNER, RALPH H., AND LEWIS M. KILLIAN
1957   *Collective Behavior.* Englewood Cliffs: Prentice-Hall.

WEICK, KARL E.
1969   *The Social Psychology of Organizing.* Reading, Massachusetts: Addison-Wesley.

NAME INDEX

417

SUBJECT INDEX

423

HM131.C7425
Colleagues in organization :
the social construction of
professional work